Optimizing C
with Assembly Code

Peter Gulutzan and Trudy Pelzer

R&D Publications
Lawrence, Kansas 66046

R&D Publications, Inc.
1601 West 23rd Street, Suite 200
Lawrence, Kansas 66046-2700
USA

Distributed by Prentice Hall
ISBN: 0-13-234576-5

Cover Design: T. Watson Bogaard

Table of Contents

Preface   **Why a Book
on 486 Programming?** . . . . . . **ix**

Chapter 1 —   **An Assembler Primer** **1**

The MOV Instruction; The Meaning of <memory>;
Putting MOV in a C Program; Alignment;
A Note on 32-bit Registers; Memory Variables
vs. Register Variables; Pipelines; Caching;
Segments; How Real Is A Cycle?

Chapter 2 —   **Basic Arithmetic
and Logic Operations** **43**

The ADD, SUB, OR, AND, and XOR Instructions;
Revisiting the Constant-to-Memory Rule;
Register Constants; Zeroing Registers;
Working with Byte Values; The INC and DEC
Instructions; The Secret Hi/Lo Rule; Flags;
The ADC and SBB Instructions; 8-bit <constant>
Operands; Asymmetry; Misalignment Revisited

Chapter 3 —   **Jumps:
The Assembler GOTO** **79**

The CMP Instruction; The JZ, JNZ, JP, JNP,
JC, JNC, JS, JNS, JO, and JNO Instructions;
Checking for Overflow; The JG, JGE, JL, JLE,
JA, and JBE Instructions; The JMP Instruction;
Double Jumps; Long Conditional Jumps;
Adding ASCII Numbers; Straddling Cache Lines;
The NOP Instruction; The LOOP Instruction;
The JCXZ Instruction; Loop Control Using a
Hidden Resource; Double-Byte Comparisons;
Loop Unrolling

Chapter 4 —   **Bit Shifts** **111**

The SHR, SAR, and SHL Instructions;
Step One — Make Sure the Switch is On;
Speeding Up <register> Shifts; Speeding Up
<memory> Shifts; Optimization Mirage:
Speeding Up 8-bit Shifts; Uses For
<SHR|SAR|SHL> <operand>,CL;
Shifts and Bit Fields; Compressing Using Shifts;
The ROL Instruction; The XCHG Instruction;
A Bubble Sort Without Exchanges;
The SHRD and SHLD Instructions

Chapter 5 —   **Other Instructions** **135**

The TEST Instruction; The NEG Instruction;
The NOT Instruction; The LDS and LES
Instructions; Setting Flags: The CLC, CMC
and STC Instructions; The LEA Instruction;
Casting; The CBW and CWD Instructions; The
MOVSX and MOVZX Instructions

Chapter 6 —   *Manipulating the Stack* *157*

Automatic Variables; The PUSH and POP
Instructions; The CALL and RET Instructions;
Passing Parameters; Function Calls; The Stack
and Penalties; Near Pointers vs. Far Pointers;
An Optimization Mirage

Chapter 7 —   *Multiplication Operations* . . . *179*

The IMUL Instruction; 32-Bit Multiplies;
The MUL Instruction; The FASTIMUL
Instruction

Chapter 8 —   *Division Operations* *201*

The IDIV and DIV Instructions; Shift
and Subtract — Part One; The BSR Instruction;
Shift and Subtract — Part Two; Forcing the
Compiler to Choose DIV; Dividing Signed
Integers With SAR and SHR; The Lost
Remainder Problem; The Negative Rounding
Problem; More on Rounding; The AAM
Instruction; Overflow; Dividing a 16-bit
Number by an 8-Bit Constant; Division Using
a Lookup Table

Chapter 9 —   ***Handling Intel Strings*** ***217***

The CLD and STD Instructions; Basic
Assumptions; The CMPSB, CMPSW, and
CMPSD Instructions; The LODSB, LODSW,
and LODSD Instructions; The MOVSB,
MOVSW, and MOVSD Instructions;
The SCASB, SCASW, and SCASD Instructions;
The STOSB, STOSW, and STOSD Instructions;
Cycle Times of String Instructions; C and Intel
String Instructions; Repeated Intel String
Instructions; The REP and REPNZ Prefix
Instructions; REP MOVSx; REP STOSx;
REP CMPSx; REP SCASx; The LSL Instruction

Chapter 10 —   ***Optimizing A Sort*** ***249***

Choosing a Sort Algorithm; Microsoft's
Translation of the quicksort Function;
Lab Notes

Chapter 11 —   ***C String Functions*** ***269***

Style Notes and Definitions; atoi; atol; itoa; ltoa;
strcat; strchr; strcmp; strcpy; strcspn; stricmp;
strlen; strlwr; strncat; strncmp; strncpy; strnset;
strpbrk; strrchr; strrev; strset; strspn; strstr;
strupr; The mem Functions; memcmp; memcpy;
memset; memchr

Chapter 12 —   ***Counting Cycles
with TACHO.EXE*** ***331***

Copyright; Requirements and Limitations;
How to Run TACHO.EXE; What
TACHO.EXE Displays; A Sample
TACHO.EXE Session; Benefits

Appendix A — *Quick Guide*
to Assembler Instructions
and Cycle Times *339*

Appendix B — *Quick Guide to Secret Rules*
of Assembler *383*

Appendix C — *A Routine To Determine*
What CPU Your Program
Is Running On *389*

Appendix D — *List of this Book's*
Diskette Contents *393*

Index *395*

Why a Book on 486 Programming?

This book came about as a result of our own need for complete and detailed information on optimizing code for specific CPUs. Much to our dismay, we often found that the answers to our questions on the subject were either not to be found at all or, worse, were wrong when we did find them. Frequently, rules were laboriously discovered through trial and error.

We think this book is necessary because it is the only book that explains everything an 80486 programmer would want to know. Many of the explanations about cycle times and pipeline stalls contained herein have never before been published anywhere, in any form, even by Intel.

This book is also a guide for evaluating a C compiler's optimizer. We will often illustrate — and sometimes criticize — the way three well-known compilers translate C source code into assembly object code. For the record, the three compilers we'll discuss are:

❖ Borland C++ version 3.1

❖ Microsoft Visual C++ version 2.0

❖ Symantec C++ version 7.0

We'll refer to these as the test compilers throughout this book. We don't expect that these versions will still be current by the time you read this, so this book concentrates on aspects that are common to all C compilers and that are very unlikely to change in the next year or two. The great bulk of the criticisms are for all practical purposes timeless.

Who Should Read this Book?

If you use C to write 16-bit programs (i.e., for MS-DOS or MS-Windows 3.x) that will run on computers with Intel 486 or similar CPUs and you have any interest at all in making your programs run faster, this book is for you. In it, we'll show you how to improve performance (the first thing your clients notice) using short assembler functions. You'll learn how to make many of your routines run faster by 5 percent, 10 percent or, in some cases, by as much as 60 percent.

You don't need to be familiar with assembler programming to use our tips. In fact, this book is an appropriate introductory assembly language text for C programmers. No instruction or idea is introduced without paying attention to the question: what good is this in a C program? In all cases, we try to explain *why* the result is faster if you do it our way. We think you'll find that the potential gains are worth it, especially in cases where your program will execute the improved routines many thousands of times in its lifetime. After all, you only have to read this book once.

In fact, you can even make improvements without reading the book! On the diskette in the back, you'll find replacements for commonly used functions in the standard C library (`atoi`, `memset`, `strlen`, etc.). These replacements are plug-compatible with the ones you're using now. If you use this code instead of the functions that came with your C library from Borland or Microsoft or Symantec, your program will run faster each time a replaced routine is run.

What this Book is NOT About

Because we aim to present everything that's worth knowing in our "typical" environment — MS-DOS or Windows 3.x on 486s — there won't be enough room to discuss other fascinating topics. Everything we'll present is relevant for OS/2 or other 32-bit operating systems, but none of our examples come from there. Some of what we'll present is not useful for optimizing 386s; when that happens we'll warn you but we won't apologize and we won't try to come up with 386-specific alternatives. A tiny amount of what we'll present is not useful for optimizing Pentiums; we felt that Pentium optimization is such a large topic that it merits a separate book.

Because we have a strict definition of the word "optimize," this book does not attempt to cover any of the following:

* finding and choosing a better algorithm,

* analyzing a problem,

* writing structured code,

* C++,

* operating system interface,

* case studies/anecdotes, clarity, or portability.

We acknowledge that all of these areas are important. In fact, for most people, they are more important than "optimization." That is as it should be, and that is why there are many books that discuss such topics already. This is not one of those books.

What this Book is About

The focus of this book is optimizing, which we define as making existing programs run faster by making small (not structural) changes in the source code, with secondary concern for side effects such as increased code size or decreasing comprehensibility. Here's what lies ahead:

* Chapters 1 through 9 are an assembler primer. They introduce general assembler syntax, inline assembly, registers, segmentation, prefixes, 32-bit operands, and the importance of double-word alignment. You'll learn how to do simple arithmetic, jumps and shifts, manipulate the stack, handle strings, and how the choice of data type can affect speed significantly. We'll show you tips for faster multiplying and faster dividing as well as for faster string movement. You'll also learn many Secret Rules of Assembler use that aren't clearly documented anywhere else.

❖ Chapter 10 optimizes a sort function in the full sense of the word. We start with four different sort algorithms and show you the steps to take to end up with the fastest possible program.

❖ Chapter 11 will teach you more about handling strings in assembler. We'll provide you with replacements for practically every string function in the standard C library: `strcmp`, `strlen`, `strcpy`, `stricmp`, `strupr`, `strncpy`, and so on, as well as for `atoi`, `atol`, `itoa`, and `ltoa`. These functions have been tested against the ones in the standard C libraries from Borland, Microsoft, and Symantec and are between 15 percent and 50 percent faster. Each function is an assembler listing complete with comments and discussion. All the routines work best with 486s, but none of them are dependent on 32-bit registers or 486-specific instructions. We also have replacements for `memcpy`, `memset`, `memchr`, and `memcmp` in this chapter, but this code does depend on 32-bit registers.

❖ Chapter 12 explains how to use TACHO.EXE, the cycle-counting utility program that comes on this book's diskette.

The rest of the book consists of a few appendices containing a synopsis of what we've dealt with and some further information:

❖ Appendix A is a quick guide to assembler instructions and cycle times. It lists the instructions used in this book and makes note of where our cycle times contradict those claimed for the instruction by Intel.

❖ Appendix B is a quick guide to the secret rules of assembler we tell you about in this book. Each rule is indexed to the page number it is introduced on.

❖ Appendix C is a routine that determines what CPU a program is running on. You'll find this routine on the diskette that comes with this book.

❖ And finally, Appendix D is a directory of what you'll find on this book's diskette.

Optimizing: How Not To Do It

Before we get on to our assembler primer, we'd like to put our objective for this book in perspective. Consider the case of a typical programmer ...

Belshazzar had a small array of 8-bit signed integers defined as a `char` array that he wanted to sort in ascending order. He was willing to spend a few hours on the project, provided he got a reasonably fast routine. So he wrote this conventional bubble-sort routine in C and got ready to speed it up by inserting some inline-assembly statements.

```
void bubblesort (int array[],int size)
 {
  unsigned int i;
  char temp;
  for (i=0; i<size-1;)            /* For each element of the array: */
    {
    if (array[i]>array[i+1])      /* if it's greater than the next: */
      {
      temp=array[i];              /* swap it with the next one */
      array[i]=array[i+1];
      array[i+1]=temp;
      i--;                        /* and backtrack. */
      }
    else i++;                     /* Otherwise: on to the next. */
    }
 }
```

But before Belshazzar began, his screen spat out a strange message!

MENE MENE TIKAL UPHARSIN

"Got a weird message here," bawled Belshazzar to his underling. "How about you parsing it for me? I wanna get on with my optimizing job here ..."

His underling (a fellow named Daniel) came over, took a look, clucked and declaimed a translation:

TESTED, TESTED AGAIN, WEIGHED AND FOUND WANTING

"I know all that," Belshazzar barked, "but that's a prediction of the doom of Babylon in 612 ... or something. It has no business popping up on my screen now!"

"Wrong," replied Daniel. "It's a reminder that you don't start optimizing your code until it's already good. If you must take on projects like this then:

Step I: **TEST**. Check out your algorithm. Is it appropriate?

Step II: **TEST AGAIN**. Check how your algorithm is coded.
Does it work?

Step III: **WEIGH**. Run some benchmarks, run your profiler.

Step IIII: **FIND WANTING**. *Now* you can look for flaws
to optimize away."

Whipping out his pocket Knuth, Belshazzar frowned and considered for a moment. "It says here that bubble sorts are reasonable for small arrays — that's what I've got. Sure it's appropriate! Why, everybody uses bubble sorts! Look, here's one of hundreds of examples from a book on C programming ... except, er, it looks different from mine." Belshazzar paused and read the code. "With this code I'd be resolving highly-disordered arrays more quickly without backtracking, and the smallest number will bubble all the way up to the top after the first iteration of the outer loop. Come to think of it, that's handy. I can ship out the first numbers while I'm still sorting."

"That's the first MENE," Daniel encouraged him. "You've checked out your algorithm against the competition, and you came up with a better one."

"This stuff works great," burbled Belshazzar with mounting cheeriness. "No matter what random test data I throw at it, it comes back sorted. Let's see, doesn't seem to be ruining data areas for other procs ... hey, both MENEs have disappeared from my screen! I guess that's step II out of the way now."

"Right. Why not stop there, boss? It's probably good enough now."

"Uh-uh. I ran the profiler before I started. This routine is critical. I have to do that weighing step." Saying which, Belshazzar ran a few simple timing tests. "Well ... not bad. I'd still like to have a look at what my C compiler produced and see if I can spot any problems, though. That's TIKAL out of the way and UPHARSIN coming up."

The last bits of the message disappeared. Belshazzar had averted doom — this time — by putting the optimization job in its right place: last.

If **MENE MENE TIKAL UPHARSIN** hadn't appeared on his screen, he'd have spent the next hour tweaking an inferior program that has a bug in it anyway. So far he's saved about 90 percent by doing the pre-optimization work. Now he's going to go for the last 10 percent — and that's where this book comes in. This short pause was just to remind you that our definition of optimizing is pretty restricted.

Chapter 1

An Assembler Primer

When you learn a foreign language, you start with a few common words and use them right away — you don't wait until you know everything before you try your first sentence. Our objective in this chapter is to follow this principle by providing you with a one-word assembler vocabulary.

By the time you finish this chapter, you will have the tools to be able to put useful assembler statements inside C programs merely by using a single assembler word. Even such a small vocabulary will enable you to speed up your programs (in a rather limited set of circumstances).

The word (also called instruction or command) we'll start with is the most common word in assembler — MOV.

The MOV Instruction

In an assembler statement, the syntax of MOV looks like this:

```
MOV <destination operand>,<source operand>    ;optional comment
```

The meaning of the MOV instruction is imperative:

MOVe (actually, copy) the contents of <source operand> into <destination operand>. The size of <source operand> and <destination operand> can be either 8-bits, 16-bits, or 32-bits, providing the size of <source operand> matches the size of <destination operand>.

That is, MOV is an assignment operator. Naturally, we expect every computer language to have an assignment operator. The tricky part in assembler is that there are three kinds of operand — constants, registers, and memory locations — with three different sizes — 8-bit, 16-bit, and 32-bit. MOV therefore has 15 possible forms, depending on the operands. Table 1.1 is a standardized description for each possible form.

Since we'll be using the diagram format of Table 1.1 for all instructions in this book, we want to draw attention to some of its fine points:

❖ <angle brackets> are used to indicate that you can substitute any operand of the specified type shown. An example of the type

```
MOV <16-bit register>,<16-bit constant>
```

would thus be

```
MOV AX,5
```

❖ The cycle count column shows the number of cycles that Intel says the instruction takes to execute on an Intel 486. Other CPUs differ.

Instruction Mnemonic	Destination Operand	Source Operand	Cycle Count
MOV	<8-bit register>	,<8-bit constant>	1
MOV	<8-bit register>	,<8-bit register>	1
MOV	<8-bit register>	,<byte-size memory>	1
MOV	<byte-size memory>	,<8-bit constant>	1
MOV	<byte-size memory>	,<8-bit register>	1
MOV	<16-bit register>	,<16-bit constant>	1
MOV	<16-bit register>	,<16-bit register>	1
MOV	<16-bit register>	,<word-size memory>	1
MOV	<word-size memory>	,<16-bit constant>	1
MOV	<word-size memory>	,<16-bit register>	1
MOV	<32-bit register>	,<32-bit constant>	1
MOV	<32-bit register>	,<32-bit register>	1
MOV	<32-bit register>	,<long-size memory>	1
MOV	<long-size memory>	,<32-bit constant>	1
MOV	<long-size memory>	,<32-bit register>	1

Table 1.1   Standardized description for each form of MOV.

❖ If you see the symbol !! in the cycle count column, you are looking at a cycle time which we derived by measurement, rather than the cycle count Intel says the instruction will take. That is, we timed the instruction on several 486 machines and this is the result. The !! will alert you that some manuals give a different number of cycles for the instruction. (That's not happening with MOV, but we were tempted to put a tentative !! in because some common variants take 2 cycles to execute, namely the ones that contain a <memory> operand. More on this later.)

As stated above, there are three kinds of operand you can use with MOV: constants, registers, and memory locations.

A *constant* is just an 8-bit, 16-bit, or 32-bit number. An 8-bit constant can be either unsigned (in the range 0 to 255) or signed (in the range −128 to +127). It can be represented as an integer (e.g., 5, 25, −13, etc.) or as any character enclosed in single quotes (e.g., 'A', '%', ' ', etc.). A 16-bit constant can be either unsigned (in the range 0 to 65535) or signed (in the range −32768 to +32767) and, of course, can only be represented as an integer. A 32-bit constant can be either unsigned (in the range 0 to 2^{32}) or signed (in the range -2^{31} to $+2^{31}$) and must be represented as a long integer. Only MOV's <source operand> can be a constant, which should be no surprise — you can't say

```
5=mema;
```

in C either.

A *register* is normally one of seven 16-bit variables named AX, BX, CX, DX, SI, DI, and BP. You can think of these variables as memory operands but they have this important characteristic: they are stored inside the CPU. Although all these registers are 16-bit values, the first four (AX, BX, CX, and DX) also allow you to refer directly to their top or bottom (8-bit) halves by taking the first letter of the register name and following it with either the letter H (for the high byte of the register) or the letter L (for the low byte of the register). Thus:

AH is the high byte and AL is the low byte of the AX register

BH is the high byte and BL is the low byte of the BX register

CH is the high byte and CL is the low byte of the CX register

DH is the high byte and DL is the low byte of the DX register

(There are also some 32-bit registers, which we'll discuss later.)

The following instruction illustrates a MOV of a constant (5) to a register (AX):

```
MOV AX,5    ;i.e., put a 5 in the AX register
```

The following examples illustrate some MOVs of 16-bit registers to 16-bit registers:

```
MOV AX,BX    ;i.e., Put the contents of BX in AX
MOV CX,BP    ;i.e., Put the contents of BP in CX
MOV SI,DI    ;i.e., Put the contents of DI in SI
```

These examples show some MOVs of 8-bit registers to 8-bit registers:

```
MOV AH,BL    ;i.e., Put the low byte of BX in the high byte of AX
MOV DL,BH    ;i.e., Put the high byte of BX in the low byte of DX
```

Remember that it is illegal to MOV a 16-bit register (or constant) into an 8-bit register and vice versa since the <source> and <destination> operands are not the same size. The following are therefore illegal instructions:

```
MOV AL,AX    ;ILLEGAL
MOV DH,256   ;ILLEGAL
MOV CX,DL    ;ILLEGAL
```

A *memory location* is a reference to a location in RAM. The reference can be a name or it can be indirect, via a pointer. To get the address of a memory location, put the directive OFFSET in front of the memory location's name. (Note: we won't concern ourselves with how to declare these memory locations using assembler, since you already know how to do that in C. To reference a C variable in assembler, just use the C name.)

The following instruction illustrates a MOV of a constant to a memory location:

```
MOV mema,5    ;i.e., Put a 5 in memory location mema
```

The following examples illustrate a MOV of a register to a memory location:

```
MOV mema,AL    ;i.e., Put the contents of AL in mema
MOV memb,DX    ;i.e., Put the contents of DX in memb
```

These examples show some MOVs of a memory location to a register:

```
MOV AL,mema          ;i.e., Put the contents of mema in AL
MOV DX,memb          ;i.e., Put the contents of memb in DX
MOV BX,OFFSET mema   ;i.e., Put the address of mema in BX
```

Finally, the next set of instructions illustrates a MOV from one memory location to another. The procedure is a trifle roundabout because it isn't possible to say:

```
MOV <memory>,<memory>    ;ILLEGAL
```

in assembler. Instead, one has to MOV <register>,<memory>, then MOV <memory>,<register>, as follows:

```
MOV AL,mema    ;i.e., Put the contents of mema into
MOV memb,AL    ;memb via register AL
```

The numeric value in a register can be an address. For traditional reasons, only four registers (BX, SI, DI, and BP) can be used as pointers. To indicate that a register is being used as an indirect reference to a memory location, put square brackets ([ ]) around the register name, as follows:

```
MOV DI,OFFSET mema    ;i.e., Put the address of mema in DI
MOV AX,[BX]           ;i.e., Put (memory location pointed to by BX) in AX
MOV [BX],AX           ;i.e., Reverse of above statement
```

Simple arithmetic with a constant can also be done on a pointer register:

```
MOV AL,[BX+5]    ;i.e., Put (memory location pointed to by BX plus 5) in AX
```

In this example, if BX is 0, then [BX+5] is a reference to memory location 5, and AL becomes the value found at that location. (Note: the constant used can be negative, e.g., [BX-1] is the same as [BX+65534]. But don't try to use [BX-SI]. Some assemblers will incorrectly accept [BX-SI] as if it's a legal addressing mode instead of rejecting it as a syntax error.)

To show the effect more clearly, the following C program shows C references to pointers side by side with the assembler output containing pointer registers.

```
C                       Assembler
char mema;
char *memp;
void main ()
{
   *memp=5;             MOV BX,memp
                        MOV [BX],5
   memp=&mema;          MOV memp,OFFSET mema
   mema=*memp;          MOV BX,memp
}                       MOV AL,[BX]
                        MOV mema,AL
```

The Meaning of <memory>

The <memory> component of an assembler instruction can take seven different forms, which, in turn, can be broken out into three major addressing modes — the Register Pointer Mode, the Register Pointer plus Constant Mode, and the Register Pointer Doubled Mode.

There is one form of the Register Pointer Mode addressing method. It involves the use of the register pointers [BX], [SI], and [DI]. (It does not include the use of [BP], because [BP] is always interpreted as [BP+0]; this is the second addressing method.)

There are three forms of the Register Pointer plus Constant Mode addressing method. The first involves the use of a 16-bit constant. The second involves the use of the register pointers [BP], [BX], [SI], and [DI] plus an 8-bit constant. The third involves the use of the register pointers [BP], [BX], [SI], and [DI] plus a 16-bit constant.

There are also three forms of the Register Pointer Doubled Mode addressing method. The first involves the use of a combination of the register pointer [BP] with either [SI] or [DI] or a combination of the register pointer [BX] with either [SI] or [DI]. The second involves the use of these same combinations plus an 8-bit constant. The third involves the use of these same combinations with a 16-bit constant.

The addressing modes and the allowable formats are shown in Table 1.2, along with the cost in bytes used for each format (n8 means an 8-bit signed constant in the range −128 to +127; n16 means a 16-bit unsigned constant in the range 0 to 65535).

Table 1.2 is important for two reasons:

(1) The choice of addressing mode affects the instruction's size. A size difference can mean a speed difference: smaller instructions will be fetched faster. But we're not recommending that you memorize the addressing mode sizes in order to predict precisely how big the whole instruction is. It's easier to just assemble it and check the resulting size. Still, if it suits your purposes, the first 256 bytes of global memory should be a commonly used array, since `array[n]` would end up being a shorter instruction if the `offset` of `array` is less than 256.

(2) The choice of addressing mode affects the instruction's cycle count. Although the basic `MOV` instruction takes 1 cycle to execute on a 486, some addressing modes can add a 1 or more cycle penalty to the execution time. The cycle count is important when looking for performance gains, and we never omit pointing out factors that affect cycle count throughout this book. We call most of these factors SECRET RULES, since they are not well documented (sometimes they're not documented at all) in the common literature. The SECRET RULES don't apply only to the `MOV` instruction; they apply to all assembler instructions. We're introducing the SECRET RULES here because the `MOV` instruction gives us enough information about assembler to be able to exemplify them.

We have discovered two SECRET RULES that pertain to memory addressing modes.

Addressing Method	Formats Allowed	Size
Register Pointer Mode	`[BX],[SI],[DI]`	1 byte
Register Pointer plus Constant Mode	`[n16],[BP]`	2 bytes
	`[BP+n8],[BX+n8],[SI+n8],[DI+n8]`	2 bytes
	`[BP+n16],[BX+n16],[SI+n16],[DI+n16]`	3 bytes
Register Pointer Doubled Mode	`[BP+SI],[BP+DI],[BX+SI],[BX+DI]`	1 byte
	`[BP+SI+n8],[BP+DI+n8]`	2 bytes
	`[BX+SI+n8],[BX+DI+n8]`	2 bytes
	`[BP+SI+n16],[BP+DI+n16]`	3 bytes
	`[BX+SI+n16],[BX+DI+n16]`	3 bytes

Table 1.2   Memory addressing methods.

◆ SECRET "CONSTANT-TO-MEMORY" RULE:
If you move a constant to a Register Pointer plus Constant Mode memory location, you lose 1 cycle.

Most of the examples in this book refer to memory locations by their C variable names, since that's the clearest way to reference them. It's also the Register Pointer plus Constant Mode addressing format: the C variable name is translated to a 16-bit constant address, shown in Table 1.2 as [n16]. Thus, this C program:

```
int mema;
void main ()
{
 mema=5;
}
```

is affected by the Constant-to-Memory Rule because an assembler will translate the body of this program, the C statement mema=5; to:

```
MOV mema,5    ;!2 cycles (Constant-to-Memory Rule)
```

This instruction takes 2 cycles — the 1 cycle used by an ordinary MOV, plus the 1-cycle penalty for moving a constant to memory via the Register Pointer plus Constant Mode addressing method. (Note the way we have indicated a penalty exists in the comment. When you see an exclamation mark preceding a cycle count, this means a penalty has been applied to the instruction. The SECRET RULE that applied the penalty is noted in parentheses at the end of the comment.)

Because a register movement is not affected by the Constant-to-Memory Rule, the following set of instructions would be just as fast:

```
MOV AX,5      ;1 cycle
MOV mema,AX   ;1 cycle
```

By the way, the following quote from Kernighan & Ritchie's *The C Programming Language* provides an optimization tip which is no longer viable:

> "Any operation which can be achieved by array subscripting can also be done with pointers. The pointer version will generally be faster ..."

If this statement were true, the program on the left might be faster than the program on the right:

```
/* POINTER VERSION */        /* ARRAY SUBSCRIPT VERSION */
char mema[10];               char mema[10];
int *memp=&mema[0];
void main ()                 void main ()
{                            {
  *(memp+7)=5;                 mema[7]=5;
}                            }
```

In fact, though, the test compilers translate the critical statement for the pointer version program as:

```
MOV [BX+7],5    ;!2 cycles (Constant-to-Memory Rule)
```

and translate the critical statement for the array subscript version program as:

```
MOV mema+7,5    ;!2 cycles (Constant-to-Memory Rule)
```

The pointer version is thus not faster than the array subscript version after all — the addresses involved are both the Register Pointer plus Constant Mode. Because the 486's addressing modes have similar costs, and because modern C compilers aren't quite so easily fooled, the optimization tip "use pointers rather than array subscripts" should be regarded as obsolete. So beware of such tips: the real difference in an instruction's size and/or speed lies in the access mode that the compiler uses in its translation.

◆ SECRET "REGISTER-POINTER-DOUBLED" RULE:
If you use an address that contains two registers, you lose 1 cycle.

All the Register Pointer Doubled addressing modes in Table 1.2 contain two registers and are therefore affected by the Register- Pointer- Doubled Rule. The source involved doesn't have to be a constant; this rule affects any instruction that contains a Register Pointer Doubled address in either the source *or* the destination. Still, this situation isn't anywhere near as common as the Constant-to-Memory Rule situation.

It's conceivable that a C compiler could use Register Pointer Doubling for the following program:

```
char mema;
char *memb;
int memc;
void main ()
{
  *(memb+memc)=mema;
}
```

For this example, it would be possible to translate the C instruction *(memb+memc)=mema; into:

```
MOV AL,mema         ;1 cycle
MOV BX,memb         ;1 cycle
MOV SI,memc         ;1 cycle
MOV [BX+SI],AL      ;!2 cycles (Register-Pointer-Doubled Rule)
```

but in fact, the test compilers simply add the value of memc to BX. So don't worry that the Register-Pointer-Doubled Rule is ruining your program now, but do keep it in mind for the future.

Putting MOV in a C Program

You now know how to use the assembler MOV instruction. The only question that remains, then, is how to put this knowledge to use within a C program.

To embed assembler instructions in C programs (or, using the correct terminology, to use *inline assembly* in C programs), it is merely necessary to precede such instructions with the keyword __asm and end them with a semicolon, as shown in the following C program:

```
char mema;
void main ()
{
   __asm MOV mema,5;     /* asm is preceded by 2 underline characters */
   printf("The value of mema is: %d\n",mema);
}
```

Exercise: compile and execute this program using your C compiler. You don't have to use any special switches to do so. When you execute the program, you will see that mema is 5.

(Note: glancing at this simple program, you might think that it would be preferable to do the assignment in C:

```
mema=5;
```

instead of in assembler:

```
__asm MOV mema,5;
```

and, of course, you would be right. The C statement not only does the same thing as the assembler instruction, it actually *is* the same thing, since the C compiler will take the C statement mema=5; and translate it to the assembler instruction MOV mema,5. You can get your C compiler to give you an assembler listing, using the /S switch in Borland, the /Fa switch in Microsoft, and the –cod switch in Symantec.)

Optimization Example #1

The following example implements the best code for assigning a constant to two integers in global memory, based on what has been discussed so far.

```
#include <time.h>                        /* This is a timing program */
int mema,memb;                           /* These are the two integers */
void main ()
{
  long l,dl;                             /* These are for the timing */

  dl=time(0);                            /* Get the current time */
  for (l=0; l<50000000; ++l)             /* This is a timing loop */
  {
    memb=mema=1;                         /* This is the critical line */
  }
  printf("%ld seconds\n",time(0)-dl);    /* Display the elapsed time */
}
```

To optimize this program, we compiled it using the test compilers and various switches and examined the assembler output each time. We found that the critical line, the C statement memb=mema=1; was translated in one of three ways:

```
Translation #1            Translation #2          Translation #3
(Microsoft, Borland)      (Borland /O2 switch)    (Symantec,Microsoft /Ox switch)
MOV mema,1                MOV mema,1              MOV AX,1
MOV AX,mema               MOV memb,1             MOV mema,AX
MOV memb,AX                                      MOV memb,AX
57 seconds                54 seconds             51 seconds
```

> ## Timing Displays
> *A word about timing displays throughout this book. The times you see come from a Dell 486/33Mhz. Each test was run in different orders and from different memory locations. We will normally show code without the timing loop around it and simply say "code x is 10 percent faster than code y" or that "there is a 10 percent gain if you use code x." Though we urge you to do your own tests, we are confident that you will get similar results on similar equipment.*

In this example, the amount of the gain is vastly understated, since the time shown is the time it took to run the entire program, including the startup and loop control statements. Comparing cycle counts only, Translations #1 and #2 both take 4 cycles while Translation #3 takes 3 cycles — that is, the cycle gain in the body of the loop is exactly 25 percent. This is a result of the Constant-to-Memory Rule. Apparently Microsoft and Symantec already know this particular secret rule but don't expect everybody to. Borland didn't.

If you're a Borland programmer, then, here's an optimization tip based on our timing tests and the Constant-to-Memory Rule. It's just a matter of replacing one C statement with two lines of inline assembly code. (This sort of quick fix is sometimes called a *spot optimization* or *peephole optimization*.)

```
#include <time.h>               /* This is a variant of the above, */
int mema,memb;                  /* which speeds up Borland C. We */
void main ()                    /* saw that Borland doesn't produce */
{                               /* the fastest code option even if */
 long l,d1;                     /* the /O2 switch (optimize all) */
                                /* is on, so we'll force the issue. */
 d1=time(0);                    /* Instead of memb=mema=1; embed */
 for (l=0; l<50000000; ++l)     /* the assembler instructions which */
 {                              /* we know are faster. */
   __asm MOV AX,1;
   __asm MOV memb,AX;
 }
 printf("%ld seconds\n",time(0)-d1);
}
```

The inline assembly code replacement used above is not pretty, which is why we only suggest using this method for Borland's compiler — other compilers will produce this output anyway if you set the switches right.

The output produced is not the smallest either (in fact it's 1 byte larger than what Borland produces with its /O2 switch). But it is faster, and speed is our main concern in an optimization tip.

This is also a very little optimization tip, but then, all we had to work with was MOV. As you build your assembler vocabulary, you're going to see more SECRET RULES and peephole optimization tips. In the end, they're going to add up to a lot.

Alignment

Here's a program containing two loops which move C int variables. If the program is compiled with Borland C (using the default compile switches for MS-DOS) the second loop will run 20 percent faster than the first loop.

```
struct c
{
 char c1;
 int i1;
 char c2;
 int i2;
} s;
void main ()
{
 long l;
 for (l=1; l<10000000; ++l) s.i1=0;
 for (l=1; l<10000000; ++l) s.i2=0;
}
```

The programs's two loops look similar and, in fact, the underlying assembler instructions are precisely the same for both. The reason that the second loop is faster than the first is that the int variable s.i1 is *misaligned.*

Definition: "a data item is aligned when its address is a multiple of its byte length." We've seen this in print a few times, but it isn't quite accurate.

Intel says that a 0-mod-four address is an address that divides evenly by 4, e.g., addresses of 0, 4, 8, 12, and so on. If a variable is to be aligned, it must fit within a 0-mod-four address memory block. For example, a word starting at address 1 takes up 2 bytes (1 and 2) and is therefore aligned since the memory block ends at byte 3. However, a word starting at address 3 would take up bytes 3 and 4 and is therefore misaligned since byte 4 is the start of a new 0-mod-four address memory block.

When using MOV, the penalty for misalignment is 3 cycles. Further, there is an additional 1-cycle penalty if you read a misaligned word and then access (read or write) another misaligned word. So it's worth it to keep the following in mind:

if (((address+1)%4)==0) then don't put a word at that address;
if ((address%4)!=0) then don't put a double-word at that address;

The example above is atypical. To persuade a C compiler to set up a misaligned int, it is necessary to have the following set of circumstances:

(1) With Borland C, use the default switch instead of the /A switch. (Borland C is the only compiler which does not word-align structure elements by default.)

(2) Define a structure. C compilers will begin assigning global variables on an even boundary (the even address in question will generally be 2 because no variable can have an address of 0). They will assign all the word size and double-word size variables first. That is, regardless of the order of the variables in your program's source code, the actual storage will have ints and longs and unsigneds, and then chars. With this scheme, it's impossible to get a word size variable on an odd address unless the word is in a structure and is preceded by an odd number of char elements.

(3) Ensure the word overlaps a double-word boundary. It's not enough to access a word at location 5+6, 9+10, 13+14, 17+18, 21+22 etc. — there's no penalty there. You have to access a word at location 3+4, 7+8, 11+12, 15+16, 19+20, and so on. That is, the second byte of the word must be at a location which is divisible by 4.

(4) Run on a genuine Intel inside computer.

Based on this, it must appear your C programs won't encounter misalignment unless you go out of your way to bring trouble on yourself. That's true. However, this warning is necessary precisely because there *are* situations, especially when using string pointers, when it appears that accessing a full word is as fast as accessing a byte. Programmers thus *will* go out of their way to bring trouble on themselves if they don't watch out for misalignment.

A Note on 32-bit Registers

The following piece of C code copies a `long int` variable to another `long int`:

```
/* 32-bit Example #1 */
long int mema,memb;
void main ()
{
 mema=memb;
}
```

A C compiler will translate the C statement `mema=memb;` to something like:

```
;32-bit Example #1 Translation
MOV AX,memb
MOV mema,AX
MOV AX,memb+2
MOV mema+2,AX
```

That is, the (16-bit) compiler is moving 16 bits at a time. On a 32-bit computer, it's possible to move 32 bits at a time, using an *extended register*:

```
MOV EAX,memb
MOV mema,EAX
```

The 32-bit `EAX` register is the extended `AX` register, that is, `EAX`'s bottom 16 bits are the same 16-bit `AX` register we've used before. All the registers we've already used can be extended this way (`EAX`, `EBX`, `ECX`, `EDX`, `ESI`, `EDI`, and `EBP`), but their use is restricted as follows:

(1) You can't use a 32-bit register if you don't have a 32-bit computer.

(2) You can't use a 32-bit register when running an old version of OS/2 or a "DOS compatibility box" under an old version of OS/2. (We haven't seen it in action but have heard reports that OS/2 1.x would not save the top half of the register when it interrupted a process.)

(3) You have to tell the assembler that you're using a 32-bit register. If you use Borland TASM or Microsoft MASM, put the directive `.486` before the 32-bit instruction(s), as follows:

```
.486                 ;Accept 486 instructions, e.g., 32-bit
    MOV EAX,memb     ;EAX is 32 bits
    MOV mema,EAX     ;EAX is 32 bits
```

The C inline assembler is unfortunately not as sophisticated. If you're using this method and Symantec C, there's no problem — preface the assembler instruction with __asm and terminate with a semicolon, e.g.:

```
__asm MOV EAX,memb    ;EAX is 32 bits
```

If you're using Borland C, put a prefix byte (DB 66h, called the *operand size override prefix* by Intel) prior to a regular 16-bit instruction, as follows:

```
__asm DB 66h;        /* Prefix byte meaning 32-bit item follows */
__asm MOV AX,memb;   /* 16-bit instruction will be treated as 32-bit */
__asm DB 66h;        /* Prefix byte meaning 32-bit item follows */
__asm MOV mema,AX;   /* 16-bit instruction will be treated as 32-bit */
```

If you're using Microsoft C, use the same method, but replace DB with _emit, e.g.:

```
__asm _emit 66h;     /* Directive meaning 32-bit item follows */
__asm MOV AX,memb;   /* 16-bit instruction will be treated as 32-bit */
```

(There are other complications with inline assembler. In this book, though, we'll avoid them by using only register-to-register and memory-to-register MOVs.)

Once we've checked to ensure that the use of 32-bit registers is allowed in our environment, we can amend the 32-bit Example #1 program so that it uses only two instructions (the prefix byte doesn't count as an instruction) to move memb into mema, as follows:

```
/* 32-bit Example #2 */
long int mema,memb;
void main ()
{
  __asm DB 66h;
  __asm MOV AX,WORD PTR memb;
  __asm DB 66h;
  __asm MOV WORD PTR mema,AX;
}
```

Since the inline assembler routine in this program uses two fewer instructions than the 32-bit Example #1 translation shown on page 15, we might expect the Example #2 program to be the faster of the two programs. This, however, is an *optimization mirage*. The 32-bit Example #2 program is actually *slower* than our first program. There are two reasons for the slowdown.

❖ The first reason is that the alignment's wrong. Although mema and memb are aligned on a word boundary (which is fine when doing a 16-bit move), they are not aligned on a double-word boundary. When 32 bits are moved at a time, there is a large cost from such misalignment.

❖ The second reason is that the mode's wrong. When the default mode is 16 bits (as in ordinary MS-DOS and Windows 3.x applications), the DB 66h prefix has to be added every time a 32-bit instruction is to be executed. The prefixed MOV instruction takes 2 cycles, rather than the 1 cycle needed for an unprefixed MOV (all other things being equal).

If we fixed the 32-bit Example #2 program's alignment problem and ran it on a 386, we would have a 21 percent gain because the 386 has to pay an extra penalty for accessing memory. Thus, halving the number of memory accesses makes the program faster. On a 486 though, the access is going to the 486's cache memory and so no such penalty applies. So, if you have a 486 you will not gain by doing a 32-bit MOV in a 16-bit application, even if you access memory on a double-word alignment. The "easy" 32-bit speedup tricks are, unfortunately, a thing of the past.

There are, however, still some real advantages in 32-bit instructions. The big opportunity areas are:

(1) You can use *any* 32-bit register as an OFFSET register. In 16-bit, you can only use BX, SI, DI, and BP. In 32-bit, this is legal:

```
MOV EAX,OFFSET mema
MOV [EAX],AX
```

(2) You can address using (for example) AX*2, AX*4, AX*8, AX*4 + EBX, and so on, providing the top 16 bits are 0. This adds a lot of flexibility, although at the cost of 1 cycle.

(3) You have a fast-access storage area, namely the top 16 bits of each register, that the compiler makers never use — so there's no conflict.

These factors don't really come into play until we start to use a larger instruction repertoire, but you'll see us taking advantage of 32-bit registers more and more as we progress.

Memory Variables vs. Register Variables

In the program below there are two loops, both of which do the same thing. The second loop is 50 percent faster than the first, though, because it works on a *register variable* (i.e., a variable assigned to a register) rather than a *memory variable* (i.e., a variable assigned to memory). (This is a Borland C test with the optimization switch turned off during compilation. If the optimization switch is on, then `mema` becomes a register variable as well. Microsoft and Symantec automatically put both `mema` and `memb` into registers.)

```
void main ()
{
 int mema=0;
 register int memb=0;
 long i;

 for (i=0; i<8000000; ++i) ++mema;      /* 30 seconds */
 for (i=0; i<8000000; ++i) ++memb;      /* 15 seconds */
}
```

The performance gain when using a register variable is so high that we'd like to be able to use only register variables in all our programs. But there just aren't enough registers to go around (remember, in 16-bit mode there are only seven). Register variables are thus a precious resource and it is important to use them wisely.

When speaking of register variables, Borland's manual says only that:

> "... since Borland C++ does a good job of placing variables in registers, it is rarely necessary to use the **register** keyword." (*Borland C++ 3.0 Programmer's Guide*, page 45)

Borland has good reason to talk so smugly: the automatic assignment of register variables is quite reasonable when compilation takes place with the optimization (/O2) switch on. However, Borland also has some undocumented rules about the use of register variables, which we'll list here so you won't get stung in the few cases where their optimization falls down.

❖ Variables are not used as registers if they're defined as `static`, if they're referenced by a `*pointer`, if they're not declared in the procedure declaration, or if they're only referenced once. These exclusions are unexceptionable.

❖ Double-word variables, e.g., `long int` or `void far *`, are never placed in register variables. If you want to use a 32-bit register (with `SI:DI`), you must use inline assembly.

❖ The program on the left (using `int`) will run faster than the program on the right (using `char`):

```
int memc;                          char memc;
int main ()                        int main ()
{                                  {
  register int mema;                 register char mema;

  mema=memc;                         mema=memc;
  getch();                           getch();
  return (mema);                     return (mema);
}                                  }
```

because `int mema` is in a register but `char mema` is not, even though the code specifically assigns mema as a register variable. There are three reasons for this.

• First, the C compiler interprets the `register` keyword as a hint rather than as a directive. If the compiler doesn't like the hint, the hint is ignored without warning.

• Second, the main function contains a call to another function — `getch`. To the C compiler, `getch` is a black box. There is no way of knowing what `getch` will do, and particularly there is no way of knowing what registers `getch` will change. It isn't safe to move a value to any register, call `getch`, and expect the value in the register to remain unchanged unless the register involved is `SI` or `DI` — the C compiler knows that no function is allowed to change the `SI` register or the `DI` register. Because of this, `SI` and `DI` are the only two registers that the C compiler can use as register variables.

• Third, `SI` and `DI` are full 16-bit size registers. They cannot be referenced a byte at a time as `AX`, `BX`, `CX`, and `DX` can. Because of this, the C compiler cannot use `SI` or `DI` as byte-size register variables.

If a function calls a function, the C optimizer has only two registers available and both of these registers are 16-bit. The fact is quite significant in a general sense; it means that adding a single function call is far more costly than the cost of the function itself because the C optimizer's options become restricted. In a particular sense, you'll sometimes find that register char variables cannot be kept in registers. Another example: the code on the left is faster than the code on the right:

```
int auto_test_1 ()                    int auto_test_1 ()
{                                      {
  auto_test_1();                         auto_test_1();
  toupper('a');                        }
}                                      int auto_test_1 ()
int auto_test_1 ()                     {
{                                      char    a;
char    a;                             int     i;
int     i;                             for (i=0;i<N;++i) if x[i]<0 a=i;
for (i=0;i<N;++i) if x[i]<0 a=i;       toupper('a');
}                                      }
```

Since the code on the left has no procedure, the DL register is used.

❖ When assigning variables to registers, priority is given to variables which appear in loops or which are referenced more than once. But when all other things appear equal, priority is given on a first-declared-first-served basis, e.g.:

```
int auto_test ()
{
long memi;
int mema,memb,memc;

for (memi=0; memi<10; ++memi) toupper(mema++);
for (memi=0; memi<10; ++memi) toupper(memb++);
for (memi=0; memi<100000000; ++memi) toupper(memc++);
}
```

In this example, memi is not a register variable (because it's long), mema and memb are register variables (because they got defined first), and memc is not a register variable (because only SI and DI are available as scratch registers and they've already been used). If the declaration was:

```
int mema,memb;
register int memc;
```

or simply:

```
int mema,memc,memb;
```

then memb would not be a register variable but mema and memc would be. Since memc is used far more often than memb, the code should ensure that memc rather than memb is a register variable; the procedure would be twice as fast.

Pipelines

For most programmers, the details of 486 pipelines aren't terribly important, but a brief discussion of the matter can help explain why certain things go wrong.

Think of a MOV instruction as having 4 different stages.

(1) Fetch the instruction.

(2) Fetch the source operand.

(3) Perform an operation — this is the actual execution.

(4) Store the destination.

Each of these stages requires 1 cycle to complete, so a 486 should use up 4 cycles to do a MOV instruction. However, the cycle count shown for MOV at the beginning of this chapter is only 1 cycle.

This seeming contradiction is explained if you think of a 486 as having four separate processors — one does the instruction fetching, one does the source operand fetching, one performs the operation, and one stores the destination.

Since these little processors are all doing their jobs simultaneously, while Processor Number 3 is actually performing a MOV, Number 2 is already fetching the source operand of the next instruction, and Number 1 is already fetching the next instruction after that. When Number 4 stores the destination of the MOV just performed, Number 3 will be ready to perform the next operation because the fetching has already been done, and so on.

Processor Number 3 is usually the only bottleneck. Not every instruction can be performed in 1 cycle like MOV can; we'll be describing many instructions later that need several cycles to complete. But that doesn't cause any problem when it comes to predicting how long an instruction will take. When we said that

```
MOV <register>,<register>
```

takes 1 cycle, we meant that Processor Number 3 takes 1 cycle for the actual execution of the instruction. Providing that Number 1, Number 2, and Number 4 get their jobs done while Number 3 is working on its problem —

and they usually can — the actual elapsed time is really and measurably 1 cycle, or one thirty-three-millionth of a second on a 33MHz machine.

If it were possible to use the words "they *always* can" instead of "they *usually* can" in the above description, it wouldn't be necessary to discuss this pipeline process at all. But delays can and do happen. We know of six situations that can stall the pipeline. There may be others that nobody knows about. Apparently, Intel is not eager to publicize such matters.

The first chance to have a pipeline stall is when Processor Number 1 (henceforth called the "Prefetcher") fails to get the next instruction in time to pass it on. This situation is easy to arrange: if the Prefetcher is always busy getting the *next* instruction, putting a goto (or the assembler equivalent) in the code stalls things because it means the next instruction isn't needed yet — the object of the jump is needed instead.

The second chance to have a pipeline stall is when the Prefetcher has to fetch long instructions while Processor Number 3 (the "Executer") is performing quick instructions that take only 1 or 2 cycles each.

The third chance to have a pipeline stall is when the contents of the source or destination operand isn't available. Register operands are right on the chip and are usually available instantaneously, but memory operands are far off in the RAM. It could take more than 1 cycle to access them. The 486 design solves this by caching (more on this later).

The fourth chance to have a pipeline stall is when Processors Number 2 and Number 4 (the "Opfetchers") can't fetch a memory location because they don't know the address. This can happen with (for example) the MOV instruction because MOV can refer to a memory address using a register, e.g., MOV AX,[BX] or MOV [BX],5. In most cases, the Opfetcher knows what BX is, so it also knows the address of what it must fetch. Thus, all runs smoothly until this pair of instructions comes along:

Instruction 1:   MOV BX,AX
Instruction 2:   MOV AX,[BX]

Here, the value in the BX register is being set by the Executer in Instruction 1. Since the Opfetcher must know what's in BX before it can do its job, it cannot fetch the [BX] memory location for Instruction 2 until the Executer finishes. Since the Opfetcher must wait, the operations are not simultaneous. The result is that the Opfetcher's time must be added on to the usual cycle count when the length of time this pair of instructions will take is calculated. This situation, which Intel sometimes calls the "address generation interlock," provides us with our next SECRET RULE.

◆ **SECRET "REGISTER-ADDRESS" RULE:**
If you set a register value just before using the register for an address, you lose 2 cycles. Further, if you set a register value, then execute any 1-cycle instruction, and then use the register for an address, you lose 1 cycle.

The Register-Address Rule is illustrated in the following program:

```
int memj,memk;
void main ()
{
 register int *memi;
 memi=&memj;
 *memi=5;
 memk=6;
}
```

Some C compilers will translate the body of this program into:

```
MOV SI,OFFSET memj
MOV [SI],5               ;pipeline stall!
MOV memk,6
```

The program is faster if the MOV memk,6 instruction is moved to just after the MOV SI,OFFSET memj instruction because the Prefetcher then has SI's value when it reaches MOV [SI],5 — eliminating the stall. Since this can't be guaranteed using C, use inline assembler to speed up the program:

```
int memj,memk;
void main ()
{
 register int memi;
 __asm MOV SI,OFFSET memj;
 __asm MOV memk,6;
 __asm MOV [SI],5;
}
```

The Register-Address Rule doesn't apply within the same instruction, so instructions like MOV BX,[BX] and MOV SI,[SI] have no penalty.

If you use 32-bit registers, the Register-Address Rule is less injurious — it ordinarily involves only a 1-cycle penalty, and there is no penalty at all if a 1-cycle instruction intervenes between the setting and use of a register.

The fifth chance to have a pipeline stall is a variant of the fourth and has different penalties depending on the situation. It's our next SECRET RULE.

◆ **SECRET "BYTES-AND-POINTERS" RULE:**
If you move a value to a byte register, then use any instruction that runs in precisely 1 cycle, then use a register pointer such as [BX] or [SI+n], you lose a cycle. Further, if you move a value to a byte register, then move a value to another byte register, then use an address register, you lose 2 cycles. (The only known exception to this is the use of: MOV <Register Pointer plus Constant memory addressing mode>,<constant>).

The Bytes-and-Pointers Rule affects the following sets of instructions:

```
MOV DL,5            ;The first instruction moves to a byte register
MOV AX,[BX]         ;The second instruction runs in 1 cycle
MOV CX,[BX+2]       ;The third instruction uses [BX] — penalty!

MOV DL,5            ;This is affected, the penalty of using the
ADD [BX+SI],AX      ;double-register comes at the start — penalty!
```

The following sets of instructions, on the other hand, are not affected:

```
MOV DL,5            ;This is not affected because the intervening
MOV [BX+2],0        ;instruction takes 2 cycles
MOV [BX+4],DL

MOV DL,5            ;This is not affected because [BX+5] is a Register
MOV CX,[BX+2]       ;Pointer plus Constant memory addressing mode
MOV [BX+5],5
```

This seemingly innocent piece of code is a particularly disastrous example of the rules described in this section:

```
char *memp;
void main ()
{
 *memp+=5;
}
```

If all optimization switches are set, Borland translates the C statement
*memp+=5; into:

```
MOV BX,memp    ;1 cycle
MOV AL,[BX]    ;!3 cycles (Register-Address Rule)
ADD AL,5       ;1 cycle (adds 5 to AL — see Chapter 2)
MOV [BX],AL    ;!3 cycles (Bytes-and-Pointers Rule
```

The first thing to notice about this result is that MOV AL,[BX]
follows MOV BX,memp — and there's a 2-cycle penalty for that,
according to the Register-Address Rule. The second thing to notice is
that MOV [BX],AL gets the full force of the Bytes-and-Pointers Rule, which
adds another 2-cycle penalty. In total, then, *memp+=5; takes 8 cycles.

If Borland had known about the penalties, the C statement would
instead be translated:

```
MOV BX,memp    ;1 cycle
MOV AX,5       ;1 cycle
ADD [BX],AL    ;!4 cycles
```

which takes only 6 cycles. (Note: there is no way to tell if the Bytes-
and-Pointers Rule is affecting performance by looking at C code, so we
only mention this obscure possibility for the sake of completeness.)

The sixth, and final, chance to have a pipeline stall involves using the
low and high halves of the same register in successive instructions. A
16-bit register, such as AX, is really kept as a unit, so Processor Number
2 (the source fetcher) can occasionally have trouble getting AL if Number
4 (the destination storer) is storing AH but doesn't know what AL is.
Fortunately, using something as simple as:

```
MOV AL,1
MOV AH,2
```

won't cause the trouble. To cause the stall you have to use particular
register combinations or particular instructions; due to the complications,
the details are best dealt with when we've finished discussing arithmetic
in Chapter 2 (see the Secret Hi/Lo Rule).

Caching

In our discussion of pipeline stalls, we mentioned that the 486 design
solves the problem of memory operand access by caching. We now return
to that subject.

All 486s have a cache on the chip. The computer manufacturer usually adds a RAM cache too, which is also good but tends to mask the effects of Intel's on-chip cache. Caches are wonderful things. The most wonderful part about them is that it isn't necessary to worry much about how they work.

One very important fact about the 486's cache is that the size of the cache line is 16 bytes. This means that if a program accesses a byte[memx] in an array, the 486 will not read in just 1 byte of the RAM. It will transfer a full 16 bytes into its cache. Then, when the program accesses byte[memx+1], the 486 won't access RAM at all because the needed value is in the cache already. (The exception is when byte[memx] mod-16 is 15. Then, of course, byte[memx] is the last byte in the cache line, and byte[memx+1] is the first byte of the next cache line.)

Since there are many cache lines, a loop can't be sped up by simple tricks like keeping all memory accesses within certain 16-byte blocks. It does help to know, though, that addresses which are evenly divisible by 16 (0-mod-16 addresses) have an important meaning as cache line boundaries.

486 caches are unified, which means that both code and data are kept in the same cache. Generally, it isn't necessary to worry about the code caching: the Prefetcher usually has plenty of time to read in the next 16 bytes of code before the program reaches it. The exception is when the code is instructed to jump somewhere else (i.e., when the code includes the equivalent of a goto) or if every instruction accesses memory — since the cache is unified, the code Prefetcher can't get at the cache at the same time that an instruction is explicitly reading or writing to memory.

We call this the *Unified Cache Penalty* — since the prefetch queue is 32 bytes long (the 16 bytes the Prefetcher has just read plus the 16 bytes waiting in the cache) and since data references have priority over code references, a series of data references (i.e., memory accesses) will exhaust the prefetch queue and cause a stall. For example, if 15 MOV AX, [BX] instructions are strung in a row, at some point Intel will have to stall for 1 or 2 cycles because the Prefetcher hasn't had a chance to get at the cache. This rarely happens, though. Typically, it works out that memory-access instructions are mixed in with other instructions (e.g., MOV AX, DX) and in that case the penalty won't happen. To avoid the Unified Cache Penalty then, change code order so an instruction that doesn't reference data is intersticed between those that do.

Another, far more frequently encountered, penalty is the *Write-through Cache Penalty*. To see this penalty in action, string five MOV [BX],AX instructions together:

```
MOV [BX],AX     ;1 cycle
MOV [BX],AX     ;1 cycle
MOV [BX],AX     ;1 cycle
MOV [BX],AX     ;1 cycle
MOV [BX],AX     ;!2 cycles — penalty applies here
```

(Note: you may see this penalty at a different point — it varies depending on the type of 486 chip.)

When the 486 writes to memory, it really *does* a write to memory. With some caching systems that's not true: only the cache is changed, *not* the RAM. But a normal Intel 486 changes both the cache *and* the RAM — that's what write-through means.

In a strict write-through system, writing instructions are always slower than reading instructions. That's not true with 486s though. A 486 holds off on writing for a short while, hoping you'll do something else so that the write-through can be performed in the background. If you don't give the machine a chance — if you *do* write five times in a row — the 486 gives up waiting and you get hit with a 1-cycle penalty.

The conclusion that writes are slower than reads in a write-through system may at first appear spurious. After all, the instruction MOV AX,[SI], which does a "read from memory (to a register)" takes 1 cycle, as does the instruction MOV [SI],AX, which does a "write to memory (from a register)". Since most simple instructions are symmetric like MOV is, our first impulse was to say that reading from memory takes the same amount of time as writing to memory. But let's suppress that impulse until we examine some more data.

Here's an example of a simple test of the cache. The cache on our Intel 486 has a size of 8,192 bytes (sizes vary but 8Kb is normal), and the caching algorithm is "throw out the Least Recently Used data" (LRU caching algorithm). Therefore, to defeat Intel caching, it's merely necessary to move through data in a forward direction, through a buffer that's bigger than 8Kb. We wrote a program with two loops that move in a cache-defeating way. The two loops are precisely the same except that one reads from memory while the other writes to memory.

When we run the program, the "reading" loop takes 11 cycles, while the "writing" loop takes 8 cycles, on average. In other words, writing is faster than reading when the cache is defeated on a typical 486. Upon reflection, we think this makes sense, because when executing a MOV [SI],AX instruction, the 486 doesn't care whether or when the contents of the AX register actually reach the memory location. A good analogy here is that of football. A football quarterback throws a ball, then moves on immediately to the next task (such as hiding from a tackler). As far as he is concerned, the throwing ends when the ball is in the air. Now consider the receiver, who waits for the ball to arrive. From his perspective, the throwing time includes the time the ball is in the air and does not end until the ball arrives in his hands. A "write" operation is a throw, a "read" operation is a reception, and therefore writes are faster than reads because during writes the 486 has a quarterback's perspective.

This describes the normal situation: usually writes and reads take the same time, but sometimes writes will look a little faster if the cache mechanism is being overloaded. Some 486s, though, don't behave this way. We've taken the most extreme example from the variety of 486s that we tested; here's what we saw (for comparison we show the cycle times on a "normal" machine too; ADD, XCHG, PUSH, and REP STOSW are all write operations, more on them later):

Instruction Executed	Regular 486/33 Time in Seconds	Anomalous 486DX2/66 Time in Seconds
ADD [SI],1	4	25
XCHG [SI],AX	10	52
PUSH AX	1	18
MOV CX,2 ... REP STOSW	20	59

As the figures in the Anomalous column show, writing to memory incurs a huge penalty, between 21 and 42 cycles, on typical instructions. It would thus be easy to write programs which worked faster on the 33MHz benchmark machine than on the so-called "double speed" DX2. Yet the DX2 performed all other tasks (reads, jumps, register-to-register comparisons, etc.) in precisely the number of cycles that one would expect. So, usually a 486DX2 takes the same number of cycles to perform a task as a 486DX, and therefore it's twice as fast (because most operations take place within the chip so the DX2 can operate at its clock-doubled speed). But the exception to the rule is so significant that we recommend caution. You should assume that your target machines might include a 486DX2 like the one we tested, and therefore take it as a "rule of thumb" that reads are faster than writes even though the evidence of your senses appears to contradict this.

What follows from this conclusion? Once again, it's worth recommending that you use registers rather than memory locations to store temporary values. In extreme situations, save the contents of a register by moving it to another register.

◆ **SECRET "CACHE-SMASH" RULE:**
If you access several memory addresses which are exactly or nearly 800h bytes (2048 decimal) apart, you risk a huge penalty. The penalty is usually between 70 and 90 cycles but may be masked if the computer has an external cache.

The Cache-Smash Rule has to do with the way that Intel manages the cache. At the nethermost level, a level application programs never see, Intel uses a 32-bit physical address which has 3 parts:

"tag"	"index"	"byte"
21 bits	7 bits	4 bits
xxxxxxxxxxxxxxxxxxxxx	xxxxxxx	xxxx

The lowmost 4 bits (the byte bits) reference individual bytes within the cache line. Since cache lines are 16 bytes long, bytes within the cache line can be addressed with a 4-bit address.

The higher-order index bits and tag bits get their names from some Intel documents which describe the details of the Intel cache structure. The details don't matter here. The only important thing is that tag and index are distinct. If two addresses have different tag bits, but the index bits are the same, there is a chance of derailing Intel's cache manager. Since the bottom 16 bits of Intel's physical address are simply the offset address, a small-model C program can check if two variables, mema and memb, meet the criterion with this statement condition:

```
if (((&mema&0x7F0)==(&memb&0x7F0))&&((&mema&0x0F800)!=(&memb&0x0F800)))
```

The following C statements illustrate the Cache-Smash Rule. They reference several addresses which are 2048 bytes apart (note that the addresses don't always have to be precisely 2048 bytes apart because the byte bits don't count in Intel's calculation). memp is a pointer to a char array.

```
mema=*memp;
mema=*(memp+2048);
mema=*(memp+4096);
mema=*(memp+8192);
```

In assembler the relevant lines look like:

```
MOV AX,[BX]           ;mema=*memp; (compiler has already loaded BX)
MOV mema,AX
MOV AX,[BX+2048]      ;mema=*(memp+2048);
MOV mema,AX
MOV AX,[BX+4096]      ;mema=*(memp+4096);
MOV mema,AX
MOV AX,[BX+8192]      ;mema=*(memp+8192);
MOV mema,AX
```

The penalty for these statements is between 70 and 90 cycles (the amount varies depending on the state of the cache beforehand). The lines are 1,000 percent slower than the very similar:

```
mema=*memp;
mema=*(memp+2000);
mema=*(memp+4000);
mema=*(memp+8000);
```

The Cache-Smash Rule is hard to detect but easy to avoid. Don't jump all over memory with a few instructions, and be especially careful when dealing with buffers whose size is an exact multiple of 2048.

Intel's cache design is efficient. By their own claims, only 10 percent of memory accesses are cache misses. That is, 90 percent of the time the memory you're after is already in the cache. Note that this figure applies to data and code memory combined, though. Since execution almost always proceeds sequentially from one code instruction to the next (or repeats loops) it's easy to get a good hit rate for code. We assume that if we considered data alone, more than 10 percent of memory accesses would be cache misses.

One thing the cache design is *not*: it's not predictable. True, Intel uses a modification of the popular least recently used (LRU) caching method, but this modification is imprecise: the 486 allots only 3 bits for the frequency-of-use field. And although the total Intel cache size is almost always 8Kb (which makes for 512 cache lines of 16 bytes each), you can't really depend on this always being true. Many Cyrixes, for instance, have smaller caches (as little as 1Kb in size) and some of the newer chips, the 486DX4 for instance, have larger caches, ranging up to 16Kb in some cases. Calculating precisely what will happen with the cache on any machine is therefore a huge job that's probably not worth doing. Personally, we'll just rely on Intel and do our best not to muck things up.

Segments

The MOV AX, [BX] instruction uses the BX register as an address. Since BX is a 16-bit register, the maximum address is (2**16 − 1) = 65535. That is, the maximum space available is 64Kb if 16-bit addressing is used. Because of this, it is necessary to use segments once MS-DOS and Windows 3.x programs reach a significant size.

What is a segment? A segment is a block of memory up to 64Kb in size (but it can be smaller).

A segment identifier is a 16-bit word that identifies the segment (in real mode it contains the segment's absolute address but we're not going to get into that; for this discussion, assume the identifier is an arbitrary number). A segment register is one of four registers — CS (Code Segment), DS (Data Segment), ES (Extra Segment), and SS (Stack Segment) — which contains a segment identifier (actually there are others, but they're almost never used). A segmented address is an address that contains not only the <memory> operand (which is really just the 16-bit offset within a segment), but also a reference to the segment register.

Ordinarily, memory accesses are in the Data Segment. The assembler notation for this is DS:. For almost all addressing modes, DS: is implicit, thus, the instructions MOV AX, [BX] and MOV AX,DS: [BX] are equivalent. There is one exception: when using the BP register, SS: is implicit. Thus, the instructions MOV AX, [BP] and MOV AX,SS: [BP] are equivalent but MOV AX,DS: [BP] is not. (Up until now, we haven't had to talk about BP's vagaries because we've simply assumed that the program is the C small model. In the small model, the DS and SS registers just happen to contain the same identifier value.)

Some examples of MOV instructions using segmented addresses are:

```
MOV AX,CS:[BX]   ;move the value pointed to by BX in the CS segment to AX
MOV ES:mem,AX    ;move AX to the variable named mem in the ES segment
MOV AX,DS:mem+5  ;move the word at location mem+5 in the DS segment to AX
```

The instruction used to load the ES register looks like an ordinary MOV, but in fact there are four special forms involved, as shown in Table 1.3.

(Notice that it isn't possible to say MOV <segment-register>,<constant>; there are certain restrictions involving segment registers. Notice also that all segment-register MOVs take 3 cycles. This contrasts with regular MOVs which take 1 cycle. It also contrasts a fair bit with some assembler reference guides which claim that `MOV <segment-register>,<memory>` takes 9 cycles. Those guides assume you use 32-bit mode.)

Moving to a segment-register does not stall the pipeline for the next instruction, so don't worry about losing a cycle with:

```
MOV DS,DX      ;3 cycles
MOV AX,mem     ;1 cycle
```

These instructions will take the expected 4 cycles.

In this book, we are not going to work on the problem of how to establish what segments and identifiers are available to the program; C compilers handle that chore. We'll just concern ourselves with the problems that segment addressing brings. We'll begin with this C program:

```
int far *memp;
void main ()
{
    int   memi;

    *memp=memi;
}
```

In this program, `memp` is a far pointer, which means it's a 32-bit item containing both the offset and the segment identifier. (Don't worry about how `memp`'s segment came into existence; assume the C compiler handles that chore, e.g., inside a `farmalloc` function). The best way to translate the `*memp=memi;` function is:

```
;*memp=memi; Translation #1
MOV BX,WORD PTR memp          ;1 cycle
MOV ES,WORD PTR memp+2        ;3 cycles
MOV AX,WORD PTR [BP-2]        ;1 cycle
MOV WORD PTR ES:[BX],AX       ;2 cycles
```

In this translation, the words `WORD PTR` are a directive to remove ambiguity; we're explicitly telling the assembler to use a 16-bit word for

Instruction Mnemonic	Destination Operand	Source Operand	Cycle Count
`MOV`	`<16-bit register>`	`,<segment-register>`	3
`MOV`	`<word-size memory>`	`,<segment register>`	3
`MOV`	`<segment-register>`	`,<16-bit register>`	3
`MOV`	`<segment-register>`	`,<word-size memory>`	3

Table 1.3   Standardized description for <segment-register> `MOV` instructions.

memp. (BYTE PTR tells the assembler to use a byte and DWORD PTR tells the assembler the operand is 32 bits long.) Since memp is actually 32 bits long, we must explicitly override what the assembler would assume in this case.

Translation #1 of *memp=memi; takes 7 cycles: 1 cycle for the ordinary command MOV BX,WORD PTR memp; 3 cycles for MOV ES,WORD PTR memp+2; 1 cycle for MOV AX,WORD PTR [BP-2]; and another 2 cycles for MOV WORD PTR ES:[BX],AX. The reason this last instruction takes 2 cycles is that it's actually *two* instructions. This is another SECRET RULE.

◆ **SECRET "PREFIX" RULE:**
Whenever you use a segment override (CS: or DS: or ES: or SS:), the assembler will begin with a 1-byte, 1-cycle instruction (the segment override instruction). Although generally used and referred to as a prefix, the segment override is really a separate instruction, and it can exist independently.

Knowing this, do we have any options when translating *memp=memi;? Yes, but all the options are bad ones:

❖ First option: dismiss any thought of using instructions that change the SS or CS registers. At this stage, and possibly forever, the values in these registers should be held sacred and inviolable. CS: and SS: can be used as segment overrides, but that's it.

❖ Second option: if you notice that your C compiler is using a special instruction, LES, to do this job, cancel it — the C compiler is making a mistake. You will save 4 cycles by replacing LES with two MOVs, as illustrated in our translation. (We'll cover LES and other "instructions of dubious utility" in Chapter 5.)

❖ Third option: load DS instead of ES. The DS register is one of the registers that can't be changed permanently because DS is the register used by the C code for memory storage. Unless DS is restored after the assembler work is done, the C code is unable to use any near pointers or other memory variables. To solve this, save DS's value before *memp=memi; and restore DS's value when done. For example, the following code uses DX as the save register:

```
;*memp=memi; Translation #2
MOV DX,DS                        ;3 cycles ;Save a copy of DS in DX
MOV BX,WORD PTR memp             ;1 cycle
MOV DS,WORD PTR memp+2           ;3 cycles
MOV AX,WORD PTR [BP-2]           ;1 cycle
MOV WORD PTR [BX],AX             ;1 cycle
MOV DS,DX                        ;3 cycles ;Restore DS from DX
```

This translation saves 1 cycle because MOV WORD PTR [BX],AX doesn't need a segment override instruction. DS: is assumed, and there is no penalty for using it with [BX]. However, MOV DX,DS and MOV DS,DX are both 3-cycle instructions, so this translation (which uses 12 cycles) is not as good as Translation #1 (which uses 7 cycles). The advantage of using ES is that its contents don't need to be saved — the C compiler doesn't demand that. This clearly overrides the 1-cycle disadvantage of the Prefix Rule.

We won't, however, give up on DS too quickly, since using it does save 1 cycle each time memp is referenced. If the program references memp more than once between the time DS is saved and restored, there is a cumulative saving. After seven references to memp, the cumulative saving (7 cycles) is greater than the time spent saving and restoring DS (6 cycles). This is the glimmering of a very significant optimization, which we'll see some huge gains from in Chapter 6, where we discuss the use of near and far pointers in greater detail.

The Prefix Rule doesn't affect just segment overrides. Other prefixes added to assembler instructions include the 32-bit operand size override (i.e., the DB 66h prefix byte discussed earlier), the 0Fh override added to certain instructions (see Chapter 3), and the REP and REPNZ prefixes that can be added to Intel string instructions (see Chapter 9). Each of these will add 1 cycle to an instruction's usual cycle count because of the Prefix Rule.

There is one other SECRET RULE having to do with segment overrides and other prefixes.

◆ SECRET "PREFIX-WAIVER" RULE:
There is no charge for using a prefix if the previous instruction takes more than 1 cycle unless the previous instruction is JMP or CALL (see Chapters 3 and 6). This rule is cumulative so that if, for example, an instruction has 2 prefixes and the previous instruction takes 3 or more cycles, both prefixes are free.

For example, a MOV DWORD PTR [BX+4],0 instruction moves a constant to a Register Pointer plus Constant address (cost: 2 cycles) and the operation is 32-bit so there is a DB 66h operand size override prefix (cost: 1 cycle, usually). If the instruction is executed twice, it speeds up:

```
MOV DWORD PTR [BX+4],0    ;!3 cycles (Prefix Rule)
MOV DWORD PTR [BX+4],0    ;2 cycles (no charge for the prefix)
```

In the next example, the third instruction, MOV [BX],AL, gets hit by the Bytes-and-Pointers Rule so it takes 2 cycles. Because of this, the fourth instruction, MOV ES:[BX],AL, takes only 1 cycle: there is no charge for using the segment-override prefix ES::

```
MOV AL,5         ;1 cycle
MOV DX,5         ;1 cycle
MOV [BX],AL      ;!2 cycles (Bytes-and-Pointers Rule)
MOV ES:[BX],AL   ;!1 cycle — the prefix is free
```

In the following code, the first instruction is MOV DX,ES, which takes 3 cycles. MOV ES:[BX],EAX has two prefixes: the ES: segment-override prefix and the DB 66h 32-bit prefix. Ordinarily, of course, the MOV itself takes 1 cycle, and so does each prefix, for a total of 3 cycles. Not so here; both prefixes are free because of the Prefix-Waiver Rule:

```
MOV DX,ES        ;3 cycles
MOV ES:[BX],EAX  ;1 cycle
```

The following code shows a counter-example of this rule. In this code the "previous" instruction is Instruction #1's MOV [BX],55 which is a 1-cycle instruction. The ES: portion of Instruction #1 is actually the instruction before that and so Instruction #2's prefix is not free:

```
Instruction #1: MOV ES:[BX],55    ;2 cycles
Instruction #2: MOV ES:[BX],55    ;2 cycles
                                  ; (ES: is not free)
```

To take advantage of the Prefix-Waiver-Rule, put any instructions that use segment overrides or 32-bit operands after slow (multi-cycle) instructions. If you can change the order of instructions this way, you will save the cycle(s) normally used by the prefixes.

By the way, instructions on extended registers are not fully affected by the Register-Address Rule. That is:

```
MOV BX,DX       ;1 cycle
MOV AX,[BX]     ;!3 cycles (Register-Address Rule)
```

causes a 2-cycle penalty, but

```
MOV EBX,EDX     ;!2 cycles (Prefix-Rule)
MOV AX,[BX]     ;!2 cycles (Register-Address Rule)
```

causes only a 1-cycle stall — so both of these instruction pairs take 4 cycles.

We've talked about cycle times a lot in this chapter and are now at the point where we can show you how we measured them. Before we do though, we'll just repeat some of the minor points about segments that tend to become traps if you forget about them:

❖ MOVs involving segment registers take 3 cycles.

❖ CS: and DS: and ES: and SS: are, in effect, 1-cycle instructions.

❖ BP is used for accessing memory in the SS segment, not the DS segment.

❖ CS and SS should never be changed.

❖ DS should only be changed if the cumulative savings from its use is greater than the cost (6 cycles) of its use.

How Real Is A Cycle?

By definition, a 33 MHz 486DX computer does 33 million cycles in one second, so we can use the word "cycle" as if it's a fairly precise unit of time, namely one thirty-three-millionth of a second — or one twenty-five-millionth of a second on a 25 MHz machine, one sixty-millionth of a second on a 60 MHz machine, and so forth.

Also by definition, a typical MOV instruction takes 1 cycle — Intel says so, and they define the processor. At this point however, we want to address the question: is Intel telling the "Truth"? This is, of course, rather a paranoid way of putting it, but so far in this chapter we've had to describe a lot of complications in cycle counting when using MOV — and Intel didn't tell us about all of them. Why should we trust them on the basic assumption?

To answer the question, we actually set out to time 27 MOV instructions. We put as much variety as we could get into our MOV timings. The instruction size varied from 2 to 6 bytes; the predicted time varied from 1 to 6 cycles. When doing our timings, the initial conditions were that the BX register pointed to a memory location named mem. mem contained a 16-bit value, OFFSET mem — that is, mem pointed to itself. The memory location mem+2 also contained OFFSET mem, as did memory location mem+7. mem was an aligned address, therefore mem+7 was not. The SI register contained 0. Table 1.4 shows our results.

The figures for the Actual Seconds column come straight from the computer's clock. To get the figures for the Actual Seconds column, we ran each instruction 10 times, then put it in a loop that repeated 3.3 million times. We also had to time an empty loop (a loop that does nothing 3.3 million times), so that we'd have a base figure to subtract from each instruction's timing. The number shown in Table 1.4 for each instruction timed is the net figure and is therefore an actual statement of the number of seconds a repeated-and-looped instruction takes on a real machine.

The Size column of Table 1.4 shows the size of the instruction in bytes. The Predicted Cycles column shows the theoretical number of cycles the instruction should take; the footnotes in this column refer to factors which cause cycles to be lost. Remember that each instruction is repeated 10 times, so the figure in this column is the total predicted cycle count divided by 10, that is, it's the average. (You might find this column interesting for an exercise: try to figure out why the predicted cycle time is as stated without peeking at the footnotes.)

We decided to mix two factors into our test situation because:

(a) Since each instruction repeats 10 times, the loop is not tight; it will be larger than a cache line in most cases. (Repeating instructions rather than jumping back and doing them again is called loop unrolling.)

(b) Since each loop repeats 3.3 million times, it takes up enough time for the PC's imprecise clock to measure the results with reasonable precision. Notice that 10 times 3.3 million is 33 million, so a 1-cycle instruction like MOV DL,5 should take 1 second if our 33 MHz computer is really doing 33 million cycles per second.

Instruction	Size (bytes)	Predicted Cycles	Actual Seconds
MOV DL,5	2	1.0	0.94
MOV EAX,EAX	2	2.0 [5]	1.93
MOV AX,[BX+SI]	2	2.0 [3]	1.93
MOV AX,ES	2	3.0	2.92
MOV ES,BX	2	3.0	2.92
MOV BX,[BX+SI]	2	3.8 [3]	3.69
MOV AX,1000	3	1.0	0.95
MOV AX,[BX+2]	3	1.0	1.05
MOV AX,ES:[BX]	3	2.0 [4]	1.93
MOV AX,[BX+SI+2]	3	2.0 [3]	2.04
MOV [BX+SI],50	3	2.0 [3] [3a]	1.99
MOV ES,[BX+2]	3	3.0	2.92
MOV AX,[BX+7]	3	4.0 [1]	4.89
MOV BX,[BX+SI+2]	3	4.0 [2] [3]	3.86
MOV ES,[BX+SI+2]	3	4.0 [3]	3.91
MOV ES,ES:[BX]	3	3.1	3.03
MOV ES,[BX+SI+7]	3	7.0 [1] [3]	6.87
MOV BX,[BX+SI+7]	3	7.0 [1] [2] [3]	6.77
MOV [BX],5000	4	1.3 [7]	1.43
MOV [BX+7],50	4	2.0 [6]	1.94
MOV ES:[BX],50	4	2.0 [2]	1.93
MOV BX,ES:[BX+2]	4	2.9 [2a] [4]	3.03
MOV ES:[BX+2],DS	4	3.1 [4a]	3.03
MOV AX,ES:[BX+7]	4	5.0 [1] [4]	5.17
MOV [BX+SI+2],1000	5	2.0 [3] [3a]	1.93
MOV [BX+SI+7],1000	5	5.0 [1] [3] [3a]	4.90
MOV EAX,1000	6	2.0 [5]	1.93

Footnotes:

[1]: Lose 3 cycles for a misaligned address

[2]: Lose 2 cycles for using address register just after loading

[2a]: Lose 1 cycle for using address register 1 cycle after loading

[3]: Lose 1 cycle for double indexing

[3a]: Since double-indexing penalty is in effect, do not lose 1 cycle for moving a constant to a Register Pointer plus Constant memory address

[4]: Lose 1 cycle for using a segment prefix in the memory address

[4a]: Prefix penalty is waived on all instructions except the first

[5]: Lose 1 cycle for using a 32-bit register prefix

[6]: Lose 1 cycle for moving a constant to a Register Pointer plus Constant memory address

[7]: Too many moves to memory in a row -- Cache Write-though Penalty

Table 1.4   Timing MOV.

For the reasons stated, the figures in the Predicted Cycles and Actual Seconds columns should be approximately the same. We can draw the following conclusions from Table 1.4's data:

❖ The Predicted Cycles and the Actual Seconds figures match within a few percent. Sure, there's a little bit of a noise factor present — perhaps 33 million isn't a precise number, perhaps the PC's 8254 timer chip is not set right, perhaps some external hardware is occasionally interrupting. We aren't going to worry about such an insignificant amount of noise — we think there's enough solid data here for some firm conclusions.

❖ The numbers show that we shouldn't have doubted the honest folks at Intel. However, many of the Predicted Cycle times were actually based on our own analysis and contradict Intel's documentation. We think this justifies our detailed discussions of Cycle Times, which are now proven to be real.

❖ Cycle times are real. If you know the cycle times, you can predict the actual time a loop will take — with, of course, some provisos.

The first proviso is the complexity of the prediction. We've already discussed a number of situations affecting cycle times — pipeline stalls and penalties and misalignment — and we'll be adding to them in the rest of this book. So we'll ask you to take this on faith for now: you don't need to worry about the complexity. As a reward for reading this book, we'll supply you with a computer program that handles the whole business of figuring out the Predicted Cycles (TACHO.EXE on this book's diskette).

The second proviso is the size of the loops in our tests. None of them are more than 60 bytes long. That's small enough that the whole code is in cache. If the whole code were not in the cache, cache time would be significant and the code would run slower than the cycle times indicate — to a small but unpredictable degree.

In fact, in tests with very long loops, we saw that when the number of cycles is greater than the number of bytes, the actual and predicted figures are still close to matching (usually within 20 percent). When the number of cycles is much less than the number of bytes — that is, when an instruction is fast but lengthy — the actual figure can be 50 percent or 100 percent greater than the simple cycle count would indicate. These results confirm that the Prefetcher cannot keep up with the Executer when the former has to fetch many bytes and the latter has little work to do.

We repeated the Table 1.4 test on several machines and found that the Actual Seconds column remained the same for every machine tested, but that the memory-writing instruction times varied if the machine was a 486SX or a clock-doubled DX2. We expected that, because such times are affected greatly by the memory interface. Nevertheless, we have a rough indicator of fetching's effect on instructions outside loops: divide the number of cycles by the number of bytes in the instruction. We'll use this ratio in the next chapters to decide between two assembler instructions that do the same thing.

Where You Are

This chapter is lengthy because we've tried to give you a true assembler primer. You now have a one-word assembler vocabulary and the framework in which to use it to help you improve the performance of your C programs. Since performance isn't just based on efficient movement of variables stored in memory, we'll expand this vocabulary in the next few chapters. Before we do, though, we'll review what we've discussed so far.

In this chapter, you learned:

❖ how to assign values from a constant, register, or memory variable to a register or memory variable with MOV, and how to use inline assembly to put MOV directly into your C programs by prefacing it with __asm and terminating it with a semicolon;

❖ to identify and use the seven basic 16-bit registers — AX, BX, CX, DX, SI, DI, and BP, the seven basic 32-bit registers — EAX, EBX, ECX, EDX, ESI, EDI, and EBP, and the four basic 16-bit segment registers — CS, DS, ES, and SS;

❖ that the 8-bit high and low halves of the AX, BX, CX, and DX registers can be directly referred to by appending the letter H (high half) or the letter L (low half) to the first letter of each register's name;

❖ that the BX, SI, DI, and BP registers can be used as pointers;

❖ the three forms of memory addressing modes — Register Pointer Mode, Register Pointer plus Constant Mode, and Register Pointer

Doubled Mode — and how they affect the size and speed of assembler instructions;

❖ the advantages of using register variables over memory variables;

❖ how misalignment of memory addresses, the 486 pipeline, and the 486 cache can cause your code to stall — and what to do to avoid this.

And finally, you learned seven SECRET RULES of assembler that will help you speed up your code:

◆ **SECRET "CONSTANT-TO-MEMORY" RULE:**
If you move a constant to a Register Pointer plus Constant Mode memory location, you lose 1 cycle.

◆ **SECRET "REGISTER-POINTER-DOUBLED" RULE:**
If you use an address that contains two registers, you lose 1 cycle.

◆ **SECRET "REGISTER-ADDRESS" RULE:**
If you set a register value just before using the register for an address, you lose 2 cycles. Further, if you set a register value, then execute any 1-cycle instruction, and then use the register for an address, you lose 1 cycle.

◆ **SECRET "BYTES-AND-POINTERS" RULE:**
If you move a value to a byte register, then use any instruction that runs in precisely 1 cycle, then use a register pointer such as [BX] or [SI+n], you lose 1 cycle. Further, if you move a value to a byte register, then move a value to another byte register, then use an address register, you lose 2 cycles. (The only known exception to this is the use of: MOV <Register Pointer plus Constant memory addressing mode>,<constant>).

◆ **SECRET "CACHE-SMASH" RULE:**
If you access several memory addresses which are exactly or nearly 800h bytes (2048 decimal) apart, you risk a huge penalty. The penalty is usually between 70 and 90 cycles but may be masked if the computer has an external cache.

◆ SECRET "PREFIX" RULE:

Whenever you use a segment override (CS: or DS: or ES: or SS:), the assembler will begin with a 1-byte, 1-cycle instruction (the segment override instruction). Although generally used and referred to as a prefix, the segment override is really a separate instruction, and it can exist independently. Other prefixes that this rule applies to are the 32-bit operand override prefix, the 0Fh prefix, the REP prefix, and the REPNZ prefix.

◆ SECRET "PREFIX-WAIVER" RULE:

There is no charge for using a prefix if the previous instruction takes more than 1 cycle unless the previous instruction is JMP or CALL. This rule is cumulative so that if, for example, an instruction has 2 prefixes and the previous instruction takes 3 or more cycles, both prefixes are free.

Chapter 2

Basic Arithmetic and Logic Operations

Now that you have a basic grounding in assembly language, let's add a few more common instructions to your vocabulary.

The ADD, SUB, OR, AND, and XOR Instructions

In an assembler statement, the syntax of these five arithmetic and logic instructions looks like this:

```
ADD <destination operand>,<source operand>     ;optional comment

SUB <destination operand>,<source operand>     ;optional comment

OR  <destination operand>,<source operand>     ;optional comment

AND <destination operand>,<source operand>     ;optional comment

XOR <destination operand>,<source operand>     ;optional comment
```

All five instructions have the same basic syntax as MOV, and the same rules apply:

❖ The <source operand> can be an 8-bit, 16-bit, or 32-bit memory operand, register, or constant.

❖ The <destination operand> can be an 8-bit, 16-bit, or 32-bit memory operand or register (but not a constant).

❖ The <destination operand> and the <source operand> must have matching sizes unless the <source operand> is an 8-bit constant. An <8-bit constant source operand> can be matched with an 8-bit, 16-bit, or 32-bit <destination operand>.

❖ A memory operand can't be used for both <source operand> and <destination operand>, that is,

```
ADD <memory>,<memory>      ;ILLEGAL
SUB <memory>,<memory>      ;ILLEGAL
OR  <memory>,<memory>      ;ILLEGAL
AND <memory>,<memory>      ;ILLEGAL
XOR <memory>,<memory>      ;ILLEGAL
```

are illegal, just as

```
MOV <memory>,<memory>      ;ILLEGAL
```

is illegal.

Any C programmer familiar with the operators +, −, |, &, and ^ already knows what the assembler instructions ADD, SUB, OR, AND, and XOR do. The meaning of the instructions is as follows:

ADD: ADD the contents of <source operand> to the contents of <destination operand>.

SUB: SUBtract the contents of <source operand> from the contents of <destination operand>.

OR: Calculate the inclusive OR of the contents of <destination operand> and <source operand> and place the results in <destination operand>. OR is a bitwise logical operator — each bit of the result is 0 if both corresponding bits of the two operands are 0; otherwise, each bit is 1.

AND: AND the contents of <destination operand> with the contents of <source operand> and place the results in <destination operand>. AND is a bitwise logical operator — each bit of the result is 1 if both corresponding bits of the two operands are 1; otherwise, each bit is 0.

XOR: Calculate the eXclusive OR of the contents of <destination operand> and <source operand> and place the results in <destination operand>. XOR is a bitwise logical operator — each bit of the result is 1 if the corresponding bits of the two operands are different; each bit is 0 if the corresponding bits of the two operands are the same.

All five instructions have 19 possible forms, depending on the operands used. Table 2.1 is a standardized description for each possible form of ADD, SUB, OR, AND, and XOR.

The following instructions illustrate some of these forms:

```
ADD AX,BX        ;i.e., Add the BX register to the AX register
SUB CX,55        ;i.e., Subtract 55 from the CX register
OR SI,mem        ;i.e., Or the SI register with memory location mem
AND mem,DI       ;i.e., And the memory location mem with the DI register
XOR mem,BP       ;i.e., Exclusive-or the memory location mem with BP
```

Instruction Mnemonic	Destination Operand	Source Operand	Cycle Count
<ADD|SUB|OR|AND|XOR>	<8-bit register>	,<8-bit constant>	1
<ADD|SUB|OR|AND|XOR>	<8-bit register>	,<8-bit register>	1
<ADD|SUB|OR|AND|XOR>	<8-bit register>	,<byte-size memory>	2
<ADD|SUB|OR|AND|XOR>	<byte-size memory>	,<8-bit constant>	3
<ADD|SUB|OR|AND|XOR>	<byte-size memory>	,<8-bit register>	3
<ADD|SUB|OR|AND|XOR>	<16-bit register>	,<8-bit constant>	1
<ADD|SUB|OR|AND|XOR>	<16-bit register>	,<16-bit constant>	1
<ADD|SUB|OR|AND|XOR>	<16-bit register>	,<16-bit register>	1
<ADD|SUB|OR|AND|XOR>	<16-bit register>	,<word-size memory>	2
<ADD|SUB|OR|AND|XOR>	<word-size memory>	,<8-bit constant>	3
<ADD|SUB|OR|AND|XOR>	<word-size memory>	,<16-bit constant>	3
<ADD|SUB|OR|AND|XOR>	<word-size memory>	,<16-bit register>	3
<ADD|SUB|OR|AND|XOR>	<32-bit register>	,<8-bit constant>	1
<ADD|SUB|OR|AND|XOR>	<32-bit register>	,<32-bit constant>	1
<ADD|SUB|OR|AND|XOR>	<32-bit register>	,<32-bit register>	1
<ADD|SUB|OR|AND|XOR>	<32-bit register>	,<long-size memory>	2
<ADD|SUB|OR|AND|XOR>	<long-size memory>	,<8-bit constant>	3
<ADD|SUB|OR|AND|XOR>	<long-size memory>	,<32-bit constant>	3
<ADD|SUB|OR|AND|XOR>	<long-size memory>	,<32-bit register>	3

Table 2.1 Standardized description for each form of ADD, SUB, OR, AND, and XOR.

Besides their basic syntax, ADD, SUB, OR, AND, and XOR have a lot in common. Their relevance to C is obvious because they all have precise equivalents in C. For example, if mema and memb are two integers, then:

```
mema=(memb+5); is the same as
     { __asm MOV AX,memb; __asm ADD AX,5; __asm MOV mema,AX; }

mema=(memb-5); is the same as
     { __asm MOV AX,memb; __asm SUB AX,5; __asm MOV mema,AX; }

mema=(memb|5); is the same as
     { __asm MOV AX,memb; __asm OR  AX,5; __asm MOV mema,AX; }

mema=(memb&5); is the same as
     { __asm MOV AX,memb; __asm AND AX,5; __asm MOV mema,AX; }

mema=(memb^5); is the same as
     { __asm MOV AX,memb; __asm XOR AX,5; __asm MOV mema,AX; }
```

Two useful things to note about these instructions are:

(a) ADDing a register to itself — e.g., ADD AX,AX — has the effect of doubling the contents of the register. This is helpful in multiplication operations.

(b) ORing or ANDing a register with itself — e.g., OR AX,AX or AND AX,AX — results in the register retaining the value it started with.

Table 2.1 shows that some arithmetic operations are faster than others. Combined with what you already know about MOV time, you can use this information to make programs go faster — or at least, to prevent them from slowing down, which is the usual effect of the traps we'll explore in this chapter.

Revisiting the Constant-to-Memory Rule

In Chapter 1, we discovered that MOV <memory>,<constant> takes an extra cycle if <memory> uses a Register Pointer plus Constant addressing mode. The Constant-to-Memory Rule applies to all the arithmetic instructions too, in the same way, so:

```
ADD mem,5      ;penalty applies, this is a 4-cycle instruction
SUB [BX+5],5   ;penalty applies, this is a 4-cycle instruction
OR [BX],5      ;no penalty (Register Pointer mode), so 3 cycles only
```

The extended form of the Constant-to-Memory Rule applies in the following program:

```
int mema;
long i;
void main ()
{
  for (i=0; i<8000000; ++i)
  {
    mema+=3;
  }
}
```

There are two ways to translate the C statement mema+=3;. The slow way is on the right, and the fast way is on the left, below:

```
MOV AX,mema      ;3 bytes, 1 cycle      ADD    mema,3 ;5 bytes, !4 cycles
ADD AX,3         ;3 bytes, 1 cycle
MOV mema,AX      ;3 bytes, 1 cycle
```

Although intuitively it might appear that the single ADD mema,3 instruction should be faster as well as smaller, the translation on the left is actually faster because it takes advantage of the fact that ADD <register>,<constant> takes only 1 cycle, while ADD <memory>,<constant> takes 4 cycles because of the Constant-to-Memory Rule. So, in the tight loop in this example program, you would gain 5 percent (1 cycle) by replacing ADD mema,3 (which is what all compilers generate) with

```
__asm MOV AX,mema;
__asm ADD AX,3;
__asm MOV mema,AX;
```

If you use an old Borland, Microsoft, or Symantec compiler, you can do this speedup without having to resort to inline assembly by changing the program so it reads:

```
int mema;
long i;
void main ()
{
  for (i=0; i<8000000; ++i)
  {
    mema=mema+3;
  }
}
```

Borland v3.1, Microsoft v5.0, and Symantec v6.0 will translate the relevant line, mema=mema+3; of this program into the optimal 3 lines of assembler code shown above. The newer versions of the compilers, on the other hand, aren't so easily fooled. The optimizers now detect that mema=mema+3; is equivalent to mema+=3; and generate consistent output — ADD mema, 3 — making it necessary to use inline assembly to get the gain.

While we're on the subject of SECRET RULES introduced in the last chapter, the Bytes-and-Pointers Rule combined with the Register-Address Rule ensures the code on the left is faster than the code on the right:

```
MOV DI,OFFSET mema    ;1 cycle      MOV    DI,OFFSET mema    ;1 cycle
ADD CX,5              ;1 cycle      ADD    CL,5              ;1 cycle
MOV AX,[DI]           ;!2 cycles    MOV    AX,[DI]           ;!3 cycles
```

In both these cases, the Register-Address Rule causes a 1-cycle penalty for using the register pointer [DI] 1 cycle after changing DI. If the intervening 1-cycle instruction also changes a byte register (like ADD CL, 5), the penalty is 2 cycles. The stall caused by the Register-Address Rule acts like a 1 cycle "penalty instruction" and so the conditions are met for the Bytes-and-Pointers Rule as well.

Before we go any further, we'd like to put our suggestions in context by providing you some warnings and basic assumptions to keep in mind.

◆ #1 WARNING!

Remember that our suggestions are for Intel 486 machines. The arithmetic is different on other machines and the difference is especially relevant to this example. For instance, on a 386, ADD mema, 3 takes 7 cycles, but MOV AX, mema + ADD AX, 3 + MOV mema, AX takes a total of 8 cycles (in fact, things get worse because no 386s except the 386SL had caches).

◆ **#2 WARNING!**
The gain in cycles comes at the expense of size, e.g., our optimized version of the last program takes 9 bytes instead of 5 bytes. We expect the gains to be bigger inside tight loops and, as we explained in the last chapter, we believe in optimizing tight loops for speed, not size. (For the record, we decide between two alternative instruction sequences this way: if the code is not in a tight loop, then divide the instruction-size ratio by the cycle-count ratio. In the above example, the instruction sizes are 5 and 9 bytes and the cycle counts are 3 and 4, respectively; so our division is (5/9) / (3/4) = 0.74. Our rule of thumb is, if the result of the division is a lot less than 1, don't use the "faster" alternative. We can't be precise about what "a lot less than 1" means, but 0.74 is enough in this case. By the way, we'd never use this tip outside a loop; it wouldn't pay.)

◆ **#3 WARNING!**
The gain only appears for Register Pointer plus Constant addressing modes. The instruction ADD [BX],3 takes only 3 cycles, so if the original C statement is something like (*mema)+=3; then our suggested translation would not provide an improvement. We're assuming that you think a 5 percent performance gain is worth the time it'll take you to look up the rule and make sure you're using it right.

None of these warnings vitiate the fact that the statement mema+=3; can be sped up in what we think is a typical situation. Sure, there are always special circumstances; we're not pretending these assumptions are unfalsifiable truths. But if we don't make them now, we'd have to repeat tediously "WARNING! WARNING!" in every paragraph of this book. Just take it as implied: for every tip we give, you have to decide if your circumstances are special and not hold it against us that our assumptions are so brutal. These warnings will not be repeated.

Register Constants

Remember that for the MOV instruction we found a way to speed code up for the case where a constant was used several times, as in

```
mema=5;
memb=5;
memc=5;
. . . .
```

We used register constants to get a gain with MOV, and we want to look at using them again because constants are even more expensive with arithmetic instructions than they are with MOV.

The arithmetic involved is straightforward. Every time you ADD (or SUB or OR or AND or XOR) a register constant to memory rather than performing the same operation on an actual constant to memory, you save 1 or 2 cycles. For example, the following sets of instructions perform the same operation — the C statement mema=(mema|3)+3;. The slow way is on the right; the fast way is shown on the left:

```
MOV AX,mema    ;1 cycle        OR    mema,3    ;3 cycles
OR AX,3        ;1 cycle        ADD   mema,3    ;3 cycles
ADD AX,3       ;1 cycle
MOV mema,AX    ;1 cycle
```

The gain from the code on the left is 33 percent (2 cycles) despite the extra instructions. In this case, though, the compiler vendors don't generate the wrong stuff so we don't have a quickie optimization tip like we did with our MOV example. This is just something to keep in mind when you're writing complete routines in assembler.

As another example, the following function combines MOV with ADD instructions. The original C source program looks like this:

```
int mema;
int *memp;
void main ()
{
    mema=*(memp++);
}
```

The test Borland C and older Microsoft and Symantec compilers translate the C statement mema=*(memp++); into (adding 2 to the pointer because the size of an integer is 2 bytes):

```
MOV BX,memp          ;1 cycle
MOV AX,[BX]          ;!3 cycles (Register-Address Rule)
MOV mema,AX          ;1 cycle
ADD memp,2           ;!4 cycles (Constant-to-Memory Rule)
```

This translation provides an opportunity for a gain. Since there's a register containing memp's value, the translation can be replaced (using inline assembler) with:

```
__asm MOV BX,memp;    /* 1 cycle */
__asm MOV AX,[BX];    /* !3 cycles */
__asm ADD BX,2;       /* 1 cycle */
__asm MOV memp,BX;    /* 1 cycle */
```

This replacement would deliver a 33 percent gain by saving 3 cycles. Once again, the test Microsoft and Symantec compilers recognize that the ADD should be moved. Symantec, however, can be forced into generating the same un-optimal translation as Borland if the C statement mema=*(memp++); in the above program is replaced with:

```
mema=*memp;
++memp;
```

so be wary how you use C's ++ operator.

If mem3 is a pointer and mem2 is a constant, they should be picked interstitially, e.g., for the expression mem1=mem2+(*mem3); the instructions on the left are faster than the instructions on the right:

```
MOV BX,mem3   ;1 cycle      MOV BX,mem3   ;1 cycle
MOV AX,mem2   ;1 cycle      MOV AX,[BX]   ;!3 cycles
ADD AX,[BX]   ;2 cycles     ADD AX,mem2   ;2 cycles
MOV mem1,AX   ;1 cycle      MOV mem1,AX   ;1 cycle
```

Here the gain occurs due to address resolution. Notice that all automatic variables are pointer references — they become [BP-reference].

Zeroing Registers

It is often necessary to set a register's value to 0. The straightforward (and intuitive) way to set (for example) the CX register's value to 0 is:

```
MOV CX,0                ;3 bytes, 1 cycle
```

Two other, shorter, methods are also possible:

```
SUB CX,CX               ;2 bytes, 1 cycle
```

and

```
XOR CX,CX               ;2 bytes, 1 cycle
```

SUB <16-bit register>,<16-bit register> and XOR <16-bit register>,<16-bit register> are both shorter than MOV <16-bit register>,0 even though all three instructions take the same number of cycles. The XOR alternative is perhaps a trifle more popular, but its use is really a matter of taste. A typical C case where a register needs to be set to 0 is:

```
int mema,memb,memc;
void main ()
{
    mema=memb=memc=0;
}
```

All C compilers will translate the body of this program to something like:

```
XOR AX,AX
MOV memc,AX
MOV memb,AX
MOV mema,AX
```

that is, compilers will choose XOR — the optimal way — to zero the 16-bit register variable.

It's harder to illustrate zeroing an 8-bit register because, as we observed in Chapter 1, compilers tend to ignore the directive register for byte-sized variables. However, the following program shows a situation where an 8-bit register needs to be zeroed:

```
char mema,memb,memc;
void main ()
{
    mema=memb=memc=0;
}
```

A compiler can choose from three different ways to zero an 8-bit register:

```
Method #1: MOV AL,0        ;Borland's choice — 2 bytes, 1 cycle
Method #2: XOR AL,AL       ;Microsoft's choice — 2 bytes, 1 cycle
Method #3: XOR AX,AX       ;Symantec's choice — 2 bytes, 1 cycle
```

In this case, the `MOV AL,0` instruction is optimal. Although all three instructions need the same amount of space and cycles when looked at in isolation, we think that `MOV`'s clarity gives it an advantage. Further, note that we also said that the three instructions need the same amount of resources *in isolation* — Method #3 is subject to a penalty due to the Secret Hi/Lo Rule, which we'll discuss later in this chapter.

For now though, just keep in mind that for 8-bit registers, `MOV <8-bit register>,0` does the job without wasting bytes and it's more clear. Why use a trick when it gains nothing?

Working with Byte Values

If you frequently have to work with a particular pair of byte elements, you can speed up the process by defining the variables as two elements of a character array and accessing them as a word (using a character array will guarantee the elements stay together). For example, the following C code, which doesn't use an array

```
char mema1,mema2;
char mema3,mema4;
void main ()
{
   mema3=mema1;mema4=mema2;
}
```

becomes

```
MOV AL,mema1       ;1 cycle
MOV mema3,AL       ;1 cycle
MOV AL,mema2       ;1 cycle
MOV mema4,AL       ;1 cycle
```

Using inline assembler and a character array, the program looks like this

```
char    mema1[2];
char    mema3,mema4;
{
  __asm    MOV    AX,WORD PTR mema1;      /* 1 cycle */
  __asm    MOV    mema3,AL;              /* 1 cycle */
  __asm    MOV    mema4,AH;              /* 1 cycle */
}
```

and uses 1 less cycle. The actual gain in a tight loop is about 10 percent. The instructions have to be in precisely this order or the gain will disappear.

The INC and DEC Instructions

In an assembler statement, the syntax of these two arithmetic instructions looks like this:

```
INC <destination operand>      ;optional comment
DEC <destination operand>      ;optional comment
```

Once again, the meaning of each instruction is imperative:

INC: INCrement the contents of <destination operand> by 1.

DEC: DECrement the contents of <destination operand> by 1.

Unlike the other assembler instructions described so far, INC and DEC have no <source operand> because the amount to be added or subtracted from <destination operand> is fixed at 1. The <destination operand> can be either an 8-bit, 16-bit, or 32-bit memory operand or a register (but not a constant). Thus, INC and DEC have six possible forms, depending on the operands used. Table 2.2 is a standardized description for each possible form.

Instruction Mnemonic	Destination Operand	Cycle Count
<INC|DEC>	<8-bit register>	1
<INC|DEC>	<byte-size memory>	3
<INC|DEC>	<16-bit register>	1
<INC|DEC>	<word-size memory>	3
<INC|DEC>	<32-bit register>	1
<INC|DEC>	<long-size memory>	3

Table 2.2   Standardized description for each possible form of INC and DEC.

The following instructions illustrate these forms:

```
INC    AX         ;i.e., Add 1 to the AX register
DEC    mem        ;i.e., Subtract 1 from memory location mem
```

There are exact equivalents for INC and DEC in C: the ++ operator and the -- operator. For example, the program on the left and the program on the right do the same thing:

```
int    mema;               int    mema;
void main ()               void main ()
{                          {
  ++mema;                    __asm inc mema;
  --mema;                    __asm dec mema;
}                          }
```

INC and DEC also have exact equivalents in assembler, i.e., INC AX appears to be exactly equivalent to ADD AX, 1 and DEC AX appears to be exactly equivalent to SUB AX, 1. There are, however, three reasons why INC / ADD and DEC / SUB should not be used interchangeably:

❖ Reason 1: Because there's no explicit <source operand>, INC and DEC are always shorter than their ADD and SUB equivalents.

❖ Reason 2: Since there's no explicit constant, INC and DEC are not subject to the Constant-to-Memory Rule. This makes INC <memory> and DEC <memory> 1 cycle faster than ADD <memory>, 1 and SUB <memory>, 1 in many cases.

❖ Reason 3: INC and DEC ignore the carry flag. This won't look like an advantage until we discuss uses for the carry flag later in this chapter, but it is.

Kernighan and Ritchie's *The C Programming Language* has this to say about C's ++ operator:

> "You could write nc = nc + 1 but ++nc is more concise *and often more efficient.*" (our italics).

Perhaps the authors thought the ++ operator gave a useful hint to the compiler that a special instruction should be used for incrementing — this might have been true in the past. Our own tests, however, show that it makes no difference whether a program uses mema+=1; or ++mema; to increment — C compilers will generate the translation INC mema regardless. Similarly, they will generate the translation DEC mema for both mema-=1; and --mema;.

Speaking of efficiency, because <INC|DEC> <memory> are 3-cycle instructions, two of the tips we gave for speeding up the <ADD|SUB|OR|AND|XOR> instructions don't apply to either INC or DEC.

For instance, there is no point in using a register constant that contains 1 to speed up incrementing or decrementing; i.e., replacing INC <memory> with ADD <memory>,<register constant=1> and replacing DEC <memory> with SUB <memory>,<register constant=1> provides no gain because ADD <memory>,<register> and SUB <memory>,<register> are also 3-cycle instructions.

There is also no point in replacing

```
INC <memory>     ;3 cycles, 2 bytes
```

with

```
MOV AX,[SI]      ;1 cycle, 2 bytes
INC AX           ;1 cycle, 1 byte
MOV [SI],AX      ;1 cycle, 2 bytes
```

Though both sets of instructions take 3 cycles, the second set takes a minimum of 3 more bytes depending on the addressing mode used. That being the case, it's unfortunate that Borland does precisely this replacement. Microsoft and Symantec correctly translate ++mema; into INC mema.

Replace ADD with INC (and SUB with DEC) wherever possible. For instance:

```
SUB AX,1                    ;1 cycle, 3 bytes
```

can be replaced with

```
DEC AX                      ;1 cycle, 1 byte
```

and

```
ADD WORD PTR mema,256       ;4 cycles, 6 bytes
```

can be replaced with

```
INC BYTE PTR mema+1         ;3 cycles, 4 bytes
```

(Remember that the high byte of the memory word mema is the second byte. On Intel machines the low byte is stored first.)

It is not, however, correct to overkill by replacing

```
ADD AX,2                        ;1 cycle, 3 bytes
```

with

```
INC AX                          ;1 cycle, 1 byte
INC AX                          ;1 cycle, 1 byte
```

though. If you ever see such code, you're looking at a trick that was once a good optimization tip for 386s. Remove it.

The `INC` instruction is frequently seen when a pointer is being incremented during a pass through one or two arrays. As an example of a common misconception, we contrived this odd-looking example in C:

```
/* Program #1 — odd-looking original */
char mema[100],memb[100];
void main ()
{
  char *mempa,mempb;
  for (mempa=mema,mempb=memb;mempa<mema+99;)
  {
    *(mempa+1)=*(mempb+1); ++mempa; ++mempb;
  }
}
```

A second version of this program appears, at first, to be better:

```
/* Program #2 — "improved" version */
char mema[100],memb[100];
void main ()
{
  register char *mempa,*mempb;
  for (mempa=mema,mempb=memb;mempa<mema+99;)
  {
    *(mempa++)=*(mempb++);
  }
}
```

The second program, which is certainly doing the same thing, appears to be improved because it *appears* to have eliminated a redundant addition to the pointers mempa and mempb — but that's a delusion. Let's look at the actual assembly code that Borland's C compiler produces for the body of the loop when all optimization switches are on:

```
     ;Program #1 Translation of *(mempa+1)=*(mempb+1); ++mempa; ++mempb;
MOV AL,[DI+1]                   ;1 cycle
MOV [SI+1],AL                   ;1 cycle
INC SI                          ;1 cycle
INC DI                          ;1 cycle
```

```
          ;Program #2 Translation of *(++mempa)=*(++mempb);
INC SI                      ;1 cycle
INC DI                      ;1 cycle
MOV AL,[DI]                 ;!3 cycles (Register-Address Rule)
MOV [SI],AL                 ;1 cycle
```

(In both cases, Borland translates the mempa and mempb pointers to the registers SI and DI.)

The two translations show that Program #1 is actually faster than Program #2. There are two reasons for this:

❖ First, since assembler allows addresses to be formed using a combination of registers and constants (e.g., [SI+1] and [DI+1]), C expressions of the type *(pointer + constant) do not result in expensive assembler ADD instructions. (Remember also that earlier we said C's ++ operator will generally result in an INC.) Furthermore, as we said in Chapter 1, addressing [SI+1] costs nothing more than addressing [SI], so the apparent redundant addition to the pointers in Program #1 doesn't actually cost anything.

❖ Second, the "improved" code in Program #2 increments the DI register just before it uses DI as a pointer. This violates the Register-Address Rule, causing the Opfetcher processor to stall the pipeline. The result is a 2-cycle penalty.

This example shows why we like to stress "what the C compiler is likely to produce given such-and-such-a-circumstance." We want to alert you to apparent improvements in the C code like the one in Program #2. If you keep what the compiler does with the code in mind, you won't be fooled by such "improvements."

The Secret Hi/Lo Rule

The Hi/Lo Rule is a four-part rule that affects performance in many different situations. This is probably the first time the full Hi/Lo Rule has been published anywhere and you can see why — 'tain't easy to figure out!

◆ **SECRET "HI/LO" RULE:**

Part 1:
((If you execute two consecutive instructions which contain references to the same 16-bit register or to the high and low halves of a 16-bit register)
and (the first instruction changes one half of the register)
and (the second instruction is MOV
and either
   ((the source operand is the other half of the register)
   or (the source operand is the entire register)))
then you lose 1 cycle.)

Part 2:
((If you execute two consecutive instructions which contain references to the same 16-bit register or to the high and low halves of a 16-bit register)
and (the first instruction changes one half of the register)
and (the second instruction does ARITHMETIC
and either
   ((the source or the destination is the other half of the register)
   or (the source or the destination is the entire register))
and (neither source nor destination is a <memory> operand))
then you lose 1 cycle.)

Part 3:
((If you execute two consecutive instructions which contain references to the same 16-bit register or to the high and low halves of a 16-bit register)
and (the first instruction changes the entire register)
and (the second instruction is MOV
   and (the source operand is the high half of the register))
then you lose 1 cycle.)

Part 4:
((If you execute two consecutive instructions which contain references to the same 16-bit register or to the high and low halves of a 16-bit register)
and (the first instruction changes the entire register)
and (the second instruction does ARITHMETIC
  and (either source or destination is the high half of the register)
   and (neither source nor destination is a <memory> operand))
then you lose 1 cycle.)

The essence of the Hi/Lo Rule is: Be wary if you're accessing two halves of the same 16-bit register in two successive instructions. The pairings to watch out for are:

```
AH/AL    (both part of AX)
BH/BL    (both part of BX)
CH/CL    (both part of CX)
DH/DL    (both part of DX)
```

Using the AX register and its two halves AH and AL as an example then, the Hi/Lo Rule means that:

❖ if (destination of instruction #1 is AH)
   and
   (instruction #2 is MOV)
   and
   (source of instruction #2 is AL or AX)
   then 1-cycle penalty

❖ if (destination of instruction #1 is AL)
   and
   (instruction #2 is MOV)
   and
   (source of instruction #2 is AH or AX)
   then 1-cycle penalty

❖ if (destination of instruction #1 is AX)
   and
   (instruction #2 is MOV)
   and
   (source of instruction #2 is AH)
   then 1-cycle penalty

❖ if (destination of instruction #1 is AH)
    and
    (instruction #2 is ARITHMETIC)
    and
    (source of instruction #2 is AL or AX)
    and
    (destination of instruction #2 is not <memory>)
    then 1-cycle penalty

❖ if (destination of instruction #1 is AL)
    and
    (instruction #2 is ARITHMETIC)
    and
    (source of instruction #2 is AH or AX)
    and
    (destination of instruction #2 is not <memory>)
    then 1-cycle penalty

❖ if (destination of instruction #1 is AH)
    and
    (instruction #2 is ARITHMETIC)
    and
    (destination of instruction #2 is AL or AX)
    and
    (source of instruction #2 is not <memory>)
    then 1-cycle penalty

❖ if (destination of instruction #1 is AL)
    and
    (instruction #2 is ARITHMETIC)
    and
    (destination of instruction #2 is AH or AX)
    and
    (source of instruction #2 is not <memory>)
    then 1-cycle penalty

* if (destination of instruction #1 is AX)
  and
  (instruction #2 is ARITHMETIC)
  and
  (source of instruction #2 is AH)
  and
  (destination of instruction #2 is not <memory>)
  then 1-cycle penalty

* if (destination of instruction #1 is AX)
  and
  (instruction #2 is ARITHMETIC)
  and
  (destination of instruction #2 is AH)
  and
  (source of instruction #2 is not <memory>)
  then 1-cycle penalty

You should note two things about this listing:

* At this point, ARITHMETIC means any one of ADD, SUB, OR, AND, XOR, INC, and DEC. There are also a few more instructions which do arithmetic by implication and are therefore subject to the Hi/Lo Rule. We'll note these instructions as we come to them.

* Naturally, BX, CX, and DX can be substituted for AX in all of the above cases, provided you also substitute the relevant high and low portions of the register — that is, BH for AH and BL for AL, etc. — in each case.

In its simplest form, the Hi/Lo Rule means that

```
DEC CH      ;1 cycle
DEC CL      ;!2 cycles
```

is slower than

```
DEC CH      ;1 cycle
DEC DL      ;1 cycle
```

because the second instruction is an arithmetic instruction and CH is the correspondent of CL, but DL is not — Part 2 of the rule.

It also means that

```
MOV AL,mem    ;1 cycle
XOR AH,AH     ;!2 cycles
```

is slower than

```
MOV AL,mem    ;1 cycle
MOV AH,0      ;1 cycle
```

because XOR is an arithmetic instruction that uses the other half of the AX register, but MOV is not an arithmetic instruction and MOV's source is not part of the AX register — Parts 1 and 2 of the rule.

Other examples of instruction pairs that fall afoul of the rule are:

```
MOV AL,DL     ;AH and AL are pairings, second instruction is arithmetic
XOR AH,AH

MOV AL,DL     ;AH and AL are pairings, second instruction AH is source
MOV DH,AH

OR DH,8       ;DH is part of DX, second instruction DX is source
MOV mem,DX

OR AL,AL      ;AL and AH are pairings, second instruction AH is source
MOV DL,AH
```

(Notice, in the last example, that Intel regards OR AL,AL as an instruction that changes the AL register, even though it ends up with the same value it started with.)

The following instruction pairs, on the other hand, do not fall afoul of the Hi/Lo rule:

```
OR DX,8       ;Second instruction changes low half of DX, not high half
OR DL,8

OR DH,8       ;Second instruction is not arithmetic and DL is not source
MOV DL,8

OR DH,8       ;OR and MOV aren't really consecutive,
MOV ES:mem,DX ;the ES: prefix override instruction intervenes
```

As with most rules, there are some exceptions to the Hi/Lo Rule. While the rule does apply even if most other penalties (misalignment, 32-bit register, segment override) are already in effect, one case where the Hi/Lo Rule does not apply is when the Register-Address Rule is in effect. That is, in the sequence:

```
MOV BL,BL     ;1 cycle
MOV [BX],BH   ;!3 cycles
```

the second instruction takes only 3 cycles (1 cycle for the MOV and a 2-cycle penalty for the use of a register for an address right after changing it). The Hi/Lo Rule does not take away an additional cycle.

Another exception is when the second instruction in a sequence is a MOV with a segment register as the destination operand, e.g.:

```
XOR AL,AL                ;1 cycle
MOV ES,AX                ;3 cycles
```

Although the source of the MOV is the other half of the register being changed by the XOR, the second instruction takes only the 3 cycles that a MOV of a 16-bit register into a segment register would normally take. Once again, the Hi/Lo Rule does not take away an additional cycle.

The Hi/Lo Rule also has no effect on a few instructions which, by definition, can only work with the AX register (or its components, AH and AL). As these instructions come up in later chapters, we'll make note of the fact that they are exempt.

We'll be showing you further examples of the Hi/Lo Rule in varying degrees of complication throughout this book — it just keeps popping up. And, although we don't expect you to try and memorize the rule (our cycle counting program, TACHO.EXE, on the diskette that comes with this book, lets you know when it's in operation), you might find it useful to note the page number the rule is printed on as a reference.

One possible way to evade the Hi/Lo Rule is to use a 16-bit register even though the use of an 8-bit register is allowed. For example, the code on the left is 1 cycle faster than the code on the right because it evades the Hi/Lo Rule:

```
AND AX,255    ;1 cycle          MOV AH,0    ;1 cycle
DEC AL        ;1 cycle          DEC AL      ;!2 cycles
```

Another possible safeguard is to use MOV rather than 8-bit arithmetic:

```
DEC AL        ;1 cycle          DEC AL      ;1 cycle
MOV AH,0      ;1 cycle          XOR AH,AH   ;!2 cycles
```

The best ways to avoid the Hi/Lo Rule, though, are to either (a) use a different set of registers, (b) reverse the instruction order, or (c) interpose some other instruction between the two offenders.

By the way, if you're using 32-bit mode, the Hi/Lo Rule also applies to this combination of instructions:

```
ADD BX,5
MOV EDX,EBX
```

The reason for this is that, when a 32-bit register is being used, its lower half is the usual 16-bit register. In this example then, the 16-bit BX register is the lower half of the EBX register. ADD BX,5 changes the lower half — MOV EDX,EBX changes the entire register — and there is a 1 cycle penalty just like there is when BL and BX are used in similar circumstances.

Note that this applies only in 32-bit mode. In 16-bit mode, the MOV EDX,EBX instruction implies a DB 66h prefix instruction and so the MOV doesn't really immediately follow the ADD, as we noted earlier with the 32-bit operand size override prefix in our examples of instruction sets that don't fall afoul of the rule.

Flags

The 486, in common with all Intel 80x86 machines, has one 16-bit flags register (or status register) that can be illustrated as follows:

Bit No.	15	14	13	12	11	10	9	8	7	6	5	4	3	2	1	0
Flags Register					O	D	I	T	S	Z		A		P		C

In this illustration, the blank bits are reserved bits and normally have a value of 0. The others are the carry, parity, auxiliary carry, zero, sign, trap, interrupt enable/disable, direction, and overflow status flags, respectively. When a flag bit is 0, the flag is OFF. When a flag bit is 1, the flag is ON.

The flag values are primarily of concern for conditional jump instructions, which we'll discuss in the next chapter (in this context, conditional means "if flag(s) is/are on/off" and jump means goto — it isn't possible to MOV directly to or from the flags register, and MOV's effect on the flags register is undefined). However since many assembler instructions change certain bits, or flags, in the flags register, we'll introduce the concept now.

For example, while <flags register> can't be used as an operand in a typical assembler instruction, the flags register is being changed indirectly every time the arithmetic instructions ADD, SUB, OR, AND, XOR, INC, and DEC are executed.

The main arithmetic flags are the zero, parity, sign, carry and overflow flags. (The auxiliary carry flag is also an arithmetic flag but isn't useful for any of the operations we describe in this book.) These flags all reflect characteristics of the arithmetic instruction's <destination operand>.

The zero flag is set (that is, turned either ON or OFF) by ADD, SUB, OR, AND, XOR, INC, and DEC. The zero flag goes ON if the <destination operand> becomes 0. If, for example, the AX register contains 5, then instructions like ADD AX,-5 (5-5==0) or SUB AX,5 (5-5==0) or AND AX,0 (5&0==0), or XOR AX,AX (5^5==0) would all turn the zero flag ON. On the other hand, instructions like ADD AX,5 (5+5!=0) or OR AX,0 (5^0!=0) or DEC AX (5-1!=0) would turn the zero flag OFF.

The parity flag is set by ADD, SUB, OR, AND, XOR, INC, and DEC. The parity flag goes ON if the low byte of the <destination operand> has an even number of 1 bits. To visualize this, think of the destination as a binary number. The 16-bit AX register with a 5 in it looks like this:

```
0000 0000 0000 0101
```

Since there are two "1 bits" (an even number) in the lower half of this register, the parity is even. An instruction like SUB AX,0 would not change the register, and so it would turn the parity flag ON. On the other hand, an instruction like DEC AX would result in this register:

```
0000 0000 0000 0100
```

and the parity flag would go OFF because of the uneven number of 1 bits in the lower half of the register.

The sign flag is set by ADD, SUB, OR, AND, XOR, INC, and DEC. The sign flag goes ON if the highest bit in the <destination operand> becomes 1. This highest bit, also called the sign bit, may or may not have a meaning. For example, is the binary number

```
1111 1111 1111 1111
```

a signed value (that is, −1) — or is it an unsigned value (that is, +65535)? This question can't be answered just by looking at the sign flag because the sign flag just indicates whether or not the sign bit is ON (as it is in this case). The number in question is a negative number (−1) if the word was defined as a `signed int` and a positive number (+65535) if the word was defined as an `unsigned int`. Regardless, if this number is incremented, the result is 0 and the sign flag goes OFF. If the number is decremented, the high bit remains 1 and the sign flag goes ON.

The carry flag is set by `ADD` and `SUB` and is cleared (that is, turned OFF) by `OR`, `AND`, and `XOR`. Although `INC` and `DEC` are also arithmetic instructions, they do not change the carry flag — they ignore it. (Note: "ignoring the carry flag" means it isn't touched at all; this is not the same effect that `AND`, `OR`, and `XOR` have, which is to always turn the carry flag OFF.) The carry flag goes ON when an overflow occurs.

For example, when the `ADD` and `SUB` instructions are executed, the carry flag goes ON if a bit gets shifted out. This concept goes clear back to the second grade arithmetic problem:

```
 24
+9
——
```

In grade 2, such problems were solved one column at a time. The first operation, add the 4 to the 9, gave a result of 13. Since 13 is a two-column result, the lower part — the 3 — was written in the ones column and the higher part — the 1 — was carried forward to the tens column. The carried amount was then added to the tens column, so the final step was to add the 1 to the 2 and write the result in the tens column.

This same concept ensures that whenever two binary numbers are added, there will be a carry value of either 0 or 1. If the carry value is 0, the carry flag goes OFF. If the carry value is 1, the carry flag goes ON.

Whenever two binary numbers are subtracted on the other hand, there will be a borrow value (remember how 24–9 was solved in grade 2). Because the borrow value is the reverse of the carry value, if the borrow value is 0 (that is, if a borrow took place) the carry flag goes ON. If the borrow value is 1 (that is, if there was no need to borrow), the carry flag goes OFF.

Thus, while the following two sets of instructions give precisely the same result

```
MOV AX,0          MOV AX,0
ADD AX,-5         SUB AX,5
```

the set of instructions on the left (using ADD) turns the carry flag OFF, and the set of instructions on the right (using SUB) turns the carry flag ON.

The overflow flag is set by ADD, SUB, INC, and DEC and is cleared by OR, AND, and XOR. Like the carry flag, the overflow flag goes ON when an overflow occurs. For example, the following C program displays "garbage"

```
unsigned int mema,memb;
void main ()
{
  mema=50000; memb=50000; mema+=memb; printf("mema=%d\n",mema);
}
```

because, since the result of (50000+50000=100000) is too large to fit in a 16-bit memory variable, the printf can only display the 16 lowest bits of the result.

As we said earlier, the carry flag signals that such an overflow has occurred. If the ADD of two unsigned numbers is too large, the carry flag goes ON. Further, if the SUB of two unsigned numbers is too small (for example because 5 is being subtracted from 3), the carry flag also goes ON.

This program also displays "garbage"

```
signed int mema,memb;
void main ()
{
  mema=30000; memb=30000; mema+=memb; printf("mema=%d\n",mema);
}
```

but the carry flag does not go ON because the result (30000+30000=60000) is still small enough to fit in a 16-bit variable. In other words, the carry flag is only a signal for overflow of unsigned integers. For signed integers, we need to know if the second-highest bit (masked by 0x4000) has overflowed into the highest bit (masked by 0x8000), thus changing the "sign." This information is signaled by the status of the overflow flag.

Technically the overflow flag signals "an exclusive OR of the carryout of the highest and second-highest bits." A simpler explanation is — when you do arithmetic and the result is garbage because of an overflow into a higher order bit, the overflow flag goes ON. If there is no overflow, the overflow flag goes OFF.

As a final example which shows how all five flags are affected by a set of instructions, consider the following piece of assembler code:

```
MOV AL,7
MOV BL,4
SUB AL,BL
```

The result of these three instructions is an AL register with a value of 3 (7–4=3). In binary, this result is 0000 0011. How does this affect the flags register?

❖ Since the result is not zero, SUB AL,BL sets the zero flag OFF.

❖ Since the result is not signed (that is, the most significant bit is not 1) SUB AL,BL sets the sign flag OFF.

❖ Since the result has an even number (two) of 1 bits in the lower half of the register, SUB AL,BL sets the parity flag ON.

❖ Since the subtract operation didn't have to do a borrow (7 is greater than 4), SUB AL,BL sets the carry flag OFF.

❖ Finally, since the subtract operation doesn't overflow, SUB AL,BL sets the overflow flag OFF.

The ADC and SBB Instructions

Now that we've talked about how the ADD and SUB instructions set the carry flag in the flags register, we can introduce two more arithmetic instructions — ADC and SBB.

ADC: **AD**d with **C**arry.

SBB: **S**u**B**tract with **B**orrow.

The arguments, cycle times, and end result of these two instructions are precisely the same as those of ADD and SUB — with one exception. The difference between {ADC, SBB} and {ADD, SUB} lies in their use of the carry flag. While the ADD and SUB instructions only set the carry flag ON and OFF, ADC and SBB both set the carry flag *and* use its status as input.

In an assembler statement, the syntax of ADC and SBB looks like this:

```
ADC <destination operand>,<source operand>    ;optional comment
SBB <destination operand>,<source operand>    ;optional comment
```

As with AND and SUB, the <source operand> for ADC and SBB can be either an 8-bit, 16-bit, or 32-bit memory operand, register, or constant, and the <destination operand> can be either an 8-bit, 16-bit, or 32-bit memory operand or register (but not a constant). A memory operand can't be used for both <source operand> and <destination operand>, and as usual, the size of the <source operand> must match the size of the <destination operand> unless the <source operand> is an 8-bit constant. An <8-bit constant source operand> can be matched with an 8-bit, 16-bit, or 32-bit <destination operand>. ADC and SBB both set the carry, overflow, parity, sign, and zero flags.

The meaning of the instructions is as follows:

ADC: ADd with Carry the contents of <source operand> to the contents of <destination operand>, i.e., test the status of the carry flag when adding.

SBB: SuBtract with Borrow the contents of <source operand> from the contents of <destination operand>, i.e., test the status of the carry flag when subtracting.

Both instructions have 19 possible forms, depending on the operands used. Table 2.3 is a standardized description for each possible form.

When would the ability to use the carry flag matter in an arithmetic operation? In the rules of assembler use, we've repeatedly said that the size of the <source> and <destination> operands of each instruction must match. This means, for example, that it isn't possible to ADD <16-bit register>,<8-bit register> or to SUB <8-bit register>,<16-bit register>, e.g., the following are both illegal instructions:

```
ADD BX,AL            ;ILLEGAL
SUB AH,DX            ;ILLEGAL
```

Sometimes, of course, it is necessary to be able to ADD (or SUB) two incompatibly-sized values. There are two ways to get around the problem.

First, the following code, which ultimately adds 2 16-bit values together, could be utilized:

```
MOV BX,255   ;16-bit number,        binary 0000 0000 1111 1111
MOV AL,1     ;Bottom 8-bits of AX,  binary           0000 0001
XOR AH,AH    ;Set top of AX to 0, AX=binary 0000 0000 0000 0001
ADD BX,AX    ;Result BX=256,        binary 0000 0001 0000 0000
```

But let's presume that for some reason it isn't possible to use all 16 bits of AX. In the previous section, we said that the ADD instruction sets the carry flag ON if the high-order bit gets carried out. For example, if BX contains 255 and AL contains 1, then ADD BL,AL will put a 0 in the BL register (since BL is the lower half of BX) and set the carry flag ON. The fact that (255+1) is not really equal to 0 now becomes significant. One natural use of the carry flag is to use ADC to *carry in* the carry flag to another register, for example BH (the higher half of BX), as follows:

```
MOV BX,255 ;16-bit number        binary 0000 0000 1111 1111
MOV AL,1   ;Bottom 8-bits of AX  binary           0000 0001
ADD BL,AL  ;Result: BL=0, BX=0   binary 0000 0000 0000 0000 carry flag ON
ADC BH,0   ;Result: BH=1, BX=256 binary 0000 0001 0000 0000 carry flag OFF penalty!
```

In this set of instructions, ADC took the fact that the carry flag was ON to mean that a carry from the lower half to the upper half of BX was required and performed this operation before carrying out the operation of adding 0 to the register (0 is added so that the end result is (255+1)

Instruction Mnemonic	Destination Operand	Source Operand	Cycle Count
<ADC|SBB>	<8-bit register>	,<8-bit constant>	1
<ADC|SBB>	<8-bit register>	,<8-bit register>	1
<ADC|SBB>	<8-bit register>	,<byte-size memory>	2
<ADC|SBB>	<byte-size memory>	,<8-bit constant>	3
<ADC|SBB>	<byte-size memory>	,<8-bit register>	3
<ADC|SBB>	<16-bit register>	,<8-bit constant>	1
<ADC|SBB>	<16-bit register>	,<16-bit constant>	1
<ADC|SBB>	<16-bit register>	,<16-bit register>	1
<ADC|SBB>	<16-bit register>	,<word-size memory>	2
<ADC|SBB>	<word-size memory>	,<8-bit constant>	3
<ADC|SBB>	<word-size memory>	,<16-bit constant>	3
<ADC|SBB>	<word-size memory>	,<16-bit register>	3
<ADC|SBB>	<32-bit register>	,<8-bit constant>	1
<ADC|SBB>	<32-bit register>	,<32-bit constant>	1
<ADC|SBB>	<32-bit register>	,<32-bit register>	1
<ADC|SBB>	<32-bit register>	,<long-size memory>	2
<ADC|SBB>	<long-size memory>	,<8-bit constant>	3
<ADC|SBB>	<long-size memory>	,<32-bit constant>	3
<ADC|SBB>	<long-size memory>	,<32-bit register>	3

Table 2.3 A standardized description for each possible form of ADC and SBB.

rather than some other value). If the carry flag had been OFF, of course, ADC would not have performed any differently than ADD. (Note, by the way, the "penalty!" notation on the ADC instruction. ADC and SBB are also subject to the Hi/Lo Rule because they are arithmetic instructions.)

Another example of using ADC to carry in the carry flag is in the case of the C statement mem1=mem2+mem3; (mem1 is long and both mem2 and mem3 are char):

```
XOR AX,AX            ;Sets AX to 0
MOV mem1+2,AX        ;Moves AX to mem1+2
MOV AL,mem3          ;Moves mem3 to AL (lower half of AX)
ADD AL,mem2          ;Adds mem2 (8-bit char) to AL
ADC AH,0             ;Take carry from ADD and add to AH
MOV mem1,AX          ;Move AX to mem1
```

SBB and SUB work the same way. If the carry flag is ON, SBB borrows and subtracts. If the carry flag is OFF, SBB doesn't borrow when subtracting. For example, in the case of the C statement mem1-=mem2; (mem1 is long, mem2 is char):

```
MOV AL,mem2              ;Move mem2 to AL
SUB BYTE PTR mem1,AL     ;Subtract AL from low-most byte of mem1
SBB BYTE PTR mem1+1,0    ;Borrow from next-most byte and subtract 0
SBB WORD PTR mem1+2,0    ;Borrow from top-most word and subtract 0
```

8-bit <constant> Operands

For all arithmetic instructions with a <constant> operand, the <constant> can be either an 8-bit, 16-bit, or 32-bit constant. This means, for example, that ADD CX,5 is one byte shorter than ADD CX,5000 because the number 5 can be stored in 8 bits but the number 5000 cannot be. (Note: we're talking about a signed 8-bit constant in this context. If <constant> is outside the range −128 to +127, one more byte is needed.)

It's amusing to see that the instruction ADD DX,128 is one byte longer than the equivalent instruction SUB DX,-128. But for practical purposes our information about 8-bit <constant> operands is only useful in the context of the logical instructions OR, AND, and XOR.

There are three tricks for saving bytes with OR, AND, and XOR — but one of them is obsolete.

Trick 1: Use the AL register. For example, it happens that AND AL,8 is one byte shorter than AND BL,8. The same is true for OR and XOR.

Trick 2: Use `OR EDX,-1` rather than `MOV EDX,-1` to put the value –1 into a 32- bit register. It happens that `OR <32-bit register>,-1` is one byte shorter than `MOV <32-bit register>,-1`.

Trick 3: Use a byte operand rather than a word operand. It used to be true that `OR BL,8` was one byte shorter than `OR BX,8` — and that the same was true for the other arithmetic instructions, including `AND` and `XOR` — in the days of 80286s and earlier machines. Since there's really only one bit involved in either case, though, the two instructions are nearly equivalent, except that they might set different flags. This trick is simpler nowadays — just make sure that you let your assembler or compiler know that your target machine is at least a 386 (by putting the `.486` directive in your program or using the appropriate compiler switches). 386s and 486s have built-in short forms of all the arithmetic instructions we discussed so far so that, for example

```
OR <16-bit register>,<constant>
```

is the same size as

```
OR <8-bit register>,<constant>
```

and so on.

As an example of this, suppose mem is a 16-bit integer that needs to be `OR`ed with a constant or `XOR`ed with a constant. If the constant in question is 255 or less, a natural assumption would be that a compiler would generate the following code (the value of the constant is 5):

```
OR mem,5
XOR mem,5
```

Microsoft and Symantec, however, do not generate these instructions. Instead, they generate:

```
OR BYTE PTR mem,5
XOR BYTE PTR mem,5
```

Remember that the directive `BYTE PTR` preceding mem is a cast. It means mem is a byte. (Our first set of instructions could have used `WORD PTR mem` to explicitly indicate mem is a word, but since mem is defined as `int`, that's default anyway — an `int` *is* a word.) In this situation, Microsoft and Symantec obviously feel that using a word operand is redundant since the top 8 bits of mem cannot be affected by the operation anyway (remember that OR and XOR can't turn the carry flag ON), and so they've chosen to save some space.

(By the way, if you code in assembler rather than C, Borland's TASM provides you with pseudo-instructions for using byte operands rather than word operands when the constant size is 8 bits or less. SETFLAG is the optimized OR, MASKFLAG is the optimized AND, and FLIPFLAG is the optimized XOR. These pseudo-instructions look especially useful because most TASM reference guides have an error. They imply that 8-bit <constant> operands don't work on 80286s. They do work.)

Despite the space savings — even for OR and XOR — there are two reasons why it's better to use the 386/486-specific short variant on a word operand (as in our first example) rather than use a byte operand which represents half of the word (the method chosen by Microsoft and Symantec).

❖ First, the right flags won't be set unless you use a word operand. This might become significant in later instructions.

❖ Second, if you use word operands, you will not be as likely to run into the penalty imposed on an arithmetic instruction by the Hi/Lo Rule. Although using a byte operand might still be worthwhile when you know the operand is on a misaligned address, a better solution is to align the address correctly and continue to use a word operand. (Note, by the way, that OR AX,OFF00h is better than MOV AH,-1 if you're trying to avoid the Hi/Lo Rule.)

The short variants of the arithmetic instructions won't work on 80286s, and in one case they are not really the shortest possible code, i.e.,

```
<arithmetic instruction> AL,<8-bit constant>
```

is even shorter than

```
<short-variant-arithmetic-instruction> AX,<8-bit constant>
```

But those exceptions aside, you will gain if you force the short variant in your code.

Asymmetry

Remember that arithmetic instructions take 2 cycles when the <destination> is a register and the <source> is a memory operand. MOV <register>,<memory>, on the other hand, takes only 1 cycle. This means that symmetrical arithmetic expressions may not be equivalent in terms of performance. For example, this pair of instructions:

```
MOV AX,[BX]     ;1 cycle
ADD AX,10       ;1 cycle
```

is faster than this pair:

```
MOV AX,10       ;1 cycle
ADD AX,[BX]     ;2 cycles
```

The C compiler vendors are aware of this fact. It doesn't matter whether your code uses the C statement mema=memb+10; or whether it uses the reverse, mema=10+memb;. Both statements will translate to:

```
MOV AX,memb     ;1 cycle
ADD AX,10       ;1 cycle
MOV mema,AX     ;1 cycle
```

When a C compiler sees the statement mema=10-memb; on the other hand, it knows the expression order can't be reversed. In this case, the translation has to be:

```
MOV AX,10       ;1 cycle
SUB AX,memb     ;2 cycles
MOV mema,AX     ;1 cycle
```

The curious corollary to this is that mema=10+memb; runs faster than mema=10-memb;. You can't do anything about that, but you can help C along when there are logical expressions, such as mema=(10&memb);. This statement is translated as:

```
MOV AX,10       ;1 cycle
AND AX,memb     ;2 cycles
MOV mema,AX     ;1 cycle
```

Since every C compiler will take 4 cycles for this by doing the `MOV AX,10` first and the `AND AX,memb` second, it's faster to say `mema=(memb&10);`, which is translated as:

```
MOV AX,memb    ;1 cycle
AND AX,10      ;1 cycle
MOV mema,AX    ;1 cycle
```

In general, then, put constants after variables when performing arithmetic operations.

Misalignment Revisited

In Chapter 1 we talked about the 3-cycle penalty inherent in misaligning addresses. Misalignment costs in arithmetic too. The `ADD`, `ADC`, `SUB`, `SBB`, `OR`, `AND`, and `XOR` instructions have a 3-cycle penalty if the address of the <source operand> is misaligned and a 6-cycle penalty if the address of the <destination operand> is misaligned. The `INC` and `DEC` instructions also have a 6-cycle penalty if the <destination operand> is misaligned. So it behooves you to ensure that your memory addresses are properly aligned. In fact, we'll add another SECRET RULE to your repertoire.

◆ **SECRET "MISALIGNMENT" RULE:**
   If your <source operand> is misaligned, you lose at least 3 cycles. If your <destination operand> is misaligned, you lose at least 6 cycles.

Where You Are

The uses to which you can put assembler have grown in number. In this chapter, you learned:

❖ how and when to add and subtract values from constants, registers or memory variables to and from registers and memory with `ADD`, `ADC`, `INC` and `SUB`, `SBB`, `DEC`;

❖ how to perform logic operations on registers and memory with `OR`, `AND`, `XOR`;

❖ how to use register constants to speed up code and how to save bytes in logic operations;

❖ about the flags register and how arithmetic operations affect the carry, overflow, parity, sign, and zero flags.

And finally, you learned another two SECRET RULES of assembler that will help you speed up your code:

◆ **SECRET "HI/LO" RULE:**

Part 1:
((If you execute two consecutive instructions which contain references to the same 16-bit register or to the high and low halves of a 16-bit register)
and (the first instruction changes one half of the register)
and (the second instruction is MOV
and either
   ((the source operand is the other half of the register)
   or (the source operand is the entire register)))
then you lose 1 cycle.)

Part 2:
((If you execute two consecutive instructions which contain references to the same 16-bit register or to the high and low halves of a 16-bit register)
and (the first instruction changes one half of the register)
and (the second instruction does ARITHMETIC
and either
   ((the source or the destination is the other half of the register)
   or (the source or the destination is the entire register))
and (neither source nor destination is a <memory> operand))
then you lose 1 cycle.)

Part 3:
((If you execute two consecutive instructions which contain references to the same 16-bit register or to the high and low halves of a 16-bit register)
and (the first instruction changes the entire register)
and (the second instruction is MOV
    and (the source operand is the high half of the register))
then you lose 1 cycle.)

Part 4:
((If you execute two consecutive instructions which contain references to the same 16-bit register or to the high and low halves of a 16-bit register)
and (the first instruction changes the entire register)
and (the second instruction does ARITHMETIC
    and (either source or destination is the high half of the register)
    and (neither source nor destination is a <memory> operand))
then you lose 1 cycle.)

◆ **SECRET "MISALIGNMENT" RULE:**
If your <source operand> is misaligned, you lose at least 3 cycles.
If your <destination operand> is misaligned, you lose at least 6 cycles.

Jumps — The Assembler GOTO

This chapter is about the main loop-control instructions in assembler — the conditional and unconditional jumps. We'll start with an instruction that's often associated with conditional jumps — CMP.

The CMP Instruction

In an assembler statement, the syntax of the CMP instruction looks like this:

```
CMP <destination operand>,<source operand>      ;optional comment
```

Once again, the syntax is familiar and the same rules apply. The <source operand> can be an 8-bit, 16-bit, or 32-bit memory operand, register, or constant. The <destination operand> can be an 8-bit, 16-bit, or 32-bit memory operand or register (but not a constant). The <destination operand> and the <source operand> must have matching sizes unless the <source operand> is an 8-bit constant — an <8-bit constant source operand> can be matched with an 8-bit, 16-bit, or 32-bit <destination operand>. And finally, a memory operand can't be used for both <source operand> and <destination operand>. CMP sets the carry, overflow, parity, sign, and zero flags.

The meaning of CMP is imperative:

CoMPare the contents of <source operand> to the contents of <destination operand>.

CMP acts exactly like the SUB instruction, except that it doesn't change the <destination operand> by actually writing to it. Nevertheless, CMP's effect on the flags register is the same effect as a SUB would have in the same circumstances — if <destination operand> becomes 0, CMP sets the zero flag; if the low byte of <destination operand> has an even number of 1 bits, CMP sets the parity flag; if <destination operand> is signed, CMP sets the sign flag; and if a bit gets shifted out on the left, CMP sets the carry flag.

CMP has 19 possible forms, depending on the operands used. Table 3.1 is a standardized description for each possible form of CMP.

Instruction Mnemonic	Destination Operand	Source Operand	Cycle Count
CMP	<8-bit register>	,<8-bit constant>	1
CMP	<8-bit register>	,<8-bit register>	1
CMP	<8-bit register>	,<byte-size memory>	2
CMP	<byte-size memory>	,<8-bit constant>	2
CMP	<byte-size memory>	,<8-bit register>	2
CMP	<16-bit register>	,<8-bit constant>	1
CMP	<16-bit register>	,<16-bit constant>	1
CMP	<16-bit register>	,<16-bit register>	1
CMP	<16-bit register>	,<word-size memory>	2
CMP	<word-size memory>	,<8-bit constant>	1
CMP	<word-size memory>	,<16-bit constant>	2
CMP	<word-size memory>	,<16-bit register>	2
CMP	<32-bit register>	,<8-bit constant>	1
CMP	<32-bit register>	,<32-bit constant>	1
CMP	<32-bit register>	,<32-bit register>	1
CMP	<32-bit register>	,<long-size memory>	2
CMP	<long-size memory>	,<8-bit constant>	1
CMP	<long-size memory>	,<32-bit constant>	2
CMP	<long-size memory>	,<32-bit register>	2

Table 3.1   A standardized description of each possible form of CMP.

The following instructions illustrate some of these forms:

```
CMP CX,55   ;i.e., compare the CX register with the constant 55
CMP SI,mem  ;i.e., compare the SI register with memory location mem
CMP mem,DI  ;i.e., compare memory location mem with the DI register
CMP mem,BP  ;i.e., compare the memory location mem with BP
CMP mem,55  ;i.e., compare memory location mem with 55
```

Since CMP has the same effect on the flags register as SUB does, if the BL register contains a 5, then

```
CMP BL,5
```

sets the zero flag ON. (The zero flag always goes ON if the source and destination are the same, that is, if the zero flag goes ON the comparison was equal.) The instruction also sets the parity flag OFF, the sign flag OFF, and the carry flag OFF.

Some forms of CMP (those with a memory operand as the <destination>) are faster than the equivalent SUB instruction, so CMP is preferable to SUB when what you're really looking for is the flag values. Because of its equivalency with SUB, CMP is also considered to be an arithmetic instruction. This means that it is subject to the usual 1-cycle penalty for using Register Pointer plus Constant or Register Pointer Doubled addressing modes, and to the usual 1-cycle penalty for triggering the Hi/Lo Rule. For example:

```
ADD DX,5     ;1 cycle, changing the entire register
CMP DH,1     ;!2 cycles, arithmetic on top half of register
```

CMP <memory>,<register> and CMP <register>,<memory> are interchangeable if the object is to compare for equality (formally: the zero flag gets set the same way regardless of the form you choose). By convention you will see the first form more often, e.g., CMP [BX],AX rather than CMP AX,[BX]. This convention arose because CMP <memory>,<register> was faster than CMP <register>,<memory> on 386s.

CMP is normally used to set the flags register in preparation for a conditional jump. That being the case, we'll defer further illustrations of CMP into the next section.

The JZ, JNZ, JP, JNP, JC, JNC, JS, JNS, JO, and JNO Instructions

In C, programs are full of `if (conditional-expression)` types of statements. The assembler equivalent to all of these is "if (flag is on) goto ...," or "if (flag is off) goto ...."

It's as simple as that. These two phrases describe the whole toolkit (except for a couple of obsolete instructions which we'll dismiss at the end of this chapter). Simple as they are, though, C compiler makers have been able to translate all the complexities of C conditions into assembler's conditional jump instructions.

The flags in question are the zero, parity, carry, sign, and overflow flags we described in Chapter 2. Since any flag can be either ON (true) or OFF (false), there are 10 possible flag situations: zero ON, zero OFF, parity ON, parity OFF, carry ON, carry OFF, sign ON, sign OFF, overflow ON, and overflow OFF. One conditional jump instruction exists for each of these 10 situations — JZ, JNZ, JP, JNP, JC, JNC, JS, JNS, JO, and JNO.

In an assembler statement, the syntax of these 10 instructions looks like this:

```
JZ    <8-bit target>    ;optional comment
JNZ   <8-bit target>    ;optional comment
JP    <8-bit target>    ;optional comment
JNP   <8-bit target>    ;optional comment
JC    <8-bit target>    ;optional comment
JNC   <8-bit target>    ;optional comment
JS    <8-bit target>    ;optional comment
JNS   <8-bit target>    ;optional comment
JO    <8-bit target>    ;optional comment
JNO   <8-bit target>    ;optional comment
```

In each case, the instruction mnemonic consists of the letter J (standing for Jump or `goto`), an optional letter N (standing for Not, i.e., "if it's false" or "if the flag is OFF, that is, Not ON") and the first letter of the name of the flag — zero, parity, carry, sign, or overflow — that the instruction tests. None of the conditional jump instructions changes any flags in the flags register.

The meaning of each of these instructions is imperative:

JZ: Jump to <target> if zero flag ON.

JNZ: Jump to <target> if not zero flag ON (that is, if flag OFF).

JP: Jump to <target> if parity flag ON.

JNP: Jump to <target> if not parity flag ON (that is, if flag OFF).

JC: Jump to <target> if carry flag ON.

JNC: Jump to <target> if not carry flag ON (that is, if flag OFF).

JS: Jump to <target> if sign flag ON.

JNS: Jump to <target> if not sign flag ON (that is, if flag OFF).

JO: Jump to <target> if overflow flag ON.

JNO: Jump to <target> if not overflow flag ON (that is, if flag OFF).

Thus,

```
JZ label
```

jumps to label if the zero flag is ON, and

```
JNZ label
```

jumps to label if the zero flag is OFF. The <target> can be any label and is actually an 8-bit offset from the current code location. That is,

```
JNZ 50
```

does not mean jump to location 50. It means jump forward 50 or jump to the location that's 50 bytes past the current location.

Because the <target> can only be a label, these instructions have only one possible form. Table 3.2 is a standardized description for these jump instructions.

Except for the last four, each conditional jump instruction also has an alternate name, as shown in Table 3.2. The alternate name is supposed to be a helpful mnemonic, and many programmers use the alternate if it's meaningful in the context. For instance, in this sequence:

```
CMP AL,0
JZ label
```

you may prefer to think of JZ as meaning "Jump if the zero flag is ON." And in this sequence, which uses the alternate name:

```
CMP AL,5
JE label
```

you may prefer to think of JE as meaning "Jump if compare was Equal." In either case the meaning to the computer is the same: equality is decided by the zero flag. In the end, the instruction mnemonic you use is really a personal preference based on whether you see the instruction as a test of flags or as a test of logic.

Instruction Mnemonic	Alternate Mnemonic	Target	Cycle Count
JZ	JE	<nearby_label>	3 if jump, 1 if no jump
JNZ	JNE	<nearby_label>	3 if jump, 1 if no jump
JP	JPE	<nearby_label>	3 if jump, 1 if no jump
JNP	JPO	<nearby_label>	3 if jump, 1 if no jump
JC	JB	<nearby_label>	3 if jump, 1 if no jump
JNC	JAE	<nearby_label>	3 if jump, 1 if no jump
JS		<nearby_label>	3 if jump, 1 if no jump
JNS		<nearby_label>	3 if jump, 1 if no jump
JO		<nearby_label>	3 if jump, 1 if no jump
JNO		<nearby_label>	3 if jump, 1 if no jump

Table 3.2   Standardized description of 10 conditional jump instructions.

Similarly,

* JNZ is equivalent to JNE "Jump if Not Equal."

* JP is equivalent to JPE "Jump if Parity Even" (if the parity flag is ON that means the parity is even).

* JNP is equivalent to JPO "Jump if Parity Odd."

* JC is equivalent to JB "Jump if Below" (if the carry flag is ON that might mean the last subtract had to borrow). This instruction is used for unsigned comparisons.

* JNC is equivalent to JAE "Jump if Above or Equal." This instruction is used for unsigned comparisons.

A word on the distinction between "Less than" and "Below" in these descriptions. Suppose the hexadecimal value 0FFFFh is in the AX register, and 1 is in the BX register. Then

```
CMP AX,BX
```

will return with the sign flag ON (because in hexadecimal 0FFFFh − 1 = 0FFFEh and the top bit is set) but with the carry flag OFF (no carrying was required). In terms of logic, the sign flag ON means "Less than 0," that is, AX is less than BX, considering that these are signed numbers. But AX is "Above" BX if both are considered as unsigned numbers, and that's what the carry flag indicates. To sum it up: check the carry flag after comparing unsigned numbers; check the sign flag after comparing signed numbers. If one operand is signed and the other is unsigned, the translation is JB.

In this next example, JC is used to check the carry flag for an overflow:

```
ADD AL,1
JC label
```

Here, the letter C (in JC) clearly implies that the point is to check what the previous instruction did to the carry flag. JC's alternate, JB, might be used in this case:

```
SUB AL,2
JB label
```

where the letter B (in JB) clearly implies that the point is this is being done as an unsigned comparison. In this example, the jump will happen if AL is either 0 or 1 (because then the carry flag is set ON) and the way we like to look at it is that 0 and 1 are "Below" 2.

The following set of instructions tests whether all the bits masked by 2026h are on in register DX:

```
AND DX,2026h
CMP DX,2026h
JZ label            ;if zero flag is ON, all bits were on
....                ;if zero flag is OFF, one of the bits was not on
```

To test whether the top 2 bits of register DX are both 0 or both 1, use this pair of instructions:

```
ADD DX,0
JO label   ;if overflow flag is ON, both bits 0 or 1
....       ;if overflow flag is OFF, the two bits have different values
```

Conditional jumps are important to the performance of a C routine because, although you might build a C routine without goto statements, C's if and while statements usually get translated to conditional jumps as well. Consider the following C program:

```
int mema;
void main ()
{
 if (mema==5) goto labelb;
 mema=5;
labelb:;
}
```

A compiler will translate the body of this program to:

```
CMP mema,5
JZ labelb
MOV mema,5
labelb:
```

In this program:

```
unsigned mema;
void main ()
{
 if (mema<7) mema=7;
}
```

The slightly more complicated statement `if (mema<7) mema=7;` generates:

```
CMP mema,7      ;!3 cycles
JAE label       ;3 cycles if jump, 1 cycle if no jump
MOV mema,7      ;!2 cycles
label:
```

(Note the penalties for the Constant to Memory Rule violation.) The translation generated, by the way, is slower than this one:

```
    __asm MOV AX,7;       /* 1 cycle */
    __asm CMP mema,AX;    /* 2 cycles */
    __asm JAE  label;     /* 3 cycles if jump, 1 cycle if no jump */
    __asm MOV mema,AX;    /* 1 cycle */
label: ; }
```

Remember: whenever you see the same constant appearing twice, there's a chance you'll gain by putting the constant in a register. The gain on this one was 1 cycle, or about 16 percent.

Checking for Overflow

`JO` might be used to check the status of the overflow flag in the following situation:

```
signed int mema,memb;
void main ()
{
  mema=30000; memb=30000; mema+=memb; printf("mema=%d\n",mema);
}
```

A compiler will translate the main expression of this program as:

```
MOV AX,mema
ADD AX,memb
MOV mema,AX
```

Note that this translation would `MOV` a "garbage" value into `mema` because the result of the addition (30000+30000=60000) causes an overflow and the compiler *doesn't bother to check for this!* (Remember that for signed integers, we need to know if the second-highest bit (masked by 0x4000) has overflowed into the highest bit (masked by 0x8000), thus changing the "sign." This information is signaled by the status of the overflow flag, which is set here by the `ADD` instruction.) You can avoid this situation by replacing the compiler's translation with the following inline assembly routine:

```
__asm MOV AX,mema;
__asm ADD AX,memb;
__asm JO overflow_routine;
__asm MOV mema,AX;
```

With this code in the program, the JO instruction checks the overflow flag and, since its condition is true, jumps the code to overflow_routine. Thus, mema doesn't get changed.

The JC instruction can be used to check the carry flag for an overflow of unsigned integers in the same way.

By the way, if you're adding an 8-bit number which is probably 0, consider that this code:

```
ADD BYTE PTR memb,0      ;!4 cycles
JNC labelx1              ;3 cycles if jump, 1 cycle if no jump
INC BYTE PTR memb+1      ;3 cycles
labelx1:
```

is faster if the jump takes place (and just as fast if no jump takes place) than:

```
ADD BYTE PTR memb,0      ;!4 cycles
ADC BYTE PTR memb+1,0    ;!4 cycles
```

The penalties in both sets of code are the result of the Constant-to-Memory Rule.

The JG, JGE, JL, JLE, JA, and JBE Instructions

So far, we've only discussed instructions that jump to a specified routine if the state of a single flag (the zero, parity, carry, sign and overflow flags) in the flags register is either ON or OFF. Some of these flags, though, have states which are related — for example, the carry and zero flags. Because of this, assembler also provides conditional jump instructions that test the state of more than one flag and make the decision to jump based on the state of them all. The instructions we'll look at are: JG, JGE, JL, JLE, JA, and JBE. None of these instructions change any flags in the flags register.

In an assembler statement, the syntax of these six instructions looks like this:

```
JG   <8-bit target>    ;optional comment
JGE  <8-bit target>    ;optional comment
JL   <8-bit target>    ;optional comment
JLE  <8-bit target>    ;optional comment
JA   <8-bit target>    ;optional comment
JBE  <8-bit target>    ;optional comment
```

The meaning of each of these instructions is imperative:

JG: Jump to <target> if Greater.

JGE: Jump to <target> if Greater or Equal.

JL: Jump to <target> if Less.

JLE: Jump to <target> if Less or Equal.

JA: Jump to <target> if Above.

JBE: Jump to <target> if Below or Equal.

In other words:

❖ JG jumps to <target> if the zero flag is OFF and the status of the sign flag equals the status of the overflow flag. This instruction is used for signed comparisons.

❖ JGE jumps to <target> if the status of the sign flag equals the status of the overflow flag. This instruction is used for signed comparisons.

❖ JL jumps to <target> if the status of the sign flag is not equal to the status of the overflow flag. This instruction is used for signed comparisons.

❖ JLE jumps to <target> if the zero flag is ON or if the status of the sign flag is not equal to the status of the overflow flag. This instruction is used for signed comparisons.

❖ JA jumps to <target> if the zero flag and the carry flag are both OFF. This instruction is used for unsigned comparisons.

❖ JBE jumps to <target> if either the zero flag or the carry flag is ON. This instruction is used for unsigned comparisons.

As with the other conditional jump instructions, the <target> can be any label and is actually an 8-bit offset from the current code location. Because there is only this one option, these instructions have only one possible form. Table 3.3 is a standardized description for this form.

The multi-flag conditional jump instructions are especially useful for handling double (or more) jump decision trees. We'll provide some examples in a later section, but first it's necessary to look at assembler's *non* conditional jump instruction.

The JMP Instruction

JMP stands for goto — the jump is always made regardless of the status of the flags register. We're showing this unconditional jump form now because it really doesn't make sense to have JMP without conditional jumps — unless you've found a practical purpose for infinite loops! There are actually multiple forms of unconditional jump, depending on how far away the target is (within 127 bytes, within 65536 bytes, in a far segment, etc.). But in a book about inline assembly and tight loops the other forms are irrelevant, so we won't discuss them here.

In an assembler statement, the syntax of the JMP instruction looks like this:

```
JMP <16-bit target>    ;optional comment
```

The meaning of JMP is imperative:

JuMP to <target>.

Instruction Mnemonic	Target	Cycle Count
JG	<nearby_label>	3 if jump, 1 if no jump
JGE	<nearby_label>	3 if jump, 1 if no jump
JL	<nearby_label>	3 if jump, 1 if no jump
JLE	<nearby_label>	3 if jump, 1 if no jump
JA	<nearby_label>	3 if jump, 1 if no jump
JBE	<nearby_label>	3 if jump, 1 if no jump

Table 3.3   Standardized description of conditional jump instructions that test the state of more than one flag.

Once again, the <target> can be any label. Unlike the conditional jump instructions, though, JMP's <target> is actually a 16-bit offset from the current code location. As usual, JMP doesn't change any flags in the flags register.

Because the <target> can only be a label, JMP has only one possible form. Table 3.4 is a standardized description for this form.

C compilers typically start to generate JMPs when if statements start to get complicated, especially when such statements are combined with else statements. For example, the C statement if (mema==5) mema=3; else mema=6; would be translated as follows (mema is a register variable, namely SI in this case):

```
            CMP SI,5          ;1 cycle
            JZ ax_equals_5    ;3 cycles if jump, 1 cycle if no jump
            MOV SI,6          ;1 cycle
            JMP short done    ;3 cycles
ax_equals_5:
            MOV SI,3          ;1 cycle
done:
```

This example illustrates how the unconditional JMP fits in: if the code splits into two possible execution threads which rejoin each other (in this case, at done:). Another way to do this without splitting or using the JMP instruction is:

```
            CMP SI,5          ;1 cycle
            MOV SI,3          ;1 cycle
            JNZ ax_equals_5   ;3 cycles if jump, 1 cycle if no jump
            MOV SI,6          ;1 cycle
ax_equals_5:
```

This shorter alternative takes 4 cycles (or 6 cycles if no jump occurs) to do the same thing the original translation took 7 (or 9) cycles to do. The savings is possible because the MOV instruction does not change any flags, so the conditional jump can be deferred to two instructions after the CMP.

Instruction Mnemonic	Target	Cycle Count
JMP	<distant_label>	3

Table 3.4   Standardized description of JMP.

Double Jumps

Double jumps are necessary in situations where a decision tree has more than two possible branches. Such situations introduce another SECRET RULE.

◆ **SECRET "DOUBLE-JUMP" RULE:**
If a conditional jump instruction whose condition is false (i.e., the jump is not done) is immediately followed by a second jump instruction, you lose 1 cycle on the second jump instruction unless the next instruction that is executed after that begins on a 0-mod-8 address.

Imagine a 3-way condition: if AX=5 thing #1 must happen, if AX>5 thing #2 must happen, and if AX<5 thing #3 must happen. The arrangement is quite simple (assume AX has a value of 3):

```
        (if signed comparison)     (if unsigned comparison)
line_1: CMP AX,5                   CMP AX,5
line_2: JZ do_thing_1              JZ do_thing_1
line_3: JG do_thing_2              JA do_thing_2
line_4: JL do_thing_3              JB do_thing_3
```

In this example, the instruction in line_4 (JL or JB, depending on whether the comparison is signed or unsigned) is really redundant because if the comparison hasn't returned *equal* or *greater than*, then it must have returned *less than*. But the immediate question is — how long does it take to reach line_4, if the value in the AX register is 3? That is, how many cycles are needed for the three instructions CMP AX,5, JZ and JA, and CMP AX,5, JZ and JG?

Our form/cycle count charts suggest these instructions should take 3 cycles — CMP <register>,<constant> is always a 1-cycle instruction, and since all conditional jumps take 1 cycle when the jump doesn't happen, line_2 and line_3 should each take another cycle. (Conditional jumps take 3 cycles if the jump happens, but in this case the conditions are false: AX=3 is not equal to or bigger than 5.) So: 1 + 1 + 1 = 3 cycles. The application of the Double-Jump Rule, however, makes the actual cycle count 4.

As another example, consider the following C program:

```
int mema;
void main ()
{
  register int memc;
  for (memc=0; memc<100; memc+=2) mema+=memc;
}
```

All C compilers will translate the body of this program to something like:

```
        XOR SI,SI    ;or AX or DX — the choice of register can vary
labelx:ADD mema,SI
        ADD SI,2
        CMP SI,100
        JB labelx
```

Although the choice of JB rather than JL is surprising since memc is signed, it's safe enough in this case. The really interesting point in this code is that all the compilers chose XOR to zero the 16-bit register variable.

Long Conditional Jumps

Of course, a second jump won't be reached unless the first jump is a conditional jump and the condition implied by it is false. But the Double-Jump Rule does apply to this situation:

```
                CMP ...
                JZ nearby_location    ;3 cycles if jump, 1 cycle if no jump
                JMP distant_location ;!4 cycles (this is the JNZ option)
nearby_location:                      ;this is the JZ option
```

At first, this may look like a contrived example to bump into the Double-Jump penalty and waste some cycles, but it's not. Such code is a common sight, because sometimes distant_location is so far away that it can't be reached with a conditional jump.

Remember that the conditional jump's <target> is actually an 8-bit offset (as opposed to the non-conditional JMP's 16-bit offset <target>) from the current code location. That is,

```
JNZ 50
```

does not mean jump to location 50, it means jump forward 50 or jump to the location that's 50 bytes past the current location. When designing the 80386 (and later) chips, Intel decided that jump instructions could be shorter if jumps are relative offsets rather than absolute locations. In fact, if the offset is between −128 and +127, the offset is only 1 byte long.

Usually, only the short form of conditional jump is relevant because (by definition), the start of a tight loop won't be more than 127 bytes away from the end of the loop. If the jump target is further away though, one of two things will happen.

One route that could be taken — choice (a) — is that a compiler will first try to produce the usual conditional jump instruction. For example, if JZ is the conditional jump instruction being used, the compiler will try to produce:

```
CMP AL,5
JZ distantlabel
```

which requires 3 cycles if AL equals 5 and 1 cycle if AL does not equal 5. If, however, distantlabel is too far away, the compiler will then produce:

```
CMP AL,5
JNZ tmplabel
JMP distantlabel
tmplabel:
```

which is logically the same thing. Notice, though, that if AL equals 5 these three instructions will take 5 cycles to get to distantlabel — 1 cycle wasted by the JNZ which is false, 3 cycles for the JMP, and 1 extra cycle for the Double-Jump Rule penalty incurred.

The other route that could be taken — choice (b) — is when the compiler is enabled for 386 or 486 code production. If this is the case, the compiler can produce the long form of the conditional jump instruction. With the long form, the offset is a 16-bit word rather than the usual 8-bit byte, so the <target> can be up to 65535 bytes before or after the current code location. Thus, if JZ is the conditional jump instruction being used, the compiler will be able to produce:

```
CMP AL,5
JZ distantlabel
```

and use only 3 cycles (or 1 cycle if the condition is false) for the jump.

Choice (a) should have disappeared with the 80286 but is regrettably extant and flourishing. When you see your compiler producing it, edit so that the jump will be choice (b). The caveat to this is: even though choice (b) is better than choice (a), it is not a free pass for 386 and 486 programmers to make loops as big as they want because of another SECRET RULE.

◆ **SECRET "LONG-JUMP" RULE:**
If you use the long form of conditional jump, you lose 1 cycle whether or not the jump happens, unless the previous instruction (which can't be JMP or CALL) takes more than 1 cycle. That is, the long form takes 4 cycles if the condition is true and 2 cycles if the condition is false, subject to the Prefix-Waiver Rule.

The Long-Jump Rule is actually another example of the Prefix Rule we introduced in Chapter 1 because a jump to a far address results in a 0Fh (extended instruction set) prefix being added to the jump instruction (remember that the addition of a prefix costs 1 byte and 1 cycle unless the Prefix-Waiver Rule is also in effect). This means you should avoid jumping to far away places. If your loop is not concise, its conditional jumps will take more cycles.

Wherever there's a prefix there's also an optimization opportunity with the Prefix-Waiver Rule. For example the instructions on the left are faster than the instructions on the right and do precisely the same thing:

```
MOV AX,ES        ;3 cycles       CMP  CX,1          ;1 cycle
CMP CX,1         ;1 cycle        MOV  AX,ES         ;3 cycles
JZ distantlabel  ;3 or 1 cycles  JZ   distantlabel  ;!4 or 1 cycles
```

Adding ASCII Numbers

Suppose you have a large set of ASCII numbers — a pretty probable supposition, considering that many database files contain numbers in ASCII — and need to add them up. Here's a simple answer:

```
void main ()
{
 totaller=0;
 for (;;)
   {
   totaller+=atol(...);
   }
 printf("total is: %d\n",totaller);
}
```

The problem with this program is that even a fast _atol routine (like the one we supply in Chapter 11) is slow. A better way is to do the addition without doing a conversion, as in this program:

```
void main ()
{
 char totaller[10+1];
 strcpy(totaller,"00000000");        /* initialize the totaller */
 for (;;)  {
  x=strlen(p1);                       /* x = size of string */
      __asm MOV SI,10;                /* SI = offset of end of totaller */
      __asm MOV DI,x;                 /* DI = offset of end of string */
  labela:__asm DEC SI;                /* --SI, no test for overflow, */
                                      /* it's "impossible" */
      __asm DEC DI;                   /* --DI, test this time because */
                                      /* it's "inevitable" */
      __asm JL  labelc;               /* if DI < 0, that means */
                                      /* we've finished this one */
      __asm MOV AL,[p1+DI];
      __asm MOV CL,totaller[SI];
      __asm SUB CL,"0";               /* DIGITS ONLY PLEASE! */
      __asm ADD AL,CL;
      __asm CMP AL,"9";               /* check for carry */
      __asm JA  labelb;
      __asm MOV totaller[SI],AL;
      __asm JMP labela;               /* Now do the next digit */
  labelb:__asm SUB AL,"9";
      __asm MOV totaller[SI],AL;
      __asm MOV AL,totaller[SI-1];    /* See Note 1, below */
      __asm DEC SI;                   /* --> prev in totaller */
      __asm INC AL;                   /* the amount carried is 1 */
      __asm CMP AL,"9";
      __asm JA  labelb;               /* we carried again */
      __asm MOV totaller[SI],AL;
      __asm JMP labela;
   labelc:  ;  }
 printf("total is: %s\n",totaller);
}
```

Note 1: The "natural" thing to do is decrement the pointer first and then use it, i.e.:

```
__asm DEC SI;
__asm MOV AL,[SI];
```

Instead, we reverse the order to avoid a Register-Address Rule penalty.

Straddling Cache Lines

In Chapter 1 we talked about the perils of straddling cache lines for data accesses and concluded that the danger of being penalized is not great unless you're accessing more than 2 bytes at a time. Unfortunately, that's precisely what the Prefetcher is doing (remember that the cache reads 16 bytes at a time), so the penalty can apply for code. This results in another SECRET RULE.

◆ **SECRET "CACHE-STRADDLING" RULE:**
If you jump to an instruction which straddles a 16-byte boundary (that is, an instruction which begins in one cache line and ends in the next cache line), you lose 2 cycles. Further, if you jump to a one-cycle instruction which doesn't straddle but is followed by an instruction which either straddles or begins in a new 16-byte boundary (i.e., the two instructions together straddle) you lose 1 cycle.

In other words, given this situation:

```
       JMP label
       ....
label: <instruction #1>
       <instruction #2>
```

the Cache-straddling Rule can be illustrated as follows:

```
IF <instruction #1> straddles THEN !2 cycle penalty
ELSE IF <instruction#1> takes 1 cycle
    AND ( <instruction #2> straddles
          OR <instruction #2> begins on new boundary)
    THEN !1 cycle penalty
```

If you want maximum speed, then, you have to determine if the objects of jump instructions are aligned and force alignment if they are not. Remember though, mere misalignment is usually not serious: what you are looking for is a pipeline stall.

While there is no standard easy way to tell a C compiler to generate 16-byte code alignment, with an assembler you can force alignment on 16-byte boundaries with the assembler directive `ALIGN 16`, which aligns the next instruction's address on a 0-mod-16 address (the directive doesn't work with inline assembly). For example, this pair of instructions:

```
ALIGN 16
MOV AX,5
```

·assures that `AX` is aligned on the next 0-mod-16 address available. This method is not very precise, though, since it isn't always necessary to align on a 16-byte boundary. It's only necessary to do so if there is a danger of straddling the cache lines. To evaluate this danger, you need to know whether the first instruction in a loop — the instruction that is frequently jumped to — ends at or straddles a 16-byte boundary. Finding out whether an instruction ends at or straddles a 16-byte boundary is not easy, but there are some tools available.

With Microsoft C, use the /Fc option to generate a combination of an assembler and a machine-code listing. The leftmost column of the listing is the machine address. With Borland C and Symantec C, it's necessary to use the debuggers that come with these packages to get this information (for details, refer to the relevant documentation provided by the compiler vendor). While such listings don't provide the absolute address, it's safe to presume that the listed module begins at a 16-byte boundary. So, if you see a straddle in the listing then there really is a straddle at runtime.

One way to test code alignment is to insert test code(s) into the C program at the places that should be aligned on 0-mod-16 addresses. As test code, we suggest the following line, which will display the letter A on the screen at runtime if (and only if) the code is misaligned.

```
#if TESTING
  __asm DB 0E8h,00h,00h,058h,0A9h,03h,00h,90h,90h,90h,90h;
#endif
```

The terse signaling method is necessary to ensure a necessary feature — the test code itself must be precisely 16 bytes long, else it would disrupt the very factor being tested. Do not use this test code with 32-bit programs, do not use it twice within the same C function, do not use it in C functions that do not already have some inline assembly code, and remember to turn `TESTING` off in any production version of your program.

Data accesses get priority over code accesses. If the address you jump to is moving to <memory> then the Prefetcher won't get a chance to load the next cache line of code in advance and there's a penalty. For example:

```
ALIGN 16
        MOV AX,DX    ;offset 0 1 cycle  size: 2
labelx: MOV [BX],AX  ;offset 2 1 cycle  size: 2
        MOV [BX],AX  ;offset 4 1 cycle  size: 2
        MOV [BX],AX  ;offset 6 1 cycle  size: 2
        MOV [BX],AX  ;offset 8 1 cycle  size: 2
        MOV [BX],AX  ;offset 10 1 cycle  size: 2
        MOV [BX],AX  ;offset 12 1 cycle  size: 2
        MOV [BX],AX  ;offset 14 1 cycle  size: 2
        MOV AX,DX    ;offset 16 !3 cycles NEW CACHE LINE penalty
        JMP labelx   ;offset 18 3 cycles
```

Wherever you have a label (the object of a jump or a call), delay instructions that change memory locations if at all possible. Intel's advice on this matter is: ALIGN 16 every label. That way you're bound to be OK by the time you get to the next cache line.

Once you find out that a straddle or new cache line penalty is going on, you can stop it by putting in some instructions that do absolutely nothing just to fill up the code until the critical loop begins — a cumbersome process which is not worth doing until the very final stages of a programming project. Assembler's no-operation instruction is called NOP.

The NOP Instruction

In an assembler statement, the syntax of the NOP instruction looks like this:

```
NOP     ;optional comment
```

The meaning of NOP is:

No OPeration.

NOP has neither a <source operand> nor a <destination operand> and has no effect on the flags register. It is a 1-byte instruction with only one possible form. Table 3.5 is a standardized description for this form.

Instruction Mnemonic	Cycle Count
NOP	1

Table 3.5 Standardized description of NOP.

NOP is useful when it's necessary to line code up on 16-byte boundaries. It's also useful when you want to set a breakpoint but you don't have a labeled address for the breakpoint location. For instance, you can add 3 NOPs to the code you're debugging, load the program with DEBUG.COM, and search for the location by searching for 90h 90h 90h (90h is the machine code for NOP).

It's too bad that assemblers aren't imaginative — they'll always generate one or more NOPs when they see EVEN (an assembler directive meaning "ALIGN 2") or ALIGN 16. This doesn't matter if the code is never executed, but if the program falls through to the code on the way to the loop-alignment point there are sometimes better instructions to use as filler. For example, a 1-byte prefix can be useful provided it has no real effect:

```
        MOV DS,AX    ;we have a slow instruction              ;3 cycles
        NOP          ;filler instruction to force alignment ;1 cycle
@@loop: MOV [BX],DX  ;aligned on 16-byte boundary            ;1 cycle
        ...
```

In this code, NOP can be replaced with DB 3Eh (the DS: prefix), which will execute in 0 cycles because of the Prefix-Waiver Rule:

```
        MOV  DS,AX     ;3 cycles
        DB   3Eh       ;0 cycles
@@loop: MOV  [BX],DX   ;1 cycle
        ...
```

For a multiple-byte filler, don't use a string of NOPs. Here are some other instructions which "do nothing" and use up more than one byte in the process:

```
MOV BP,BP              ;2 bytes, 1 cycle
DB 08Dh,0AEh,00h,00h   ;4 bytes, 1 cycle
```

Apart from that, your main use of NOP should be to cause your compiler to avoid generating useless NOPs, something Symantec C takes care of automatically. With Borland and Microsoft C, you can only be sure of this if you compile with one of the /O switches.

The LOOP Instruction

In an assembler statement, the syntax of the LOOP instruction looks like this:

```
LOOP      <8-bit target>                  ;optional comment
```

The meaning of LOOP is imperative:

Decrement the CX register by 1. If CX is not equal to 0, jump to LOOP's <target>.

LOOP is a conditional jump instruction which doesn't use the status of the flags register to make the decision to jump. As usual, <target> can be any label, and LOOP has no effect on the flags register. Because this is the only option, LOOP has only one possible form. Table 3.6 is a standardized description for this form.

The LOOP instruction will subtract 1 from the CX register without affecting the flags register. Then, if the CX register is not 0, the instruction at <label> is executed — that is, the effect is the same as:

```
JMP <label>
```

if CX doesn't equal zero after the decrement. If the CX register is 0 after the decrement, the jump is not performed. Instead, execution falls through to the next instruction.

LOOP is nearly an obsolete instruction because there's a faster alternative. Consider these two assembler code snippets, both of which move the contents of the BX register to the AX register 50 times and end up with CX = 0.

```
        MOV CX,50    ;1 cycle            MOV   CX,50    ;1 cycle
labelx: MOV AX,BX    ;1 cycle   labelx:  MOV   AX,BX    ;1 cycle
        DEC CX       ;1 cycle            LOOP  labelx   ;7 cycles
        JNZ labelx   ;3 cycles
```

Instruction Mnemonic	Target	Cycle Count
LOOP	<nearby_label>	7 if jump, 6 if no jump!!

Table 3.6   Standardized description of LOOP.

The code on the left is 60 percent faster than the code on the right. The two snippets are not precisely equivalent because DEC changes the flags register and LOOP doesn't. But if the status of the flags register doesn't matter, LOOP is useless on 486s. The compiler makers apparently know this, since they never generate LOOP instructions when translating loops in C statements.

The JCXZ Instruction

In an assembler statement, the syntax of the JCXZ instruction looks like this:

```
JCXZ    <8-bit target>    ;optional comment
```

The meaning of JCXZ is imperative:

Jump to <target> if CX register equals 0.

JCXZ is another conditional jump instruction which doesn't use the status of the flags register to make the decision to jump. Once again, <target> can be any label and JCXZ has no effect on the flags register. Because this is the only option, JCXZ has only one possible form. Table 3.7 is a standardized description for this form.

Unlike LOOP, JCXZ does not affect the contents of CX. The instruction merely jumps to the instruction at <label> if the CX register equals 0. JCXZ is becoming obsolete — we mention it only to show you what it used to be used for and what instructions should now be used instead.

It's common to use the CX register for loop control, so one often sees JCXZ at the start of a loop. For example, there are two ways to OR an array of words with 1. The first way, shown below, can produce an incorrect result (the number of words is in a variable named memno):

```
        MOV CX,memno
labelx: OR [BX],1
        ADD BX,2
        LOOP labelx
```

Instruction Mnemonic	Target	Cycle Count
JCXZ	<nearby_label>	8 if jump, 5 if no jump

Table 3.7   Standardized description of JCXZ.

To see why this code is wrong, consider what would happen if memno = 0 (which should mean the loop will be executed zero times). On the very first iteration, the LOOP instruction will decrement the CX register from 0 to –1 or (expressed as an unsigned number) 65,535 — so the loop will end up being executed 65,536 times! To correct this, insert a JCXZ just before the loop starts, thus:

```
        MOV CX,memno      ;1 cycle
        JCXZ labely       ;5 or 8 cycles
labelx: OR [BX],1         ;3 cycles
        ADD BX,2          ;1 cycle
        LOOP labelx       ;2 or 6 cycles
labely: ...
```

Although this example uses LOOP, which is unoptimal code, we think unoptimal code fits fine in a discussion of JCXZ because JCXZ is unoptimal too due to another SECRET RULE.

◆ **SECRET "JCXZ-COSTS-MORE" RULE:**
JCXZ costs 5 cycles more if true, and 4 cycles more if false, than the other conditional jump instructions.

The JCXZ-Costs-More Rule means that

```
OR CX,CX
JNZ label
```

is faster than

```
JCXZ label
```

We call the JCXZ-Costs-More Rule a "secret" because according to the information provided by Borland in their *Turbo Assembler Quick Reference Guide*, JCXZ is like any conditional jump instruction — it should take 3 cycles if true (that is, the jump should be performed) and 1 cycle if false. The actual cost though, as shown in Table 3.7, is 8 cycles if the condition is true and 5 cycles if CX is not 0. Intel's documentation is correct on this point.

The fastest way to do the OR an array loop is to replace both the JCXZ and the LOOP instructions (and, while we're optimizing, to use a register rather than a constant to OR with), thus:

```
          MOV CX,memno      ;1 cycle
          OR CX,CX          ;1 cycle
          JZ labely         ;1 or 3 cycles
          MOV AX,1          ;1 cycle
labelx:   OR [BX],AX        ;3 cycles
          ADD BX,2          ;1 cycle
          DEC CX            ;1 cycle
          JNZ labelx        ;1 or 3 cycles
labely:
```

This loop provides a gain of 2 cycles, or 20 percent over the original loop.

The JCXZ instruction is useful if the status of the flags in the flags register must be preserved, otherwise it should be replaced. We have not found a case where a C compiler generates a JCXZ instruction.

Loop Control Using a Hidden Resource

MOV is a symmetric instruction: MOV <memory>,<register> takes the same number of cycles as MOV <register>,<memory> (provided that <memory> is in cache, is properly aligned, and avoids all the other hazards we discussed in Chapter 1).

With the arithmetic instructions, however, this symmetry disappears. Not only is ADD <register>,<memory> 1.5 times faster than ADD <memory>,<register> (2 cycles vs. 3 cycles), but ADD <register>,<constant> is 3 times faster than ADD <memory>,<constant> (1 cycle vs. 3 cycles) — and in fact it's often four times faster because the memory addressing mode is commonly of the Register Pointer plus Constant or Register Pointer Doubled types (1-cycle penalty).

Under the circumstances, "put the most frequently used variables in registers" is sound advice. The problem with this is that often there are more variables than there are registers. However, in a sense, there are really twice as many registers as you might think because all registers are 32 bits long.

A 16-bit application almost never uses the top half of a 32-bit register. In fact, you can be sure that your 16-bit C compiler never uses the top half. This gives you a "hidden resource" that can be used without the slightest possibility that the C compiler might want to use the top half for its own purposes. Though it costs 1 cycle to use a 32-bit register in 16-bit mode, the benefit outweighs the cost if the other choice is to use memory.

Here's an example which uses a 16-bit memory variable for loop control (assume that registers AX, BX, CX, DX, SI, DI, and BP are used up during the body of the loop marked with ...).

```
        MOV mem,500h     ;2 cycles
loop:...
        DEC mem          ;3 cycles
        JGE loop         ;3 cycles (assuming jump is done)
```

The same loop using the high part of the EAX register looks like this:

```
        AND EAX,0FFFFh         ;!2 cycles (Prefix Rule)
        OR EAX,(-500h)*1000h   ;2 cycles
loop: ...
        ADD EAX,1*10000h       ;2 cycles
        JS loop                ;3 cycles (assuming jump is done)
```

Not only does this method give you more registers to use, the control part of the loop saves 1 cycle.

While we're on the subject of arithmetic, the standard way to add a 16-bit constant to a 32-bit number takes 8 cycles. This method depends on the fact that ADD sets the carry flag ON if (mem + <constant> > 0FFFFh). The carry flag then gets added in on the second instruction, with ADC, e.g.:

```
ADD WORD PTR mem,<constant>     ;4 cycles
ADC WORD PTR mem+2,0            ;4 cycles
```

The following alternative code will do the same job in either 7 cycles (if the jump occurs) or 8 cycles (if no jump occurs):

```
        ADD WORD PTR mem,<constant>     ;4 cycles
        JNC labelx                      ;1 or 3 cycles
        INC WORD PTR mem+2              ;3 cycles
labelx: ...
```

The gain provided by this alternative code comes from the fact that mem is a Register Pointer plus Constant memory addressing mode. If a Register Pointer memory addressing mode is used, the gain disappears since ADD <register>,<constant>, ADC <register>,<constant> and INC <register> are all 3-cycle instructions.

This alternative code will also add a 16-bit number to a 32-bit number. The method takes either 5 or 11 cycles:

```
ADD DWORD PTR mem,<constant> ;5 cycles or !11 cycles
```

This method is the fastest of the three — but only if you can make sure that mem is double-word aligned. The 6-cycle penalty applies if mem is not aligned. It's important, then, to check all the alternatives before you use the carry flag in ADC or SBB.

Double-Byte Comparisons

The code on the left is 10 percent faster (on average) than the code on the right (despite the Hi/Lo Rule penalty):

```
MOV AL,mema   ;1 cycle        CMP mema,1  ;2 cycles
MOV AH,memb   ;1 cycle        JZ labela1  ;3 cycles or 1 cycle
CMP AX,0101h  ;!2 cycles      CMP memb,1  ;2 cycles
JZ labela1    ;3 cycles or 1 cycle   JZ labela1  ;3 cycles or 1 cycle
```

MOV is faster than CMP and there's always a way to make use of that.

Loop Unrolling

There are three general ways to go about adding 1 to every third byte in an array 12 times: looping, duplicating, or hybrid (both looping and duplicating). These methods are:

```
        ;Pure Looping:
        MOV BX,3        ;1 cycle
        MOV CX,12       ;1 cycle
labela: INC mema[BX]    ;3 cycles
        ADD BX,3        ;1 cycle
        DEC CX          ;1 cycle
        JNZ labela      ;3 or 1 cycles  ;Total cycles: 97 Savings: -0-

        ;Hybrid — Duplicated Once:
        MOV BX,3        ;1 cycle
        MOV CX,12       ;1 cycle
labela: INC mema[BX]    ;3 cycles
        INC mema[BX+3]  ;3 cycles
        ADD BX,6        ;1 cycle
        SUB CX,2        ;1 cycle
        JNZ labela      ;3 or 1 cycles  ;Total cycles: 62 Savings: 36%
```

```
                ;Hybrid — Duplicated Three Times:
                MOV   BX,3           ;1 cycle
                MOV   CX,12          ;1 cycle
        labela: INC mema[BX]         ;3 cycles
                INC mema[BX+3]       ;3 cycles
                INC mema[BX+6]       ;3 cycles
                INC mema[BX+9]       ;3 cycles
                ADD BX,12            ;1 cycle
                SUB CX,4             ;1 cycle
                JNZ labela           ;3 or 1 cycles  ;Total cycles: 53 Savings: 45%

                ;Pure Duplicating:
        INC mema[3]                  ;3 cycles
        INC mema[6]                  ;3 cycles
        INC mema[9]                  ;3 cycles
        INC mema[12]                 ;3 cycles
        INC mema[15]                 ;3 cycles
        INC mema[18]                 ;3 cycles
        INC mema[21]                 ;3 cycles
        INC mema[24]                 ;3 cycles
        INC mema[27]                 ;3 cycles
        INC mema[30]                 ;3 cycles
        INC mema[33]                 ;3 cycles
        INC mema[36]                 ;3 cycles      ;Total cycles: 36 Savings 63%
```

In these illustrations, each duplication of the payload (the `INC mema[BX]` instruction) is called a *loop unroll*. The Hybrid — Duplicated Once example has thus been unrolled once, the Hybrid — Duplicated Three Times example has been unrolled three times, and the final example, Pure Duplicating, has been unrolled 11 times, or *fully unrolled.*

Loop unrolling is crude, obvious, and one of the easiest ways to shave off a few cycles in any program. Every time you use a loop unroll, you save the cost of the loop-control instructions (in this case, the increment of the pointer, the decrement of the counter, and the conditional jump). The savings can look impressive when the loop is unrolled once — 36 percent in this example. But note that we did not gain an additional 36 percent even when the loop was completely unrolled — there's a law of diminishing returns that sets in fast.

The absolute limit of loop unrolling's usefulness is when it costs more to fetch the additional instructions than is being saved by eliminating the loop control. This absolute limit is a number somewhere between 20 and 60 loop unrolls, depending on the relative cost of the payload and loop-control instructions and the size of the cache. As a practical limit, we suggest a maximum of 20 loop unrolls.

Review Exercise

The following code snippet is supposed to count the number of words which are greater than 256 in an array mema, which is 16 words long. We're going to phrase this exercise in the form of a puzzle — how many improvements can you make?

Rules: Do not use any registers except CX and BX. Loop unrolling is not allowed. When the routine ends, CL must contain the correct count. Assume the program will be compiled for small model C with all switches in an off state.

Score: Two points for every saved cycle, 1 point for every saved byte. The top score is 17 points but anything over 10 is excellent. The answers follow the program.

```
struct {
 char memx;
 unsigned int mema[300];
    }
void main ()
{
        __asm MOV CH,16;            /* Hint: how many moves are */
                                    /* needed? */
        __asm MOV CL,0;             /* Hint: registers or constants? */
        __asm MOV BX,OFFSET mema;   /* Hint: how can a pipeline stall? */
one:    __asm CMP WORD PTR [BX],255; /* Hint: what's mema[0]'s address? */
        __asm JBE two;              /* Hint: what's the carry flag */
                                    /* for? */
        __asm ADD CL,1;             /* Hint: what is INC good for? */
two:    __asm ADD BX,2;
        __asm SUB CH,1;             /* Hint: what is DEC good for? */
        __asm CMP CH,0;             /* Hint: what else sets the zero */
                                    /* flag? */
        __asm JNZ one;
}
```

Answers:

(1) Score 1 point if you noticed that the first two MOV instructions can be done with MOV CX,1000h to save 1 byte. Do not award yourself another point for saving a cycle unless you missed point (3).

(2) Subtract 2 points if you thought of XOR CL,CL to clear the CL register. This instruction is not smaller than MOV CL,0 and it's slower because it triggers the Hi/Lo Rule.

(3) There is a 2-cycle penalty for changing BX's value and then using BX as an addressing register in the very next instruction. Score 2 points

if you thought of moving the MOV BX,OFFSET mema instruction up to the start of the program (you'll still have a 1-cycle penalty if the next instruction is MOV CX,1000h).

(4) Score zero points if you thought of using a register variable. It wouldn't do any good, because [BX] is a Register Pointer memory access mode. Score 4 points if you thought of CMP BYTE PTR [BX+1],0 which avoids memory alignment trouble — the way the struct is set up, misalignment might happen at a 3-cycle cost.

(5) Score 1 point if you replaced ADD CL,1 with INC CL. Score 6 points if you replaced lines 5 and 6 with ADC CL,0 — you'd save 2 bytes and either 1 or 3 cycles by removing the conditional jump (estimated average: 2).

(6) Score zero points if you replaced ADD BX,2 with ADD BL,2 or two INC BX instructions. ADD BX,2 is the one instruction that can't be improved.

(7) Score 1 point if you replaced SUB CH,1 with DEC CH — that saves 1 byte.

(8) Score four points if you removed the CMP CH,0 instruction — CMP CH,0 is logically unnecessary because the zero flag was set by the previous instruction. This saves 2 bytes and 1 cycle.

Where You Are

In this chapter, you learned:

❖ how to write goto routines in assembler with the conditional jump instructions JZ, JNZ, JP, JNP, JC, JNC, JS, JNS, JO, JNO, JG, JGE, JL, JLE, JA, JBE, LOOP, and JCXZ and the unconditional jump instruction JMP;

❖ how to use the CMP instruction to simulate a SUB without actually changing the register or memory variable;

❖ how to test code alignment and use NOP to avoid the penalties applied to misaligned addresses;

❖ how to manage loop control with the high half of a 32-bit register — a hidden resource.

And finally, you learned another four SECRET RULES of assembler that will help you speed up your code:

◆ **SECRET "DOUBLE-JUMP" RULE:**
If a conditional jump instruction whose condition is false (i.e., the jump is not done) is immediately followed by a second jump instruction, you lose 1 cycle on the second jump instruction unless the next instruction that is executed after that begins on a 0-mod-8 address.

◆ **SECRET "LONG-JUMP" RULE:**
If you use the long form of conditional jump, you lose 1 cycle whether or not the jump happens, unless the previous instruction (which can't be JMP or CALL) takes more than 1 cycle. That is, the long form takes 4 cycles if the condition is true and 2 cycles if the condition is false, subject to the Prefix-Waiver Rule.

◆ **SECRET "CACHE-STRADDLING" RULE:**
If you jump to an instruction which straddles a 16-byte boundary (that is, an instruction which begins in one cache line and ends in the next cache line), you lose 2 cycles. Further, if you jump to a one-cycle instruction which doesn't straddle, but is followed by an instruction which either straddles or begins in a new 16-byte boundary (i.e., the two instructions together straddle) you lose 1 cycle.

◆ **SECRET "JCXZ-COSTS-MORE" RULE:**
JCXZ costs 5 cycles more if true, and 4 cycles more if false, than the other conditional jump instructions.

Chapter 4

Bit Shifts

This chapter is about the assembler shift instructions — the instructions that shift and rotate bits left and right. We'll look at the SHR, SAR, SHL, SHLD, SHRD, ROL, and XCHG instructions.

The SHR, SAR, and SHL Instructions

In an assembler statement, the syntax of the SHR, SAR, and SHL instructions looks like this:

```
SHR <destination operand>,<bit-count operand>     ;optional comment
SAR <destination operand>,<bit-count operand>     ;optional comment
SHL <destination operand>,<bit-count operand>     ;optional comment
```

The <bit-count operand> can be the CL register or an 8-bit constant. This is the number of bits that are to be shifted in the <destination operand>. The <destination operand> can be either an 8-bit, 16-bit, or 32-bit memory operand or register.

The meaning of these instructions is imperative:

SHR: SHift <destination operand> to the Right by <bit-count operand> bits.

SAR: Shift <destination operand> to the Arithmetic Right by <bit-count operand> bits.

SHL: SHift <destination operand> to the Left by <bit-count operand> bits.

SHR and SAR shift the bits in <destination operand> to the right, moving the low-order bit into the carry flag. (This effectively divides the <destination operand> by 2.) The difference between SHR and SAR is their effect on the topmost (sign) bit of the <destination operand>. SHR sets the sign bit to 0 and is therefore used to shift right an unsigned value. SAR leaves the sign bit in the same state it was in before the shift and is therefore used to shift right a signed value.

SHL shifts the bits in <destination operand> to the left, moving the high-order bit into the carry flag and clearing the low-order bit.

SHR, SAR, and SHL have 18 possible forms, depending on the operands used. Table 4.1 is a standardized description for each possible form (note that the constant 1 is considered to be different from other constants).

We've already described SHR, SAR and SHL's effect on the carry flag. These three instructions also set the zero, parity, and sign flags according to the result of the operation. If <bit-count operand> is 0, though, SHR, SAR, and SHL do not affect any of the flags in the flags register.

Instruction Mnemonic	Destination Operand	Bit-Count Operand	Cycle Count
<SHR|SAR|SHL>	<8-bit register>	,CL	3
<SHR|SAR|SHL>	<byte-size memory>	,CL	4
<SHR|SAR|SHL>	<8-bit register>	,1	3
<SHR|SAR|SHL>	<byte-size memory>	,1	4
<SHR|SAR|SHL>	<8-bit register>	,<8-bit constant>	2
<SHR|SAR|SHL>	<byte-size memory>	,<8-bit constant>	4
<SHR|SAR|SHL>	<16-bit register>	,CL	3
<SHR|SAR|SHL>	<word-size memory>	,CL	4
<SHR|SAR|SHL>	<16-bit register>	,1	3
<SHR|SAR|SHL>	<word-size memory>	,1	4
<SHR|SAR|SHL>	<16-bit register>	,<8-bit constant>	2
<SHR|SAR|SHL>	<word-size memory>	,<8-bit constant>	4
<SHR|SAR|SHL>	<32-bit register>	,CL	3
<SHR|SAR|SHL>	<long-size memory>	,CL	4
<SHR|SAR|SHL>	<32-bit register>	,1	3
<SHR|SAR|SHL>	<long-size memory>	,1	4
<SHR|SAR|SHL>	<32-bit register>	,<8-bit constant>	2
<SHR|SAR|SHL>	<long-size memory>	,<8-bit constant>	4

Table 4.1   Standardized description of SHR, SAR, and SHL.

The overflow flag is affected only if <bit-count operand> is the constant 1. In this case, SHL clears the overflow flag if the high-bit of the shifted result is the same as the result on the carry flag (that is, if the top 2 bits of <destination operand> were originally the same), SAR clears the overflow flag for all single shifts, and SHR sets the overflow flag to the high-order bit of <destination operand>.

As with most assembler instructions, the shift instructions also have C equivalents. A C compiler will usually translate C's >> operator into an assembler shift-right instruction and will translate C's << operator into an assembler shift-left instruction. For example:

```
int mema;
unsigned int memb;
void main ()
{
  mema=mema<<2;      /* becomes SHL mema,2 */
  mema=mema>>2;      /* becomes SAR mema,2 */
  memb=memb<<2;      /* becomes SHL memb,2 */
  memb=memb>>2;      /* becomes SHR memb,2 */
}
```

SHR and SAR have uses as divide-by-2 instructions and SHL has uses as a multiply-by-2 instruction. This book's chapters on multiplying and dividing have some examples of multiple shift instructions for that purpose. In this chapter, though, we'll concentrate on the shifting itself. Because the alternative forms of shift instructions overlap in function, there is a good chance that the assembler, the C compiler, or you yourself will pick an inefficient form without noticing.

Step One — Make Sure the Switch is On

The 8086 does not support the <shift> <register>,<constant> and <shift> <memory>, <constant> forms of the shift instructions. As a result, C compilers always execute instructions like

```
SHL <operand>,5     ;2 cycles if <register>, 4 cycles if <memory>
```

via the CL register, as follows:

```
MOV CL,5            ;1 cycle
SHL <operand>,CL    ;3 cycles if <register>, 4 cycles if <memory>
```

Assemblers are even worse. Borland TASM, for instance, defaults to the <shift> <register>,1 and <shift> <memory>,1 forms — using as many instructions as are needed to make the necessary shift:

```
SHL <operand>,1    ;3 cycles if <register>, 4 cycles if <memory>
SHL <operand>,1    ;3 cycles if <register>, 4 cycles if <memory>
SHL <operand>,1    ;3 cycles if <register>, 4 cycles if <memory>
SHL <operand>,1    ;3 cycles if <register>, 4 cycles if <memory>
SHL <operand>,1    ;3 cycles if <register>, 4 cycles if <memory>
```

By default, then, compilers and assemblers will use a long-winded alternative because the short way was not legal in the days of the 8086. To correct this tendency, tell your compiler that the processor is post-8086 with the /2 switch for Borland C, the /G2 switch for Microsoft C, and the −2 switch for Symantec C, or use the .486 directive in assembler.

Speeding Up <register> Shifts

SHL <register>,1 requires 3 cycles. ADD <register>,<register> takes 1 cycle. The code on the left is thus faster than the code on the right:

```
ADD DX,DX    ;2 bytes, 1 cycle          SHL DX,1    ;2 bytes, 3 cycles
```

In a binary system, shifting 1 bit left is the same as multiplying by 2. Doubling a number by adding it to itself is also the same as multiplying by 2. ADD <register>,<same register> is thus always equivalent to SHL <register>,1 — the two instructions even have the same effect on the zero and carry flags — and has the added advantage of being 2 cycles faster. The following program:

```
int mema,memb;
void main ()
{
 mema=memb<<1;
}
```

would be faster if the C statement mema=memb<<1; was replaced with inline assembler instructions as follows:

```
int mema,memb;
void main ()
{
 __asm MOV AX,memb;
 __asm ADD AX,AX;
 __asm MOV mema,AX;
}
```

There is, however, a potential trap if this trick is tried with 8-bit operands:

```
MOV AL,[BX]    ;1 cycle
ADD AL,AL      ;1 cycle
MOV [BX],AL    ;!3 cycles
```

This example falls afoul of the Bytes-and-Pointers Rule.

Shifting the other way, SHR <register>,1 also requires 3 cycles. But the SHR <register>,<constant> instruction requires only 2 cycles — and <constant> can be any value, *including* 1.

This is not a case where the same instruction has two different cycle times. SHR <operand>,1 and SHR <operand>,<constant> are actually two different instructions at the machine opcode level. The problem is that the instructions are not distinguishable at the assembler level, and so all assemblers generate the machine opcode of the first instruction for them both. By doing so, they save 1 byte — and waste 1 cycle. The same situation applies with SAR (and with SHL, but replacing SHL with ADD negates this possibility anyway).

To correct for this behavior, you can enter machine code directly. This is not an elegant solution, but it does the job. We'll show you how with DB, which stands for Deposit Byte.

DB is not a true instruction but means "deposit a byte exactly as shown." DB is followed by a hexadecimal literal. Hexadecimal literals in assembler always consist of leading 0s (necessary if the first digit of the literal is not 0 through 9), the value itself, and a trailing letter h. These are the codes you need (all three instructions in each column are needed to replace the related assembler instruction):

```
SHR AX,1  SHR BX,1  SHR CX,1  SHR DX,1  SHR SI,1  SHR DI,1  SHR BP,1
DB 0C1h   DB 0C1h   DB 0C1h   DB 0C1h   DB 0C1h   DB 0C1h   DB 0C1h
DB 0E8h   DB 0EBh   DB 0E9h   DB 0EAh   DB 0EEh   DB 0EFh   DB 0EDh
DB 001h   DB 001h   DB 001h   DB 001h   DB 001h   DB 001h   DB 001h


SHR AL,1  SHR AH,1  SHR BL,1  SHR BH,1  SHR CL,1  SHR CH,1  SHR DL,1  SHR DH,1
DB 0C0h   DB 0C0h   DB 0C0h   DB 0C0h   DB 0C0h   DB 0C0h   DB 0C0h   DB 0C0h
DB 0E8h   DB 0ECh   DB 0EBh   DB 0EFh   DB 0E9h   DB 0EDh   DB 0EAh   DB 0EEh
DB 001h   DB 001h   DB 001h   DB 001h   DB 001h   DB 001h   DB 001h   DB 001h


SAR AX,1  SAR BX,1  SAR CX,1  SAR DX,1  SAR SI,1  SAR DI,1  SAR BP,1
DB 0C1h   DB 0C1h   DB 0C1h   DB 0C1h   DB 0C1h   DB 0C1h   DB 0C1h
DB 0F8h   DB 0FBh   DB 0F9h   DB 0FAh   DB 0FEh   DB 0FFh   DB 0FDh
DB 001h   DB 001h   DB 001h   DB 001h   DB 001h   DB 001h   DB 001h
```

SAR AL,1	SAR AH,1	SAR BL,1	SAR BH,1	SAR CL,1	SAR CH,1	SAR DL,1	SAR DH,1
DB 0C0h	DB 0C0h	DB 0C0h	DB 0C0h	DB 0C0h	DB 0C0h	DB 0C0h	DB 0C0h
DB 0F8h	DB 0FCh	DB 0FBh	DB 0FFh	DB 0F9h	DB 0FDh	DB 0FAh	DB 0FEh
DB 001h	DB 001h	DB 001h	DB 001h	DB 001h	DB 001h	DB 001h	DB 001h

For example, consider this C program:

```
unsigned int mema,memb;
void main ()
{
 memb=mema/2;
}
```

All compilers will translate the C statement memb=mema/2; into:

```
MOV AX,mema     ;1 cycle
SHR AX,1        ;3 cycles
MOV memb,AX     ;1 cycle
```

You can save 1 cycle by forcing the SHR AX,<constant=1> variant of SHR, like this:

```
unsigned int mema,memb;
void main ()
{
 __asm MOV AX,mema;     /* 1 cycle */
 __asm DB 0C1h;
 __asm DB 0E8h;
 __asm DB 001h;         /* 2 cycles in all */
 __asm MOV memb,AX;     /* 1 cycle */
}
```

Incidentally, there is an easier way to do this if you use a true assembler (such as Borland TASM or Microsoft MASM), as opposed to the inline assembler that comes with your C compiler. The method involves using a macro to create your own instruction. Macros are beyond the scope of this book, so we'll just provide you with a small routine which you can add to the start of your assembler program:

```
SHR486 macro operand,shiftcount
       SHR operand,2
       ORG $ - 1
       DB shiftcount
       ENDM
SAR486 macro operand,shiftcount
       SAR operand,2
       ORG $ - 1
       DB shiftcount
       ENDM
```

We won't explain the ORG command in this book. All you have to know to use this code is that it provides you with two macros for faster 1-bit register shifts. So whenever you have to shift a register one bit to the right, e.g.:

```
SHR AX,1        or        SAR AX,1
```

use this instruction instead:

```
SHR486 AX,1    or        SAR486 AX,1
```

and you save 1 cycle. Warning: don't use these macros for anything but registers! Speeding up 1-bit memory shifts is another matter.

Speeding Up <memory> Shifts

Compared with the MOV or ADD instructions, the shift instructions are not very fast, and <SHR|SAR|SHL> <memory>,<constant> is the slowest of the lot — at least 4 cycles (more on this later). Our tip for speeding up <memory> shifts is simple, then. Don't do them.

Avoiding SHL <memory>,1 is easy. In the last section you learned the trick for shifting a register 1 bit to the left — add the register to itself. To shift a memory operand 1 bit to the left, all you have to do is move the memory to a register, use the Add-to-Self trick, and move back again. For example, the code on the left is faster than the code on the right and does the same thing:

```
MOV AX,[BX]     ;1 cycle        SHL [BX],1    ;4 cycles
ADD AX,AX       ;1 cycle
MOV [BX],AX     ;1 cycle
```

Although the code on the left is longer, there is a speed gain of 25 percent.

The gain could be even bigger. At the beginning of this section, we noted that SHL <memory>,<constant> takes *at least* 4 cycles. This is the time shown in Table 4.1 and, in the example above (where the constant is 1), it's true. But SHL <memory>,<constant> often takes 5 cycles to execute due to the Constant-to-Memory Rule. Remember that when you MOV a constant to a memory location, i.e.:

```
MOV <memory>,<constant>
```

you get penalized 1 cycle if the addressing mode is anything other than [BX], [SI], or [DI]. This rule also applies when you use the

<shift> <memory>,<constant> form of the shift instructions, so these instructions take not 4, but 5 cycles:

```
SHR BYTE PTR [BX+4],4    ;!penalty
SHL WORD PTR mem,2       ;!penalty
```

The Constant-to-Memory Rule does not apply if the <constant> is 1, that is, <SHR|SAR|SHL> <memory>,1 is never penalized. Since the Constant-to-Memory Rule's penalty doesn't apply to Register Pointer addresses either, these are four-cycle instructions as expected:

```
SHR BYTE PTR [BX],4
SHL WORD PTR [SI],2
```

To avoid <SHR|SAR|SHL> <memory>,<constant other than 1>, use the same MOV to/from memory/register trick but replace the ADD you used when the constant is 1 with a SHL <register>,<constant> instruction:

```
MOV AX,[BX+2]    ;1 cycle        SHL [BX+2],3    ;5 cycles
SHL AX,3         ;2 cycles
MOV [BX+2],AX    ;1 cycle
```

C compilers may or may not do this for you. For example, consider this C program:

```
int mema;
void main ()
{
  mema=mema>>5;
}
```

With the 286 switches on but all optimizing switches off, the C statement mema=mema>>5; is usually translated as:

```
MOV AX,mema    ;1 cycle
SAR AX,5       ;2 cycles
MOV mema,AX    ;1 cycle
```

that is, our optimization tip is followed. With the optimizing switches on, however, this unoptimal translation is usually generated:

```
SAR mema,5    ;5 cycles
```

Borland doesn't fall into this trap, but Microsoft and Symantec both produce SAR mema,5 if any optimizing switch at all is used — even if we explicitly say we want to optimize for speed rather than size. We've observed that this is often the case — given a choice, Microsoft and Symantec will try to save code space even if the Constant-to-Memory Rule is violated in the process.

Optimization Mirage: Speeding Up 8-bit Shifts

On an 80286, the code on the left is faster than the code on the right:

```
MOV AH,AL     ;2 cycles     SHL AX,8     ;5 cycles
XOR AL,AL     ;2 cycles
```

On a 486 though, the 286 optimized code on the left takes 3 cycles and the straightforward SHL instruction on the right takes only 2 cycles. This is normally not a problem because modern compilers correctly generate SHL <operand>,8 if given a chance. But a related "optimization" comes up in this case:

```
unsigned int mema,memb;
void main ()
{
 memb=mema>>8;
}
```

Compilers will translate the C statement memb=mema>>8; in one of two ways:

```
Borland and Symantec                Microsoft
MOV AX,WORD PTR mema ;1 cycle       MOV AL,BYTE PTR mema+1 ;1 cycle
SHR AX,8             ;2 cycles      SUB AH,AH              ;!2 cycles
MOV WORD PTR memb,AX ;1 cycle       MOV WORD PTR memb,AX   ;!2 cycles
```

Borland and Symantec just produce the most obvious code. Microsoft, on the other hand, comes up with a tour de force — realizing that an 8-bit shift is effectively equal to moving the low half of a register to the high half and then zeroing the low half. Unfortunately, this triggers the Hi/Lo Rule, so the result of Microsoft's imaginative leap is that a penalty is applied to both the second and third instructions.

Still, Microsoft is on the right track. If the translation would use words instead of bytes, memb=mema>>8; could take only 3 cycles:

```
MOV AX,WORD PTR mema+1     ;1 cycle
AND AX,255                 ;1 cycle
MOV memb,AX                ;1 cycle
```

While we're on the subject, you should note that SHR, SAR, and SHL are also considered to be arithmetic instructions for the purposes of the Hi/Lo Rule as long as the <bit-count operand> is not 1 or the CL register. Thus, while

```
MOV DH,5      ;1 cycle
SHL DX,5      ;!3 cycles
```

triggers a penalty, the following combination does not

```
MOV CH,5      ;1 cycle
SHR AX,CL     ;3 cycles — no penalty
```

and neither does:

```
MOV CH,5      ;1 cycle
SAR CX,1      ;3 cycles — no penalty
```

Uses For <SHR|SAR|SHL> <operand>,CL

Table 4.1 shows that <SHR|SAR|SHL> <memory>,CL always takes precisely the same amount of time as <SHR|SAR|SHL> <memory>,<constant>. Therefore, it is always faster to use <SHR|SAR|SHL> <memory>,<constant> to shift by a constant value (unless you can avoid the Hi/Lo Rule by doing so) because then an extra cycle isn't used up in moving a bit value to shift into CL. For example, the code on the left is faster than the code on the right:

```
SHL [BX],5     ;4 cycles       MOV CL,5       ;1 cycle
                               SHL [BX],CL    ;4 cycles
```

The same is true if the <destination operand> is a register, since <SHR|SAR|SHL> <register>,CL takes 1 cycle more than <SHR|SAR|SHL> <register>,<constant>. For example, the code on the left is faster than the code on the right:

```
SHL  AX,5      ;2 cycles       MOV CL,5       ;1 cycle
                               SHL AX,CL      ;3 cycles
```

Despite this, there are two cases where <SHR|SAR|SHL> <memory>,CL has a use. The first is when you don't know the amount to shift in advance. Consider this example:

```
int mema,memb;
void main ()
{
 mema=mema<<memb;
}
```

The test C compilers translate mema=mema<<memb; into:

```
MOV AX,mema      ;1 cycle
MOV CL,memb      ;1 cycle
SHL AX,CL        ;3 cycles
MOV mema,AX      ;1 cycle
```

which is not ideal. It is faster to translate into:

```
MOV CL,memb      ;1 cycle
SHL mema,CL      ;4 cycles
```

The second case where <SHR|SAR|SHL> <memory>,CL has a use is in the following program, which shifts two integers in the same direction:

```
int mema,memb;
void main ()
{
 mema=mema>>5;
 memb=memb>>5;
}
```

The body of this program is often translated as:

```
SAR mema,5       ;5 cycles
SAR memb,5       ;5 cycles
```

Given the discussion earlier, this translation is better:

```
MOV AX,mema      ;1 cycle
SAR AX,5         ;2 cycles
MOV mema,AX      ;1 cycle
MOV AX,memb      ;1 cycle
SAR AX,5         ;2 cycles
MOV mema,AX      ;1 cycle
```

In this case, though, the following translation takes even fewer cycles:

```
MOV  CX,5        ;1 cycle
SAR  mema,CL     ;4 cycles
SAR  memb,CL     ;4 cycles
```

Once again, the principle is: whenever you see the same constant value used twice (which in this case is true of the constant 5), look for an opportunity to put the constant in a register.

Shifts and Bit Fields

C compilers will use SHL and SHR when assigning to and from bit fields. As an example, consider the following C code, which contains a bit field structure:

```
struct person
 {
 char name[12];
 unsigned married:1,sex:2,elderly:1;
 }
folk[1000];
unsigned int mema;
void main ()
{
 folk[0].sex=0;
 folk[0].sex=3;
 folk[0].sex=mema;
 mema=folk[0].sex;
}
```

Let's examine how various C compilers handle this code — especially how they make use of SHR and SHL. When translating the C statement folk[0].sex=0; the three test compilers all generate:

```
AND BYTE PTR folk+12,0F9h     ;!4 cycles (Constant-to-Memory Rule)
```

This is clever. The compilers have rearranged the structure so as to put bits on byte boundaries where possible. Because of this `folk[0].sex` doesn't happen to really be the first byte of the `folk` array, nor does it need to be. For moving the value 0 to the 2 bits at the location masked by 6, each compiler hits on the best idea — AND the byte with ~(6), that is, with 0F9h. However, note the penalty applied by the Constant-to-Memory Rule. Once again, this type of translation can be improved using a register instead of the memory operand:

```
MOV AL,BYTE PTR folk+12      ;1 cycle
AND AL,0F9h                  ;1 cycle
MOV BYTE PTR folk+12,AL      ;1 cycle
```

When translating `folk[0].sex=3;` the compilers generate:

<u>Borland</u>
```
AND BYTE PTR folk+12,249 ;!4 cycles
OR BYTE PTR folk+12,6    ;!4 cycles
```

<u>Microsoft and Symantec</u>
```
OR BYTE PTR folk+12,6 ;!4 cycles
```

In this translation, Borland's AND is redundant. Microsoft and Symantec correctly realize that the constant constitutes all the possible bits in the bit field. As usual, the Constant-to-Memory Rule penalty could be avoided.

The C statement `folk[0].sex=mema;` is translated as follows:

<u>Borland</u>
```
MOV AX,mema                  ;1 cycle
AND AX,3                     ;1 cycle
AND BYTE PTR folk+12,249     ;!4 cycles
SHL AL,1                     ;3 cycles
OR BYTE PTR folk+12,AL       ;3 cycles
```

<u>Microsoft</u>
```
MOV AL,mema                  ;1 cycle
SHL AL,1                     ;3 cycles
XOR AL,folk+12               ;2 cycles
AND AX,6                     ;!2 cycles
XOR folk+12,AX               ;3 cycles
```

<u>Symantec</u>
```
MOV AX,mema                  ;1 cycle
AND AX,3                     ;1 cycle
SHL AX,1                     ;3 cycles
MOV CX,folk+0Ch              ;1 cycle
AND CL,0F9h                  ;1 cycle
OR AX,CX                     ;!2 cycles
MOV folk+0Ch,AX              ;1 cycle
```

These translations could be improved. The compilers all generate `SHL <register>,1` which is an inferior instruction on 486s (remember to tell your compiler that the processor is post-8086 to correct this tendency). The usual ignorance of the Hi/Lo Rule is apparent in the Microsoft and Symantec code. In addition, all three compilers are doing arithmetic twice on a memory operand rather than loading a register for more speed. Based on these observations, we would improve the compilers' translations as follows (taking Borland for our example):

```
MOV AX,mema                ;1 cycle
AND AX,3                   ;1 cycle
MOV CL,BYTE PTR folk+12    ;1 cycle
AND CL,249                 ;1 cycle
ADD AL,AL                  ;1 cycle
OR AL,CL                   ;1 cycle
MOV BYTE PTR folk+12,AL    ;1 cycle
```

A typical `SHR` usage is generated by each compiler when translating the final line of our C program, `mema=folk[0].sex;`:

```
Borland
MOV AL,BYTE PTR folk+12    ;1 cycle
SHR AX,1                   ;3 cycles
AND AX,3                   ;1 cycle
MOV mema,AX                ;1 cycle

Microsoft
MOV AL,BYTE PTR folk+12    ;1 cycle
AND AX,6                   ;!2 cycles
SHR AL,1                   ;3 cycles
MOV mema,AX                ;!2 cycles

Symantec
MOV AX,folk+0Ch            ;1 cycle
SHR AX,1                   ;3 cycles
AND AX,3                   ;1 cycle
MOV mema,AX                ;1 cycle
```

Borland and Symantec generate 6 cycle translations. Microsoft's translation uses an extra 2 cycles merely because the `SHR` and `AND` instructions are transposed, triggering the Hi/Lo Rule twice. Symantec's translation also differs from both the others because it starts with `MOV AX` rather than `MOV AL`. We thought at first that they'd do the same thing even if the operand is misaligned and thus trigger a penalty, but that turned out not to be the case. Symantec is pretty sensible about the way `folk.sex[]` is allocated so in this simple case, misalignment is not too likely.

Compressing Using Shifts

There are 26 letters in the English alphabet. Since 26 is less than $2**5$, any single letter can be stored in a 5-bit "byte." Further, strings that contain only uppercase letters or the standard C terminator byte (\0) can be compressed so that every 16-bit word contains three 5-bit letters, instead of two 8-bit letters. This saves space, but — more importantly — allows you to move and compare three letters at a time. Such a C string can be compressed using the following code, which uses only nine of the assembler instructions introduced so far:

```
.486                            ;Allow 486 instructions
        MOV BX,OFFSET string     ;Use BX as the input pointer
        MOV CX,DI                ;Use CX to save the contents of DI
        MOV DI,BX                ;Use DI as the output pointer
looper: MOV AL,[BX]              ;Get the next byte from the input string
        SUB AL,040h              ;Subtract the ASCII code for 'A'
        JL end0
        SHL AX,11                ;Shift the letter 11 bits left
        MOV DX,AX                ;Now high 5 bits of DX have the first byte
        MOV AL,[BX+1]            ;Get the next byte from the input string
        SUB AL,040h              ;Subtract the ASCII code for 'A'
        JL ender                 ;(If the byte was less than 'A', it was '\0')
        AND AX,01Fh              ;Get rid of the last byte which is still in AH
        SHL AX,5                 ;Shift the second byte 5 bits to the left
        OR DX,AX                 ;Now bits 5-9 of DX have the second byte
        MOV AL,[BX+2]            ;Get the next byte from the input string
        SUB AL,040h              ;Subtract the ASCII code for 'A'
        JL ender                 ;(If the byte was less than 'A', it was '\0')
        OR DX,AX                 ;Now bits 10-14 of DX have the third byte
        MOV [DI],DX              ;Store 16-bit word containing all 3 bytes
        ADD BX,3                 ;Point to the next byte triplet in the input
        ADD DI,2                 ;Point to the next 16-bit word in the output
        JMP looper               ;Repeat
end0:   XOR DX,DX                ;Ended on a 3-byte boundary:
                                 ;dump a 0 word
ender:  MOV [DI],DX              ;We've reached the '\0' byte. Store last word.
        MOV DI,CX                ;Restore the original value of DI
.8086                           ;Don't allow 486 instructions any more
```

Some notes on this routine:

❖ This code assumes the input string contains only uppercase letters or \0. The subtraction and the check for the \0 byte could thus be combined in a single instruction.

❖ The initialization instruction MOV BX, OFFSET string is at the start so that at least one instruction falls between the pointer's setup and its use.

❖ AND AX, 01Fh is used to clear the bits that are left over from the previous instruction. We could have used XOR AH, AH or MOV AH, 0 but would have lost 1 cycle due to the Hi/Lo Rule if we had.

❖ The routine does 3 bytes at a time, which is a reasonable amount of loop unrolling and fits with the way the input is handled. Remember that MOV AL,[BX], MOV AL,[BX+1], and MOV AL,[BX+2] are all 1 cycle instructions. If BX was incremented for every byte, cycles would be wasted.

The ROL Instruction

In an assembler statement, the syntax of the ROL instruction looks like this:

```
ROL <destination operand>,<bit-count operand>    ;optional comment
```

The <bit-count operand> can be the CL register or an 8-bit constant. This is the number of bits that are to be rotated in the <destination operand>. The <destination operand> can be either an 8-bit, 16-bit, or 32-bit memory operand or register.

The meaning of ROL is imperative:

ROtate <destination operand> to the Left by <bit-count operand> bits.

ROL has no exact equivalent in C, although the Symantec library function _rotl does the same job (much, much slower). The ROL instruction is like a SHL (SHift Left), but the bits that get shifted out on the left get shifted in on the right.

ROL has 18 possible forms, depending on the operands used. Table 4.2 is a standardized description for each possible form of ROL (note that the constant 1 is considered to be different from other constants).

ROL's effect on the flags register is to put the value of the rotated bit into the carry flag and — only if the <bit-count operand> is the constant 1, to XOR the carry flag bit after the rotation with the high-order result bit and put the XOR result into the overflow flag. ROL has no effect on the parity, sign, and zero flags.

As long as the <bit-count operand> is not 1 or the C L register, R O L is also an arithmetic instruction as far as the Hi/Lo Rule is concerned. For example, there is a 1-cycle penalty for this combination

```
MOV AH,5      ;1 cycle
ROL AL,2      ;!3 cycles
```

but not for

```
MOV CH,5      ;1 cycle
ROL AX,CL     ;3 cycles — no penalty
```

or

```
MOV CH,5      ;1 cycle
ROL CX,1      ;3 cycles — no penalty
```

Instruction Mnemonic	Destination Operand	Bit-Count Operand	Cycle Count
ROL	<8-bit register>	,CL	3
ROL	<byte-size memory>	,CL	4
ROL	<8-bit register>	,1	3
ROL	<byte-size memory>	,1	4
ROL	<8-bit register>	,<8-bit constant>	2
ROL	<byte-size memory>	,<8-bit constant>	4
ROL	<16-bit register>	,CL	3
ROL	<word-size memory>	,CL	4
ROL	<16-bit register>	,1	3
ROL	<word-size memory>	,1	4
ROL	<16-bit register>	,<8-bit constant>	2
ROL	<word-size memory>	,<8-bit constant>	4
ROL	<32-bit register>	,CL	3
ROL	<long-size memory>	,CL	4
ROL	<32-bit register>	,1	3
ROL	<long-size memory>	,1	4
ROL	<32-bit register>	,<8-bit constant>	2
ROL	<long-size memory>	,<8-bit constant>	4

Table 4.2   Standardized description for each possible form of R O L.

The relatively expensive ROL <register>,1 format is easily avoided. The code on the left is faster than the code on the right:

```
ADD DL,DL    ;1 cycle       ROL DL,1    ;3 cycles
ADC DL,0     ;1 cycle
```

and is equivalent because ADD DL,DL shifts DL 1 bit left (and sets the carry flag ON if the top-most bit was a 1), and ADC DL,0 puts a 1 in the low-most bit if the carry flag is ON.

Another way to speed up 1 bit ROLs is to use the ROL <register>,<constant> form, which uses 2 cycles. This form can be forced by putting the appropriate machine opcodes in — the same method we showed earlier for SHR, SAR, and SHL. However, since the ADD + ADC method also uses 2 cycles and is an easier way to replace ROL, we won't publish the machine-code chart for 1-bit ROLs in this book.

We have found only one use for ROL: to swap two halves of a register. That is, the command ROL AX,8 takes the high part of AX (the AH register) and puts it in the low part of AX (the AL register). At the same time, it also puts the AL register's contents in the AH register. The same is true for the BX, CX, and DX registers (and also for SI, DI, and BP, even though their halves can't be directly accessed). One other instruction can also be used to swap the high and low halves of the AX, BX, CX, and DX registers — XCHG.

The XCHG Instruction

In an assembler statement, the syntax of the XCHG instruction looks like this:

```
XCHG <first operand>,<second operand>    ;optional comment
```

Both the <first operand> and the <second operand> can be either an 8-bit, 16-bit, or 32-bit register or memory operand, the size of which must match. As usual, the operands in a single instruction may not both be memory operands. XCHG has no effect on the flags register.

The meaning of XCHG is imperative:

eXCHanGe the contents of <first operand> with the contents of <second operand>.

XCHG has nine possible forms, depending on the operands used. Table 4.3 is a standardized description for each possible form. Note the cycle count for the second and third forms of the instruction. Intel's documentation claims that these are 5-cycle instructions. Our measurements show otherwise (on some machines XCHG takes 8 cycles; on most machines it takes 10 cycles).

XCHG stands for exchange and does just that for its two operands: it exchanges their contents. It isn't just a shift instruction, but we introduce it here because we are showing a faster way than XCHG to exchange the top and bottom halves of a register — for example, ROL BX, 8 (a 2-cycle instruction) is faster than XCHG BL, BH (a 3-cycle instruction). If the two register operands aren't halves of the same register, though, XCHG should be utilized.

XCHG is also an expensive way to handle switches involving one register and one memory operand. In such cases, it's far better to make the switch with MOV via a spare register:

```
MOV <spare register>,<first operand>
MOV <first operand>,<second operand>
MOV <second operand>,<spare register>
```

For example, instead of

```
XCHG DX,[BX]     ;10 cycles
```

use

```
MOV AX,DX        ;1 cycle
MOV DX,[BX]      ;1 cycle
MOV [BX],AX      ;1 cycle
```

Instruction Mnemonic	First Operand	Second Operand	Cycle Count
XCHG	`<8-bit register>`	`,<8-bit register>`	3
XCHG	`<8-bit register>`	`,<byte-size memory>`	10!!
XCHG	`<byte-size memory>`	`,<8-bit register>`	10!!
XCHG	`<16-bit register>`	`,<16-bit register>`	3
XCHG	`<16-bit register>`	`,<word-size memory>`	10!!
XCHG	`<word-size memory>`	`,<16-bit register>`	10!!
XCHG	`<32-bit register>`	`,<32-bit register>`	3
XCHG	`<32-bit register>`	`,<long-size memory>`	10!!
XCHG	`<long-size memory>`	`,<32-bit register>`	10!!

Table 4.3   Standardized description for each possible form of XCHG.

If a spare register isn't available, three XOR instructions can be used for the same effect. All forms of XCHG <register>,<operand> can be done with this code:

```
XOR <register>,<operand>
XOR <operand>,<register>
XOR <register>,<operand>
```

which is also always faster than XCHG. For example, instead of

```
XCHG BP,[SI+10]    ;10 cycles
```

use

```
XOR BP,[SI+10]    ;2 cycles
XOR [SI+10],BP    ;3 cycles
XOR BP,[SI+10]    ;2 cycles
```

Since XCHG changes registers, the instruction can trigger the Hi/Lo Rule. In this case though (using the words of our description of the Hi/Lo Rule in Chapter 2), the (destination of instruction #1) is always the <second operand> — which, of course, is a destination in the sense that it gets written to as well. For example, the code on the left is faster than the code on the right because it doesn't trigger the Hi/Lo Rule:

```
XCHG AH,DH    ;3 cycles        XCHG AH,DH    ;3 cycles
MOV CX,AX     ;1 cycle         MOV CX,DX     ;!2 cycles
```

In this case, the combination of XCHG <first operand = AH> and MOV <source operand = AX> doesn't trigger the Hi/Lo Rule despite the fact the two halves of the same register are involved. On the other hand, the combination of XCHG <second operand = DH> and MOV <source operand = DX> *does* trigger the penalty — DH and DX are related registers. The penalty would normally disappear if the first instruction on the right was XCHG DH,AH. (We say "would normally disappear" instead of "will disappear" because some compilers translate XCHG DH,AH and XCHG AH,DH with the same machine opcodes, so switching the operands isn't guaranteed to work.)

In Chapter 1 we noted that there is a 1-cycle penalty for changing a byte-sized register and then using a register pointer 1 cycle later, as in:

```
MOV AL,1      ;1 cycle — changing a byte sized register
NOP           ;1 cycle — intervening instruction
MOV DX,[BX]   ;!2 cycles (Bytes-and-Pointers Rule)
```

Now, there's a complication. Some slow instructions that change byte-sized registers will also trigger a penalty if the *next* instruction refers to a register pointer. That is, a penalty is added to the instruction that refers to a register pointer even if there is no intervening 1-cycle instruction. This is another SECRET RULE.

◆ **SECRET "DELAYED-BYTES-AND-POINTERS" RULE:**
If you move a value to a byte register then use a register pointer such as [BX] or [SI+n], you lose 2 cycles if the first instruction is XCHG.

The Delayed-Bytes-and-Pointers Rule means that the code on the left is twice as fast as the code on the right, which does the same thing:

```
ROL AX,8      ;2 cycles      XCHG AL,AH    ;3 cycles
MOV [BX],AX   ;1 cycle       MOV [BX],AX   ;!3 cycles
```

Because of its cost then, the only useful XCHG is XCHG <register>,<register> in the case where the <first operand> and <second operand> are not two 8-bit halves of the same 16-bit register.

A Bubble Sort Without Exchanges

A bubble sort program can be used to put the bytes of a string in order and thus seems to be a good candidate for an instruction (such as ROL or XCHG) that exchanges bytes. We believe the following is a reasonable way to implement the classic bubble sort without using ROL or XCHG though.

```
        MOV BX,OFFSET string    ;We'll use the BX register as a pointer
loop1:  XOR CX,CX               ;We'll use the CX register as a flag
loop2:  MOV AL,[BX]
        MOV AH,[BX+1]
        CMP AL,AH
        JBE next                ;(These two bytes are already in order)
        MOV [BX],AH
        MOV [BX+1],AL
        INC CX
next:   INC BX
        CMP BX,OFFSET string+29
        JB loop2
        OR CX,CX                ;Were any interchanges done?
        JNZ loop1               ;Yes, repeat
```

Although we tried some alternatives to this code, we didn't find any that did the job better with byte-swapping instructions — sometimes the fastest instruction sequence uses neither ROL nor XCHG.

The SHRD and SHLD Instructions

In an assembler statement, the syntax of the SHRD and SHLD instructions looks like this:

```
SHRD <destination operand>,<source operand>,<bit-count operand>    ;optional comment
SHLD <destination operand>,<source operand>,<bit-count operand>    ;optional comment
```

The <bit-count operand> can be an 8-bit constant. This is the number of bits that are to be shifted in the <destination operand>. The <destination operand> can be a 16-bit or 32-bit memory operand or register. The <source operand> can be a 16-bit or 32-bit register that matches the size of <destination operand>. The <source operand> is the source of the bits that are to be shifted in and is not changed.

The meaning of these instructions is imperative:

SHRD: SHift <destination operand> to the Right Double-word by <bit-count operand> bits. Take the bits to shift in from the left (beginning with bit 31) from <source operand>.

SHLD: SHift <destination operand> to the Left Double-word by <bit-count operand> bits. Take the bits to shift in from the right (starting with bit 0) from <source operand>.

SHRD and SHLD have four possible forms, depending on the operands used. Table 4.4 is a standardized description for each possible form of SHRD and SHLD.

Instruction Mnemonic	Destination Operand	Source Operand	Bit-Count Operand	Cycle Count
<SHRD|SHLD>	<16-bit register>	,<16-bit register>	,<8-bit constant>	2
<SHRD|SHLD>	<word-size memory>	,<16-bit register>	,<8-bit constant>	3
<SHRD|SHLD>	<32-bit register>	,<32-bit register>	,<8-bit constant>	2
<SHRD|SHLD>	<long-size memory>	,<32-bit register>	,<8-bit constant>	3

Table 4.4   Standardized description for each possible form of SHRD and SHLD.

The opcode of both SHRD and SHLD begins with a 0Fh prefix, so add an extra cycle to the cycle count each time the instructions are run unless the Prefix-Waiver Rule is in effect.

SHRD and SHLD set the sign, zero, and parity flags according to the value of the operation's result, and set the carry flag to the value of the last bit shifted out. The effect on the overflow flag is undefined.

It is important to remember that, while <destination operand> gets shifted, SHRD and SHLD do *not* change <source operand>. For example, suppose the AX and BX registers contain the following bit values:

```
AX                      BX
1111 1000 0000 0000     0000 0111 1100 0000
```

If the instruction SHLD BX,AX,5 is run, the result will look like this:

```
AX                      BX
1111 1000 0000 0000     1111 1000 0001 1111
```

SHLD BX,AX,5 has shifted the BX register 5 bits to the left and taken the top-most 5 bits of AX (11111b) and put them in the low-most part of BX to replace the shifted bits. Although AX is a participant in the instruction (the replacement bits come from it), AX doesn't get shifted. To shift both operands, use a combination of SHLD and SHL:

```
SHLD BX,AX,5     ;!3 cycles (Prefix Rule)
SHL AX,5         ;2 cycles
```

In their C manual, the Microsoft people present this as an example of optimization (the idea is to shift a double-word left 12 bits):

```
      OR  CL,CL     ;1 cycle
      JZ  end       ;3 or 1 cycles
loop: SHL AX,1      ;3 cycles
      RCL BX,1      ;3 cycles
      DEC CL        ;1 cycle
      JNZ loop      ;3 or 1 cycles
end:
```

Microsoft's example is shifting 1 bit at a time, in a loop. The first mistake in this code is the way that 1 bit is shifted each time. The SHL and RCL instructions take 6 cycles per bit (remember that C always generates the slow forms of 1 bit shift/rotate instructions). Precisely the same thing can be done with 3 cycles per bit using ADD and ADC:

```
ADD BX,BX    ;shift BX 1 bit left
ADD AX,AX    ;shift AX 1 bit left
ADC BX,0     ;what got carried out of AX goes into BX
```

Microsoft's second mistake is that they don't use SHRD and SHLD — the double shift instructions that are available on 386s, 486s, and Pentiums. The 5-bit shift example we showed above is 1,200 percent faster than Microsoft's code.

Where You Are

In this chapter, you learned:

❖ how to shift and rotate the bits in a register or memory variable to the left with SHL, SHLD, and ROL and to the right with SAR, SHR, and SHRD;

❖ how to swap the high and low halves of a register with XCHG, and how and when to speed up the process by replacing XCHG with ROL, 3 MOVs, or 3 XORs;

❖ how to speed up register shifts by replacing SHL with ADD and replacing SAR and SHR with optimal machine opcodes;

❖ how to speed up memory shifts by replacing SHL with a MOV plus ADD combination and replacing SAR and SHR with a MOV and optimal SAR/SHR combination.

And finally, you learned another SECRET RULE of assembler that will help you speed up your code:

◆ **SECRET "DELAYED-BYTES-AND-POINTERS" RULE:**
If you move a value to a byte register then use a register pointer such as [BX] or [SI+n], you lose 2 cycles if the first instruction is XCHG.

Chapter 5

Other Instructions

Up to now we've been looking at groups of assembler instructions that are connected by a theme: arithmetic, jumping, shifting, and the like. This chapter's theme is miscellaneous instructions. Each instruction we'll introduce is important in itself (albeit not as important as the ones we discussed in earlier chapters), but there isn't any overarching idea behind them.

The TEST Instruction

In an assembler statement, the syntax of the TEST instruction looks like this:

```
TEST <destination operand>,<source operand>    ;optional comment
```

The <source operand> can be either an 8-bit, 16-bit, or 32-bit constant, memory operand, or register. The <destination operand> can be either an 8-bit, 16-bit, or 32-bit memory operand or register. The <destination operand> and the <source operand> must have matching sizes and cannot both be a memory operand. TEST clears the carry and overflow flags, and sets the parity, sign, and zero flags.

The meaning of TEST is imperative:

TEST for the bit-wise logical "and" of the contents of <destination operand> and <source operand>.

TEST acts exactly like the AND instruction, except that it doesn't affect the <destination operand> by actually writing to it. TEST just sets the flags in the flags register exactly as AND would for the same operands — e.g., if the AL register has the value 193 (binary 1100 0001), TEST AL,1 will set the zero flag OFF (because 11000001&1 is 1), the sign flag OFF (because the highest bit is 0), the parity flag OFF (because there is only one 1-bit in the result), the carry flag OFF (because carrying is impossible with an AND operation), and the overflow flag OFF (because the overflow flag is always cleared by TEST).

TEST has 15 possible forms, depending on the operands used. Table 5.1 is a standardized description for each possible form of TEST.

TEST is the most symmetric of instructions: TEST AX,DX and TEST DX,AX return precisely the same result in the same amount of time. The instruction is used in the translation of this program:

```
char mema;
void main ()
{
  if ((mema&5)==0) mema=7;
}
```

Instruction Mnemonic	Destination Operand	Source Operand	Cycle Count
TEST	<8-bit register>	,<8-bit register>	1
TEST	<8-bit register>	,<8-bit constant>	1
TEST	<8-bit register>	,<byte-size memory>	2
TEST	<byte-size memory>	,<8-bit register>	2
TEST	<byte-size memory>	,<8-bit constant>	2
TEST	<16-bit register>	,<16-bit register>	1
TEST	<16-bit register>	,<16-bit constant>	1
TEST	<16-bit register>	,<word-size memory>	2
TEST	<word-size memory>	,<16-bit register>	2
TEST	<word-size memory>	,<16-bit constant>	2
TEST	<32-bit register>	,<32-bit register>	1
TEST	<32-bit register>	,<32-bit constant>	1
TEST	<32-bit register>	,<long-size memory>	2
TEST	<long-size memory>	,<32-bit register>	2
TEST	<long-size memory>	,<32-bit constant>	2

Table 5.1   Standardized description for each possible form of TEST.

A good C compiler will translate `if ((mema&5)==0) mema=7;` to:

```
TEST mema,5
JNZ labels
MOV mema,7
labels:...
```

C compilers generate TEST when/if they're smart enough to realize that an AND operation should be non-destructive. Consider this program:

```
int mema;
int memb;
void main ()
{
  if (mema&4) ++memb;
}
```

C compilers will generate similar code for the C statement `if (mema&4) ++memb;`:

```
Borland                         Microsoft, Symantec (optimized)
TEST mema,4    ;!3 cycles       TEST  BYTE PTR mema,4    ;!3 cycles
JZ labelx      ;3 or 1 cycles   JE    labelx             ;3 or 1 cycles
INC [BX]       ;3 cycles        INC   WORD PTR memb       ;3 cycles
labelx:...                      labelx:...
```

Microsoft's and Symantec's translation uses a slight optimization: TEST BYTE PTR mema,4. Borland's instruction, operating on the whole word, is 1 byte longer. There is no short form of the TEST instruction when you're comparing a 16-bit operand to what is, in effect, an 8-bit constant. Note the penalty applied by the Constant-to-Memory Rule, though. This code is a faster translation for `if (mema&4) ++memb;`:

```
MOV AL,BYTE PTR mema    ;1 cycle
TEST AL,4               ;1 cycle
JNZ labelx              ;3 cycles or 1 cycle
INC [BX]                ;3 cycles
labelx:...
```

As usual when the same constant is being used twice there are alternatives. In this case we're testing a single bit and we're adding a single bit. The alternative is:

```
MOV AL,BYTE PTR mema    ;1 cycle
SHR AL,5                ;2 cycles
ADC [BX],0              ;1 cycle
```

When two bits are being tested, there are four possible outcomes: the first bit is on and the second bit is off, or both bits are on, or the first bit is off and the second bit is on, or both bits are off. This code tests all four possibilities with a single TEST instruction, provided one of the bits is the high bit (bit 80h of the byte):

```
TEST BYTE PTR memb,80h + 40h    ;Testing two bits at once
JZ label1                       ;(Zero: both bits are off)
JPE label2                      ;(Parity even: both bits are on)
JS label3                       ;(Sign: bit 80h is on)
JMP label4                      ;(None of above: bit 40h is on)
```

This is the only case we've found where the JPE instruction has a use. The method is only valid for byte-size operands.

Testing two bits at a time is particularly useful for checking if a pointer is straddling a double-word boundary. Expressed in C, if ((address%3)==3); then the address is misaligned — so check if the last two bits of the address are both 1 bits, as follows:

```
TEST <address' register>,3
JZ labela                       ;Zero: both bits are 0
JPO labelb                      ;Parity odd: one of the bits is off
<next instruction>             ;Neither of above: misaligned address
```

If the code falls through to the next instruction, the address is misaligned.

TEST and ADD can be equivalent in some circumstances. The destructive test on the left is 1 byte shorter (but not faster) than the code on the right:

```
ADD BL,BL    ;2 bytes, 1 cycle        TEST BL,64    ;3 bytes, 1 cycle
JS label     ;2 bytes                 JNZ label     ;2 bytes
```

These two sets of instructions are equivalent in function because doubling a number (ADD BL,BL) will shift all its bits left. In this case, if the second-to-top bit is a 1, then doubling it will make the topmost bit (the sign bit) 1. This tip is useless if you must preserve the value in the register you're testing with (in this example, the BL register).

Another way to use TEST is to do a self-test. If you want to compare the CX register with 0, use this instruction:

```
TEST CX,CX
```

Not only is TEST <register>,<same register> 1 byte shorter than CMP <register>,0, it sets the zero flag and the sign flag the same way that CMP <register>,0 does so you can follow it with a conditional jump instruction like JZ or JL. Since TEST sets the sign flag, self-testing is also useful for checking whether the top bit in a byte or word is on or off. The test on the left is 1 byte shorter (but not faster) than the code on the right:

```
TEST BL,BL     ;2 bytes          TEST BL,128    ;3 bytes
JS label       ;2 bytes          JNZ label      ;2 bytes
```

These tests are equivalent because the bit being checked happens to be the sign bit so TEST sets the sign flag. Testing a register with itself takes less room than testing a register against a constant and gives you all the results you need under most circumstances. Formally: TEST CX,CX is the same as TEST CX,65535.

If you're testing with what is in effect an 8-bit constant, you can also save a byte by using an 8-bit <destination operand>. For example, the code on the left is 1 byte shorter than the code on the right and takes the same amount of time:

```
TEST AL,32                       TEST AX,32
JNZ label                        JNZ label
```

There are four instructions which set exactly the same flags: TEST, OR, AND, and XOR. For example, to set the flags based on the value in the CX register, you can use either of these instructions:

```
TEST CX,CX
OR CX,CX
AND CX,CX
XOR CX,0
```

We strongly recommend TEST for this purpose because TEST does not change CX — the <destination operand>. Since the other three instructions all change CX by writing to the register, using them instead might trigger a Hi/Lo Rule penalty or a Bytes-and-Pointers penalty in the next instruction. (Remember that Intel considers that the register has been changed even if the new value is exactly the same as the value before the operation.) Because of the Bytes-and-Pointers Rule, the instructions on the left are faster than the instructions on the right:

```
TEST AL,AL     ;1 cycle          OR AL,AL       ;1 cycle
JZ label       ;3 or 1 cycles    JZ label       ;3 or 1 cycles
MOV AX,[DI]    ;1 cycle          MOV AX,[DI]    ;!2 cycles
```

Although TEST doesn't change the <destination> register and so does not cause the next instruction to potentially suffer from the Hi/Lo Rule, TEST does imply an AND, so it is considered to be an arithmetic instruction as far as the Hi/Lo Rule is concerned. This means TEST will be penalized if it is the second instruction in a pair that "change" the high and low halves of one register. If the second instruction is TEST <register>,1 you can evade the Hi/Lo Rule by replacing it with SHR <register>,1 since SHR with a constant value of 1 as a <source operand> doesn't trigger the Hi/Lo Rule. For example, the destructive test on the left is 1 byte shorter and takes the same number of cycles as the instructions on the right:

```
MOV  BH,5     ;1 cycle                    MOV  BH,5     ;1 cycle
DB   0C0h     ;2 cycles, 3 DBs force      TEST BL,1     ;!2 cycles
DB   0EBh     ;cheaper form of SHR BL,1   JNZ label
DB   001h
JC   label
```

These sets of instructions are equivalent in function because the SHR instruction puts the last bit shifted out into the carry flag.

The NEG Instruction

In an assembler statement, the syntax of the NEG instruction looks like this:

```
NEG <destination operand>    ;optional comment
```

The <destination operand> can be either an 8-bit, 16-bit, or 32-bit memory operand or register. NEG sets the overflow, parity, sign, and zero flags. NEG also sets the carry flag unless the <destination operand> is zero. If <destination operand> is 0, NEG clears the carry flag.

The meaning of NEG is imperative:

NEGate the contents of <destination operand> with its two's complement.

The NEG instruction replaces the value of <destination operand> with its two's complement. When you NEG a positive <destination operand>, it becomes negative. When you NEG a negative <destination operand>, it becomes positive. When you NEG a zero <destination operand>, it stays 0. Intel considers NEG to be an arithmetic instruction for the purposes of the Hi/Lo Rule.

NEG has six possible forms, depending on the operands used. Table 5.2 is a standardized description for each possible form of NEG.

NEG is a useful instruction in translations of C statements like mema=mema*-1;. Some compilers will see the multiply sign and translate this expression using a costly assembler multiply instruction. To make sure that your compiler uses NEG instead, replace this type of expression with mema=-mema;. All compilers will reliably translate mema=-mema; into:

```
MOV AX,mema     ;1 cycle, 3 bytes
NEG AX          ;1 cycle, 2 bytes
MOV mema,AX     ;1 cycle, 3 bytes
```

which is much faster — but still wasteful. The Constant-to-Memory Rule doesn't apply to NEG, so it's just as fast and far smaller to do the job the simple way:

```
NEG mema        ;3 cycles, 4 bytes
```

The NOT Instruction

In an assembler statement, the syntax of the NOT instruction looks like this:

```
NOT <destination operand>    ;optional comment
```

The <destination operand> can be either an 8-bit, 16-bit, or 32-bit memory operand or register.

The meaning of NOT is imperative:

Negate One's complemenT the contents of <destination operand>.

Instruction Mnemonic	Destination Operand	Cycle Count
NEG	<8-bit register>	1
NEG	<byte-size memory>	3
NEG	<16-bit register>	1
NEG	<word-size memory>	3
NEG	<32-bit register>	1
NEG	<long-size memory>	3

Table 5.2   Standardized description for each possible form of NEG.

The NOT instruction replaces the value of <destination operand> with its one's complement, that is, it inverts the <destination operand> — all 1 bits become 0 bits and all 0 bits become 1 bits. NOT does not affect any of the flags in the flags register. If you want to complement an operand and set the flags at the same time, use XOR <destination operand>, -1. Intel considers NOT to be an arithmetic instruction for the purposes of the Hi/Lo Rule.

NOT has six possible forms, depending on the operands used. Table 5.3 is a standardized description for each possible form of NOT.

NOT is mainly used for double-word arithmetic.

The LDS and LES Instructions

In an assembler statement, the syntax of the LDS and LES instructions looks like this:

```
LDS <destination operand>,<source operand>    ;optional comment
LES <destination operand>,<source operand>    ;optional comment
```

The <source operand> can be a memory address. The <destination operand> is always an implicit segment register:16-bit register combination. The DS segment register is implicit for the LDS instruction and the ES segment register is implicit for the LES instruction. LDS and LES do not affect any of the flags in the flags register.

The meaning of LDS and LES is imperative:

LDS: Load DS:<register> with pointer from memory.

LES: Load ES:<register> with pointer from memory.

Instruction Mnemonic	Destination Operand	Cycle Count
NOT	<8-bit register>	1
NOT	<byte-size memory>	3
NOT	<16-bit register>	1
NOT	<word-size memory>	3
NOT	<32-bit register>	1
NOT	<long-size memory>	3

Table 5.3   Standardized description for each possible form of NOT.

LDS and LES read a full pointer from the <source operand> and store it in the specified <destination operand>.

LDS and LES have only one possible form. Table 5.4 is a standardized description for this form.

Intel designed the LDS and LES instructions for handling far pointers. A far pointer contains both the offset within the segment and the segment itself, so far pointers are always 32 bits long. LDS and LES provide a handy way to load both components of the pointer into registers. For example, given this code:

```
int far *memp;
int mema;
void main ()
{
 mema=*memp;
}
```

all C compilers will generate this translation for the mema=*memp; statement:

```
LES BX,memp        ;6 cycles
MOV AX,ES:[BX]     ;!3 cycles (Register-Address Rule)
MOV mema,AX        ;1 cycle
```

But this is not an optimal translation due to another SECRET RULE.

◆ **SECRET "LOAD-POINTER-WITH-MOV" RULE:**
 If you use LDS or LES instead of two MOVs to load a pointer, you lose 2 cycles.

The Load-Pointer-With-MOV Rule means this code is faster than the translation provided by a C compiler for mema=*memp;:

```
MOV BX,WORD PTR memp       ;1 cycle
MOV ES,WORD PTR memp+2     ;3 cycles
MOV AX,ES:[BX]             ;1 cycle
MOV mema,AX                ;1 cycle
```

Instruction Mnemonic	Destination Operand	Source Operand	Cycle Count
LDS	<DS:16-bit register>	,<memory address>	6
LES	<ES:16-bit register>	,<memory address>	6

Table 5.4   Standardized description of LDS and LES.

LDS and LES are thus not valuable instructions unless the objective is to save code space. Their use by C compilers is possibly a relic of the age of 386s.

Setting Flags: The CLC, CMC, and STC Instructions

In an assembler statement, the syntax of the CLC, CMC, and STC instructions looks like this:

```
CLC      ;optional comment
CMC      ;optional comment
STC      ;optional comment
```

These three instructions have neither a <source operand> or a <destination operand> because their only purpose is to directly affect the status of the carry flag. No other flags in the flags register are affected.

The meaning of CLC, CMC, and STC is imperative:

CLC: CLear Carry flag.

CMC: CoMplement Carry flag.

STC: SeT Carry flag.

CLC clears the carry flag; that is, it turns the carry flag OFF. CMC sets the carry flag to the complement of its current status; that is, if the carry flag is ON, CMC turns it OFF, and if the carry flag is OFF, CMC turns it ON. STC sets the carry flag; that is, it turns the carry flag ON.

These three instructions have only one possible form. Table 5.5 is a standardized description for this form.

STC and CLC are handy for returning a Boolean value from a subroutine. For example, the following code could be used to return either 0 or 1 to the AX register:

```
SBB AX,AX     ;1 cycle, If Carry Flag ON then AX = -1, else AX = 0
NEG AX        ;1 cycle, If AX = 0 then AX = 0, if AX = -1 then AX = 1
```

Instruction Mnemonic	Cycle Count
<CLC|CMC|STC>	2

Table 5.5 Standardized description of CLC, CMC, and STC.

But so could the following:

```
        CALL _subroutine
        JC failure                      ;_subroutine returned carry flag ON
        ...
_subroutine:
        <check for error condition>
        STC
        RET
        ...
        CLC
        RET
```

Because the Boolean value is returned in the carry flag, this code doesn't waste a register. It also saves time because the calling routine can test the return value immediately. If the flag value was returned in a register, the calling routine would have to CMP the register value to decide whether the value equals zero or not. You won't see this optimization in a standard C library, though — the firm convention is that an integral return value comes back in the AX register.

In fact, we couldn't find a C compiler that seemed to use a carry flag instruction for any reasonable purpose, except for one occurrence in Symantec's standard library, where they use CMC to negate a 32-bit number with:

```
NOT DX      ;1 cycle
NEG AX      ;1 cycle
CMC         ;2 cycles
ADC DX,0    ;3 cycles
```

This method is not as fast as the negating method we will show when we discuss multiplying in Chapter 7. In any case, TEST AX,AX clears the carry flag twice as fast as CLC so, although it uses one more byte, you should consider using it in cases where the status of the other flags in the flags register doesn't matter. Other 1-cycle instructions to set flags without changing registers include:

```
TEST SP,SP   ;sets zero flag OFF (assuming SP can never equal 0)
CMP AX,AX    ;sets zero flag ON
CMP SP,-1    ;sets carry flag ON (assuming SP can never equal 0)
```

The LEA Instruction

In an assembler statement, the syntax of the LEA instruction looks like this:

```
LEA <destination operand>,<source operand>    ;optional comment
```

The <source operand> can be a memory address. The <destination operand> can be either a 16-bit or a 32-bit register. LEA has no effect on the flags in the flags register.

The meaning of LEA is imperative:

Load (that is, copy) Effective Address from <source operand> to <destination operand>.

The LEA instruction calculates the effective address (that is, the offset) of the <source operand> and puts it in the register specified by <destination operand>. If <destination operand> is a 16-bit register and <source operand> is a 16-bit address, then LEA calculates the 16-bit effective address of <source operand> and stores it in <destination operand>. If <destination operand> is a 16-bit register and <source operand> is a 32-bit address, then LEA calculates the 32-bit effective address of <source operand> and stores the lower 16-bits in <destination operand>. If <destination operand> is a 32-bit register and <source operand> is a 16-bit address, then LEA calculates the 16-bit effective address of <source operand>, zero-extends the result, and stores it in <destination operand>. If <destination operand> is a 32-bit register and <source operand> is a 32-bit address, then LEA calculates the 32-bit effective address of <source operand> and stores it in <destination operand>.

LEA has two possible forms, depending on the operands used. Table 5.6 is a standardized description for each possible form of LEA.

There are two instructions that move constants to registers: MOV and LEA. Usually MOV is shorter, but there is one exceptional case. When

Instruction Mnemonic	Destination Operand	Source Operand	Cycle Count
LEA	<16-bit register>	,<memory address>	1
LEA	<32-bit register>	,<memory address>	1

Table 5.6   Standardized description for each possible form of LEA.

you're writing for a 16-bit target, and you want to move a constant value between 0 and 65535 to a 32-bit register, LEA is shorter. For example:

```
__asm MOV EAX,5;      /* !2 cycles, 6 bytes (Prefix Rule) */
```

is longer than:

```
__asm LEA EAX,DS:[5];    /* !2 cycles, 5 bytes (Prefix Rule) */
```

By the way, the above example glosses over two syntax problems. First, remember that with Borland C and Microsoft C, you can't reference 32-bit registers in 16-bit mode — you have to change the LEA instruction to what looks like two separate instructions:

```
__asm _emit 66h;        /* Explicit Operand Size Override Prefix for Microsoft */
                        /* Use "DB" rather than "_emit" for Borland */
__asm LEA AX,DS:[5];    /* In fact this will load the EAX register */
```

Second, no compiler will do anything with the DS: (Segment Override) prefix because DS: is meaningless with LEA instructions. And yet it must be used! Most C compilers and some assemblers will accept LEA AX,DS:[5] but reject the more obvious and legal-looking synonyms LEA AX,[5] or LEA AX,5.

LEA can be used instead of ADD in cases where you don't want the flags register to be changed by the operation. For example, LEA BX,[BX+6] performs the same operation as ADD BX,6 — both instructions take 1 cycle to add 6 to the BX register, but LEA doesn't set flags like ADD does. LEA's use in multiplying is shown in Chapter 7. Other than this, LEA doesn't have much use in 16-bit mode, not even in loading pointers. Rather than using LEA to translate C pointer=&address types of expressions, all compilers generate

```
MOV _pointer,OFFSET address
```

instead.

LEA is affected by the Register-Address Rule we introduced in Chapter 1, so the instructions on the left are faster than the instructions on the right:

```
INC BX        ;3 cycles        INC BX        ;3 cycles
MOV AX,BX     ;1 cycle         LEA AX,[BX]   ;!2 cycles
```

LEA is also affected by the Bytes-and-Pointers Rule, so the instructions on the left are faster than the instructions on the right:

```
MOV AL,0    ;1 cycle          MOV AL,0       ;1 cycle
NOP         ;1 cycle          NOP            ;1 cycle
INC DI      ;1 cycle          LEA DI,[DI+1]  ;!2 cycles
```

Although LEA contains a reference to memory, there is no penalty involved in loading a misaligned address. However, LEA is subject to a Prefetcher pipeline stall — although seven LEA SI,[BP+1000] instructions take the expected 7 cycles, eight LEA SI,[BP+1000] instructions in a row take 11 cycles — a 4 cycle penalty.

Casting

Most of the assembler instructions we've looked at expect two operands which must be the same size. MOV AX,AL and CMP BX,CL and TEST CX,<8-bit memory operand> are all illegal, because assembler won't implicitly cast the smaller operand to the larger like a C statement does. You therefore have to do explicit casting in assembler whenever two operands have different sizes. This isn't a difficult job because the operands have only three likely sizes: 8-bit, 16-bit, or 32-bit. The casting is done with CBW, CWD, MOVSX, and MOVZX.

The CBW and CWD Instructions

In an assembler statement, the syntax of the CBW and CWD instructions looks like this:

```
CBW    ;optional comment
CWD    ;optional comment
```

Neither CBW nor CWD affect the flags in the flags register.

The meaning of CBW and CWD is imperative:

CBW: Convert Byte in AL to Word in AX.

CWD: Convert Word in AX to Double-word in DX:AX.

The CBW instruction converts the signed byte in the AL register to a signed word in the AX register. It does this by extending the topmost bit (sign bit) of the AL register into all the bits of the AH register.

The CWD instruction converts the signed word in the AX register to a signed double-word in the pair of registers DX:AX. It does this by extending the sign bit of the AX register into all the bits of the DX register.

CBW and CWD have only one possible form. Table 5.7 is a standardized description for this form.

When working with 8-bit to 16-bit casting, the big advantage is that the AX, BX, CX, and DX registers can all be split easily into their higher and lower halves (e.g., AX splits into AH and AL). In this program:

```
unsigned int mema;
unsigned char memb;
void main()
{
  mema=memb;
}
```

the C compiler can therefore bring memb into a low 8-bit register (e.g., AL), clear the corresponding high 8-bit register (e.g., AH), and end up with a 16-bit register (e.g., AX) containing the right value, as shown in these translations:

```
      ;Borland's translation
MOV AL,memb                  ;1 cycle
MOV AH,0                     ;1 cycle
MOV DX,AX                    ;!2 cycles (Hi-Lo Rule)
MOV mema,DX                  ;1 cycle

      ;Microsoft's translation
MOV AL,BYTE PTR memb         ;1 cycle
SUB AH,AH                    ;!2 cycles (Hi-Lo Rule)
MOV WORD PTR mema,AX         ;!2 cycles (Hi-Lo Rule)

      ;Symantec's translation
MOV AL,memb                  ;1 cycle
XOR AH,AH                    ;!2 cycles (Hi-Lo Rule)
MOV mema,AX                  ;!2 cycles (Hi-Lo Rule)
```

Microsoft and Symantec should either have cleared the AH register with MOV AH,0 (instead of SUB AH,AH and XOR AH,AH, respectively), or they should have cleared AH prior to the MOV AL,memb instruction — they've violated the Hi/Lo Rule twice. As for Borland, the MOV DX,AX detour is a sheer waste — not only does it also violate the Hi/Lo

Instruction Mnemonic	Cycle Count
<CBW|CWD>	3

Table 5.7   Standardized description of CBW and CWD.

Rule, MOV mema,AX would accomplish the same purpose and save 1 cycle overall. Still, at least none of the three make the mistake of using AND mema,0000000011111111b; they all know that working with 16-bit constants is a slower option because of the Constant-to-Memory Rule.

The test compilers' translations of mema=memb; worked because memb is defined as an unsigned char. If memb were signed, the conversion would take a different form, probably involving the CBW instruction (remember, CBW converts AL to AX). CBW assumes that AL contains an 8-bit signed number. To convert this to a signed 16-bit number in AX, CBW does a process called *sign extending*, as follows:

❖ If AL is negative (i.e., if the most significant bit of AL is a 1), then all the bits in AH become 1. For instance, if AL contains –3 (binary 1111 1101), the most significant bit of AL is a 1 and AH is set to binary 1111 1111. The AX register thus contains binary 1111 1111 1111 1101, or –3.

❖ If AL is positive (i.e., if the most significant bit of AL is a 0), then all the bits in AH become 0. For instance, if AL contains +3 (binary 0000 0011), the most significant bit of AL is a 0 and AH is set to binary 0000 0000. The AX register thus contains binary 0000 0000 0000 0011, or +3.

CWD follows the same process when moving AX's topmost bit into the DX register.

A C compiler could use CBW to translate this program:

```
int mema;
char memb;
void main ()
{
 mema=memb;
}
```

In this case, mema=memb; translates to:

```
MOV AL,memb     ;1 cycle
CBW             ;3 cycles
MOV mema,AX     ;1 cycle
```

Since CBW is a specialized instruction which only accepts AL as the input and produces AX as the output, it can't be used to convert the BL, CL, or DL registers to a signed word. For these registers, you can use what we call the Trick Shift method to convert a byte to a word. The Trick Shift method is guaranteed to propagate a sign bit's value into an entire byte. For example, to convert BL into BX:

```
MOV BH,BL      ;1 cycle, Let the BH register equal the BL register
SHR BH,8       ;2 cycles, Shift BH 8 bits right so BH equals BL's sign bit
SBB BH,0       ;1 cycle, Subtract 0 from BH with borrow from the carry flag
```

After the eighth shift of BH, the topmost bit (the sign bit) has been shifted into the carry flag and BH will be 0 (if BL's sign bit was 0) or 1 (if BL's sign bit was 1). Then SBB BH,0 (subtract 0 from BH with borrow) will make BH equal to –1 (binary 1111 1111) if the carry flag is ON and binary 0000 0000 if the carry flag is OFF. You must enable 80486 instructions using the .486 directive to use the Trick Shift method.

Using CBW and CWD or the Trick Shift method has its advantages, but all casting — whether it's unsigned or signed — costs. The MOV AH,0 instruction takes only 1 cycle while the CBW and CWD instructions take 3 cycles and the Trick Shift takes 4 cycles. One way you can avoid such profligacy is to never define a byte in the default manner (i.e., as signed char) if the byte's sign doesn't matter. If you define the byte as unsigned char, the compiler will use MOV AH,0 rather than CBW for conversions, saving 2 cycles.

We have never seen a C compiler that produces optimum code for arithmetic expressions containing combinations of 8-bit and 16-bit signed operands. They either go into contortions to get an operand into AL in order to make CBW possible, or they do a conversion too early, forgetting that the result of an 8-bit operation can always be propagated into a 16-bit operation via the carry flag. For example, the mema=memb+memc; expression in this C program:

```
int mema;
char memb,memc;   /* memb and memc are signed by default */
void main ()
{
  mema=memb+memc;
}
```

will be translated in very similar ways (at a cost of either 11 or 12 cycles):

Borland
```
MOV AL,memb      ;1 cycle
CBW              ;3 cycles
PUSH AX          ;1 cycle
MOV AL,memc      ;1 cycle
CBW              ;3 cycles
POP DX           ;1 cycle
ADD DX,AX        ;1 cycle
MOV  mema,DX     ;1 cycle
```

Microsoft and Symantec
```
MOV AL,memb      ;1 cycle
CBW              ;3 cycles
MOV CX,AX        ;1 cycle
MOV AL,memc      ;1 cycle
CBW              ;3 cycles
ADD CX,AX        ;1 cycle
MOV mema,CX      ;1 cycle
```

(Note: The PUSH instruction puts an operand on the stack. The POP instruction takes an operand from the stack. We'll look at these instructions in detail in Chapter 6.)

Translating mema=memb+memc; with the Trick Shift method also takes 11 cycles:

```
MOV AL,memb     ;1 cycle
CBW             ;3 cycles
MOV CL,memc     ;1 cycle
SHR CL,8        ;2 cycles
SBB CL,0        ;1 cycle
ADD AX,CX       ;!2 cycles (Hi/Lo Rule)
MOV mema,AX     ;1 cycle
```

but propagating the carry flag saves another 4 cycles despite the Hi/Lo Rule penalty incurred:

```
MOV AL,memb     ;1 cycle
ADD AL,memc     ;2 cycles
MOV AH,0        ;1 cycle
SBB AH,0        ;1 cycle
MOV mema,AX     ;!2 cycles
```

By the way, none of this conversion confusion happens if all operands are defined as int or unsigned int. It's tempting, then, to never define anything as char. But there are some problems with this solution:

(1) It takes longer to access a 16-bit operand on a non-even memory address (the misalignment problem discussed in Chapter 1).

(2) While it takes no longer to move a 16-bit constant to a memory operand than an 8-bit constant, there are twice as many 8-bit registers as 16-bit registers available to make the move.

(3) Division (and sometimes multiplication) is faster with 8-bit operands, as we'll show in Chapters 7 and 8.

CWD is used when working with 16-bit to 32-bit casting. As with CBW, there's no choice of registers, but CWD can also be replaced using a variant of the Trick Shift. C compilers use CWD to translate expressions containing both int and long operands; the same general sort of problems apply as for conversions of char and int operands.

The MOVSX and MOVZX Instructions

In an assembler statement, the syntax of the MOVSX and MOVZX instructions looks like this:

```
MOVSX <destination operand>,<source operand>    ;optional comment
MOVZX <destination operand>,<source operand>    ;optional comment
```

The <source operand> can be either an 8-bit or 16-bit memory operand or register. The <destination operand> can be either a 16-bit or 32-bit register. An 8-bit <source operand> can be moved to either a 16-bit or 32-bit <destination operand>. A 16-bit <source operand> can only be moved to a 32-bit <destination operand>. Neither MOVSX or MOVZX has any affect on the flags in the flags register.

The meaning of MOVSX and MOVZX is imperative:

MOVSX: MOVe (that is, copy) with Sign-eXtension contents of <source operand> to <destination operand>.

MOVZX: MOVe with Zero-eXtension contents of <source operand> to <destination operand>.

MOVSX reads the contents of <source operand> as an 8-bit byte or a 16-bit word (as appropriate), sign-extends the value to the size of <destination operand> (either 16-bits or 32-bits), and writes the result in the register specified by <destination operand>.

MOVZX reads the contents of <source operand> as an 8-bit byte or a 16-bit word (as appropriate), zero-extends the value to the size of <destination operand> (either 16-bits or 32-bits), and writes the result in the register specified by <destination operand>.

Instruction Mnemonic	Destination Operand	Source Operand	Cycle Count
<MOVSX|MOVZX>	<16-bit register>	,<8-bit register>	3
<MOVSX|MOVZX>	<16-bit register>	,<byte-size memory>	3
<MOVSX|MOVZX>	<32-bit register>	,<8-bit register>	3
<MOVSX|MOVZX>	<32-bit register>	,<byte-size memory>	3
<MOVSX|MOVZX>	<32-bit register>	,<16-bit register>	3
<MOVSX|MOVZX>	<32-bit register>	,<word-size memory>	3

Table 5.8   Standardized description for the possible forms of MOVSX and MOVZX.

MOVSX and MOVZX have six possible forms, depending on the operands used. Table 5.8 is a standardized description for the possible forms of MOVSX and MOVZX.

The opcode of both these instructions begins with a OFh prefix so an extra cycle is used each time either instruction is run unless the Prefix-Waiver Rule is in effect.

The MOVSX and MOVZX instructions work on 386s or later processors. Their purpose is to convert 8-bit or 16-bit operands into 16-bit or 32-bit operands, either zeroing or propagating the sign in the process. For example:

```
MOVZX EAX,AL      ;Top 24 bits of EAX register become 0
MOVSX EAX,AL      ;Top 24 bits of EAX register become AL's sign
MOVZX EBX,DX      ;Lower 16 bits of EBX = DX, Higher 16 bits = 0
MOVSX ESI,BX      ;Lower 16 bits of ESI = BX, Higher 16 bits = BX's sign
```

In 16-bit mode, MOVSX and MOVZX aren't really useful for casting because CBW and CWD are generally faster. For example, CWD takes 3 cycles but MOVSX EAX,AX takes 5 cycles because of the Prefix Rule penalty for a 32-bit register and the Long-Jump Rule penalty. Also, CWD gets the upper bits into the DX register and it's easier to use the DX register than to use the upper 16 bits of the EAX register.

In 32-bit mode, MOVSX and MOVZX can take the same time as CBW and CWD because the latter instructions also have a prefix in 32-bit mode.

One example of some code which uses a 16-bit memory variable for loop control is (assume that registers AX, BX, CX, DX, SI, DI, and BP are used up during the body of the loop marked with ...):

```
        MOV mem,500h          ;!2 cycles (Constant-to-Memory Rule)
loop_label:...
        DEC mem               ;3 cycles
        JGE loop_label        ;3 cycles (assuming jump is done)
```

The same loop using the high part of the EAX register looks like this:

```
        MOVZX EAX,AX          ;!5 cycles (Prefix & Long-Jump Rules)
        OR EAX,(-500h)*1000h  ;!2 cycles (Prefix Rule)
loop_label:...
        ADD EAX,1*10000h      ;!2 cycles (Prefix Rule)
        JS loop_label         ;3 cycles (assuming jump is done)
```

You can always move a constant to a 32-bit register's top half using MOVZX to clear it and OR <shifted constant value> to set it. You can also always depend on the sign and carry flags changing appropriately when you do arithmetic on the top half of a 32-bit register, but you can't count on the zero flag being appropriately set, which is why the second loop adds to a negative number rather than decrementing a positive number as the first loop does (remember that the sign and carry flags only depend on the top half of the register, but the zero flag depends on the entire register). Despite this, the second loop saves 1 cycle for each iteration.

Three assembler instructions can be used to clear the top half of a 32-bit register to zero. One is MOVZX:

```
MOVZX EDI,DI          ;!5 cycles clear top half of EDI (Prefix Rule)
                      ;4 bytes
```

The second is LEA, which is good for the BX, SI, DI, and BP registers if you're using 16-bit mode:

```
LEA EBX,[BX]          ;!2 cycles clear top half of EBX (Prefix Rule)
                      ;3 bytes
```

The third instruction is AND, which is the best way in 32-bit mode:

```
AND EAX,0000FFFFh     ;1 cycle clear top half of EAX
                      ;6 bytes
```

Notice how MOVZX, though short, is much slower than the alternatives for "Top Half Clearing" operations.

Where You Are

In this chapter, you learned:

❖ how and when to use the TEST instruction to simulate an AND instruction without actually changing the destination register or memory variable;

❖ how to use the NEG instruction to change the value in a register or memory variable to its two's complement;

❖ how to use the NOT instruction to invert the value in a register or memory variable;

❖ how to load an effective memory address into a register with LEA and a far pointer into a segment register:register combination with LDS and LES — and how to do these loads even faster with MOV;

❖ how to set the status of the carry flag with CLC, CMC, and STC — and how to use this status to return Boolean values;

❖ how and when to cast bytes to words and words to double-words with CBW and CWD and with MOVSX and MOVZX, and how to replace these instructions when their use is either impossible or too slow.

And finally, you learned another SECRET RULE of assembler that will help you speed up your code:

◆ **SECRET "LOAD-POINTER-WITH-MOV" RULE:**
If you use LDS or LES instead of two MOVs to load a pointer, you lose 2 cycles.

Chapter 6

Manipulating the Stack

Your assembler vocabulary is now large enough that you can look at how the stack can be manipulated in assembler.

This stack-demonstration program contains an infinite loop, but it won't actually loop forever — it will end after a few centiseconds.

```
void main ()
{
        __asm MOV BP,SP;         /* line 1 */
        __asm XOR AX,AX;         /* line 2 */
        __asm MOV [BP-2],AX;     /* line 3 */
labela: __asm CMP [BP-2],AX;     /* line 4 */
        __asm JZ labela;         /* line 5 */
}
```

Some points to note about this code:

(1) The stack is SS — the Stack Segment we introduced briefly in Chapter 1. Global data is stored in DS — the Data Segment. Since all our examples so far have used the small model, it hasn't been necessary to talk about the differences between these two segment registers. In the small model, the stack and the data segment are the same, that is, DS=SS.

(2) We want to point to the location in memory that is just before SP, the Stack Pointer register, but we can't use [SP-2] as an address directly because the only registers that can be used as pointers are BX, SI, DI, and BP. The code therefore moves SP to BP in line 1.

(3) XOR AX,AX sets the AX register value to 0 in line 2. This is the usual way to clear a 16-bit register to 0.

(4) The code addresses a location in memory with [BP-2] in lines 3 and 4. We do not use SUB BP,2 and then address the location with [BP] because that is inefficient on a 486.

(5) The memory location [BP-2] is compared with CMP [BP-2],AX (in line 4, where AX is still 0 before the jump). This is faster than CMP WORD PTR [BP-2],0. The time saved is important because the comparison is in a loop.

(6) The memory location [BP-2] is compared with CMP [BP-2],AX in line 4. This puts the memory operand before the register operand.

Points (3) to (6) all relate to speed rather than the stack. We mention them anyway as an aid to developing good habits. The JZ instruction in line 5, though, *is* relevant to our discussion on the stack — JZ makes the program go back to the instruction at labela, the point where memory location [BP-2] is compared with zero. This code doesn't hang because some other code will inevitably interrupt it, and an interruption will always change what's on the stack just before SP. (The usual suspect in MS-DOS is the clock timer, which interrupts roughly every .055 seconds.)

Because your code will always be interrupted by something similar to the DOS clock timer, you should be prepared to deal with these interlopers. One method you can use is to "bar the door." If the first line in your program is:

```
__asm CLI;
```

you will prevent interruptions completely (in DOS programs only; CLI is not accepted by Windows). In fact, a CLI (CLear Interrupts flag; 5 cycles) instruction will not only make a loop such as the one shown in our example program infinite, it will ensure that pressing the traditional keyboard Control-Alt-Del sequence won't stop the loop either. Placing an STI (SeT Interrupts flag; 5 cycles) instruction after your loop will prevent this — STI allows interruptions again — but there are several disadvantages to this:

(a) the system's time-of-day clock becomes incorrect;

(b) background tasks (e.g., communication over network adapters) are disabled; and

(c) under a multitasking system, no other job can gain control.

The bar-the-door technique, then, is not highly recommended.

The alternative way to handle interruptions is to accept them — and actually make the interrupter's job easier — by making sure the SP register always has an even value. Since pointer arithmetic conventionally uses SP's value and since references to addresses with odd pointers cause alignment penalties, having an even value for SP helps. Changing the stack with DEC SP or some arbitrary function isn't quite good enough for the purpose though — we'll provide you with the correct methods during the course of this chapter.

Another way you can make the interrupter's job (and thus your own) easier is to make sure there is always some room on the stack so the interrupting job doesn't have to write over some vital data. (The phrase "some room" is admittedly imprecise — it's only a few bytes if only the clock can interrupt, but it's several hundred bytes under NetWare and Windows.) However, you do have the right to make some use of the stack. In fact, there are a variety of conventional uses.

Automatic Variables

When a program executes the assembler instruction

```
SUB SP,2
```

it temporarily reserves a word of memory for its own use, knowing that no well-behaved interrupting job will try to use memory above the Stack Pointer's value. In effect, then, a word is taken from a common memory pool for the program's exclusive use. This, in fact, is the convention that C follows with automatic variables (at least, with automatic variables that can't be put in registers). For example, if a C procedure begins like this:

```
void xproc ()
{
 char memx[100];
 ...
```

then the C compiler will generate, somewhere near the start, the instruction:

```
SUB SP,100
```

That is, the compiler will reserve 100 bytes of memory for the variable memx.

Of course, reserving memory isn't any good unless the compiler also knows the address of memx. This is provided by a pointer register. All C compilers will use BP for this purpose, so before generating SUB SP,100 the compiler will set the BP register to the current SP value. Then, throughout the procedure, memx can simply be referred to with the address [BP-100]. For example, the following code:

```
void xproc ()
{
 char memx[100];
 ...
 memx[0]='a';
 memx[2]='b';
 ...
```

is translated as

```
_xproc proc
        ...
        MOV BP,SP              ;BP is the pointer
        SUB SP,100            ;reserve 100 bytes for memx
        MOV [BP-100],'a'      ;this is location memx[0]
        MOV [BP-98],'b'       ;this is location memx[2]
        ...
```

This simple design has a flaw though. Suppose that the program needs to call another function — yproc — from within the xproc function. If yproc uses the same convention, it will also contain a MOV BP,SP instruction. Thus, when yproc returns to xproc and xproc tries to access location memx[4], the BP register will be pointing to the wrong place.

The solution to this problem is another convention. All well-behaved functions must save the value of BP when they start and must restore it when they end. There are two assembler instructions for just these purposes — PUSH and POP.

The PUSH and POP Instructions

In an assembler statement, the syntax of the PUSH and POP instructions looks like this:

```
PUSH <operand>    ;optional comment
POP <operand>     ;optional comment
```

The meaning of PUSH and POP is imperative:

PUSH: Decrement SP, PUSH <operand> onto top of stack.

POP: POP top of stack to <operand>, increment SP.

The PUSH instruction puts an operand on the stack (that is, in SS, the stack segment) without affecting the flags register. To do so, it reserves space on the stack (by subtracting from SP), then copies <operand> to the new stack location. The <operand> can be either a 16-bit or 32-bit constant, register, or memory location. (Although there is a machine opcode for pushing an 8-bit constant, doing so is a bad idea because SP should be even. Anyway, despite what Intel's documentation says, if you PUSH an 8-bit constant, the 486 will subtract 2 from the SP register, i.e., it really pushes a word onto the stack, never a byte.) PUSH decrements SP by 2 if the size of <operand> is 16 bits; otherwise SP is decremented by 4.

POP is the precise reverse of PUSH. The POP instruction takes an operand from the stack without affecting the flags register. To do so, it copies the contents from the stack location to <operand> then cancels the reserved space on the stack (by adding to SP). The <operand> can be either a 16-bit or 32-bit register or memory location (but not a constant). POP increments SP by 2 if the size of <operand> is 16 bits; otherwise SP is incremented by 4.

PUSH and POP have seven and five possible forms, respectively, depending on the operands used. Table 6.1 is a standardized description for each possible form of PUSH and POP. (Note: POP CS is not allowed on 486s.)

Instruction Mnemonic	Operand	Cycle Count
PUSH	<16-bit constant>	1
PUSH	<32-bit constant>	1
<PUSH|POP>	<16-bit register>	1!!
<PUSH|POP>	<32-bit register>	1!!
<PUSH|POP>	<segment-register>	3
PUSH	<word-size memory>	4
PUSH	<long-size memory>	4
POP	<word-size memory>	5!!
POP	<long-size memory>	5!!

Table 6.1   Standardized description for each possible form of PUSH and POP.

PUSH <constant> isn't very common, perhaps because this form of the PUSH instruction didn't appear on the original 8086 computer. It does have a few uses though. Since it's a 1-cycle instruction, PUSH 5 is faster than:

```
MOV AX,5    ;1 cycle
PUSH AX     ;1 cycle
```

so good C compilers use PUSH <constant> to pass a value to a function. For this program:

```
void function_name (int);
void main ()
{
  function_name(5);    /* passing an integer to function_name */
}
```

the translation of the call should look like this:

```
PUSH 5                ;pass a literal integer to the function
CALL function_name    ;call the function (more on this instruction later)
ADD SP,2              ;clean up the stack after regaining control
```

PUSH <constant> is also handy for moving a constant to a segment register:

```
PUSH 0    ;2 bytes, 1 cycle
POP ES    ;1 byte, 3 cycles
```

This code is slightly smaller than the popular alternative:

```
XOR AX,AX    ;2 bytes, 1 cycle
MOV ES,AX    ;2 bytes, 3 cycles
```

We said earlier that if you PUSH an 8-bit constant (such as 5, −1, or indeed any number between −128 to +127) the 486 will subtract 2 from the SP register — that is, the 486 really pushes a word onto the stack, never a byte. Intel is making it hard to misalign the stack. Similarly, if you PUSH an 8-bit constant in 32-bit mode, the 486 will subtract 4 from the ESP register because misalignment won't happen if everything is on a 4-byte boundary (0-mod-4 address).

Despite the fact that PUSH <constant> is moving a constant to memory, it doesn't trigger a Constant-to-Memory Rule penalty. That's one reason why the code on the left is faster than the code on the right:

```
MOV BP,SP    ;1 cycle         MOV BP,SP      ;1 cycle
PUSH 0       ;1 cycle         SUB SP,2       ;1 cycle
                              MOV [BP-2],0   ;!2 cycles
```

Microsoft C may clear an automatic variable using the code on the right, or something similar. It might be worthwhile to watch for such behavior.

In 32-bit mode, ESP (the Extended Stack Pointer) can be used as a pointer. This allows you to express PUSH <register> and POP <register> instructions with LEA. To wit: these two instructions do precisely the same thing as PUSH EAX (1 cycle):

```
LEA ESP,[ESP-4]     ;1 cycle, subtract 4 from ESP register
MOV [ESP],EAX       ;2 cycles, move EAX to [ESP]
```

and these two instructions do precisely the same thing as POP EAX (1 cycle):

```
MOV EAX,[ESP]       ;1 cycle, move [ESP] to EAX
LEA ESP,[ESP+4]     ;1 cycle, add 4 to ESP register
```

These pairs of instructions use LEA for addition and subtraction because the flags register isn't affected by LEA. We show these substitutions only to illustrate precisely what PUSH and POP do. The substitutions are not faster, and we're not suggesting you use them.

By the way, in a function or procedure of a 16-bit application program, it's impossible that SP could be −1. To get there, it would have to have PUSHed or CALLed while SP was equal to +1. This causes a crash. In a 16-bit program that allows no interrupts, however, SP=0 is at least conceivable. In a 32-bit Windows application program, ESP=0 is also not possible. CMP ESP,-1 is guaranteed to return carry flag ON.

The most common use of PUSH and POP is to save and then restore the values of registers or memory locations that need to be changed only temporarily. In our earlier example of a yproc procedure being called from within an xproc procedure and then returning, we wanted to save BP and then restore it for conventional reasons. Our original code, which didn't accomplish this, was:

```
_xproc proc
        . . .
        MOV  BP,SP          ;BP is the pointer
        SUB  SP,100         ;reserve 100 bytes for memx
        MOV  [BP-100],'a'   ;this is location memx[0]
        MOV  [BP-98],'b'    ;this is location memx[2]
        . . .
```

PUSH and POP can be added to this code to achieve the desired result:

```
_xproc proc
       ...
       PUSH BP           ;save the value of BP on entrance to the
                         ;function
       MOV BP,SP         ;BP is the pointer
       SUB SP,100        ;reserve 100 bytes for memx
       MOV [BP-100],'a'  ;this is location memx[0]
       MOV [BP-98],'b'   ;this is location memx[2]
       POP BP            ;restore BP's original value for the
                         ;calling function

       ...
```

In C calls, the convention is to preserve BP, SI, and DI in 16-bit mode and to preserve EBP, ESI, EDI, and EBX in 32-bit mode, so you'll find that most procedures start with PUSH and end with POP.

The secondmost common use of PUSH and POP is to simulate a MOV. There are a few assignments, for instance segment register to segment register, which are illegal, that is:

```
MOV ES,DS     ;ILLEGAL
```

is not allowed. PUSH and POP are legal though, so:

```
PUSH DS    ;1 byte, 3 cycles
POP ES     ;1 byte, 3 cycles
```

provides the intended result — the contents of DS are moved into ES. The same result can also be obtained with:

```
MOV AX,DS    ;2 bytes, 3 cycles
MOV ES,AX    ;2 bytes, 3 cycles
```

Using two MOVs to assign the contents of one segment register to another instead of PUSH and POP is fairly common because this method was faster on 386 machines. On 486's however, using two MOVs takes the same amount of time and costs an additional 2 bytes in addition to using up an extra register, so PUSH and POP should be used instead.

One case where MOV can improve performance is when the operand is a memory operand. For example, the code on the left is faster than the code on the right:

```
MOV AX,mem    ;1 cycle              PUSH mem    ;4 cycles
PUSH AX       ;1 cycle
```

The thirdmost common use of PUSH and POP is to pass parameters when calling subroutines. Calling (and returning from) subroutines is done with the CALL and RET instructions.

The CALL and RET Instructions

In an assembler statement, the syntax of the CALL and RET instructions looks like this:

```
CALL <target>    ;optional comment
RET              ;optional comment
```

The meaning of CALL and RET is imperative:

CALL: **CALL** the procedure located at <target>.

RET: **RET**urn from procedure.

CALL pushes the current code address on the stack and jumps to <target> to execute the procedure found there. The procedure must end in a RET instruction, which transfers control back to the address on the stack. This is then the address the code returns to. CALL's <target> can be a label or a 16-bit or 32-bit register or memory operand; the CALLs are all near. Neither instruction affects the flags register. Since both CALL and RET are jump instructions, they are subject to the Cache-Straddling Rule (see Chapter 3).

CALL and RET have five and one possible forms, respectively, depending on the operand used. Table 6.2 is a standardized description for the possible forms of CALL and RET.

Instruction Mnemonic	Target	Cycle Count
CALL	<distant_label>	3
CALL	<16-bit register>	5
CALL	<32-bit register>	5
CALL	<word-size memory>	5
CALL	<long-size memory>	5
RET		5

Table 6.2   Standardized description for each possible form of CALL and RET.

CALL's functionality can be expressed in these instructions:

```
PUSH $     ;$ stands for current code address
JMP label
```

but since CALL is faster than PUSH and JMP, the instruction shouldn't be replaced with this combination.

RET pops an address off the stack and jumps to it, so its functionality can be expressed in these instructions:

```
POP AX
JMP AX
```

This is just an illustration though. Don't replace RET with this combination.

C uses CALL and RET frequently. Consider the following program:

```
void xproc ()
{
 xproc();
}
void yproc ()
{
 ;
}
```

All C compilers translate this program as follows (in MS-DOS, with the small model):

```
_xproc:
        CALL _yproc
        RET
_yproc:
        RET
```

CALL <register> and CALL <memory> allow you to call via an address. If register DX contains the address of a function named funcx, then CALL DX has the same effect as CALL funcx. Pointers to functions will lead a C compiler to produce either CALL <register> or CALL <memory>. For example, consider the following program:

```
int (*comp)(int);          /* defines a pointer to a function */
int mema;
void main ()
{
 if ( (*comp)(1) ) mema=5;  /* invokes the function via the pointer */
}
```

Borland translates this to:

```
        PUSH 1                  ;pass the parameter
        CALL WORD PTR comp      ;CALL <memory>
        POP CX                  ;Borland uses this instead of ADD SP,2
                                ;the procedure returns an integer to AX
        OR AX,AX                ;testing if AX contains 0 — not best way
        JE ok                   ;if AX was 0 the zero flag will be on now
        MOV mema,5              ;we reach here only if the zero flag is off
ok: ...
```

Though it's a 5-cycle instruction, there's very little that can be done to optimize this form of CALL. Self-modifying code is faster but too tricky. If the function has only two possible addresses, then it's probably faster to use a conditional rather than a function pointer in the C code.

Earlier we said that PUSH and POP are commonly used to pass parameters when calling subroutines. Now that you know how to get to and return from a procedure, we'll return to that subject.

Passing Parameters

C passes parameters by pushing them on the stack. For example, this procedure (with the small model):

```
void xproc (int memx)
{
 yproc(memx);
}
```

is translated as:

```
_xproc:
        PUSH BP
        MOV BP,SP
        MOV CX,[BP+4]
        PUSH CX
        CALL _yproc
        POP CX
        POP BP
        RET
```

The _xproc procedure is assuming that its caller has done the same thing that _xproc itself is about to do — that is, _xproc assumes the caller used PUSH to pass the integer size variable on the stack, then used CALL to transfer control to _xproc, which, once again, saves, uses, and restores the BP register.

When we talked about automatic variables, we said the essential thing was that [BP-n] could be used to refer to the automatics' addresses. Parameters also use BP, but their addresses are referred to using [BP+n] — that is, parameters are above BP on the stack and automatic variables are below BP. (This may explain BP's name; it stands for Base Pointer because it falls in the middle.)

In our _xproc example, the stack has the original BP value at [BP+0], the address of the calling return at [BP+2], and the passed integer at [BP+4]. (These addresses would be different in compact or large models, and, if a far pointer was being passed, the offsets would also be different in all models, which is why a library of subroutines often comes in different versions depending on the model.) When _yproc gets control, its stack will look the same — except that _yproc's return address is an address within _xproc and _yproc's parameter is a copy of the parameter passed to _xproc.

When _xproc regains control from _yproc, it must do some cleanup work because the parameter that _xproc PUSHed is still lying on the stack. Our code does the cleanup with POP CX. An alternative (and perhaps better) way to do this is to use ADD SP,2, which clearly shows that our intention is to throw away the word on the stack, rather than bring it into a register.

A minor optimization opportunity arises in stack cleanup. Since the POP instruction takes the same time as the ADD SP,2 instruction, it doesn't really matter which you choose to use. If you pass two integer parameters, though, Borland C will clean up the stack with two POPs. That is, Borland will translate this original C code:

```
...
xproc(memi,memi);
...
```

to this assembler code:

```
PUSH memi
PUSH memi
CALL _xproc
POP CX
POP CX
```

You could substitute inline assembly code using ADD SP,4 instead of the two POP CX instructions and save a cycle.

By the way, the first instruction in a function often takes 1 cycle longer than expected because of another SECRET RULE, which is true only in 16-bit mode. It does not trigger a penalty if you use 32-bit mode.

◆ SECRET "CALL-PLUS-STACK-USE" RULE:
In 16-bit mode, if the first instruction after a CALL is PUSH or POP or RET, you lose 1 cycle.

The penalty applied by the Call-Plus-Stack-Use Rule is frequent because the first instruction in many functions is PUSH BP.

When passing parameters, then, the caller has to PUSH parameters, CALL the callee, and ADD to the stack to get rid of the parameters. The callee has to preserve BP with a PUSH, move the stack with a MOV BP,SP instruction, restore BP with a POP, and RET to return to the caller. That's a lot of overhead. There are a few ways that you can speed the process up. None of them are universally recommendable but all are worth a thought if the overhead is causing a problem in a particular place:

(1) Pass parameters as globals. If everything is passed via globals, the overhead is reduced by about 50 percent.

(2) Pass parameters as registers. If you use Symantec C, for example, you can tell the compiler to use registers for passing the first two integer parameters. SI and DI will be used to do so — but since the compiler has to preserve and then restore SI and DI by pushing and popping them as well, the gain is slight.

(3) Pass the return address as a global. This works only if the procedure is non-recursive and requires that you keep track of which global variable is associated with which procedure. The result would look like this:

```
int xproc_return_address;
void main ()
{
        __asm MOV WORD PTR xproc_return_address,OFFSET labelb;
        __asm JMP labelb;
labelb:...;
}
void xproc ()
{
        ...
        __asm JMP WORD PTR xproc_return_address;
}
```

The combination is cheaper than CALL, and the JMP in xproc is cheaper than RET.

(4) Use SP rather than BP to address parameters and automatic variables. This works only if you don't do anything deep within the procedure that would change SP. Using SP depends on the fact that ESP can be used as a 32-bit pointer — before you use SP, then, make sure the top bits of ESP are 0 or you'll be addressing somewhere unexpected. The code on the right shows this "improved" method; the code on the left is the conventional method:

```
_xproc:                          _xproc:
        PUSH BP                  .486
        MOV BP,SP                        AND ESP,0FFFFh
        MOV AX,[BP+4]                    MOV AX,[ESP+2]
        ...                      .8086
        POP BP                           ...
        RET                              RET
```

Using SP rather than BP is a method that comes into its own when the program is a true 32-bit application.

Note: You may have noticed that most of the examples in this book use global variables rather than automatics. We've done this because we can predict with confidence that the global variable is in memory, but a compiler with a good optimizer could store an automatic variable in a register instead. Of course, storing an automatic in a register isn't bad — in fact it's very good — but it makes a comparative illustration impossible because we can't depend on all compilers storing the same way.

Function Calls

In the small model, a C compiler handles a function call with a single parameter with:

```
PUSH <parameter>
CALL <function>
```

When the function is entered, the top of the stack looks like this:

16-bit or 32-bit parameter
16-bit or 32-bit return address

A function that returns a 16-bit value uses the AX register. A function that returns a 32-bit value uses DX : AX. When entering a function, there are two ways to get the parameter into the AX register so it can be manipulated. The conventional method is on the left and the tricky way (which saves 2 cycles) is on the right:

```
_xproc:                                  _xproc:
     PUSH BP           ;!2 cycles             POP DX     ;!2 cycles
     MOV BP,SP         ;1 cycle               POP AX     ;1 cycle
     MOV AX,[BP+4]     ;!3 cycles             PUSH AX    ;1 cycle
     ...                                      PUSH DX    ;1 cycle
     POP BP            ;1 cycle               ...
     RET               ;5 cycles              RET        ;5 cycles
```

Another way to save a cycle is to replace the second line (MOV BP, SP) in the _xproc code on the left with MOV EBP, ESP (1 cycle because of the Prefix-Waiver Rule). Because this move is to a 32-bit register, the following MOV AX, [BP+4] instruction is then hit with a 1-cycle Register-Address Rule penalty, rather than a 2-cycle Register-Address Rule penalty.

PUSH won't work on (8-bit) char variables because PUSH is a 16-bit instruction. However, compilers won't use CBW to pass a char parameter. The relevant line in this program:

```
char mema;
void mem2(char);
void main ()
{
 mem2(mema);
}
```

is translated as:

```
MOV AL,mema     ;Load only the AL register
PUSH AX         ;But push the entire AX register
CALL mem2       ;Then call the function
ADD SP,2        ;Clean up after returning from call
```

The Stack and Penalties

Remember that since many routines begin with the instruction PUSH BP in order to make BP safe for use as an address register, it's quite easy to run into the Call-Plus-Stack-Use Rule. For example:

```
int memc;
void main (int mema)
{
 memc=mema;
}
```

will translate to:

```
_main: PUSH BP          ;!2 cycles (_main is being called from somewhere)
       MOV BP,SP         ;1 cycle
       MOV AX,[BP+4]     ;!3 cycles (Register-Address Rule)
       MOV memc,AX       ;1 cycle
       POP BP            ;1 cycle
       RET               ;5 cycles
```

Most procedures with parameters will get such penalties. If you have an initialization type of instruction that could fit before the PUSH BP or before the MOV AX,[BP+4], such an instruction would effectively cost 0 cycles.

Besides the Call-Plus-Stack-Use Rule, two other rules may cause you to lose cycles when manipulating the stack. Both are variations of secret rules which we've already introduced.

◆ **SECRET "CHANGE-SP-THEN-USE-STACK" RULE:**
If the first instruction after an explicit change to SP is PUSH or POP or RET, you lose 2 cycles. If the first instruction after an explicit change to ESP is PUSH or POP or RET, you lose 1 cycle.

The Change-SP-Then-Use-Stack Rule is a variation of the Call-Plus-Stack-Use Rule. Since the PUSH, POP, and RET instructions all implicitly use SP to address the stack, it isn't surprising to find that changing the SP "pointer" also involves a penalty. Note, however, that the stack-changing instruction must be explicit — e.g., MOV SP,SP or ADD SP,0 or the like. Two PUSHes in a row will not trigger the penalty.

◆ SECRET "HI/LO-PUSH" RULE:
If an instruction that changes one half of a register is immediately followed by a PUSH of an entire register, you lose 1 cycle.

The Hi/Lo-Push Rule is an extension of the basic Hi/Lo Rule. (This is not surprising when you consider that PUSH is really an "arithmetic" instruction because it subtracts from the SP register. However, the reasoning is not complete; POP adds to the SP register but does not trigger the penalty.) For example, the penalty is triggered by these instructions:

```
MOV AH,5      ;1 cycle
PUSH AX       ;!2 cycles
```

Merely using the BP register can also trigger a penalty. In reality, there is no such instruction as:

```
MOV BYTE PTR [BP],5     ;looks like a 1 cycle instruction
```

Although an assembler will accept such an instruction, all addressing with the BP register is really done with a displacement — even if the displacement is 0. What the assembler actually executes is:

```
MOV BYTE PTR [BP+0],5     ;!2 cycles (Constant-to-Memory Rule)
```

As we said in Chapter 1, [BP] is really [BP+0] and is thus a Register Pointer plus Constant memory addressing mode. MOV [BP],<constant> therefore triggers the Constant-to-Memory Rule's penalty.

Near Pointers vs. Far Pointers

The three loops in the following program do exactly the same thing, but the timings vary a large amount. The comments show the times achieved with Borland C.

```
#define PSIZE 2000
void main ()
{
 char far *memf;
 char near *memn;
 char huge *memh;
 char buffer[PSIZE];
 int memi;
 long meml;

 for (meml=1; meml<(8000000*2)/PSIZE; ++meml)
 {                            /* 6 seconds */
  for (memi=0,memn=buffer; memi<PSIZE; ++memi,++memn) *memn=*memn;
 }
 for (meml=1; meml<(8000000*2)/PSIZE; ++meml)
 {                            /* 15 seconds */
  for (memi=0,memf=buffer; memi<PSIZE; ++memi,++memf) *memf=*memf;
 }
 for (meml=1; meml<(8000000*2)/PSIZE; ++meml)
 {                            /* 43 seconds */
  for (memi=0,memh=buffer; memi<PSIZE; ++memi,++memh) *memh=*memh;
 }
}
```

The program shows that a memory access with a near pointer is more than twice as fast as an access with a far pointer, and that a memory access with a far pointer is more than twice as fast as an access with a huge pointer. It's clearly worthwhile to use near pointers whenever feasible. (Sometimes this requires you to be explicit about it. Remember that in the compact and large memory models, the default pointer type is always far.)

Since the access time difference between the pointer types is more than 100 percent, it's tempting to state a formula: *If you are going to access every byte in a far buffer more than once, you will save time by copying to a near buffer, processing, and copying back again.*

For example, in the following program the second loop is 30 percent faster than the first loop despite the overhead of the _fmemcpy.

```
#define PSIZE 2000
void main ()
{
 char far *memf;
 char near *memn;
 int memi;
 long meml;

 memf=farmalloc(PSIZE);
 for (meml=1; meml<(8000000*2)/PSIZE; ++meml)
  {                           /* 13 seconds */
  for (memi=0,memf=far_buffer; memi<PSIZE; ++memi,++memf)
   {
   if (*memf++==5) *memf=0;
   }
  }
 for (meml=1; meml<(8000000*2)/PSIZE; ++meml)
  {                           /* 10 seconds */
  _fmemcpy(near_buffer,far_buffer,PSIZE);
  for (memi=0,memn=near_buffer; memi<PSIZE; ++memi,++memn)
   {
   if (*memn++==5) *memn=0;
   }
  _fmemcpy(far_buffer,near_buffer,PSIZE);
  }
 farfree(far_buffer);
}
```

The difference in speed between a near pointer and far pointer looks like a classic *storage hierarchy* situation, with near memory at the top, followed by far memory, then RAM disk, then hard disk, then diskette or CD-ROM, etc. And just as we move data from a diskette file to hard disk before working on them, we might move data from far memory to near memory before working on them — one level up the hierarchy. This is only a helpful illusion, though. The far *memory* isn't slower — it's the far *pointers* that are slower, so here is the same loop once again. This time only the default segment is being changed.

```
#define PSIZE 2000
void main ()
{
 char far *memf;
 char near *memn;
 int memi;
 long meml;

 memf=farmalloc(PSIZE);
 for (meml=1; meml<(ITERATIONS*2)/PSIZE; ++meml)
  {                              /* 8 seconds */
  __asm PUSH DS;
  __asm MOV AX,WORD PTR memf;
  __asm MOV memn,AX;
  __asm MOV AX,WORD PTR memf+2;
  __asm MOV DS,AX;
  for (memi=0; memi<PSIZE; ++memi,++memn)
   {
   if (*memn++==5) *memn=0;
   }
  __asm POP DS;
  }
 farfree(far_buffer);
}
```

Note: after we change the DS register in this code, we do not refer to anything in the default data segment (memi and memn are automatics, so they are not in the default data segment), we do not call any functions, and we do only simple arithmetic and comparison. If we had to do anything more complicated, we wouldn't risk changing DS — we'd do a copy despite the additional cost.

An Optimization Mirage

Suppose a program loop is simultaneously going through two arrays of bytes. It's quite common in optimization books to see a tip that, in effect, tells you to replace the code on the left with the code on the right:

```
          PUSH DI                         PUSH DI
          MOV CX,16                       MOV CX,16
          MOV BX,OFFSET mema               MOV BX,OFFSET mema
          MOV DI,OFFSET mema               MOV DI,OFFSET mema
label_aa: MOV AX,[BX]                      SUB BX,DI
          MOV [DI],AX            label_aa: MOV AX,[BX+DI]
          INC DI                           MOV [DI],AX
          INC BX                           INC DI
          DEC CX                           DEC CX
          JNZ label_aa                     JNZ label_aa
          POP DI                           POP DI
```

The idea looks very clever. In the original code (on the left), both the BX and the DI registers are incremented. But if DI is subtracted from BX before the loop is entered, then [BX+DI] will represent the correct address. For example, at the start BX equals OFFSET mema, after the SUB BX,DI instruction BX equals (OFFSET mema - DI), and when the loop is entered the address [BX+DI] equals (OFFSET mema - DI) + DI, which correctly reduces to (OFFSET mema), the address we want. The scheme means that it's no longer necessary to increment the BX register inside the loop that starts at label_aa:. The loop is shorter by one instruction, and books which suggest this tip claim the revised code (on the right) is faster.

We found no evidence of this claim when we timed the original and revised code on a 486. We believe, as stated in Chapter 1, that double-indexing slows things down.

Where You Are

This chapter discussed how the stack — that is, SS, the Stack Segment — is conventionally manipulated by C functions and procedures and how you can ensure this process runs smoothly. Specifically, you learned:

❖ how to speed up your code by using near pointers instead of far pointers;

❖ that the convention C follows with automatic variables is to use SP — the Stack Pointer — to reserve memory and to use BP — the Base Pointer — as the pointer register which contains the memory address so that [BP-n] will always refer to the appropriate address location;

❖ that well-behaved functions will preserve BP's value by using PUSH to save the value at the beginning and using POP to restore the value at the end of the function to ensure that the entire program always gets the right value for BP;

❖ that besides preserving BP, it is conventional for C calls to preserve SI and DI in 16-bit mode and to preserve EBP, ESI, and EDI in 32-bit mode;

❖ that C functions always return 16-bit values to AX and 32-bit values to DX:AX;

❖ that C also passes parameters by pushing them on the stack so that [BP+n] will always refer to the appropriate address location — and how to speed up this process;

❖ how to call a subroutine with the CALL instruction and to return from a subroutine with the RET instruction;

❖ how to save cycles in stack clean-up.

And finally, you learned another three SECRET RULES of assembler that will help you speed up your code:

◆ **SECRET "CALL-PLUS-STACK-USE" RULE:**
In 16-bit mode, if the first instruction after a CALL is PUSH or POP or RET, you lose 1 cycle.

◆ **SECRET "CHANGE-SP-THEN-USE-STACK" RULE:**
If the first instruction after an explicit change to SP is PUSH or POP or RET, you lose 2 cycles. If the first instruction after an explicit change to ESP is PUSH or POP or RET, you lose 1 cycle.

◆ **SECRET "HI/LO-PUSH" RULE:**
If an instruction that changes one half of a register is immediately followed by a PUSH of an entire register, you lose 1 cycle.

Chapter 7

Multiplication Operations

Multiplication in assembler is done with the IMUL and MUL instructions.

The IMUL Instruction

In an assembler statement, the syntax of the IMUL instruction can involve either one, two, or three explicit operands. The three forms of IMUL look like this:

```
IMUL <source operand>                                         ;optional comment
IMUL <destination operand>,<source operand>                   ;optional comment
IMUL <destination operand>,<source operand_1>,<source operand_2>   ;optional comment
```

IMUL performs signed multiplication. In the first form of the instruction — IMUL <source operand> — the <source operand> can be either an 8-bit, 16-bit, or 32-bit register or memory operand. If <source operand> is 8-bit, IMUL multiplies <source operand> with the value of the AL register and places the result in the AX register. If <source operand> is 16-bit, IMUL multiplies <source operand> with the value of the AX register and places the result in the DX:AX register combination. If <source operand> is 32-bit, IMUL multiplies <source operand> with the value of the EAX register and places the result in the EDX:EAX register combination. This is the earliest form of IMUL, available on 8086 machines.

In the second form of the instruction —
IMUL <destination operand>,<source operand> — the
<source operand> can be an 8-bit constant or a 16-bit or 32-bit register
or memory operand, and the <destination operand> can be a 16-bit or
32-bit register. In this form, IMUL multiplies <source operand> with
<destination operand> and places the result in <destination operand>. If
<destination operand> is 16-bit, <source operand> must be either 8-bit
or 16-bit. If <destination operand> is 32-bit, <source operand> must be
either 8-bit or 32-bit. This form of IMUL became available with the 386.

In the third form of the instruction —
IMUL <destination operand>,<source operand_1>,<source operand_2>
— <source operand_2> is a sign-extended 8-bit constant and <source operand_1>
can be either a 16-bit or 32-bit register or memory operand. The
<destination operand> can be either a 16-bit or 32-bit register and must
match the size of <source operand_1>. If <source operand_1> is 16-bit,
IMUL multiplies the word in <source operand_1> with <source operand_2>
and places the result in the 16-bit <destination operand>. If
<source operand_1> is 32-bit, IMUL multiplies the double-word in
<source operand_1> with <source operand_2> and places the result in
the 32-bit <destination operand>. This form of IMUL became available with
the 286.

Despite what it does, IMUL is not considered to be an arithmetic
operation for the purposes of the Hi/Lo Rule.

The meaning of IMUL is imperative:

Integer (signed) MULtiply the contents of <source operand> with
either AL, AX, or EAX and place the result in the corresponding implied <destination operand> AX, DX:AX or EDX:EAX.

or

Integer (signed) MULtiply the contents of <source operand> with the contents of <destination operand> and place the result in <destination operand>.

or

Integer (signed) MULtiply the contents of <source operand_1>
with the contents of <source operand_2> and place the result in
<destination operand>.

IMUL's effect on the sign, zero, and parity flags is undefined. IMUL clears the overflow and carry flags under the following conditions (if these conditions aren't met, the overflow and carry flags are turned ON):

IMUL FORM	TURNS OVERFLOW & CARRY FLAGS OFF IF
1: 8-bit reg/mem	AL = sign-extend of AL to 16-bits
1: 16-bit reg/mem	AX = sign-extend of AX to 32-bits
1: 32-bit reg/mem	EDX:EAX = sign-extend of EAX to 32-bits
2: 16-bit reg,16-bit reg/mem	result fits exactly in 16-bit register
2: 32-bit reg,32-bit reg/mem	result fits exactly in 32-bit register
3: 16-bit reg,16-bit reg/mem,constant	result fits exactly in 16-bit register
3: 32-bit reg,32-bit reg/mem,constant	result fits exactly in 32-bit register

IMUL has 16 possible forms, depending on the operands used. Table 7.1 is a standardized description for each possible form of IMUL.

The following instructions illustrate some of these forms:

```
IMUL BL                       ;AX = AL*BL
IMUL WORD PTR mem             ;DX:AX = AX*mem
IMUL ECX                      ;EDX:EAX = EAX*ECX
IMUL DX,CX                    ;DX = DX*CX
IMUL EBX,DWORD PTR mem        ;EBX = EBX*mem
IMUL AX,CX,5                  ;AX = CX*5
IMUL EAX,DWORD PTR mem,18     ;EAX = mem*18
```

Instruction Mnemonic	Destination Operand (Result) =	Source_1 Operand (Multiplicand) *	Source_2 Operand (Multiplier)	Cycle Count
IMUL			<8-bit register>	13 to 18
IMUL			<byte-size memory>	13 to 18
IMUL			<16-bit register>	13 to 26
IMUL			<word-size memory>	13 to 26
IMUL			<32-bit register>	13 to 42!!
IMUL			<long-size memory>	13 to 42!!
IMUL	<16-bit register>		,<8-bit constant>	13 to 26
IMUL	<16-bit register>		,<16-bit register>	13 to 26
IMUL	<16-bit register>		,<word-size memory>	13 to 26
IMUL	<32-bit register>		,<8-bit constant>	13 to 42
IMUL	<32-bit register>		,<32-bit register>	13 to 42
IMUL	<32-bit register>		,<long-size memory>	13 to 42
IMUL	<16-bit register>	,<16-bit register>	,<8-bit constant>	13 to 26
IMUL	<16-bit register>	,<word-size memory>	,<8-bit constant>	13 to 26
IMUL	<32-bit register>	,<32-bit register>	,<8-bit constant>	13 to 42
IMUL	<32-bit register>	,<long-size memory>	,<8-bit constant>	13 to 42

Table 7.1   Standardized description for each possible form of IMUL.

For the first time, our form chart doesn't show that an instruction takes a specific number of cycles. Instead, each form of IMUL takes anywhere from 13 cycles to the number of cycles shown at the high end of the range in the Cycles Count column. The number of cycles you can expect depends on the binary magnitude of the instruction's multiplier (that is, the previous power of 2 closest to the value of the multiplier — a multiplier with a value of 2 has a magnitude of 1, a multiplier with a value of 4 has a magnitude of 2, a multiplier with a value of 8 has a magnitude of 3, and so on.) The formula for the number of cycles is:

cycles = 13 or (11 + (magnitude of multiplier)), whichever is higher

For operations involving a 32-bit operand, add an extra cycle for the 32-bit operand override prefix. For the second form of IMUL, add an extra cycle for a 0Fh prefix for instructions of the type:

```
IMUL <16-bit register>,<16-bit register>
IMUL <16-bit register>,<word-size memory>
IMUL <32-bit register>,<32-bit register>
IMUL <32-bit register>,<long-size memory>
```

These Prefix Rule penalties are subject to being waived by the Prefix-Waiver Rule.

For example, IMUL BX means DX:AX will be set to the result of AX (multiplicand) * BX (multiplier). If BX has a value of 18, its magnitude is 4 and IMUL BX takes the higher of 13 cycles or (11+4=15) cycles. The chart below gives the magnitude and cycle count for multiplier values from zero to 255:

MULTIPLIER VALUE	MAGNITUDE	CYCLE COUNT
0 to 7	up to 2	13
8 to 15	3	14
16 to 31	4	15
32 to 63	5	16
64 to 127	6	17
128 to 255	7	18
256 to 511	8	19
512 to 1,023	9	20

If the multiplier is a negative constant, IMUL's speed is erratic. In almost all cases our cycle-count formula applies the same for +<constant> and –<constant>. For instance, the code on the left takes the same number of cycles as the code on the right:

```
MOV AX,mem    ;1 cycle          MOV AX,mem    ;1 cycle
MOV DX,22     ;1 cycle          MOV DX,-22    ;1 cycle
IMUL DX       ;15 cycles        IMUL DX       ;15 cycles
```

The exceptions to the formula are that most small negative numbers (–1, –5, –10, etc.) take 1 cycle longer than their positive counterparts and that negations of powers of 2 (–8, –16, –32, etc.) take 3 cycles longer than their positive counterparts. For instance, the code on the left is 3 cycles faster than the code on the right:

```
MOV AX,mem    ;1 cycle          MOV AX,mem    ;1 cycle
MOV DX,64     ;1 cycle          MOV DX,-64    ;1 cycle
IMUL DX       ;17 cycles        IMUL DX       ;20 cycles
```

Multiplication is a symmetrical operation; the order of the operands has no effect on the result. That is, the expressions 5*15 and 15*5 both produce the same answer, so programmers don't care which one of the two is used, and neither does a C compiler. Another SECRET RULE, though, is that assembler *does* care.

◆ **SECRET "MULTIPLY-BIG-TO-SMALL" RULE:**
Multiplication works faster if the value of <source operand_1> — the multiplicand — is greater than the value of <source operand_2> — the multiplier. This is true whether the multiplicand is specified or merely implied (i.e., AL, AX, EAX, or the <destination operand>).

You can use this rule to speed up IMUL by ensuring your first operand is larger than the second operand.

IMUL is also affected by the method of memory addressing you chose for a memory operand. If you use a Register Pointer plus Constant memory location with IMUL <register>,<memory>,<constant> the Constant-to-Memory Rule will apply the usual 1-cycle penalty. Because it is such a slow instruction, IMUL is also affected by the Delayed-Bytes-and-Pointers Rule, but this time the penalty involved is only 1 cycle. In fact, all the assembler multiplication and division instructions are subject to this 1-cycle penalty, so we'll re-state the rule here in an expanded form.

◆ **SECRET "DELAYED-BYTES-AND-POINTERS" RULE:**
If you move a value to a byte register then use a register pointer such as [BX] or [SI+n], you lose 2 cycles if the first instruction is XCHG. If you move a value to a byte register then use a register pointer such as [BX] or [SI+n], you lose 1 cycle if the first instruction is IMUL or MUL (see below) or IDIV or DIV (see Chapter 8).

C statements of the general form mema=memb*memc; are resolved with IMUL instructions (assuming mema, memb, and memc are integers). Generally, though, one sees that the earliest form of IMUL is used:

```
MOV AX,memb      ;1 cycle
IMUL memc        ;13 to 18 cycles
MOV mema,AX      ;1 cycle, Ignore overflow in DX
```

but the expression could more easily be stated as

```
IMUL AX,memc     ;13 to 26 cycles, Cheaper if memc <1024
```

on 386 and 486 machines. The real problem, though, is simple: IMUL is too expensive an instruction to use in evaluating simple expressions. The compilers aren't completely unaware of this. Borland, for example, will translate the C expression mema=mema*2; into:

```
MOV AX,mema      ;1 cycle
SHL AX,1         ;3 cycles
MOV mema,AX      ;1 cycle
```

which isn't perfect, but it does use SHL instead of IMUL, saving 8 cycles. But Borland only uses this trick for powers of 2. When the expression is mema=mema*3; Borland simply uses the standard instruction:

```
MOV AX,mema      ;1 cycle
MOV DX,3         ;1 cycle
IMUL DX          ;13 cycles
MOV mema,AX      ;1 cycle
```

We're not going to give up so easily. Multiplying by constants is so common, and the potential gain is so substantial, that we think it's worth analyzing the problem and coming up with a general solution.

IMUL takes at least 13 cycles while ADD takes only 1 cycle. One might suppose that it is just as fast to implement mema=memb*13; with one MOV and 12 ADD instructions, as it is to use one IMUL instruction. We timed this supposition and found out that it's actually even faster to replace the IMUL. The code on the left takes 1 cycle less than the code on the right:

```
MOV AX,BX      ;1 cycle              IMUL AX,BX,13      ;14 cycles
ADD AX,BX      ;1 cycle
ADD AX,BX      ;1 cycle
ADD AX,BX      ;1 cycle
ADD AX,BX      ;1 cycle
ADD AX,BX      ;1 cycle
ADD AX,BX      ;1 cycle
ADD AX,BX      ;1 cycle
ADD AX,BX      ;1 cycle
ADD AX,BX      ;1 cycle
ADD AX,BX      ;1 cycle
ADD AX,BX      ;1 cycle
ADD AX,BX      ;1 cycle
```

With a bit of subtlety, ADD can be used to multiply by 13 even more quickly. AX can be added to itself three times (that is, $AX = AX \wedge 3$), then BX can be added to the result five times. This takes only 9 cycles, far fewer than IMUL ever can:

```
MOV AX,BX      ;1 cycle
ADD AX,AX      ;1 cycle
ADD AX,AX      ;1 cycle
ADD AX,AX      ;1 cycle
ADD AX,BX      ;1 cycle
ADD AX,BX      ;1 cycle
ADD AX,BX      ;1 cycle
ADD AX,BX      ;1 cycle
ADD AX,BX      ;1 cycle
```

Even this can be improved on though. The three ADD AX,AX instructions can be replaced by one SHL AX,3 instruction, saving 1 cycle. Better yet, they can be replaced by a SHL AX,4 instruction, under the reasoning that multiplying by 16 and then subtracting 3 times is faster than multiplying by 8 and then adding 5 times. Multiplying by 13 now takes 6 cycles:

```
MOV AX,BX      ;1 cycle
SHL AX,4       ;2 cycles
SUB AX,BX      ;1 cycle
SUB AX,BX      ;1 cycle
SUB AX,BX      ;1 cycle
```

An alternative that also takes 6 cycles effectively multiplies BX by 3 before subtracting BX from AX. This destroys the BX register — something the IMUL instruction wouldn't do — and can't be used if the source and result registers are the same. Nevertheless, it's a legitimate final stroke:

```
MOV AX,BX    ;1 cycle
SHL AX,4     ;2 cycles
SUB AX,BX    ;1 cycle, in effect, multiply BX by 1
ADD BX,BX    ;1 cycle, in effect, multiply BX by 2
SUB AX,BX    ;1 cycle, subtract BX from AX after "multiplying by 3"
```

The rules for multiplying by a constant are:

(1) Find the next power of 2 which is greater than the constant and the last power of 2 which is less than the constant. Choose the power of 2 that is closest to the constant to work with. For instance, for a constant of 13, the next power of 2 is 16 and the last power of 2 is 8. The power closest to 13 is 16 and this is the power to work with.

(2) Use ADD or SHL to multiply the <destination operand> by the power chosen in step (1).

(3) Calculate the remainder; that is, the difference between the chosen power and the constant (for instance, $16 - 13 = 3$). The remainder might be positive, negative, or zero. If the remainder is 0, the multiplication is complete.

(4) For any remainder other than 0, find the closest power of 2 for the remainder, using the same method as in step (1). For instance, with a remainder of 3, the nearest power is 2 and the remainder of the remainder is thus 1. All you can do at this stage is ADD or SUB, so if this amount is large then you will have to use the IMUL instruction after all.

(5) Use ADD or SHL to multiply the remainder by the power chosen in step (4).

(6) Use ADD or SUB to add or subtract the multiplied remainder to/from the <destination operand>.

Using this process, the following code can be substituted for IMUL when multiplying by numbers from 2 to 10. The code uses the case where <source operand> is a register — this allows use of the instruction ADD <source>,<source>. The gains shown are a comparison with the IMUL instruction.

```
*2 (gain: 11 cycles)         *3 (gain: 10 cycles)              *4 (gain: 10 cycles)
MOV AX,source   ;1 cycle     MOV AX,source      ;1 cycle      MOV AX,source      ;1 cycle
ADD AX,AX       ;1 cycle     ADD AX,AX          ;1 cycle      ADD AX,AX          ;1 cycle
                             ADD AX,source      ;1 cycle      ADD AX,AX          ;1 cycle


*5 (gain: 9 cycles)          *6 (gain: 8 cycles)              *7 (gain: 9 cycles)
MOV AX,source   ;1 cycle     MOV AX,source      ;1 cycle      MOV AX,source      ;1 cycle
ADD AX,AX       ;1 cycle     ADD AX,AX          ;1 cycle      SHL AX,3           ;2 cycles
ADD AX,AX       ;1 cycle     ADD AX,AX          ;1 cycle      SUB AX,source      ;1 cycle
ADD AX,source   ;1 cycle     ADD source,source  ;1 cycle
                             ADD AX,source      ;1 cycle


*8 (gain: 11 cycles)         *9 (gain: 10 cycles)             *10 (gain: 9 cycles)
MOV AX,source   ;1 cycle     MOV AX,source      ;1 cycle      MOV AX,source      ;1 cycle
SHL AX,3        ;2 cycles    SHL AX,3           ;2 cycles     SHL AX,3           ;2 cycles
                             ADD AX,source      ;1 cycle      ADD source,source  ;1 cycle
                                                              ADD AX,source      ;1 cycle
```

This process has been automated by Borland TASM and Microsoft MASM using a special instruction macro called FASTIMUL, which we'll discuss at the end of this chapter.

By the way, be wary with expressions like mema=mema*-1; — some compilers will see the multiply sign and translate the expression using an IMUL. For example, only Microsoft translates an expression that multiplies a long integer with –1 as:

```
NEG memb          ;3 cycles
ADC memb+2,0      ;4 cycles
NEG memb+2        ;3 cycles
```

To make sure your compiler uses the less expensive NEG instruction to resolve mema=mema*-1; types of expressions, use expressions of the type mema=-mema; instead. All compilers will reliably translate mema=-mema; into:

```
MOV AX,mema       ;1 cycle
NEG AX            ;1 cycle
MOV mema,AX       ;1 cycle
```

which is much faster. (This wastes bytes though. See our note on this point in the discussion of NEG in Chapter 5. It's better to force NEG mema.)

32-Bit Multiplies

This code multiplies two long integers mema and memb, yielding a long integer memc:

```
long int mema,memb,memc;
void main ()
{
 memc=mema*memb;
}
```

Multiword multiplying is complex-looking. The 16-bit instructions to resolve memc=mema*memb; are:

```
MOV AX,WORD PTR mema         ;Multiply low 16 bits of mema
IMUL WORD PTR memb           ;by low 16 bits of memb.
MOV WORD PTR memc,AX         ;memc = result, which is in DX:AX
MOV WORD PTR memc+2,DX
MOV AX,WORD PTR mema+2       ;Multiply high 16 bits of mema
IMUL WORD PTR memb+2         ;by high 16 bits of memb.
ADD WORD PTR memc+2,AX       ;Add result to memc
```

The translation is more straightforward when instructions with 32-bit operands are used:

```
MOV EAX,DWORD PTR mema       ;Multiply all 32 bits of mema
IMUL DWORD PTR memb          ;by all 32 bits of memb.
MOV DWORD PTR memc,EAX       ;memc = result, EAX is the low 32 bits
```

The gain is 38 percent. Since some C compilers won't generate this translation, the following is the same program except that memc=mema*memb; is replaced with inline assembly:

```
long int mema,memb,memc;
void main ()
{
  __asm DB 66h;
  __asm MOV AX,WORD PTR mema;
  __asm DB 66h;
  __asm IMUL WORD PTR memb;
  __asm DB 66h;
  __asm MOV WORD PTR memc,AX;
}
```

The MUL Instruction

In an assembler statement, the syntax of the MUL instruction looks like this:

```
MUL <source operand>    ;optional comment
```

MUL performs unsigned multiplication. This is its major difference with IMUL, which performs signed multiplication. The other difference between the two instructions is that MUL has no optional syntax forms.

MUL's <source operand> can be either an 8-bit, 16-bit, or 32-bit register or memory operand. If <source operand> is 8-bit, MUL multiplies <source operand> with the value of the AL register and places the result in the AX register. If <source operand> is 16-bit, MUL multiplies <source operand> with the value of the AX register and places the result in the DX : AX register combination. If <source operand> is 32-bit, MUL multiplies <source operand> with the value of the EAX register and places the result in the EDX : EAX register combination.

Despite what it does, MUL, like IMUL, is not considered to be an arithmetic operation for the purposes of the Hi/Lo Rule. MUL is, however, affected by the Delayed-Bytes-and-Pointers Rule. The penalty involved for violating the rule is 1 cycle.

The meaning of MUL is imperative:

(unsigned) MULtiply the contents of <source operand> with either AL, AX, or EAX and place the result in the corresponding implied <destination operand> AX, DX : AX or EDX : EAX.

MUL's effect on the sign, zero, and parity flags is undefined. MUL clears the overflow and carry flags if the upper half of the operation's result is 0 — that is, when a byte operand is multiplied by AL and the result placed in AX, both flags are turned OFF if the AH value is 0; when a word operand is multiplied by AX and the result placed in DX : AX, both flags are turned OFF if the DX value is 0; and when a double-word operand is multiplied by EAX and the result placed in EDX : EAX, both flags are turned OFF if the EDX value is 0 — otherwise the overflow and carry flags are turned ON.

MUL has six possible forms, depending on the operands used. Table 7.2 is a standardized description for each possible form of MUL.

The following instructions illustrate these forms:

```
MUL BL              ;AX = AL*BL
MUL BYTE PTR mem    ;AX = AL*mem
MUL CX              ;DX:AX = AX*CX
MUL WORD PTR mem    ;DX:AX = AX*mem
MUL ECX             ;EDX:EAX = EAX*ECX
MUL DWORD PTR mem   ;EDX:EAX = EAX*mem
```

As with IMUL, our form chart doesn't show that MUL takes a specific number of cycles. Instead, each form of MUL takes anywhere from 13 cycles to the number of cycles shown at the high end of the range in the Cycles Count column. The number of cycles you can expect depends on the same formula (and the corollaries to it) we described earlier for IMUL, that is:

cycles = 13 or (11 + (magnitude of multiplier)), whichever is higher

MUL is also affected by the Multiply-Big-to-Small Rule. This means that the code on the left is faster than the code on the right:

```
MOV BX,37      ;1 cycle         MOV AX,37      ;1 cycle
MOV AX,4000    ;1 cycle         MOV BX,4000    ;1 cycle
MUL BX         ;16 cycles       MUL BX         ;22 cycles
```

In C code:

```
unsigned   mema=37,memb=4000,memc;
void main ()
{
 memc=mema*memb;
}
```

Instruction Mnemonic	Source Operand (Multiplier)	Cycle Count
MUL	<8-bit register>	13 to 18
MUL	<byte-size memory>	13 to 18
MUL	<16-bit register>	13 to 26
MUL	<word-size memory>	13 to 26
MUL	<32-bit register>	13 to 42
MUL	<long-size memory>	13 to 42

Table 7.2   Standardized description for each possible form of MUL.

This program will run faster if the C statement memc=mema*memb; is replaced with memc=memb*mema; because all compilers will move the first operand (mema) into AX and multiply by the second operand (memb) — the compilers don't know which operand is bigger, nor is there any way to influence which operand will be loaded first. Usually you won't know either, but if you know enough about the data to make a reasonable guess, your gain will be about 10 percent to 30 percent.

Compilers will improperly resolve mema=memb*memc; if mema is an integer but memb and memc are chars. Their deficiencies can be touched up with a bit of inline assembler:

```
__asm MOV AL,memb;
__asm MUL BYTE PTR memc;
__asm MOV mema,AX;
```

This is not a major problem, though, since expressions like mema=memb*memc; don't occur too frequently. A far more common occurrence is implicit multiplication by an unsigned constant, hidden in C addresses like memb[3] or memb[memx][5]. In the case of memb[3] there may be a multiplication depending on memb's type — if memb is an int, multiply by 2 to get the offset; if memb is a long, multiply by 4; and so on. In the case of memb[memx][5] the value of memx must be multiplied by some constant no matter what memb's type is. The nature of the problem is simple: MUL is too expensive an instruction to use in evaluating such addresses and should be replaced with inline assembler routines using ADD, SHL, MOV, SUB, and NEG as we've shown. Alternatively, define arrays so that the size of each element of the array is a power of 2, using filler bytes as necessary. This will ensure that your compiler will use shift instructions rather than MUL to calculate array addresses.

The FASTIMUL Instruction

FASTIMUL is a pseudo-instruction (actually a macro) supported by Borland TASM and Microsoft MASM. FASTIMUL is the same syntactically as the three-operand version of the assembler IMUL instruction but in fact resolves to a combination of assembler MOV, SHL, ADD, SUB, and (if multiplying by a negative number) NEG instructions.

In an assembler statement, the syntax of the FASTIMUL instruction looks like this:

```
FASTIMUL <destination operand>,<source operand_1>,<source operand_2> ;optional comment
```

FASTIMUL performs signed multiplication with a constant — <source operand_2> is a sign-extended 8-bit constant and <source operand_1> can be either a 16-bit or 32-bit register or memory operand. The <destination operand> can be either a 16-bit or 32-bit register and must match the size of <source operand_1>. If <source operand_1> is 16-bit, FASTIMUL multiplies the word in <source operand_1> with <source operand_2> and places the result in the 16-bit <destination operand>. If <source operand_1> is 32-bit, FASTIMUL multiplies the double-word in <source operand_1> with <source operand_2> and places the result in the 32-bit <destination operand>.

The meaning of FASTIMUL is imperative:

FAST Integer (signed) MULtiply the contents of <source operand_1> with the contents of <source operand_2> and place the result in <destination operand>.

FASTIMUL has four possible forms, depending on the operands used. Table 7.3 is a standardized description for each possible form of FASTIMUL.

Because it resolves to different combinations of assembler instructions, FASTIMUL may or may not be subject to the Hi/Lo Rule. Its effect on the flags in the flags register and the number of cycles used up by the operation is also undefined — both depend on exactly how each individual operation is resolved. You can be sure that FASTIMUL will be faster than IMUL, but your code must be able to tolerate the fact that the source register is destroyed and the flags won't necessarily be the same after the operation.

Instruction Mnemonic	Destination Operand (Result) =	Source_1 Operand (Multiplicand) *	Source_2 Operand (Multiplier)	Cycle Count
FASTIMUL	<16-bit register>	,<16-bit register>	,<8-bit constant>	undefined
FASTIMUL	<16-bit register>	,<word-size memory>	,<8-bit constant>	undefined
FASTIMUL	<32-bit register>	,<32-bit register>	,<8-bit constant>	undefined
FASTIMUL	<32-bit register>	,<long-size memory>	,<8-bit constant>	undefined

Table 7.3   Standardized description for each possible form of FASTIMUL.

Borland TASM 3.0's FASTIMUL is far from optional. These are the defects we found in it:

(1) FASTIMUL is tuned for 386s. On a 386 the SHL and ADD instructions take more cycles (and the IMUL instruction takes fewer cycles) than on a 486. There are many cases where TASM 3.0 decides — mistakenly — that the operation resolves into so many SHLs and ADDs that it's cheaper to use a standard IMUL instruction.

(2) You can't change the tuning because the FASTIMUL macro's source code is not supplied.

(3) FASTIMUL generates the instruction SHL <register>,1 even though the instruction ADD <register>,<register> is faster.

(4) When it generates SHL <memory>,1 FASTIMUL uses the wrong machine code.

(5) FASTIMUL uses NEG and ADD to do subtractions where a simple SUB would suffice.

(6) FASTIMUL gives the wrong results when <source operand_1> and <destination operand> are the same. Optimization is impossible in such circumstances but an error message would be nice.

(7) FASTIMUL doesn't work with 8-bit registers. Neither does IMUL itself, of course, but the limitation isn't necessary when one is using SHL and ADD.

These defects can all be corrected. Listing 7.1 (see page 196) does just that — it is a macro that does the fastest possible multiplies on 486s. As macros go, this is a very long and complex one — it uses tricks like defining macros within macros, determining whether a macro operand is a register and what its size is, finding the most significant byte in a constant, using the fastest variant of SHL <operand>,1, and using alternate code depending on CPU type. Macros are beyond the scope of this book, so if you skip this listing you will not suffer in later chapters. We've tried to make it as clear as possible, though, and anyone interested in macros may find some instructive methods herein which are far from intuitive or obvious.

Although (regrettably) you cannot use a macro like ZOOMIMUL (see Listing 7.1) with inline assembly, there's an easy fix: use it with Borland TASM or Microsoft MASM, get a listing of the code with the macros expanded, and copy the expanded code into your C program. To make this easier, the diskette at the back of this book contains ZOOMIMUL.ASM, as well as a code listing of ZOOMIMUL.ASM results for all constants up to 2000.

By the way, there are one-instruction replacements for the ZOOMIMUL suggestions if <source operand_1> is a register and <source operand_2> is one of the constants 2, 3, 4, 5, 8, or 9:

```
LEA AX,[EBX*2]          ;AX = BX * 2 5% faster than ZOOMIMUL
LEA AX,[EBX*2+EBX]      ;AX = BX * 3 15% faster than ZOOMIMUL
LEA AX,[EBX*4]          ;AX = BX * 4 slower than ZOOMIMUL
LEA AX,[EBX*4+EBX]      ;AX = BX * 5 slower than ZOOMIMUL
LEA AX,[EBX*8]          ;AX = BX * 8 same speed as ZOOMIMUL
LEA AX,[EBX*8+EBX]      ;AX = BX * 9 slower than ZOOMIMUL
```

In 16-bit mode, only the multiply-by-2 and multiply-by-3 calculations involving LEA can beat the operations resolved using ADD and the shift instructions. In 32-bit operating systems, the LEA instructions deliver more. Since 32-bit addressing is not a feature of normal MS-DOS or Windows 3.x, we merely note the possibility.

Ending on a warning note, we have to emphasize that ZOOMIMUL is for Intel 486s only. On 386s the possibility of gain is somewhat less frequent because SHL, ADD, and IMUL use different numbers of cycles. And Cyrix claims that on their 486 clone the IMUL instruction is 4 times faster than on an Intel 486 — a fact that would make ZOOMIMUL useless whenever the CYCLECOUNTER value reached 5 or more.

Where You Are

In this chapter, you learned:

❖ how to do signed multiplication with IMUL and unsigned multiplication with MUL;

❖ how the order of your operands will affect the multiplication instruction's speed;

❖ how to speed up multiplication by avoiding IMUL and MUL as much as possible, either by using the FASTIMUL macro or by using combinations of MOV, ADD, NEG, and shift instructions — especially when your multiplier is a constant.

And finally, you learned two more SECRET RULES of assembler that will help you speed up your code:

◆ **SECRET "MULTIPLY-BIG-TO-SMALL" RULE:**
Multiplication works faster if the value of <source operand_1> — the multiplicand — is greater than the value of <source operand_2> — the multiplier. This is true whether the multiplicand is specified or merely implied (i.e., AL, AX, EAX, or the <destination operand>).

◆ **SECRET "DELAYED-BYTES-AND-POINTERS" RULE:**
If you move a value to a byte register then use a register pointer such as [BX] or [SI+n], you lose 2 cycles if the first instruction is XCHG. If you move a value to a byte register then use a register pointer such as [BX] or [SI+n], you lose 1 cycle if the first instruction is IMUL, MUL, IDIV, or DIV.

Listing 7.1   ZOOMIMUL.ASM

```
;*** LISTING OF ZOOMIMUL.ASM start ***
;--- Doesn't work for non-register arguments
;--- Doesn't work if source operand = destination operand

;ZOOMIMUL
;Copyright (c) 1994 by Ocelot Computer Services Inc. All rights reserved.

NEARESTPOWEROF2 macro value  ;; This is nested within ZOOMIMUL
foo enum f1=value
NEXTPOWEROF2 = WIDTH foo
LASTPOWEROF2 = (NEXTPOWEROF2-1)

DISTANCETONEXTPOWEROF2 = ((1 SHL NEXTPOWEROF2) - value)
DISTANCETOLASTPOWEROF2 = (value - (1 SHL LASTPOWEROF2))

if (DISTANCETOLASTPOWEROF2 LE DISTANCETONEXTPOWEROF2)
POWEROF2 = LASTPOWEROF2
else
POWEROF2 = NEXTPOWEROF2
endif

 endm

;Shift left by a power of 2, but replace SHL with more efficient instructions
;if possible. If you know that the program will only be running on 386s or
;486s, specify .386 or .486 before calling! We can use a much better shifting
;instruction if we know it's a 386 or 486. SHL_X is for use with registers.
SHL_X macro arg,shiftcount,argsize
SHIFT_CYCLECOUNTER = 0
if (shiftcount EQ 0)     ;;Do nothing for a zero-shift.
 exitm
 endif
;;Determine if arg is a register.
SHLEQA = $
 if argsize
 DEC word ptr arg
 else
 DEC byte ptr arg
 endif
SHLEQB = $
SHLEQC = (SHLEQB - SHLEQA)
ORG SHLEQA
if (SHLEQC LE 2)
 ARG_IS_A_REGISTER = 1
else
 ARG_IS_A_REGISTER = 0
endif

FAST_SHL = 0
if (@CPU AND 8)
 if (shiftcount GT 2)
  FAST_SHL = 1
 endif
 if (ARG_IS_A_REGISTER EQ 0)
  FAST_SHL = 1
 endif
endif
```

Listing 7.1 ZOOMIMUL.ASM (continued)

```
if (FAST_SHL)
 SHLEQD = $
 if argsize
  SHL word ptr arg,shiftcount
 else
  SHL byte ptr arg,shiftcount
  endif
 if (ARG_IS_A_REGISTER)
  SHIFT_CYCLECOUNTER = SHIFT_CYCLECOUNTER + 2
 else
  SHIFT_CYCLECOUNTER = SHIFT_CYCLECOUNTER + 3
  endif
 if (shiftcount EQ 1)
  SHLEQJ = $
  if argsize
 MOV word ptr arg,77
  else
 MOV byte ptr arg,77
  endif
 SHLEQK = $
 ARG_IS_8_BIT = 0
  if ((SHLEQK - SHLEQJ) EQ 2)
 ARG_IS_8_BIT = 1
  endif
 if (ARG_IS_A_REGISTER EQ 0)
 if ((SHLEQK - SHLEQJ) EQ 3)
 ARG_IS_8_BIT = 1
  endif
 ;;Can be 4 if mode switch for 32-bit (the 66h byte)!
 endif
 ORG SHLEQK
 SHLEQE = $
 ORG SHLEQD
 if ARG_IS_8_BIT
 DB 0C0h
 else
 DB 0C1h
 endif
 ORG SHLEQE
 DB 1
 endif
else
 rept shiftcount
  if ARG_IS_A_REGISTER
  ADD arg,arg
  SHIFT_CYCLECOUNTER = SHIFT_CYCLECOUNTER + 1
  else
  if argsize
   SHL word ptr arg,1
  else
   SHL byte ptr arg,1
   endif
  SHIFT_CYCLECOUNTER = SHIFT_CYCLECOUNTER + 4
  endif
  endm
endif
endm
```

Listing 7.1 ZOOMIMUL.ASM (continued)

```
ZOOMIMUL macro destination_r,source_rm,value
;; Determine if destination register is a byte or a word, e.g. if AL or AX.
;; Since MOV AL,77 is a two-byte instruction and MOV AX,77 is a three-byte
;; instruction and MOV EAX,77 is even more, we can find out by emitting
;; MOV <destination_r>,77 and then checking whether it's two bytes or not.
;; We ORG so as to write over the instruction. Set DESTINATION_IS_WORDSIZE
;; to TRUE if it's not byte size.
EQUA1 = $
 MOV destination_r,77
if (($-EQUA1) EQ 2)
 DESTINATION_IS_WORDSIZE = 1 ;;destination_r is a word
 word_or_byte_ptr equ <word ptr>
else
 DESTINATION_IS_WORDSIZE = 0 ;;destination_r is a byte
 word_or_byte_ptr equ <byte ptr>
endif
 ORG EQUA1

;; Determine if source and destination. are the same thing. We won't find out
;; if we've used EQU to give the same register two different names and we're
;; using the different names now, but that scenario sounds somewhat unlikely.
IFIDNI <destination_r>,<source_rm>
 DESTINATION_EQ_SOURCE = 1
else
 DESTINATION_EQ_SOURCE = 0
endif

;; Determine mode. If it's 32-bit mode then MOV AX,77 will cause an
;; extra byte to be generated (for the 66h prefix).
EQAC1 = $
 MOV AX,77
EQAC2 = $
EQAC3 = (EQAC2-EQAC1)
if (EQAC3-2)
 MODE_IS_32_BIT = 1
else
 MODE_IS_32_BIT = 0
endif
 ORG EQAC1

;; Determine if source_rm is a register (again, just by looking at the $s).
;; If it's a register, we can act on it directly without needing to MOV.
EQAB1 = $
 MOV word_or_byte_ptr source_rm,77
EQAB2 = $
EQAB3 = (EQAB2-EQAB1)
SOURCE_IS_REGISTER = 0  ;; Initially, assume source is not a register
if DESTINATION_IS_WORDSIZE
if MODE_IS_32_BIT
if (EQAB3-?)
 SOURCE_IS_REGISTER = 1
endif
else
if (EQAB3-?)
 SOURCE_IS_REGISTER = 1
endif
endif
else
if (EQAB3-3)
 SOURCE_IS_REGISTER = 1
endif
endif
```

Listing 7.1   ZOOMIMUL.ASM (continued)

```
ORG EQAB1

if (value EQ 0)
 XOR destination_r,destination_r
 CYCLECOUNTER = 1
 exitm
endif

;; We only need to move the source to the destination if it's not already
;; equal to it. ZOOMIMUL would generate a MOV instruction here regardless.
if DESTINATION_EQ_SOURCE
else
 MOV destination_r,source_rm
 CYCLECOUNTER = 1
endif

if (value LT 0)
 absolutevalue =-value
else
 absolutevalue=value
 endif

if (ABSOLUTEVALUE GT 128)    ;;Check for certain overflow
 errif (DESTINATION_IS_WORDSIZE EQ 0) "Value > Maximum Byte Value"
 errif (ABSOLUTEVALUE GT 32768) "Value > Maximum Word Value"
 ;;!!! But it could be a 32-bit register !!!
 endif

;; Now figure out the nearest power of 2. See the macro def before this one.
 NEARESTPOWEROF2 absolutevalue

;; Generate the shifts for POWEROF2. If it's a 1-bit shift, ADD is faster.
;; We can do far more efficient shifting if .386 or .486 is specified!
 SHL_X destination_r,POWEROF2,DESTINATION_IS_WORDSIZE
 CYCLECOUNTER = CYCLECOUNTER + SHIFT_CYCLECOUNTER

newvalue = (absolutevalue - (1 SHL POWEROF2)) ;;Something close to this.

if (newvalue LT 0)
 newvalue=-newvalue
 add_or_sub macro arg1,arg2
  SUB arg1,arg2
  endm
else
 add_or_sub macro arg1,arg2
  ADD arg1,arg2
  endm
endif
```

Listing 7.1 ZOOMIMUL.ASM (continued)

```
if (newvalue GT 0)
 NEARESTPOWEROF2 newvalue
 finalvalue = (newvalue - (1 SHL LASTPOWEROF2))
  if (finalvalue GT 13)
    CYCLECOUNTER = 100
  else
  rept finalvalue
 ADD_OR_SUB destination_r,source_rm
 CYCLECOUNTER = CYCLECOUNTER + 1
 endm
 if (LASTPOWEROF2 GT 0)
  SHL_X source_rm,LASTPOWEROF2,DESTINATION_IS_WORDSIZE
  CYCLECOUNTER = CYCLECOUNTER + SHIFT_CYCLECOUNTER
  endif
   ADD_OR_SUB destination_r,source_rm
  CYCLECOUNTER = CYCLECOUNTER + 1
  endif
endif

if (value LT 0)
 NEG destination_r
 CYCLECOUNTER = CYCLECOUNTER + 1
endif

;; Determine how many cycles our shifts and adds use up. If it looks like a
;; bigger amount than we'd take with IMUL, use IMUL. This form of IMUL will
;; work on a 286, only with an 8086 do we have extra work.
if (CYCLECOUNTER GT 13)     ;; or 18?? or 26??
 ORG EQAB1
if (@Cpu AND 4)
 ;;WON'T WORK IF 8-BIT. But values up to 128 would never reach here?
 IMUL destination_r,source_rm,value
else
 PUSH AX
 PUSH DX
 MOV AX,value
 IMUL word_or_byte_ptr source_rm
 POP DX
 POP AX
endif
 endif

 PURGE add_or_sub
 endm

;*** LISTING OF ZOOMIMUL.ASM ends ***
```

Chapter 8

Division Operations

Division in assembler is done with the IDIV, DIV, and AAM instructions.

The IDIV and DIV Instructions

In an assembler statement, the syntax of the IDIV and DIV instructions looks like this:

```
IDIV <source operand>    ;optional comment
DIV <source operand>     ;optional comment
```

The inputs to a divide instruction are the divisor (what you're dividing by) and the dividend (what you're dividing). The outputs from a divide instruction are the quotient (what the result is) and the remainder (what's left over). Divide instructions always include the divisor — this is the <source operand> in the syntax diagram. The dividend, the quotient, and the remainder, however, are *not* specified — they are implicitly some combination of the AX and DX registers, depending on the divisor's size.

IDIV performs signed division with the <source operand> as the divisor. IDIV's dividend must be sign-extended. DIV performs unsigned division with the <source operand> as the divisor. For both instructions, the dividend, quotient, and remainder are implicitly assigned to fixed registers based on the size of the divisor. The <source operand> can be either an 8-bit, 16-bit, or 32-bit register or memory operand.

If <source operand> is 8-bit, the AH register must contain the sign-extension of the AL register if you want to use the IDIV instruction. For 8-bit divides, IDIV and DIV divide the value of the AX register by the value of <source operand> and place the result in the AL register. The remainder is placed in the AH register.

If <source operand> is 16-bit, the DX register must contain the sign-extension of the AX register if you want to use the IDIV instruction. For 16-bit divides, IDIV and DIV divide the value of the DX : AX register combination by the value of <source operand> and place the result in the AX register. The remainder is placed in the DX register.

If <source operand> is 32-bit, the EDX register must contain the sign-extension of the EAX register if you want to use the IDIV instruction. For 32-bit divides, IDIV and DIV divide the value of the EDX : EAX register combination by the value of <source operand> and place the result in the EAX register. The remainder is placed in the EDX register.

Despite what they do, IDIV and DIV are not considered to be arithmetic operations for the purposes of the Hi/Lo Rule. Because they are such slow instructions, though, IDIV and DIV are affected by the Delayed-Bytes-and-Pointers Rule. The penalty involved for violating the rule is 1 cycle.

The meaning of IDIV and DIV is imperative:

IDIV: Integer (signed) DIVide the value of the implied sign-extended <dividend> AX, DX : AX or EDX : EAX by the value of <source operand> and place the result in the corresponding implied <destination operands> AL (remainder to AH), AX (remainder to DX) or EAX (remainder to EDX).

DIV: (unsigned) DIVide the value of the implied <dividend> AX, DX : AX or EDX : EAX by the value of <source operand> and place the result in the corresponding implied <destination operands> AL (remainder to AH), AX (remainder to DX) or EAX (remainder to EDX).

Intel's documentation states that the effect of IDIV and DIV on the flags in the flags register is undefined. In fact, though, the 486 chip sets the zero flag and the carry flag ON if there is a remainder and OFF if there is no remainder. Do not depend on the state of any of the flags after doing a division.

IDIV and DIV have six possible forms, depending on the operands used. Table 8.1 is a standardized description for each possible form of IDIV and DIV.

The following sets of instructions illustrate some of these forms:

```
MOV AX,5       ;divide 5
MOV CL,2       ;by 2
IDIV CL        ;Result: AL contains 2, AH contains 1

XOR DX,DX
MOV AX,0100h   ;divide 0x00000100
MOV CX,0100h   ;by 0x0100
DIV CX         ;Result: AX contains 1, DX contains 0
```

IDIV and DIV are both slow instructions that will trigger a Delayed-Bytes-and-Pointers Rule penalty. For example:

```
DIV CL         ;16 cycles
MOV DX,[BX]    ;!2 cycles (Delayed-Bytes-and-Pointers Rule)
```

The speed of a DIV instruction, in cycles, is always 8 + (number of bits in the divisor) — that is 8 + (8-bits) for a total of 16 cycles if <source operand> is an 8-bit register or byte-size memory operand. DIV is also the only arithmetic instruction which takes the same time regardless of whether <source operand> is a register or a memory operand. IDIV instructions are slower: they always take 11 + (number of bits in the divisor) cycles, plus 1 more cycle if the divisor is a memory operand. Thus, division is slower even than multiplication and an order of magnitude slower than all other arithmetic instructions. Because of this, we're going to devote correspondingly more space to the quest for various tricks that can speed up division.

Instruction Mnemonic	Source Operand (Divisor)	Cycle Count
IDIV	<8-bit register>	19
IDIV	<byte-size memory>	20
IDIV	<16-bit register>	27
IDIV	<word-size memory>	28
IDIV	<32-bit register>	43
IDIV	<long-size memory>	44
DIV	<8-bit register>	16
DIV	<byte-size memory>	16
DIV	<16-bit register>	24
DIV	<word-size memory>	24
DIV	<32-bit register>	40
DIV	<long-size memory>	40

Table 8.1   Standardized description for each possible form of IDIV and DIV.

Shift and Subtract — Part One

In Chapter 7, we suggested that if you were multiplying with a constant, you could replace IMUL and MUL with combinations of SHL and ADD instructions to save cycles. IDIV and DIV are in a similar position — they are both very expensive instructions to use. Since a divide instruction is the reverse of a multiply instruction, is it possible to get the same effect with combinations of SHR and SUB instructions and so save cycles again?

To see if such a replacement works better than using IDIV and DIV, it's first necessary to normalize the divisor and the dividend — that is, to shift both operands so that the highest 1-bit is in the same position of both bytes, words or double-words (as the case may be). Once this is done, the bits must be compared and shifted one bit at a time.

Normalizing the operands is a long process. First, find out where the highest 1-bit is. Knowing the position of a number's highest 1-bit is the same as knowing the binary magnitude of the number. In the binary number 0000 0000 0000 0011, for example, the highest 1-bit is in bit position 1 (counting backwards from the beginning of the word, the lowest position is 0), in the binary number 0100 1111 0000 0000 the highest 1-bit is in bit position 14, and in the binary number 1000 0000 0000 0000 the highest 1-bit is in bit position 15. The following routine finds the highest 1-bit in the AX register and puts it in the CX register:

```
        PUSH AX        ;Save current value of AX
        XOR CX,CX      ;Begin with the assumption that magnitude is 0
        TEST AX,AX     ;Don't enter the loop if AX's initial value is 0
        JZ labelb      ;(if it's 0, we'll end up with CX = 0)
labela: INC CX
        ADD AX,AX
        JNC labela
        DEC CX
labelb: POP AX         ;Restore original value of AX
```

When the routine ends, CX has the position of AX's highest 1-bit — at a tremendous cost. It takes 6 cycles to set up the loop and another 5 cycles for every ADD instruction in the loop. If AX's highest 1-bit is in position 0, this routine uses up 86 cycles before it can tell you that. Since the whole idea is to save cycles, the routine would be far better if assembler had some quicker way to find a value's highest 1-bit. The BSR instruction does just this job.

The BSR Instruction

In an assembler statement, the syntax of the BSR instruction looks like this:

```
BSR <destination operand>,<source operand>    ;optional comment
```

BSR scans the bits in <source operand> from the most significant (highest) bit to the least significant (lowest) bit and writes the bit index of the first 1-bit found into <destination operand>. The <source operand> can be either a 16-bit or 32-bit register or memory operand. The <destination operand> can be either a 16-bit or 32-bit register and must match the size of the <source operand>.

The meaning of BSR is imperative:

Bit Scan the contents of <source operand> in Reverse.

BSR turns the zero flag ON if all the bits scanned are 0; otherwise it turns the zero flag OFF. BSR's effect on the overflow, sign, parity, and carry flags is undefined.

BSR has four possible forms, depending on the operands used. Table 8.2 is a standardized description for each possible form of BSR.

A raft of bit-scan and bit-test instructions were added to assembler with the Intel 386 chip; we won't pay excessive attention to them in this book because they have very few known uses. BSR, for example, has only one use — to find a number's binary magnitude — and it's dreadfully slow. BSR takes 6 cycles to set up, another 3 cycles for each bit it has to scan, and 1 more cycle in most cases for a prefix penalty (which we won't get into here). Still, BSR CX, AX puts AX's magnitude in CX a lot faster than the loop shown earlier, so we'll use it to continue the process of normalizing a division instruction's operands.

Instruction Mnemonic	Destination Operand	Source Operand	Cycle Count
BSR	<16-bit register>	,<16-bit register>	6 to 55!!
BSR	<16-bit register>	,<word-size memory>	7 to 56!!
BSR	<32-bit register>	,<32-bit register>	6 to 103
BSR	<32-bit register>	,<long-size memory>	7 to 104

Table 8.2   Standardized description for each possible form of BSR.

Shift and Subtract — Part Two

The following routine, called _DIV, is the classic Shift and Subtract method for doing division operations without using the IDIV or DIV instructions:

```
                        ;unsigned DIV(unsigned dividend,unsigned divisor);
            public _DIV ;Compare _div function in standard C library
_DIV proc
        PUSH BP
        MOV BP,SP
        MOV BX,[BP+6]   ;BX = divisor, an unsigned integer
        MOV DX,[BP+4]   ;DX = dividend, an unsigned integer
.386
        BSR AX,BX       ;BSR (Bit Scan Reverse) gives the offset of
        BSR CX,DX       ;the highest 1 bit: the power-of-2 magnitude.
.8086
        SUB CX,AX       ;CX = difference in dividend-divisor magnitude
        MOV AX,0        ;AX = quotient, initial value = 0
        JL @@ret        ;(divisor > dividend, so just return 0)
        SHL BX,CL       ;Shift divisor left by magnitude difference.
        INC CX          ;We'll use (difference+1) as our loop control.
@@2:    ADD AX,AX       ;Shift AX one bit position to the left
        CMP BX,DX       ;If shifted divisor is now less than or equal
        JA @@3          ;to shifted dividend, we put a 1 bit in the
        SUB DX,BX       ;least-most-significant-quotient-bit position
        OR AL,1         ;and subtract the dividend from the divisor,
@@3:    SHR BX,1        ;otherwise dividend's unshifted next go-round.
        LOOP @@2        ;Loop for every bit of the magnitude.
@@ret:  POP BP
        RET             ;return AX = quotient
_DIV endp
```

We think the _DIV routine is worth illustrating. If you read it carefully you will see that the actual Shift and Subtract loop takes only 10 cycles per bit, so there might be some chance of using a variation of _DIV in some circumstances. In real life, though, the chances of knowing the magnitude of both the dividend and the divisor in advance is very poor, so the two BSR instructions in the routine drive the cost up. For general purposes then, the Shift and Subtract _DIV routine can't substitute for the IDIV or DIV instructions. Since a simple Shift and Subtract substitution won't work, a better method needs to be found to save cycles in division operations. One way to save cycles is to force your compiler to use DIV rather than IDIV when translating division operations. Another way to save cycles is to replace DIV and IDIV with SAR and SHR in cases where subtraction isn't involved (more on this later). A third way to save cycles when you're specifically dividing an 8-bit number by 10 is to use the AAM instruction, which we will introduce shortly.

Forcing the Compiler to Choose DIV

It's not a secret, but neither is it a well-known fact, that DIV works faster (by 1 cycle) than IDIV on the same numbers. This is a lesson for C programmers who casually declare a variable as int without considering whether the variable can ever be a negative (signed) number. For example:

```
int memi,memj;     /* memi and memj range is 1 to 500 */
void main ()
{
 memj=memi/10;
}
```

This program would run faster if the first line was unsigned memi,memj;.

Dividing Signed Integers With SAR and SHR

Dividing by 2-to-the-nth-power is equivalent to shifting *n* bits to the right. For example, if AX contains 12 and CL contains 4 (i.e., 2 to the power of 2), then:

```
DIV CL
```

will result in AL equals 3 and AH equals 0 (the remainder). In other words, after 16 cycles, AX will equal 3. The same result is achieved in only 2 cycles with:

```
SHR AX,2
```

We'd like to unreservedly recommend that when dividing by a value equal to a power of 2 (e.g., 2, 4, 8, 16, 32, 64, etc), you use a shift-right instruction rather than a divide instruction — but there are two problems with this recommendation.

The Lost Remainder Problem

The first problem is the *lost remainder* problem. When a shift right is executed, the bits shifted off past the right end of the operand — into oblivion — are the remainder. If you need to know the division's remainder (or modulus), an extra step is needed. For example, these instructions will divide AX by 4 without losing the remainder — putting the quotient in AX and the remainder in DX:

```
MOV DX,AX        ;we'll use DX for the remainder
AND DX,(4-1)     ;AND DX with (divisor minus 1)
SHR AX,2         ;divide AX by 4
```

The Negative Rounding Problem

The second problem with recommending that division be replaced by shift-rights is the *negative rounding* problem. When a signed integer is to be shifted to the right, you have to use SAR instead of SHR so the sign bit will be shifted too. The negative rounding problem arises when the operation requires that SAR be executed on a negative number which is not also a power of 2. In this case, the quotient is rounded toward infinity. For example, if AX contains −13 (not a power of 2) and you divide by 4 (a power of 2, as in our recommendation) using the SAR instruction:

```
SAR AX,2
```

the result is −4. To see why this is so, think of the original 16-bit AX register value (−13) in binary form — that is, 1111 1111 1111 0011. If this number is shifted two bits to the right, SAR will bring in two 1-bits on the left because it's operating on a signed number. The result is binary 1111 1111 1111 1100 and this value is, in decimal, −4. SAR always rounds down, which is fine for positive numbers. With negative numbers though, it's necessary to round up, as IDIV does.

Microsoft and Symantec handle this problem by using IDIV instead of SAR. Borland just ignores the problem — it uses a simple SAR when dividing signed integers by powers of 2 despite the incorrect result. A faster way to solve the problem which also provides the correct answer is:

```
          TEST AX,AX     ;See if the AX register's sign bit is on
          JGE unsig      ;We could have used JNS
          ADD AX,(4-1)   ;Add (divisor - 1) to dividend
unsig: SAR AX,2          ;divide AX by 4
```

Although this method takes 5 or 6 cycles, it's still much faster than IDIV and it gives the correct answer, which is −3.

An even better solution to the rounding to infinity problem where the divisor is 2, can be expressed as: *If the number is negative, then add 1 to it.* An (inefficient) way of expressing this in C is if (number<0) ++number;. A programmer with a bit of assembler experience will express the same thing in terms of the resources available at the assembler level, that is: *Add the register's sign flag to the register itself.* Thinking this way is a trick that comes only with practice.

The most efficient path to the `mema=mema/2;` solution has three stages. The first stage is:

```
MOV AX,mema      ;1 cycle
ADD AX,8000h     ;1 cycle
SUB AX,8000h     ;1 cycle
```

At this point, the AX register has whatever value it started with (−13 in our earlier example). The only change made is to the flags register. If the original value of AX was signed, the carry flag is now ON. If AX was originally unsigned, the carry flag is now OFF. In effect, AX's sign bit has been MOVed to the carry flag. Total cost so far: 3 cycles.

The second stage to resolving `mema=mema/2;` is:

```
ADC AX,0    ;1 cycle
```

At this point, if the carry flag is OFF, then AX has gotten the same value it started with — so positive numbers stay the same. If the carry flag is ON, then ADC adds 1 to the value — so negative numbers get incremented. Total cost so far: 4 cycles.

Since adding 1 to a negative number was the stated objective, the third stage of resolving `mema=mema/2;` can do the shift:

```
DB 0C1h          ;2 cycles — this is the way to say SAR AX,1
DB 0F8h          ;using the faster SAR <register>,<constant>
DB 001h          ;variant we showed in chapter 4.
MOV mema,AX      ;1 cycle
```

Total cost to resolve `mema=mema/2;` is 7 cycles.

This three-step-method looks cryptic until you start thinking of the problem in assembler terms. Similarly, a chess neophyte will think a grandmaster's moves look weird, until the master reaches the objective and the point of the combination becomes clear. Practice thinking of `if ... then` statements as bits that are ON/1 or OFF/0, and you'll be one step closer to assembler grandmastership yourself.

Our suggested code is faster than the code generated by any C compiler that we've checked. Symantec comes closest (9 cycles) but penalizes itself by using CWD and the slow SAR variant:

```
MOV AX,mema      ;1 cycle
CWD              ;3 cycles, DX becomes -1 if AX is signed
SUB AX,DX        ;1 cycle
SAR AX,1         ;3 cycles
MOV mema,AX      ;1 cycle
```

More on Rounding

If you were programming in COBOL, you could clearly express that the result of the expression `mema/memb;` should be rounded up if the fractional part of the quotient is greater than (or perhaps equal to) 1/2. In C, however, to get a rounded division you have to get the modulus and see if it's greater than (or perhaps equal to) 1/2 of the divisor. This program does a rounded division by 10:

```c
int dividend,quotient;
void main ()
{
 quotient=dividend/10;
 if ((dividend%10)>=(10/2)) ++quotient;
}
```

All C compilers translate the body of this program into:

```
        MOV AX,_dividend    ;AX = lower 16 bits of dividend        ;1 cycle
        MOV CX,10           ;CX = divisor                          ;1 cycle
        CWD                 ;DX = upper 16 bits of dividend        ;3 cycles
        IDIV CX             ;Divide DX:AX by CX, AX=quotient       ;27 cycles
        MOV _quotient,AX    ;quotient = result of division (in AX) ;1 cycle
        MOV AX,_dividend    ;AX = lower 16 bits of dividend        ;1 cycle
        CWD                 ;DX = upper 16 bits of dividend        ;3 cycles
        IDIV CX             ;Divide DX:AX by CX, DX=remainder      ;27 cycles
        CMP DX,5            ;Is the remainder >= (10/2)?           ;1 cycle
        JLE $EX174          ;(if no, skip the INC instruction)     ;3 or 1 cycles
        INC _quotient       ;Add 1 to the quotient.                ;3 cycles
$EX174:
```

One clever optimization in this code is that the compilers only load the `CX` register once — notice that there is no `MOV CX,10` before the second `IDIV` instruction. But they miss the far more important and common fact — that `IDIV` returns both the quotient and the remainder at once. The following assembler instructions rectify that omission:

```
        MOV AX,_dividend    ;1 cycle
        MOV CX,10           ;1 cycle
        CWD                 ;3 cycles
        IDIV CX             ;27 cycles
        CMP DX,5            ;1 cycle
        JLE $EX174          ;3 or 1 cycles
        INC AX              ;1 cycle
$EX174: MOV _quotient,AX    ;1 cycle
```

This method reduces the number of cycles from 68 to 37 — a savings of nearly 50 percent.

The AAM Instruction

In an assembler statement, the syntax of the AAM instruction looks like this:

```
AAM     ;optional comment
```

The meaning of AAM is imperative:

Ascii Adjust AX register after Multiply.

AAM divides the AL register by 10, putting the quotient in the AH register and the remainder in the AL register. AAM should only be executed after executing a MUL instruction that leaves the result in the AX register. AAM sets the sign, zero, and parity flags according to the result of the operation. AAM's effect on the overflow and carry flags is undefined.

As with IDIV and DIV, AAM is not considered to be an arithmetic operation for the purposes of the Hi/Lo Rule. However, because it changes the AH and AL registers, if the instruction following AAM is either MOV or an arithmetic instruction, the Hi/Lo Rule may apply to the second instruction.

AAM has only one possible form. Table 8.3 is a standardized description for this form.

AAM is a very specialized unsigned-divide instruction. For example, if mema is a char variable, AAM can be used to translate the C expression mema=mema/10; using 18 cycles:

```
MOV AL,mema     ;1 cycle
AAM             ;15 cycles
MOV mema,AH     ;!2 cycles (Hi/Lo Rule)
```

Instruction Mnemonic	Cycle Count
AAM	15

Table 8.3   Standardized description of AAM.

This compares favorably with a 21 cycle translation that uses a DIV instruction:

```
MOV AL,mema      ;1 cycle
XOR AH,AH        ;!2 cycles (Hi/Lo Rule)
MOV CL,10        ;1 cycle
DIV CL           ;16 cycles
MOV mema,AL      ;1 cycle
```

AAM, whose machine opcode is D4 0A, is the only documented instance of the nameless "divide AL by immediate value" instruction. The opcode D4 0B means divide AL by 11 (hexadecimal 0Bh), opcode D4 0C means divide AL by 12, and so on. You could thus use the undocumented AAM variant to divide AL by any 8-bit constant — but only if you have an Intel chip! Legend has it that years ago there was a version of the IBM PC BIOS that used this trick, and a computer with that BIOS acted strangely when an engineer replaced the Intel 8086 chip with a NEC V20 8086 clone. It turned out that the V20 divided by 10 no matter what the second opcode byte was, since it never occurred to NEC's creators that anyone would ever use undocumented Intel instructions.

Overflow

When a C program divides an integer by 0, the compiler generally returns some sort of abend — the program prints "Divide overflow" and halts, for instance. The same sort of abend is returned whenever the quotient is too large to fit in the result register (AL, AX, or EAX). It's possible to re-program the divide overflow routine to do something more intelligent than print and quit, but this is rarely done in practice. It's much easier to check for overflow *before* dividing. Here's how.

If the value of AX is being divided by the value of CL, overflow will only happen if AH is greater than or equal to CL. Therefore, instead of just DIV, use:

```
CMP AH,CL
JA <overflow routine>
DIV CL
```

If the value of DX : AX is being divided by the value of CX, overflow will only happen if DX is greater than or equal to CX. Therefore, instead of just DIV, use:

```
CMP DX,CX
JA <overflow routine>
DIV CX
```

And if the value of EDX : EAX is being divided by the value of ECX, overflow will only happen if EDX is greater than or equal to ECX. Therefore, instead of just DIV, use:

```
CMP EDX,ECX
JA <overflow routine>
DIV ECX
```

Since no C compiler ever checks for overflow, it is pretty well mandatory to use inline assembly to insert division with overflow checks like the above whenever there is any possibility whatever that overflow will occur.

Dividing a 16-bit Number by an 8-bit Constant

Consider this C program:

```
int mema;
void main ()
{
 mema=mema/100;
}
```

All C compilers will translate the C statement mema=mema/100; into something like this:

```
MOV AX,mema      ;1 cycle
CWD              ;3 cycles
MOV BX,100       ;1 cycle
IDIV BX          ;27 cycles
MOV mema,AX      ;1 cycle
```

Since an 8-bit division is 8 cycles faster than a 16-bit division (remember that IDIV's cost is 11 + (number of bits) cycles), it would be far better to translate mema=mema/100; with IDIV BL if at all possible — and if you knew that mema would never be less than 0, an even better translation would use DIV BL. Keep in mind though that if, for example, the value of AX happens to be 30000, then <IDIV|DIV> BL will cause an abend (because 30000/100 = 300, too large for an 8-bit quotient) so the code must also check for overflow, as follows:

```
        MOV AX,mema        ;1 cycle
        MOV BX,100         ;1 cycle
        CMP AH,BL          ;1 cycle           Check for overflow the usual way
        JAE ak0a           ;3 or 1 cycles (if it's too big, use IDIV BX)
        IDIV BL            ;19 cycles        8-bit divide of AX by BL
        AND AX,255         ;1 cycle          MOV AH,0 would work too
        JMP short ak0b     ;3 cycles         Ready to MOV AX to mema now.
ak0a:   CWD                ;3 cycles
        IDIV BX            ;27 cycles        16-bit divide of DX:AX by BX
ak0b:   MOV mema,AX        ;1 cycle
```

This code only speeds mema=mema/100; up if the value of mema is less than 25600.

Division Using a Lookup Table

It happens that you can divide a 2-byte number 1 byte at a time by making the remainder from the first division into the high part of the dividend in the second division. For example, suppose you have an unsigned 16-bit integer mema that contains the hexadecimal number 2A24h and want to divide mema by 10h. The hard way to do so is:

```
MOV CL,10h                 ;In both steps, the divisor will be 10h
MOV AL,BYTE PTR mema+1     ;Step 1: divide high byte i.e. 2Ah by 10h
MOV AH,0                   ;so AX = 002Ah
DIV CL                     ;AL quotient will = 2, AH remainder will = A
MOV BYTE PTR mema+1,AL
MOV AL,BYTE PTR mema       ;Step 2: divide low byte i.e. 24h by 10h
                           ;Remember: AH still has A in it so AX = 0A24h
DIV CL                     ;AL quotient will = A2, AH remainder will = 4
MOV BYTE PTR mema,AL
```

At the end of these instructions, mema contains 02A2h, which is the right answer. Byte-at-a-time divisions are easily extensible to 32-bit, 64-bit, or even 128-bit dividends. There are certainly much faster ways of doing this particular operation — DIV CX and SHR AX,4 spring to mind — but the exercise does show you another way to divide a 16-bit number in two 8-bit steps. This becomes important when you consider two of the laws of mathematics.

One law of mathematics states that there are only 256 possible divisors in 8-bit arithmetic. The maximum dividend size can be greater than that because in Step 2 the high 8 bits of the dividend are the remainder from the previous step — but even that is not a large number. Another law of mathematics states that no remainder can ever be as large as the divisor — so if the divisor is 10, the maximum divisor size in Step 2 must be (256 * 10) – 1. This number is small enough that it's quite easy to make a cheat sheet and replace the division instructions with instructions that just look up the answers on the cheat sheet. This code creates and uses a lookup table for dividing an 8-bit number by an 8-bit constant (in this case, by the constant 10):

```
char quotients[10*256];
char remainders[10*256];
void main ()
{
    __asm MOV  CX,10;                              /* table creation starts here */
    __asm MOV  BX,(10*256)-1;
labelx:__asm MOV  AX,BX;
    __asm XOR  DX,DX;
    __asm DIV  CX;
    __asm MOV  quotients[BX],AL;
    __asm MOV  remainders[BX],DL;
    __asm DEC  BX;
    __asm JGE  labelx;                             /* table creation ends here */
    ...

/* Divide — replace "Result=Value/10;" expression with this. */
    __asm MOV  BH,0;                               /* 1 cycle */
    __asm MOV  BL,BYTE PTR Value+1;                /* 1 cycle */
    __asm MOV  AH,BYTE PTR quotients[BX];          /* !3 cycles (Register-Address Rule) */
    __asm MOV  BH,BYTE PTR remainders[BX];         /* 1 cycle */
    __asm MOV  BL,BYTE PTR Value;                  /* 1 cycle */
    __asm MOV  BYTE PTR Result+1,AH;              /* 1 cycle */
    __asm MOV  AL,BYTE PTR quotients[BX];          /* !2 cycles (Bytes-and-Pointers Rule */
    __asm MOV  BYTE PTR Result,AL;                 /* 1 cycle */
    ...
```

The Divide Using Table Lookup method takes 11 cycles. This compares favorably with DIV CX, which takes 24 cycles. Should we weigh the cost of the table creation and the size of the lookup tables against this gain? No — remember that the objective of this book is to save time with instructions that will be repeated thousands or millions of times. In that perspective, the cost of the table creation is insignificant. As for the size of quotients[] and remainders[] — anyone who needs the space can simply reallocate after finishing whatever loop the divide operations are in.

Where You Are

In this chapter, you learned:

❖ how to do signed division with IDIV and unsigned division with DIV, and how and when to use the specialized divide-by-10 instruction AAM instead;

❖ how to scan bits in a register or memory variable with BSR;

❖ how to speed up division operations where the divisor is a power-of-2 by replacing IDIV and DIV with SAR and SHR instructions;

❖ how to solve SAR's negative rounding problem and how to optimize rounded divisions;

❖ how to check for overflow before a division operation;

❖ how to use a lookup table to speed up simple division operations.

Chapter 9

Handling Intel Strings

Since this is a C book, the word *string* means a one-dimensional byte array terminated by a \0. Intel's definition differs from this. The assembler string instructions are designed to work on byte arrays or word arrays or double-word arrays — and the size is fixed. Since we're not out to change anyone's terminology, this book will use the phrase *Intel string* instead of the word string whenever we're using Intel's definition.

If you plan to use the Intel string instructions, it will be necessary to slog through several complex and arbitrary rules and warnings before you gain anything. In fact, the first warning is: There is more slogging than gaining involved in using Intel string instructions. For those who would prefer to just use the assembler vocabulary learned thus far, this chapter supplies common workarounds for all the Intel string instructions. If you're among this group, skimming this chapter should be easy. If you do plan on using Intel string instructions, be ready to be patient. It will take a fair amount of learning before you can do something useful. We'll start by introducing two instructions that affect the status of a new flag whose usefulness is by no means immediately apparent.

The CLD and STD Instructions

In an assembler statement, the syntax of the CLD and STD instructions looks like this:

```
CLD     ;optional comment
STD     ;optional comment
```

These two instructions have neither a <source operand> or a <destination operand> because their only purpose is to directly affect the status of the direction flag. No other flags in the flags register are affected.

The direction flag is not an arithmetic flag, so it isn't affected by any of the other instructions we've discussed so far. As a result it tends to be sticky: once the direction flag is ON, it stays ON. Normally, this is not relevant — the status of the flag is only important when Intel string instructions are being used.

The meaning of CLD and STD is imperative:

CLD: CLear Direction flag.

STD: SeT Direction flag.

CLD clears the direction flag; that is, it turns the direction flag OFF. If the direction flag is OFF, Intel string instructions perform auto-increment — that is, they go up by incrementing the index registers SI and/or DI. (In 32- bit mode, the index registers are ESI and EDI.) For example, if the instruction starts at address 0, it proceeds to execute up through address 1, 2, 3, 4, and so on if the direction flag is OFF.

STD sets the direction flag; that is, it turns the direction flag ON. If the direction flag is ON, Intel string instructions perform auto-decrement — that is, they go down by decrementing the index registers SI and/or DI (or ESI and/or EDI in 32-bit mode). For example, if the instruction starts at address 4, it proceeds to execute down through address 3, 2, 1, 0, −1 (0FFFFh) and so on if the direction flag is ON.

These two instructions have only one possible form. Table 9.1 is a standardized description for this form.

The direction flag is normally OFF because programs usually start at the beginning of an array and process to the array's end. You might want the direction flag ON, though, if you're moving overlapping strings or scanning for the last matching byte in a string. In fact, though, the direction flag is so rarely ON that it's easy to be lulled into the belief that the flag is always OFF — an assumption that can lead to intermittent bugs. This is one of the subtler traps of assembler programming. The Borland and Symantec C manuals say "you must ensure that the direction flag is OFF when you return from an [assembler code] procedure"; the Microsoft manual says "you must ensure that the direction flag is UNCHANGED." Microsoft doesn't follow its own advice so we'll optimistically advise that the apparent distinction here is not serious.

Before we can illustrate CLD and STD there are some basic operating assumptions about Intel string instructions which must be outlined.

Basic Assumptions

The Intel string instructions work entirely with implicit operands. Rather than allowing you to specify a <source operand> and/or a <destination operand>, each instruction assumes that these registers are used:

- The SI (Source Index) register is always used as a pointer to the Intel string where 8-bit bytes, 16-bit words, or 32-bit double-words come from — that is, SI is implicitly the <source operand pointer> in 16-bit mode. The DS (Data Segment) register is always used as the source segment so the full address is DS:SI. (Note: in 32-bit mode, it's DS:ESI.)

- The DI (Destination Index) register is always used as a pointer to the Intel string where bytes, words, or double-words are going to — that is, DI is implicitly the <destination operand pointer> in 16-bit mode. The ES (Extra Segment) register is always used as the destination segment so the full address is ES:DI. This is somewhat unusual. The only time that ES is the default is when the destination of an Intel string instruction is being referred to. In those cases, since ES is the default, there is no Prefix Rule penalty as there is when ES: is used in all other circumstances. (Note: in 32- bit mode, it's ES:EDI.)

Instruction Mnemonic	Cycle Count
<CLD|STD>	2

Table 9.1 Standardized description of CLD and STD.

❖ The AX register is always used as the <destination operand> when an Intel string instruction is going from an Intel string to a register. AX is also always used as the <source operand> when an Intel string instruction is going from a register to an Intel string. (We're using AX as convenient shorthand here — in reality, byte-size operations go to and from AL, word-size operations go to and from AX, and double-word-size operations go to and from EAX.)

❖ The CX register (or ECX register in 32-bit mode) is always used as the loop counter when a "repeated Intel string instruction" — a sort of burst mode extension of the ordinary one-operand-at-a-time instruction — is used.

The repeated Intel string instructions are the ones that really count. We regret, then, that to make them understandable we have to start with the simpler, unrepeated, Intel string instructions — CMPSx, LODSx, MOVSx, SCASx, and STOSx — which are not terribly useful.

The CMPSB, CMPSW and CMPSD Instructions

In an assembler statement, the syntax of the CMPSB, CMPSW, and CMPSD instructions looks like this:

```
CMPSB      ;optional comment
CMPSW      ;optional comment
CMPSD      ;optional comment
```

The *compare Intel string* instructions compare a byte, word, or double-word which is addressed (pointed to) by DS:SI with a byte, word, or double-word which is addressed by ES:DI, incrementing both SI and DI in the process (or decrementing them if the direction flag is ON). The registers increment or decrement by 1 if a byte is compared, by 2 if a word is compared, or by 4 if a double-word is compared. Note that 16-bit mode means that 16-bit addressing is being used (as in MS-DOS and 16-bit Windows), and 32-bit mode means that 32-bit addressing is being used (as in 32-bit Windows or OS/2). This means that, in 16-bit mode, CMPSD uses DS:SI and ES:DI just like CMPSB and CMPSW do, even though it's comparing a double-word. This is true of all the Intel string instructions.

The comparison is done by effectively subtracting the value pointed to by ES:DI from the value pointed to by DS:SI without actually changing either one. The comparison's result sets or clears the flags in the flags register (in the same way as for the CMP instruction, which also simulates a SUB). Since CMPSB, CMPSW, and CMPSD are basically just variants of one instruction, we'll refer to them collectively as the CMPSx instruction. CMPSx sets the carry, overflow, parity, sign, and zero flags according to the result of the operation but has no effect on the direction flag.

The meaning of CMPSx is imperative:

CMPSB: CoMPare String one Byte (8-bits) at a time, increment (decrement) SI and DI by 1.

CMPSW: CoMPare String one Word (16-bits) at a time, increment (decrement) SI and DI by 2.

CMPSD: CoMPare String one Double-word (32-bits) at a time, increment (decrement) SI and DI by 4.

For example, if a memory variable mema pointed to by SI contains the byte value 15, then after these instructions

```
MOV SI,OFFSET mema
MOV DI,OFFSET mema
CMPSB
```

the zero flag will be ON (because comparing something to itself must result in equality), and the SI and DI registers will point to address [mema+1] (assuming the direction flag is OFF).

These three instructions have only one possible form. Table 9.2 is a standardized description for this form.

Instruction Mnemonic	Cycle Count
<CMPSB|CMPSW|CMPSD>	8

Table 9.2   Standardized description of CMPSB, CMPSW, and CMPSD.

CMPSx can be replaced by the following sets of instructions (we're assuming the direction flag is OFF and the ES segment register value is the same as the DS segment register value, i.e., that ES=DS):

```
        ;replace CMPSB              ;replace CMPSW               ;replace CMPSD
INC DI          ;1 cycle    ADD DI,2        ;1 cycle    ADD DI,4        ;1 cycle
MOV AL,[SI]     ;1 cycle    MOV AX,[SI]     ;1 cycle    MOV EAX,[SI]    ;!2 cycles
INC SI          ;1 cycle    ADD SI,2        ;1 cycle    ADD SI,4        ;1 cycle
CMP AL,[DI-1]   ;!3 cycles  CMP AX,[DI-2]   ;2 cycles   CMP EAX,[DI-4]  ;!3 cycles
```

The replacement codes destroy the AL or AX or EAX register respectively, but in all other respects they are precisely equivalent to the CMPSx instruction. The gain is between 2 and 3 cycles, or between 25 and 38 percent. The slightly smaller gain for CMPSB is because the CMP AL,[DI-1] instruction takes 3 cycles; it is being penalized by the Bytes-and-Pointers Rule. The slightly smaller gain for CMPSD is due to the Prefix Rule penalties incurred by the MOV and CMP instructions.

The LODSB, LODSW, and LODSD Instructions

In an assembler statement, the syntax of the LODSB, LODSW, and LODSD instructions looks like this:

```
LODSB       ;optional comment
LODSW       ;optional comment
LODSD       ;optional comment
```

The *load Intel string* instructions load a byte, word, or double-word which is addressed (pointed to) by DS:SI into the AL, AX, or EAX registers respectively, incrementing SI in the process (or decrementing SI if the direction flag is ON). SI is incremented or decremented by 1 if a byte is loaded, by 2 if a word is loaded, or by 4 if a double-word is loaded. Since LODSB, LODSW, and LODSD are basically just variants of one instruction, we'll refer to them collectively as the LODSx instruction. LODSx has no effect on the flags in the flags register.

The meaning of LODSx is imperative:

LODSB: LOaD String one Byte (8-bits) at a time, increment (decrement) SI by 1.

LODSW: LOaD String one Word (16-bits) at a time, increment (decrement) SI by 2.

LODSD: LOaD String one Double-word (32-bits) at a time, increment (decrement) SI by 4.

For example, if a memory variable mema pointed to by SI contains the byte value 15, then after this instruction

```
LODSB
```

the AL register will contain 15, and the SI register will point to address [mema+1] (assuming the direction flag is OFF). The flags register will remain unchanged.

These three instructions have only one possible form. Table 9.3 is a standardized description for this form.

LODSx can be replaced by the following sets of instructions (we're assuming the direction flag is OFF):

```
    ;replace LODSB              ;replace LODSW              ;replace LODSD
MOV AL,[SI]     ;1 cycle    MOV AX,[SI]     ;1 cycle    MOV EAX,[SI]    ;!2 cycles
LEA SI,[SI+1]   ;1 cycle    LEA SI,[SI+2]   ;1 cycle    LEA SI,[SI+4]   ;1 cycle
```

The replacement codes are precisely equivalent to the LODSx instructions. Notice the choice of LEA SI, [SI+num] instead of INC SI or ADD SI,num; LEA changes no flags. The gain is 3 cycles, or 60 percent.

The MOVSB, MOVSW, and MOVSD Instructions

In an assembler statement, the syntax of the MOVSB, MOVSW, and MOVSD instructions looks like this:

```
MOVSB     ;optional comment
MOVSW     ;optional comment
MOVSD     ;optional comment
```

The *move Intel string* instructions copy a byte, word, or double-word from the address pointed to by DS:SI and store it in the address pointed

Instruction Mnemonic	Cycle Count
<LODSB|LODSW|LODSD>	5

Table 9.3   Standardized description of LODSB, LODSW, and LODSD.

to by ES:DI, incrementing both SI and DI in the process (or decrementing them if the direction flag is ON). The registers increment or decrement by 1 if a byte is moved, by 2 if a word is moved, or by 4 if a double-word is moved. Since MOVSB, MOVSW, and MOVSD are basically just variants of one instruction, we'll refer to them collectively as the MOVSx instruction. MOVSx has no effect on the flags in the flags register.

The meaning of MOVSx is imperative:

MOVSB: **MOV**e String one **B**yte (8-bits) at a time, increment (decrement) SI and DI by 1.

MOVSW: **MOV**e String one **W**ord (16-bits) at a time, increment (decrement) SI and DI by 2.

MOVSD: **MOV**e String one **D**ouble-word (32-bits) at a time, increment (decrement) SI and DI by 4.

For example, if a memory variable mema pointed to by SI contains the byte value 15, and a memory variable memb pointed to by DI contains the byte value 20, then after this instruction

```
MOVSB
```

memb will contain 15, the SI register will point to address [mema+1], and the DI register will point to address [memb+1] (assuming the direction flag is OFF). The flags register will remain unchanged.

These three instructions have only one possible form. Table 9.4 is a standardized description for this form.

MOVSx can be replaced by the following sets of instructions (we're assuming the direction flag is OFF and the ES segment register value is the same as the DS segment register value, i.e., that ES=DS):

```
          ;replace MOVSB              ;replace MOVSW                 ;replace MOVSD
MOV AL,[SI]    ;1 cycle       MOV AX,[SI]    ;1 cycle       MOV EAX,[SI]   ;!2 cycles (Prefix Rule)
MOV [DI],AL    ;1 cycle       MOV [DI],AX    ;1 cycle       MOV [DI],EAX   ;1 cycle
INC SI         ;1 cycle       ADD SI,2       ;1 cycle       ADD SI,4       ;1 cycle
INC DI         ;1 cycle       ADD DI,2       ;1 cycle       ADD DI,4       ;1 cycle
```

Instruction Mnemonic	Cycle Count
<MOVSB|MOVSW|MOVSD>	7

Table 9.4   Standardized description of MOVSB, MOVSW, and MOVSD.

The replacement codes destroy the status of the flags in the flags register as well as the AL or AX or EAX register respectively, but in all other respects the replacements are precisely equivalent to the MOVSx instruction. The gain is 3 cycles, or 43 percent.

The SCASB, SCASW, and SCASD Instructions

In an assembler statement, the syntax of the SCASB, SCASW, and SCASD instructions looks like this:

```
SCASB    ;optional comment
SCASW    ;optional comment
SCASD    ;optional comment
```

The *scan Intel string* instructions compare the value of the AL or AX or EAX registers to a byte, word, or double-word which is addressed (pointed to) by ES:DI, incrementing DI in the process (or decrementing DI if the direction flag is ON). DI is incremented or decremented by 1 if a byte is compared, by 2 if a word is compared, or by 4 if a double-word is compared.

The comparison is done by effectively subtracting the byte, word, or double-word pointed to by ES:DI from the value in AL, AX, or EAX, respectively, without actually changing either one. The comparison's result sets or clears the flags in the flags register (in the same way as for the CMP instruction, which also simulates a SUB). Since SCASB, SCASW, and SCASD are basically just variants of one instruction, we'll refer to them collectively as the SCASx instruction. SCASx sets the carry, overflow, parity, sign, and zero flags according to the result of the operation but has no effect on the direction flag.

The meaning of SCASx is imperative:

SCASB: SCAn String one Byte (8-bits) at a time, increment (decrement) DI by 1.

SCASW: SCAn String one Word (16-bits) at a time, increment (decrement) DI by 2.

SCASD: SCAn String one Double-word (32-bits) at a time, increment (decrement) DI by 4.

For example, if the AL register contains 20 and DI points to a memory variable mema which contains 15, then after this instruction

```
SCASB
```

the flags in the flags register will be set as appropriate for the operation 20–15, mema will still contain 15, and the DI register will point to address [mema+1] (assuming the direction flag is OFF).

These three instructions have only one possible form. Table 9.5 is a standardized description for this form.

SCASx can be replaced by the following sets of instructions (we're assuming the direction flag is OFF and the ES segment register value is the same as the DS segment register value, i.e., that ES=DS):

```
        ;replace SCASB                ;replace SCASW                ;replace SCASD
CMP AL,[DI]     ;2 cycles     CMP AX,[DI]     ;2 cycles     CMP EAX,[DI]     ;!3 cycles
                                                                             ;(Prefix Rule)
LEA DI,[DI+1]   ;1 cycle      LEA DI,[DI+2]   ;1 cycle      LEA DI,[DI+4]    ;1 cycle
```

The replacement codes are precisely equivalent to the SCASx instruction. Notice the choice of LEA DI,[DI+num] instead of INC DI or ADD DI,num; LEA changes no flags. The gain is 3 cycles, or 50 percent.

The STOSB, STOSW, and STOSD Instructions

In an assembler statement, the syntax of the STOSB, STOSW, and STOSD instructions looks like this:

```
STOSB    ;optional comment
STOSW    ;optional comment
STOSD    ;optional comment
```

The *store Intel string* instructions put the contents of the AL or AX or EAX registers into a byte, word, or double-word memory location which is addressed (pointed to) by ES:DI, incrementing DI in the process (or decrementing DI if the direction flag is ON). DI is incremented or decremented by 1 if a byte is stored, by 2 if a word is stored, or by 4 if a

Instruction Mnemonic	Cycle Count
<SCASB|SCASW|SCASD>	6

Table 9.5   Standardized description of SCASB, SCASW, and SCASD.

double-word is stored. Since STOSB, STOSW, and STOSD are basically just variants of one instruction, we'll refer to them collectively as the STOSx instruction. STOSx has no effect on the flags in the flags register.

The meaning of STOSx is imperative:

STOSB: STOre String one Byte (8-bits) at a time, increment (decrement) DI by 1.

STOSW: STOre String one Word (16-bits) at a time, increment (decrement) DI by 2.

STOSD: STOre String one Double-word (32-bits) at a time, increment (decrement) DI by 4.

For example, if the AL register contains 20 and DI points to a memory variable mema which contains 15, then after this instruction

```
STOSB
```

mema will contain 20 and the DI register will point to address [mema+1] (assuming the direction flag is OFF).

These three instructions have only one possible form. Table 9.6 is a standardized description for this form.

STOSx can be replaced by the following sets of instructions (we're assuming the direction flag is OFF and the ES segment register value is the same as the DS segment register value, i.e., that ES=DS):

```
        ;replace STOSB                ;replace STOSW                  ;replace STOSD
MOV [DI],AL     ;1 cycle      MOV [DI],AX     ;1 cycle      MOV [DI],EAX  ;!2 cycles (Prefix Rule)
LEA DI,[DI+1]   ;1 cycle      LEA DI,[DI+2]   ;1 cycle      LEA DI,[DI+4] ;1 cycle
```

The replacement codes are precisely equivalent to the STOSx instruction. Notice the choice of LEA DI,[DI+num] instead of INC DI or ADD DI,num; LEA changes no flags. The gain is 3 cycles, or 60 percent.

Instruction Mnemonic	Cycle Count
<STOSB|STOSW|STOSD>	5

Table 9.6   Standardized description of STOSB, STOSW, and STOSD.

Cycle Times of String Instructions

To supplement the cycle-time numbers in our charts, we add these significant notes:

(1) All the Double-word variants of the Intel string instructions will usually take 1 extra cycle because of the Prefix Rule penalty applied to the 32-bit operand override prefix. The Prefix-Waiver Rule may sometimes reduce the cycle count so that it matches the Byte and Word variants of an instruction.

(2) None of the Intel string instructions are affected by the Register-Address Rule, so there is no penalty for pairs of instructions like:

```
MOV SI,OFFSET mem     ;Changing the register used in addressing
LODSB                 ;The LODSx instruction implicitly uses SI
```

(3) None of the Intel string instructions are affected by the Hi/Lo Rule, so there is no penalty for pairs of instructions like:

```
MOV AL,5     ;Changing the low half of a 16-bit register
STOSW        ;The STOSx instruction implicitly uses AX
```

and there is also no penalty for pairs of instructions like:

```
LODSB        ;Moving to the low half of the AX register
ADD mem,AX   ;then using the whole register in arithmetic
```

C and Intel String Instructions

Purely as an illustration, the code below shows how a C compiler could translate various C statements using Intel string instructions (SI is being used to point to memp1 and DI is being used to point to memp2):

```
char mema;
char *memp1,*memp2;
{
 mema=*(memp1++);             /* LODSB | MOV mema,AL */
 *(memp1++)=*(memp2++);       /* MOVSB */
 if (*memp1++==*memp2++) goto labelx;   /* CMPSB | JZ labelx */
 if (mema!=*memp2++) goto labelx;       /* MOV AL,mema | SCASB | JNZ labelx */
 *memp2++=mema;               /* MOV AL,mema | STOSB */
}
```

The fact is, though, that with one exception, C compilers do not generate translations using Intel string instructions. The exception is the case shown here:

```
double mema;     /* mema is a double so it's 8 bytes long */
double *memp;
{
  mema=*(memp++);
}
```

The following is an edited and simplified listing of what two C compilers generated for mema=*(memp++); in this case:

```
Microsoft                              Symantec
MOV DI,OFFSET mema     ;1 cycle        MOV BX,memp         ;1 cycle
MOV SI,memp            ;1 cycle        ADD memp,8          ;!4 cycles
ADD memp,8             ;!4 cycles      MOV AX,[BX+6]       ;1 cycle
MOVSW                  ;7 cycles       MOV CX,[BX+2]       ;1 cycle
MOVSW                  ;7 cycles       MOV DX,[BX]         ;1 cycle
MOVSW                  ;7 cycles       MOV BX,[BX+4]       ;1 cycle
MOVSW                  ;7 cycles       MOV mema+6,AX       ;1 cycle
                                       MOV mema+4,BX       ;1 cycle
                                       MOV mema+2,CX       ;1 cycle
                                       MOV mema,DX         ;1 cycle
```

Notice that Symantec's code, which doesn't use MOVSW, is nearly 3 times faster than Microsoft's code.

Repeated Intel String Instructions

Since all the Intel string instructions can be replaced with faster (albeit larger) code on a 486, what good are they? Granted, they're all 1 byte instructions so they take less room than their substitutes (and are actually faster than their substitutes on 386s). Still, there isn't much use for the CMPSx or LODSx or MOVSx or SCASx or STOSx instructions in themselves. But put a repeat — REP or REPNZ — prefix in front of an Intel string instruction and the picture changes.

The REP and REPNZ Prefix Instructions

In an assembler statement, the syntax of the Intel string instructions with a REP or REPNZ prefix added looks like this:

```
REP CMPSB      ;optional comment
REP CMPSW      ;optional comment
REP CMPSD      ;optional comment
REPNZ CMPSB    ;optional comment
REPNZ CMPSW    ;optional comment
REPNZ CMPSD    ;optional comment

REP MOVSB      ;optional comment
REP MOVSW      ;optional comment
REP MOVSD      ;optional comment

REP SCASB      ;optional comment
REP SCASW      ;optional comment
REP SCASD      ;optional comment
REPNZ SCASB    ;optional comment
REPNZ SCASW    ;optional comment
REPNZ SCASD    ;optional comment

REP STOSB      ;optional comment
REP STOSW      ;optional comment
REP STOSD      ;optional comment
```

The repeated Intel string instructions repeat the same operation that the single-iteration CMPSx, MOVSx, SCASx, and STOSx instructions do, a number of times.

The meaning of REP and REPNZ is imperative:

REP: REPeat <intel MOVSx or STOSx string instruction> operation until CX register is 0.

or

REP: REPeat <intel CMPSx or SCASx string instruction> operation until CX register is 0 or while zero flag is ON.

and

REPNZ: REPeat <intel CMPSx or SCASx string instruction> operation until CX register is 0 or while Not Zero flag on (that is, while zero flag is OFF).

That is:

REP CMPSx: if CX is 0 then go on to next instruction else do a CMPSx; decrement CX by 1; if zero flag is OFF then go on to next instruction else repeat loop. Remember that, since CMPSx will either set or clear the zero flag based on the result of the operation, the flag's status prior to the REP is irrelevant to the number of iterations.

REP MOVSx: if CX is 0 then go on to next instruction else do a MOVSx; decrement CX by 1; repeat loop.

REP SCASx: if CX is 0 then go on to next instruction else do a SCASx; decrement CX by 1; if zero flag is OFF then go on to next instruction else repeat loop. Remember that, since SCASx will either set or clear the zero flag based on the result of the operation, the flag's status prior to the REP is irrelevant to the number of iterations.

REP STOSx: if CX is 0 then go on to next instruction else do a STOSx; decrement CX by 1; repeat loop.

REPNZ CMPSx: if CX is 0 then go on to next instruction else do a CMPSx; decrement CX by 1; if zero flag is ON then go on to next instruction else repeat loop. Remember that, since CMPSx will either set or clear the zero flag based on the result of the operation, the flag's status prior to the REP is irrelevant to the number of iterations.

REPNZ SCASx: if CX is 0 then go on to next instruction else do a SCASx; decrement CX by 1; if zero flag is ON then go on to next instruction else repeat loop. Remember that, since SCASx will either set or clear the zero flag based on the result of the operation, the flag's status prior to the REP is irrelevant to the number of iterations.

REP and REPNZ are 1-byte prefixes. In all cases, the CX register is replaced by the ECX register in 32-bit mode. The changing and decrementing of the CX or ECX register has no effect on the flags register.

Two alternate names for REP are REPZ — REPeat while Zero flag ON — and REPE — REPeat while Equal. An alternate name for REPNZ is REPNE — REPeat while Not Equal. (These alternate names only have a use if the Intel string instruction is CMPSx or SCASx.) These five directives are the *repeat prefixes*. The only time you'll see a repeat prefix is in combination with an Intel string instruction; putting REP, REPZ, REPE, REPNZ, or REPNE in front of other assembler instructions has no effect.

The repeated Intel string instructions have 18 possible forms. Table 9.7 is a standardized description for the possible forms of the repeated Intel string instructions, showing the different cycle counts involved for varying values of CX.

Since REP and REPNZ are prefixes, their speed is subject to the rules laid down for prefixes in Chapter 1; usually they take 1 cycle, but if the last instruction took more than 1 cycle, REP and REPNZ are free because of the Prefix-Waiver Rule. The Cycles To Initialize and/or Cycles Per Iteration columns in Table 9.7 do not show the 1 cycle that repeat prefixes usually take, so add 1 to the cycle count unless circumstances are special.

The critical thing to look at in Table 9.7 is the Cycles Per Iteration column. Consider the 3 cycles for each iteration of REP MOVSW if CX>1, for instance. That's much faster than the 7 cycles that MOVSW (without the repeat prefix) takes. So the replacement code that we showed for MOVSW can't simply be stuffed in a loop and used as a replacement for REP MOVSW: the replacement code would be slower.

Instruction Mnemonic	Cycles To Initialize	Cycles Per Iteration	Cycle Count
Forms: for CX = 0			
REP CMPSB			5
REP CMPSW			5
REP CMPSD			5
REPNZ CMPSB			5
REPNZ CMPSW			5
REPNZ CMPSD			5
REP MOVSB			5
REP MOVSW			5
REP MOVSD			5
REP SCASB			5
REP SCASW			5
REP SCASD			5
REPNZ SCASB			5
REPNZ SCASW			5
REPNZ SCASD			5
REP STOSB			5
REP STOSW			5
REP STOSD			5

Table 9.7   Standardized description for the possible forms of the repeated Intel string instructions.

As already noted, CMPSD and MOVSD and SCASD and STOSD are prefixed instructions already — a DB 66h (32-bit) prefix is added to them because they operate on double-words. This means there's usually a 1-cycle penalty per instruction. Note that it's 1 cycle per *instruction* and not 1 cycle per *iteration* — if CX is 5000, then REP STOSD is 1 cycle slower than REP STOSW, not 5000 cycles slower — because of the Prefix-Waiver Rule. Since REP STOSD moves twice as much material as REP STOSW in each iteration, this provides quite an optimization opportunity, as we'll show later.

Instruction Mnemonic	Cycles To Initialize	Cycles Per Iteration	Cycle Count
Forms: for CX > 0			
REP CMPSB	7	7	
REP CMPSW	7	7	
REP CMPSD	7	7	
REPNZ CMPSB	7	7	
REPNZ CMPSW	7	7	
REPNZ CMPSD	7	7	
REP SCASB	7	5	
REP SCASW	7	5	
REP SCASD	7	5	
REPNZ SCASB	7	5	
REPNZ SCASW	7	5	
REPNZ SCASD	7	5	
REP STOSB	7	4	
REP STOSW	7	4	
REP STOSD	7	4	
Forms: for CX = 1			
REP MOVSB			13
REP MOVSW			13
REP MOVSD			13
Forms: for CX > 1			
REP MOVSB	10!!	3	
REP MOVSW	10!!	3	
REP MOVSD	10!!	3	

Table 9.7   continued

On the other hand, penalties for misalignment apply for *every* iteration. The penalty is usually 3 cycles, but if you're using CMPSD or MOVSD, the penalty is sometimes 4 cycles, and if both index registers — SI and DI — are pointing to misaligned memory addresses, then the penalty is a full 7 cycles per iteration.

When using a REP/REPNZ prefix, remember to load the CX register first since all the repeated Intel string instructions depend on the register's value. (Again, remember that whether an Intel string instruction uses double-words or not has no bearing on the register chosen as the counter. If 16-bit addressing is being used, then CX is the counter for the byte, word, and double-word forms of all Intel string instructions.) The "is CX equal to 0" check happens at the start of the loop, which is useful — if it was at the end of the loop, there would be 65,536 iterations if CX was already 0, a situation unlikely to be correct.

REP MOVSx

REP MOVSB — REPeat MOVSB <CX> times — decrements CX with each iteration of a MOVSB instruction and stops (i.e., goes on to execute the next instruction) when CX becomes 0. Consider the common problem of moving array mema to array memb. This C program shows one way to do it:

```
int mema[5000];
int memb[5000];
int *memp1,*memp2;
void main ()
{
  for (memp1=mema,memp2=memb; memp1<mema+5000; ++memp1,++memp2)
    {
    *memp2=*memp1;
    }
}
```

All the compilers we checked translated this program differently. The best translation was:

```
        MOV _memp1,OFFSET _mema          ;!2 cycles      ;memp1=mema
        MOV _memp2,OFFSET _memb          ;!2 cycles      ;memp2=memb
$F176:  MOV BX,_memp1                    ;1 cycle        ;BX represents memp1
        MOV AX,[BX]                      ;!3 cycles      ;AX=*memp1
        MOV BX,_memp2                    ;1 cycle        ;BX now represents memp2
        MOV [BX],AX                      ;!3 cycles      ;*memp2=AX
        ADD _memp2,2                     ;!4 cycles      ;++memp2
        ADD _memp1,2                     ;!4 cycles      ;++memp1
        CMP _memp1,OFFSET _mema+10000    ;!3 cycles      ;10000 is 5000*2
        JB $F176                         ;1 or 3 cycles  ;(repeat the loop)
```

Total cycles for this translation: 4+(4,999*22)+(1*20) = 110,002. We repeat: this is the *best* translation by any C compiler that we checked.

The translation has frequent use of `memp1` and `memp2`. If `memp1` and `memp2` were <register> instead of <memory> variables, the `ADD` and `CMP` instructions would take only 1 cycle each, the two `MOV`-to-register instructions would be unnecessary, and the code wouldn't be penalized so severely — e.g., the `MOV AX,[BX]` and `MOV [BX],AX` instructions are both penalized by the Register-Address Rule, which is why they take 3 cycles instead of 1 cycle. Since the C optimizer didn't put `memp1` and `memp2` in registers on its own, it's necessary to force this behavior by defining `memp1` and `memp2` as automatics rather than as globals, as follows:

```
int mema[5000];
int memb[5000];
void main ()
{
int *memp1,*memp2;
  for (memp1=mema,memp2=memb; memp1<mema+5000; ++memp1,++memp2)
   {
   *memp2=*memp1;
   }
}
```

The translation of this code is much smaller and much faster:

```
        PUSH SI                 ;1 cycle        ;Save the SI and DI registers
        PUSH DI                 ;1 cycle        ;whenever they're used
        MOV SI,OFFSET _mema      ;1 cycle        ;SI=memp1=pointer to mema, always
        MOV DI,OFFSET _memb      ;1 cycle        ;DI=memp2=pointer to memb, always
L8:     MOV CX,[SI]             ;1 cycle        ;CX = *memp1
        MOV [DI],CX             ;1 cycle        ;*memp2 = CX
        MOV CX,2                ;1 cycle        ;ADD 2 to SI and DI
        ADD SI,CX              ;1 cycle        ;++memp1
        ADD DI,CX              ;1 cycle        ;++memp2
        CMP SI,OFFSET _mema+10000 ;1 cycle      ;Are 5000 words done?
        JB L8                  ;3 or 1 cycles   ;(if not, loop)
        POP DI                 ;1 cycle        ;Restore SI and DI registers
        POP SI                 ;1 cycle
```

Total cycles for this translation: 4+(1*10)+(4,998*9)+(1*11)+2 = 45,007 — a savings of 64,995 cycles. (Incidentally, the lines

```
MOV CX,2
ADD SI,CX
ADD DI,CX
```

are still not optimal. The instructions

```
ADD SI,2
ADD DI,2
```

are even shorter and faster.)

This translation is now at the level where tweaking the C code won't help any more — there is no way to persuade the compiler into using REP MOVSW, so do it yourself with inline assembler:

```
__asm PUSH SI;              /* 1 cycle Save the SI and DI registers */
__asm PUSH DI;              /* 1 cycle whenever they're used */
__asm MOV  SI,OFFSET _mema; /* 1 cycle SI=memp1=pointer to mema, always */
__asm MOV  DI,OFFSET _memb; /* 1 cycle DI=memp2=pointer to memb, always */
__asm MOV  CX,5000;         /* 1 cycle */
__asm REP  MOVSW;           /* 15007 cycles */
__asm POP  DI;              /* 1 cycle Restore SI and DI registers */
__asm POP  SI;              /* 1 cycle */
```

Total cycles for this code: 5+15,007+2 = 15,014. This is similar to the code that all C compiler manufacturers supply with the _memcpy function. In other words, the people who made your C compiler know that the compiler can't handle array movement efficiently; that's why they wrote the _memcpy function in assembler. The final optimization step would be to use double-words; see our own version of MEMCPY in Chapter 11.

(Note: this code assumes the direction flag is OFF and that ES=DS. To ensure this is the case, add these three lines to the beginning of your code whenever you utilize our suggestions in this chapter:

```
__asm CLD;          /* Direction flag OFF */
__asm MOV CX,DS;    /* Ensure that */
__asm MOV ES,CX;    /* ES=DS */
```

We'll assume that this is the case from now on.)

By the way, you can change REP MOVSB to REP MOVSW by simply shifting the CX register 1 bit to the right providing that the DI register is not equal to [SI+1]. Since the SHR instruction puts the shifted bit into the carry flag, there's an easy way to find out if there was a 1-byte remainder. So when CX is likely to be greater than 4 and you're not concerned with the state of the flags register, you'll always get about a 50 percent gain by replacing REP MOVSB with (assuming the direction flag is OFF):

```
         SHR CX,1     ;3 cycles          ;CX=CX/2, carry flag gets changed
         REP MOVSW    ;10+(3*CX) cycles  ;Move n/2 words instead of n bytes
         JNC labels   ;1 or 3 cycles     ;Was low-most bit a 0 for SHR?
         MOVSB        ;7 cycles          ;If low-most bit was 1, final MOVSB
labels: ...
```

(Note: this example uses `SHR CX,1` merely for purposes of illustration; remember that `DB 0C1h + DB 0E9h + DB 001h` is 1 cycle faster. The point is, there is a shift to the right.) Remember: if `DI=[SI+1]`, then `MOVSW` will not come up with the same result as two `MOVSB` instructions, so don't use this replacement if it is possible that `DI=[SI+1]`.

`REP MOVSW` can also be changed to `REP MOVSD` by shifting the `CX` register 1 bit to the right. The principles are the same as for the replace `REP MOVSB` with `REP MOVSW` optimization.

REP STOSx

`REP STOSB` — **REP**eat `STOSB` <CX> times — decrements `CX` with each iteration of a `STOSB` instruction and stops (i.e., goes on to execute the next instruction) when `CX` becomes 0. Expressing this as a C program:

```
char mema[4096];
char *memp1;
int counter;
void main ()
{
  for (memp1=mema,counter=4096-1;counter>=0;++memp1,--counter) *memp1=0;
}
```

The same program could also be expressed this way:

```
char mema[4096];
char *memp1;
int counter;
void main ()
{
  __asm MOV DI,OFFSET mema;    /* 1 cycle */
  __asm MOV CX,4096;           /* 1 cycle */
  __asm MOV AL,0;              /* 1 cycle */
  __asm REP STOSB;             /* 7+(4096*4) cycles */
}
```

Total cycles for this code: 16,394. This inline assembler example is faster than even the best optimized C code, with a 75 percent gain, but it's still not the fastest way to do the job. Remember that instructions which work on words usually take the same amount of time as instructions which work on bytes, and that's true with `REP STOSB` and `REP STOSW` as well. The following inline assembler routine gives a 90 percent gain.

```
char mema[4096];
char *memp1;
int counter;
void main ()
{
    __asm MOV DI,OFFSET mema;   /* 1 cycle, Assumes alignment on even bound */
    __asm MOV CX,4096/2;        /* 1 cycle */
    __asm MOV AX,0;             /* 1 cycle */
    __asm REP STOSW;            /* 7+(2048*4) cycles */
}
```

Total cycles for this code: 8,202.

REP STOSD costs 4 cycles per store and moves twice as much as REP STOSW. Since storing words rather than bytes improved our program so much, perhaps it can be improved even more by storing double-words rather than words. Despite the fact that the code has to ensure address misalignment can't happen, using REP STOSD instead of REP STOSW looks worth it:

```
            XOR EAX,EAX                  ;!2 cycles (Prefix Rule)
            MOV DI,buffer_we_want_zeroed ;1 cycle
            MOV CX,4096/2                ;1 cycle
            TEST DI,3                    ;1 cycle
            JZ labela                    ;1 or 3 cycles
            STOSW                        ;5 cycles
            DEC CX                       ;1 cycle
labela:     SHR CX,1                     ;2 cycles
            REP STOSD                    ;8+(1024*4) cycles
            JNC labelb                   ;1 or 3 cycles
            STOSW                        ;1 cycle
labelb:
```

Total cycles for this code: 4,117. This change delivers what the cycle-counting promises. The code is zeroing at a rate of about 2 cycles per word. The gain is 50 percent over the code that uses REP STOSW, and 95 percent over the original C program.

Let's take this one step further. Table 9.7 shows that REP MOVSx takes 3 cycles per move. This is faster than REP STOSx's 4 cycles per store, so if the code must frequently clear buffers to zero, initializing the first double-word and then moving the buffer to itself has the potential to speed things up even more. That is, replace REP STOSD with:

```
MOV [SI],EAX    ;!2 cycles ;first buffer word = 0
LEA SI,[DI+4]   ;1 cycle
REP MOVSD       ;11+(1024*3) cycles
```

This code does what it's intended to do — it zeros the buffer. However, the apparent 25 percent savings is a classic optimization mirage. Although REP MOVSx is faster than REP STOSx, it is not actually faster by 1 cycle per iteration because MOVSx is one of three 486 assembler instructions that accesses two memory operands (the others are PUSH and POP). This means MOVSx depletes the cache more quickly than the other instructions, and so cycle counts get quite unreliable when MOVSx is involved. After a series of timing tests of the above two loops, we've concluded that it's safer to think of REP MOVSx as being a 4.1-cycle instruction "in practice." (Note: despite the caching problem, REP MOVSx is faster than REP STOSx. If you move <number> bytes, then reset SI and CX, and repeat until <required number> bytes are moved, your code will still be about 20 percent faster with REP MOVSx than if you use REP STOSx. We won't illustrate this complex trick here because there's an even faster replacement for REP STOSx; see our MEMSET routine in Chapter 11.)

And finally, the fastest — and most piggish — of all clear-the-buffer tricks. In an MS-DOS program, if the task of clearing a 200-byte buffer is so important that it should get priority over everything else, this is the way to do it:

```
CLI                 ;Prevent other jobs from interrupting
MOV DX,SP           ;Save a copy of the SP register
LEA SP,[DI+200]     ;Point SP to end of buffer
PUSH EAX            ;SP-=4; [SP] = EAX
PUSH EAX            ;SP-=4; [SP] = EAX
                    ;Repeat PUSH EAX 48 more times — full
                    ;unrolling, but not over limit
MOV SP,DX           ;Restore original SP register value
STI                 ;Allow interrupts again
```

Most operating systems (including Windows95, apparently) won't let application programs use CLI, so this interesting idea has a short future. If it's possible to use it, average speed should approach about .5 cycles per byte in actual practice (that is, taking the write-through cache pipeline stall into account).

REP STOSB and REP STOSW can be changed to REP STOSW and REP STOSD, respectively, by shifting the CX register 1 bit to the right. The principles are the same as for the replace REP MOVSB with REP MOVSW and replace REP MOVSW with REP MOVSD optimization shown earlier (remember especially, that DI cannot equal [SI+1]). The following code, for example, uses STOSD instead of STOSW (assuming the direction flag is OFF).

```
        TEST DI,3       ;1 cycle            ;If address isn't double-word aligned
        JNZ labela      ;3 or 1 cycles      ;use STOSW.
        SHR CX,1        ;3 cycles           ;See note in MOVSB to MOVSW example.
        REP STOSD       ;8+(4*CX)           ;Store n/2 double-words, not n words.
        ADC CX,0        ;1 or 3 cycles      ;When we SHR'd was low-most bit a 0?
labela: REP STOSW       ;7+(4*CX) cycles    ;If low-most bit was 1: final STOSW.
labels: ...
```

The TEST DI,3 instruction is necessary here because misalignment is very possible for double-word addresses.

REP CMPSx

REP CMPSB — REPeat CMPSB <CX> times or until the last comparison returns not equal — decrements CX with each iteration of a CMPSB instruction and stops (i.e., goes on to execute the next instruction) either when CX becomes 0 or when a check of the zero flag shows its status is OFF.

REPNZ CMPSB — REPeat CMPSB <CX> times or until the last comparison returns equal — decrements CX with each iteration of a CMPSB instruction and stops (i.e., goes on to execute the next instruction) either when CX becomes 0 or when a check of the zero flag shows its status is ON.

The following code achieves precisely the same effect as REP CMPSB but is not a replacement. It is intended only to be an illustration of, conceptually, precisely how REP CMPSB works.

```
        TEST CX,CX      ;1 cycle            ;If CX contains 0, then
        JZ labelc       ;1 or 3 cycles      ;(do no comparison at all)
        PUSH AX         ;1 cycle            ;Save current AX contents
labela: MOV AL,ES:[DI]  ;2 cycles           ;AL = what ES:DI points to
        MOV AH,[SI]     ;1 cycle            ;AH = what DS:SI points to
        INC SI          ;1 cycle            ;++SI
        INC DI          ;1 cycle            ;++DI
        CMP AH,AL       ;1 cycle            ;Compare [DS:SI] to [ES:DI]
        JNZ labelb      ;1 or 3 cycles      ;(if not equal, exit loop)
        DEC CX          ;1 cycle            ;--CX
        JZ labela       ;1 or 3 cycles      ;(If CX didn't hit 0, repeat)
labelb: POP AX          ;1 cycle            ;Restore original AX contents
labelc:                                     ;flags have result of comparison
                                            ;SI and DI are past the unequal byte
```

(Note: the loop doesn't begin with MOV AH,[SI] + MOV AL,ES:[DI] to avoid the penalty imposed by the Bytes-and-Pointers Rule.)

Actually, this code fails to act precisely like REP CMPSB in one situation: If CX is 0 at the outset, then the flags register should not be changed. This highlights an interesting trap. If two strings which are 0 bytes long are being compared, it's logical to expect that since "all" the bytes are equal the result of the comparison should be a setting of the zero flag to ON. But this is not the case. Do not use the following code if there is any prospect that CX can equal 0:

```
REP CMPSB
JZ strings_not_equal
....                          ;Assume the strings are equal if code reaches here
```

Since no CMPSB takes place, there is no way of guessing the status of the flags. This is true for both REP CMPSx and REPNZ CMPSx.

REP SCASx

REP SCASB — REPeat SCASB <CX> times or until the last comparison returns not equal — decrements CX with each iteration of a SCASB instruction and stops (i.e., goes on to execute the next instruction) either when CX becomes 0 or when a check of the zero flag shows its status is OFF.

REPNZ SCASB — REPeat SCASB <CX> times or until the last comparison returns equal — decrements CX with each iteration of a SCASB instruction and stops (i.e., goes on to execute the next instruction) either when CX becomes 0 or when a check of the zero flag shows its status is ON.

REP SCASx and REPNZ SCASx have the same trap as REP CMPSx and REPNZ CMPSx — if the CX register equals 0, don't use this code:

```
REP SCASB
JZ strings_not_equal
....                          ;Assume the strings are equal if code reaches here
```

Since no SCASB takes place, there is no way of guessing the status of the flags.

The following code achieves precisely the same effect as REPNZ SCASB. Once again, this code is purely to show how REPNZ SCASB works and isn't intended to be a replacement for the instruction. (We could make it faster with loop unrolling but we'd have to unroll at least 3 times to break even with REPNZ SCASB.)

```
        TEST CX,CX        ;1 cycle          ;If CX register is 0, then
        JZ labelb         ;1 or 3 cycles    ;(do no comparison at all)
labela: CMP AL,ES:[DI]    ;!3 cycles        ;AL is set up before entry
        LEA DI,[DI+1]     ;1 cycle          ;++DI without changing flags
        JZ labelb         ;1 or 3 cycles    ;(CMP set zero flag so stop)
        DEC CX            ;1 cycle          ;--CX, setting flags thus
        JNZ labela        ;1 or 3 cycles    ;(CX isn't 0 yet so repeat)
labelb:                                     ;flags have result of comparison
                                            ;DI is past the unequal byte
```

On the other hand, you *can* replace REP SCASB with:

```
@loop1:  MOV DX,[DI]    ;1 cycle          ;Assumes correct alignment and
         CMP AL,DL      ;1 cycle          ;Assumes CX is positive and
         JZ @@loop2     ;1 cycle          ;Assumes CX is even.
         CMP AL,DH      ;1 cycle
         JZ @@loop2     ;1 cycle
         ADD DI,2       ;1 cycle
         SUB CX,2       ;1 cycle
         JG @@loop1     ;3 or 1 cycles
```

This code and REP SCASB both take 5 cycles per byte. (DX is a 16-bit register so the code above is moving words, not bytes.) The trick is, after comparing the lower 8-bit halves of the word, it's known that the lower halves are equal, so CMP AL,DH must be a comparison of the higher halves only.

REP SCASW can be replaced by:

```
@loop1:  MOV EDX,[DI]   ;!2 cycles        ;Assumes correct alignment and
         CMP AX,DX      ;1 cycle          ;Assumes CX is positive and
         JZ @@loop2     ;1 or 3 cycles    ;Assumes CX is even.
         CMP EAX,EDX    ;!2 cycles
         JZ @@loop2     ;1 or 3 cycles
         ADD DI,4       ;1 cycle
         SUB CX,4       ;1 cycle
         JG @@loop1     ;1 cycle
```

This code and REP SCASW both take 5 cycles per word. (EDX is a 32-bit register so the code above is moving double-words, not words.) Again, the trick is, after comparing the lower 16-bit halves of the double-word, it's known that the lower halves are equal, so CMP EAX,EDX must be a comparison of the higher halves only.

Because they take the same number of cycles as REP SCASx, neither of these routines is a good replacement unless (a) you unroll the loop; or (b) you're searching the block for something other than equality (for example, you could replace the JZ instructions with JA instructions — such a modification is not possible with SCASx).

You can use SCASB to find the size of a C string. Suppose you have a pointer to a C string. As in all C strings, the last byte is a null byte: \0. You want to find this last byte so you'll know where the string ends. SCASB can tell you that the size of the string 'XYZ' is three characters by telling you that \0 is the fourth character. The trick is to start with CX = 0FFFFh (that is, −1), which, as far as REP is concerned means "repeat 65,535 times." The following code uses REPNZ SCASB to search for the terminating \0 byte, then negates CX.

```
MOV AL,0           ;We're searching for '\0', so let AL = 0
MOV CX,0FFFFh      ;CX = 0FFFFh, which is -1, or which is 65535
REPNZ SCASB        ;Scan, incrementing DI and decrementing CX
NOT CX             ;Complement CX
DEC CX             ;Now CX has the offset of '\0' in the string
```

All C compilers use this trick in their implementation of _strlen. We know a faster way: load a full word into a register and then compare each half of the register with \0, as follows:

```
                ;AL = character to search for. In this case, AL contains 0.
                ;BX --> C string.
                ;BX must be aligned for this code to work properly
@@loop: MOV DX,[BX]   ;1 cycle
        CMP DL,AL     ;1 cycle
        JZ  @@end0    ;3 or 1 cycles
        ADD BX,2      ;1 cycle
        CMP DH,AL     ;1 cycle
        JNZ @@loop    ;3 or 1 cycles
        DEC BX        ;1 cycle        ;end encountered because AH=[BX]
@@end0:                               ;end encountered because AL=[BX]
```

This code is faster than code that compares a register to a string 1 byte at a time. Consider these facts: MOV takes only 1 cycle to load [BX] into DL and [BX+1] into DH, and both CMP DL,AL and CMP DH,AL take only 1 cycle each. Therefore:

```
MOV DX,[BX]     ;1 cycle
CMP DL,AL       ;1 cycle
...
CMP DH,AL       ;1 cycle
```

is faster than

```
CMP AL,[BX]     ;2 cycles
...
CMP AL,[BX+1]   ;2 cycles
```

With a lot of loop unrolling you can search in 2.5 cycles per byte — twice as fast as REP SCASB.

In some cases, there's an even faster way to search for \0:

```
                ;Assume the search is for '\0', not the general case
                ;BX --> C string.
                ;BX must be aligned for this code to work properly
@@loop: MOV DX,[BX]   ;1 cycle
        ADD BX,2      ;1 cycle
        TEST DL,DH    ;1 cycle
        JNZ @@loop    ;3 or 1 cycles
        TEST DL,DL    ;1 cycle
        JZ  @@end0    ;3 or 1 cycles
        TEST DH,DH    ;1 cycle
        JNZ @@loop    ;3 or 1 cycles
        DEC BX        ;1 cycle
@@end0:
```

The key to this code is the TEST DL, DH instruction, which will set the zero flag if *either* DL or DH equals 0 — a neat way of testing two bytes in a single instruction. Unfortunately TEST DH, DL is not precise, so if the zero flag *does* go ON, the additional tests TEST DL, DL and TEST DH, DH have to be made to see which register equals 0. Even so, if the string being checked is English text — spaces, punctuation and lowercase letters — this loop, when unrolled, takes as few as 2.1 cycles per byte.

Despite the performance gains, though, we're not advocating that you abandon REP SCASx and use replacements all the time. The routines we've shown you are too dangerous to use with any protected-mode operating environment, including Windows 3.1 in both standard or enhanced386 mode as they stand because they could trigger a General Protection Fault (GPF).

A GPF is an attempt to read or write to an address which is beyond a segment limit. For example, suppose the current data segment (the one that the DS segment register refers to) has a size of 4,095 bytes. The segment limit in this case is 4,094, that is, the last valid byte in the segment is byte number 4,094 (as usual we use base-0 arithmetic). If the \0 you're searching for is in this last byte, then eventually BX will equal 4,094 and the next MOV DX, [BX] instruction will cause a crash because this word-sized access is trying to load both byte number 4,094 and byte number 4,095. Loading byte number 4,094 is, of course, no problem (MOV DL, [BX] would work) but byte number 4,095 is beyond the segment limit and is therefore protected from any unauthorized access. (This is what the phrase "Windows runs in protected mode" means.)

MS-DOS doesn't run in protected mode so you don't have to worry about General Protection Faults when writing MS-DOS application programs. However, if you want to implement your code in a Windows program, you'll either have to use REP SCASx instead of replacements such as the ones in this chapter, or be very careful in calculating the segment limit and ensuring your code doesn't try to go beyond it. You can find the segment limit either by using the Windows API function GetSelectorLimit or (the faster way) by using the assembler instruction LSL.

The LSL Instruction

In an assembler statement, the syntax of the LSL instruction looks like this:

```
LSL <destination operand>,<source operand>    ;optional comment
```

The \<source operand\> can be either a 16-bit or 32-bit register or memory operand. The \<destination operand\> can be either a 16-bit or 32-bit register which matches the size of the \<source operand\>. LSL is strictly a protected mode instruction; it won't work inside an MS-DOS program.

The meaning of LSL is imperative:

Load Segment Limit from \<source operand\> into \<destination operand\>.

LSL turns the zero flag ON but has no effect on the other flags.

LSL has four possible forms, depending on the operands used. Table 9.8 is a standardized description for the possible forms of LSL.

LSL's opcode includes a 0Fh prefix, so an extra cycle is added each time the instruction is run unless the Prefix-Waiver Rule is in effect.

Before using LSL, you have to put a valid segment selector (e.g., a value from a segment register or memory) into the \<source operand\>. (If the segment selector is not valid, LSL turns the zero flag OFF and doesn't change the \<destination operand\>.) For example:

```
MOV AX,DS                      ;Move contents of DS into AX
LSL DX,AX                      ;Load Data Segment Limit into DX

MOV AX,WORD PTR pointer+2      ;If pointer is defined as char far *,
LSL DX,AX                      ;then pointer+2 has the segment part.
```

Instruction Mnemonic	Destination Operand	Source Operand	Cycle Count
LSL	\<16-bit register\>	\<16-bit register\>	10
LSL	\<16-bit register\>	\<word-size memory\>	10
LSL	\<32-bit register\>	\<32-bit register\>	10
LSL	\<32-bit register\>	\<long-size memory\>	10

Table 9.8   Standardized description for the possible forms of LSL.

The following routine, which uses LSL, is a replacement for Windows 3.1's GetSelectorLimit:

```
/* Function: return the segment limit. Uses inline assembly and LSL.
   Pass: segment selector
   Return: segment limit (=0 if segment selector is invalid)
   This function works only in protected mode.
*/

int GetSelectorLimit (int memp)
{
  __asm XOR AX,AX;        /* if the LSL fails, AX will remain = 0 */
  __asm MOV DX,memp;      /* Move the segment selector into DX */
  __asm DB 0Fh;           /* This is the LSL AX,DX instruction */
  __asm DB 03h;           /* — Load Segment Limit. Put the address */
  __asm DB 0C2h;          /* of the highest accessible byte into AX. */
}
```

(Note: LSL does *not* return the top limit if memp equals SS, the Stack Segment. If you want to find out the segment limit for an automatic variable, don't use LSL because automatic variables are in the Stack Segment. Instead, you could assume that the ultimate limit is the current value of SP; that is, use:

```
__asm MOV AX,SP;    /* Use instead of LSL if stack segment */ )
```

Armed with a knowledge of the segment limit, you can use our code suggestions to replace Intel string instructions even under Windows and still avoid GPFs. However, because LSL involves some cycle overhead, the replacement code won't be faster unless the string involved is at least 20 bytes long. For that reason, we won't use this trick when we implement a replacement for the _strlen function in Chapter 11. If you find that your application is searching fairly long strings on a regular basis, you'll be able to improve performance by writing your own replacement code using what we've described in this chapter.

A final note about Windows 3.1 segments: GlobalAlloc always allocates a multiple of 32 bytes, e.g., if you ask for 65 bytes, you'll get 96 bytes (always an even number). In practice, then, it should be impossible to trigger a GPF with our replacement code provided you make sure that BX is aligned at the start. There is no guarantee that this will be true forever though.

Before leaving the subject of GPFs, we need to mention an idea which should not be attempted — picking up multiple bytes at a time then testing, e.g.:

```
labela: MOV EDX,[DI]            ;!2 cycles
        CMP DL,0                ;1 cycle
        JZ labelb               ;1 or 3 cycles
        CMP DH,0                ;1 cycle
        JZ labelb               ;1 or 3 cycles
        TEST EDX,0FF0000h       ;!2 cycles
        JZ labelb               ;1 or 3 cycles
        TEST EDX,0FF000000h     ;!2 cycles
        JZ labelb               ;1 or 3 cycles
        SUB CX,4                ;1 cycle
        JNZ labela              ;1 or 3 cycles
labelb: ...
```

Unless your code will never be run under anything but MS-DOS, this shouldn't be tried because the danger of a protected mode violation is too great.

Where You Are

In this chapter, you learned:

❖ how to set and clear the direction flag with STD and CLD so that Intel string instructions would know whether to increment or decrement addresses;

❖ how to compare Intel strings with CMPSx, and how to replace CMPSx with faster code;

❖ how to load Intel strings with LODSx, and how to replace LODSx with faster code;

❖ how to move Intel strings with MOVSx, and how to replace MOVSx with faster code;

❖ how to scan Intel strings with SCASx, and how to replace SCASx with faster code;

❖ how to store Intel strings with STOSx, and how to replace STOSx with faster code;

- ❖ how to execute repeated Intel string instructions with REP CMPSx, REP MOVSx, REP SCASx, and REP STOSx and also with REPNZ CMPSx and REPNZ SCASx;

- ❖ how to replace byte instructions with word instructions and word instructions with double-word instructions as long as it isn't possible that DI=[SI+1];

- ❖ other ways to speed up your code by replacing Intel string instructions;

- ❖ how to avoid General Protection Faults by using the LSL instruction to find the segment limit.

Chapter 10

Optimizing A Sort

We're now finished with our assembler primer. The rest of this book will take a more in-depth look at how assembler can be used to improve the overall performance of a C program.

In this chapter we're going to optimize a small model C routine that sorts arrays of signed integers in ascending order. The maximum number of elements in the array is 30,000 but on average, it's a very small number: around 20. Our priorities are, in descending order:

(1) correctness;

(2) average speed;

(3) worst speed;

(4) best speed; and

(5) size. This time, we'll begin our optimizing at the beginning.

Don't we always begin at the beginning? No, not really. So far in this book, we've generally started with a set of C instructions and looked for ways to speed them up with ideas that grew from our assembler knowledge. The question of where the C program came from never came up. That question's not entirely outside the scope of this book, but until now our examples have been so simple that examining the stages needed to come up with the code wasn't necessary. In this chapter, we'll indicate the code's genesis — or rather, we'll specify where we got the four public domain C programs we'll be examining.

When we looked for code to work with in this chapter, we came across four different algorithms which will sort arrays of signed integers in ascending order. The first stage of optimizing our target program was to choose one of the algorithms to work with.

Candidate Number 1: Insertion Sort.

Source: Microsoft Visual C++ 2.0's sample file \msvc15\samples\sortdemo.c.
Advantage: it's the simplest.

```
void insertsort (int array[],int size)
{
 unsigned int i;
 char temp;
 for (i=0; i<size-1;)
 {                               /* For each element of the array: */
  if (array[i]>array[i+1])
  {                              /* if it's greater than the next: */
   temp=array[i];               /* swap it with the next one */
   array[i]=array[i+1];
   array[i+1]=temp;
   if (i!=0) i--;               /* and backtrack. */
   else i++;
  }
  else i++;
 }
}                               /* Otherwise: on to the next. */
```

Candidate Number 2: Bubble Sort.

Source: Carl Townsend, *QuickC Programming for the IBM*, Howard W. Sams, 1988

```
void bubblesort (int *array,int size)
{
 int i,j;
 int temp;
 for (i=0; i<size-1; i++)       /* From <first> to <second-last> */
 {
  for (j=i+1; j<size; j++)      /* From <current> to <last> */
  {
   if (array[i]>array[j])       /* If a pair is out of order: */
   {
    temp=array[i];              /* Swap array[i] with array[j]. */
    array[i]=array[j];
    array[j]=temp;
   }
  }
 }
}
```

Candidate Number 3: Shell Sort.

Source: Brian Kernighan and Dennis Ritchie, *The C Programming Language*, Prentice-Hall, 1978. The touted advantage: "in early stages, far-apart elements are compared ... this tends to eliminate large amounts of disorder quickly."

```
void shellsort (int v[],int n)
{
 int gap,i,j;
 int temp;
 for (gap=n/2; gap>0; gap/=2)
 {
  for (i=gap; i<n; i++)
  {
   for (j=i-gap; j>=0 && v[j]>v[j+gap]; j-=gap)
   {
    temp=v[j];
    v[j]=v[j+gap];
    v[j+gap]=temp;
   }
  }
 }
}
```

Candidate Number 4: Quicksort.

Source: R. Sedgewick, Implementing Quicksort Programs, Comm. ACM Oct.1978 and Corrigendum, Comm. ACM, June 1979 (Mr. Sedgewick has since written a complete book titled *Algorithms in C*). You don't have to understand all of this listing; it's only necessary to see that quicksort is somewhat more complex than the other three candidates.

```
void quicksort (int *base, unsigned size)
{
 int *stack[40];                        /* stack */
 int **sp;                              /* stack pointer */
 int *i, *j, *limit, *mid;              /* various array pointers */
 int element_count;
 int tmp;
 sp = stack;                            /* initialize pointer to stack */
 limit = base + size;                   /* pointer past end of array */
 for (;;)
 {                                      /* two levels of "infinite" loop */
  for (;;)
  {
   element_count = limit - base;        /* # of elements to do on this round*/
   if (element_count <= 7) break;       /* if <7 elements use insertion sort*/
   mid=base+(element_count>>1);         /* mid = halfway from start to end */
   tmp=*mid; *mid=*base; *base=tmp;     /* Exchange *mid, *base */
   i = base + 1;                        /* i starts @bottom and goes up */
   j = limit - 1;                       /* j starts @top and goes down */
   if (*i>*j)
   {                                    /* if (*i>*j): Exchange *i,*j */
        tmp=*i; *i=*j; *j=tmp;
   }
```

```
if (*base>*j)
{                                /* if (*base>*j): Exchange *base,*j */
 tmp=*base; *base=*j; *j=tmp;
}
if (*i>*base)
{                                /* if (*i>*base): Exchange *i,*base */
      tmp=*base; *base=*i; *i=tmp;
}
for (;;)
{
 do i++; while (*i < *base);     /* i goes up till it's >= base */
 do j--; while (*j > *base);     /* j goes down till it's <= base */
 if (i > j) break;               /* if j has passed i, stop looping */
 tmp=*i; *i=*j; *j=tmp;          /* Exchange *i,*j */
}
tmp=*base; *base=*j; *j=tmp;     /* Exchange *base, *j */
if (j - base > limit - i)
{                                /* If (lower section is bigger now) */
 *sp = base;                     /* "Push base" (= base when we pop) */
 *(sp+1) = j;                    /* "Push j" (= limit when we pop) */
 base = i;
}                                /* Next iteration with upper section*/
else
{                                /* If (upper section is bigger now) */
 *sp = i;                        /* "Push i" (= base when we pop) */
 *(sp+1) = limit;                /* "Push limit" (=limit when we pop)*/
 limit = j;
}                                /* Next iteration with lower section*/
 sp += 2;
}                                /* "Inc" stack pointer, 2 elements */
i = base + 1;                    /* element_count <= 7, so */
while (i < limit)
{                                /* we switch to an insertion sort */
 j = i;                          /* This part of the routine is */
 while (j > base && *(j-1)>*j)
 {                               /* very similar to insertion_sort */
  tmp=*(j-1); *(j-1)=*j; *j=tmp; /* shown earlier, so the 2 functions*/
  j--;
 }                               /* should perform about the same if */
 i++;
}                                /* the number of elements is <= 7. */
if (sp > stack)
{                                /* Is there something on the stack? */
 sp -= 2;                        /* Yes, we "Pushed." Now we "Pop." */
 base = *sp;                     /* Compare Kernighan & Ritchie's */
 limit = *(sp+1);
}                                /* push() and pop() procedures. */
else break;
}
}                                /* When the stack's empty, stop. */
```

You've probably already seen some of our candidate sort algorithms in a book or magazine article. If you did, you might recall that the number of comparisons is proportional to the square of the number of elements, or it's proportional to the log_2, or it's based on some other fairly complicated calculation. This information would be important if you knew what it costs to compare two elements or what it costs to exchange them — but you don't. The only way to find the cost out is to actually time the comparisons and exchanges. In that case, it's no more trouble to time the entire sort function, which is what we did.

We timed the four candidate sort algorithms in the usual way, using the three test C compilers and three variations of the array contents. In the first variation, all elements are in order. In the second variation, all elements are in reverse order. In the third variation, all elements equal 1 except the last element, which is 0. The results, in seconds elapsed, follow:

Test #1: at the start, all array elements are in order.
Array contains: { 1,2,3,4,5,6,7,8,9,10,11,12,13,14,15,16,17,18,19,20 }

	Borland	**Microsoft**	**Symantec**
insertsort	15	11	13
bubblesort	80	67	85
shellsort	59	59	59
quicksort	29	25	36

Test #2: at the start, all array elements are in reverse order.
Array contains: { 20,19,18,17,16,15,14,13,12,11,10,9,8,7,6,5,4,3,2,1 }

	Borland	**Microsoft**	**Symantec**
insertsort	390	219	259
bubblesort	84	75	86
shellsort	83	69	80
quicksort	38	31	44

Test #3: at the start, all array elements are in order except the last.
Array contains: { 1,1,1,1,1,1,1,1,1,1,1,1,1,1,1,1,1,1,1,0 }

	Borland	**Microsoft**	**Symantec**
insertsort	53	32	38
bubblesort	80	67	85
shellsort	63	60	61
quicksort	34	28	39

At first glance, it appeared that insertsort was the better algorithm for our purpose because insertsort is the fastest of the four when all rows are in order at the start — which might be a common circumstance for our target program. When we ran the third test, though, we saw that insertsort takes 250 percent longer if just *one* element is changed — that's just too volatile to make it a good choice. The evidence of the timing tests forces us to pick quicksort as the algorithm to use.

Let's clarify the importance of what we've just done. By the narrow definition of the word "optimize" that we've been using throughout this book, we haven't done any optimizing so far in this chapter. But we *have* made our target program faster because our original plan for this chapter was "how to optimize a bubble sort." We had a brilliant critique of the traps that C compilers encounter when they translate the `bubblesort` algorithm, and we had some suggestions ready which speeded up `bubblesort` by about 35 percent. Think of our embarrassment: we were planning on presenting a 35 percent speedup by tweaking the `bubblesort` algorithm when anyone could get a 50 percent improvement merely by replacing it with the `quicksort` algorithm!

Why didn't we start in the first place by searching the literature, compiling candidate algorithms, and running timing tests? Because that's boring! On the other hand, hacking away at a C compiler's code is like solving an easy puzzle — we enjoy it. Still, we've got an excuse: we were writing a book about optimizing using assembler tricks, so all we could think about was optimizing using assembler tricks. In our real programming lives we'd never jump to the tweaking stage before not only making sure the original C algorithm was right for the purpose it was being put to, but that it was the best possible algorithm to use.

Anyway, at this stage we've chosen an algorithm to use. Stage two of optimizing our target program involves checking the algorithm to see whether improvements can be made in the C code. Since that's beyond the scope of this book, we'll just assume that a published algorithm is the best it can be and skip this stage.

Stage three of optimizing our target program involves taking a closer look at how our compiler (we chose Microsoft as the test compiler for this chapter) translates the winning candidate. (Again, it's not necessary to understand every detail of the code. Just skim it and see if you can find some places that might be improvable given what you've read so far. Then skip ahead to our Lab Notes for what we think are the answers.)

Microsoft's Translation of the quicksort Function

The labels and code in this section come from Microsoft. The commentary is our own. The numbers just preceding the comments are the cycle times for each instruction. If a penalty affects the cycle time, the number is preceded by an exclamation mark (!). Line numbers are shown following a double dash (--) at the end of each comment.

```
_quicksort proc near
  PUSH    BP                      ;!2    ;Actually Microsoft used ENTER 92,0        --  1
  MOV     BP,SP                   ;1     ;here — a rare and useless instruction.    --  2
  SUB     SP,92 ;005Ch            ;1     ;Our PUSH + MOV + SUB are a replacement.   --  3
  PUSH    DI                      ;!2    ;DI gets popped again at program end        --  4
  PUSH    SI                      ;1     ;SI gets popped again at program end        --  5
  MOV     DX,WORD PTR [BP+4]      ;1     ;[BP+4] is passed "base" parameter          --  6
  LEA     AX,WORD PTR [BP-90]     ;1     ;C code: sp = stack;                        --  7
  MOV     WORD PTR [BP-10],AX     ;1     ;[BP-10] will hold a tmp copy of sp         --  8
  MOV     AX,WORD PTR [BP+6]      ;1     ;[BP+6] is passed "size" parameter          --  9
  ADD     AX,AX                   ;1     ;times 2 because an int is 2 bytes          -- 10
  ADD     AX,DX                   ;1     ;C code: limit = base + size;               -- 11
  MOV     WORD PTR [BP-8],AX      ;1     ;[BP-8] will hold a tmp copy of limit       -- 12
  JMP     $L238                   ;3     ;Jump to where the limit is checked         -- 13
$FC185:                                  ;The main body of the outer loop begins here -- 14
  MOV     BX,CX                   ;1     ;C code: mid=base+(element_count>>1);       -- 15
  AND     BL,254                  ;1     ;CX was initialized after $L238 label       -- 16
  MOV     SI,DX                   ;1     ;Using SI register for "base" here          -- 17
  MOV     AX,WORD PTR [BX][SI]    ;!4    ;AX = base + (element_count*2)/2            -- 18
  MOV     WORD PTR [BP-2],AX      ;1     ;[BP-2] will hold a copy of "tmp"           -- 19
  MOV     AX,WORD PTR [SI]        ;1     ;C code: tmp=*mid;*mid=*base;*base=tmp      -- 20
  MOV     WORD PTR [BX][SI],AX    ;2     ;Notice 2nd use of a double register        -- 21
  MOV     AX,WORD PTR [BP-2]      ;1                                                 -- 22
  MOV     WORD PTR [SI],AX        ;1                                                 -- 23
  LEA     DI,WORD PTR [SI+2]      ;1     ;C code: i = base+1;                        -- 24
  MOV     BX,WORD PTR [BP-8]      ;1     ;C code: j = limit-1;[BP-8] is limit        -- 25
  SUB     BX,2                    ;1     ;Using BX register for "j" here             -- 26
  MOV     AX,WORD PTR [DI]        ;1     ;C code: if (*i>*j) {                       -- 27
  CMP     WORD PTR [BX],AX        ;!3    ;Notice transposal of operands              -- 28
  JGE     $I191                   ;1/3   ;Not JAE;integers are signed                -- 29
  MOV     CX,AX                   ;1     ;C code: tmp=*i;8=*j;*j=tmp;                -- 30
  MOV     AX,WORD PTR [BX]        ;1     ;Still using BX register for j here.        -- 31
  MOV     WORD PTR [DI],AX        ;1     ;and DI register for i. Microsoft is        -- 32
  MOV     WORD PTR [BX],CX        ;1     ;using a register for "tmp" this time.      -- 33
$I191: MOV AX,WORD PTR [SI]       ;1     ;C code: if (*base>*j) {                    -- 34
  CMP     WORD PTR [BX],AX        ;2     ;At this point, SI register is base,        -- 35
  JGE     $I192                   ;3/1   ;BX register is j. AX is *base              -- 36
  MOV     CX,AX                   ;1     ;C code: tmp=*base;*base=*j;*j=tmp;         -- 37
  MOV     AX,WORD PTR [BX]        ;1     ;This exchange is similar to the one        -- 38
  MOV     WORD PTR [SI],AX        ;1     ;we did 8 lines ago. Microsoft finds        -- 39
  MOV     WORD PTR [BX],CX        ;1     ;a free register about half the time.       -- 40
$I192: MOV AX,WORD PTR [SI]       ;1     ;C code: if (*i>*base) {                    -- 41
  CMP     WORD PTR [DI],AX        ;2     ;At this point, SI register is base.        -- 42
  JLE     $L220                   ;3/1   ;DI register is i, AX is *base again.       -- 43
  MOV     CX,AX                   ;1     ;C code: tmp=*base;*base=*i;*i=tmp;         -- 44
  MOV     AX,WORD PTR [DI]        ;1     ;In repetitions like this we sometimes      -- 45
  MOV     WORD PTR [SI],AX        ;1     ;see some cases where a register gets       -- 46
  MOV     WORD PTR [DI],CX        ;1     ;loaded with the same value twice.          -- 47
$L220: MOV WORD PTR [BP+4],DX     ;1     ;Beginning of the inner for (;;) loop       -- 48
  MOV     WORD PTR [BP-4],BX      ;1     ;Using [BP-4] for j here                    -- 49
```

```
$D197: MOV SI,DX                  ;1    ;C code: do i++;while (*i < *base) ;      -- 50
       ADD DI,2                   ;1    ;DI still is i, this is the "i++" part    -- 51
       MOV AX,WORD PTR [SI]       ;!2   ;SI still is base, so AX is *base         -- 52
       CMP WORD PTR [DI],AX       ;2    ;and here we're comparing *i to *base     -- 53
       JL $D197                   ;1/3  ;(*i<*base,loop to reload SI register)     -- 54
       MOV WORD PTR [BP-6],DI     ;1    ;[BP-6] holds a tmp copy of i             -- 55
$D200: SUB BX,2                   ;1    ;BX is still j, this is the "j-- " part   -- 56
       MOV AX,WORD PTR [SI]       ;1    ;C code: do j --;while (*j > *base) ;     -- 57
       CMP WORD PTR [BX],AX       ;!3   ;and here we're comparing *j to *base     -- 58
       JG $D200                   ;1/3  ;(*j<*base,loop to check *base again)     -- 59
       CMP BX,DI                  ;1    ;C code: if (i > j) break;                -- 60
       JB $L223                   ;1/3  ;(breakout: j and i passed each other)    -- 61
       MOV DX,WORD PTR [DI]       ;1    ;C code: tmp=*i;*i=*j;*j=tmp;             -- 62
       MOV AX,WORD PTR [BX]       ;1    ;Notice that this time Microsoft is       -- 63
       MOV WORD PTR [DI],AX       ;1    ;using the DX register for tmp, which     -- 64
       MOV WORD PTR [BX],DX       ;1    ;is safe because it's about to reload     -- 65
       MOV DX,WORD PTR [BP+4]     ;1    ;DX register from [BP+4] i.e. "base."     -- 66
       JMP short $L220            ;3    ;Back to beginning of inner loop now      -- 67
$L223: MOV DX,WORD PTR [BP+4]     ;1    ;[BP+4] is passed "base" parameter        -- 68
       MOV SI,DX                  ;1    ;C code: tmp=*base;*base=*j;*j=tmp;       -- 69
       MOV AX,WORD PTR [SI]       ;!3   ;On this occasion Microsoft has run       -- 70
       MOV WORD PTR [BP-2],AX     ;1    ;out of registers to use for "tmp", so    -- 71
       MOV AX,WORD PTR [BX]       ;1    ;it presses a stack memory operand        -- 72
       MOV WORD PTR [SI],AX       ;1    ;into service. Namely: [BP-2] will        -- 73
       MOV AX,WORD PTR [BP-2]     ;1    ;be used for "tmp" in this exchange.      -- 74
       MOV WORD PTR [BX],AX       ;1                                              -- 75
       MOV DI,WORD PTR [BP-8]     ;1    ;[BP-8] is where we stored "limit"        -- 76
       MOV AX,DI                  ;1    ;C code: if (j - base > limit - i) {      -- 77
       SUB AX,WORD PTR [BP-6]     ;2    ;[BP-6] is where we stored "i"            -- 78
       AND AL,254                 ;1    ;Actually, this code means: "if          -- 79
       MOV CX,BX                  ;1    ;((j-base)&0xFFFE)>(limit-i)&0xFFFE))"    -- 80
       SUB CX,SI                  ;1    ;which is not an exact translation of     -- 81
       AND CL,254                 ;1    ;the original C code. It's harmless;      -- 82
       CMP AX,CX                  ;!2   ;base and limit both point to ints        -- 83
       JGE $I204                  ;3/1  ;so are an even number of bytes apart.    -- 84
       MOV CX,WORD PTR [BP-10]    ;1    ;[BP-10] is used for "sp" variable        -- 85
       MOV SI,CX                  ;1    ;C code: *sp = base                       -- 86
       MOV WORD PTR [SI],DX       ;!3   ;Using SI register for "sp"               -- 87
       MOV WORD PTR [SI+2],BX     ;1    ;C code: *(sp+1) = j;                     -- 88
       MOV DX,WORD PTR [BP-6]     ;1    ;[BP-6] is where we stored "i"            -- 89
       JMP short $L240            ;3    ;Go finish "PUSHing."                     -- 90
       NOP                        ;0    ;We never execute this instruction        -- 91
$I204: MOV CX,WORD PTR [BP-10]    ;1    ;[BP-10] is used for "sp" variable        -- 92
       MOV SI,CX                  ;1    ;Using SI register for "sp"               -- 93
       MOV AX,WORD PTR [BP-6]     ;1    ;C code: *sp = i;([BP-6] is i)            -- 94
       MOV WORD PTR [SI],AX       ;!2   ;The AX register still has i's value      -- 95
       MOV WORD PTR [SI+2],DI     ;1    ;C code: *(sp+1) = limit;                 -- 96
       MOV DI,BX                  ;1    ;C code: limit = j; see next line         -- 97
$L240: MOV WORD PTR [BP-8],DI     ;!3   ;[BP-8] is where we store new "limit"     -- 98
       ADD CX,4                   ;1    ;C code: sp += 2;(sizeof(int) is 2)       -- 99
$L239: MOV WORD PTR [BP-10],CX    ;1    ;[BP-10] is where store new "sp"          --100
$L238: MOV CX,WORD PTR [BP-8]     ;1    ;Here's the code where we actually check  --101
       SUB CX,DX                  ;1    ;whether element_count>>1 is greater      --102
       SAR CX,1                   ;3    ;than 7. It looks a little out of         --103
       CMP CX,7                   ;1    ;place because the original C code is     --104
       JLE $JCC236                ;3/1  ;at the start of the loop. Microsoft      --105
       JMP $FC185                 ;!4   ;has transposed it to the end here.       --106
$JCC236:                               ;C comment: /* Number of elements < 7 */  --107
       MOV CX,DX                  ;1    ;C code: i = base + 1;                    --108
       ADD CX,2                   ;1    ;Using DX for base, using CX for i,       --109
       CMP CX,WORD PTR [BP-8]     ;2    ;using [BP-8] for limit. Interestingly    --110
       JAE $FB208                 ;3/1  ;Microsoft is about to change the         --111
       MOV WORD PTR [BP+4],DX     ;1    ;parameter that we passed on the stack    --112
```

```
$FC207: MOV BX,CX                    ;1       ;C code: j = i;BX is j, CX is i              --113
        CMP BX,WORD PTR [BP+4]       ;2       ;C code:while (j>base && *(j-1)>*j) {        --114
        JBE $FB211                   ;3/1     ;(j <= [BP+4] i.e. "base" parameter)         --115
        MOV WORD PTR [BP-6],CX       ;1       ;using [BP-6] to store new "i" value         --116
$FC210: MOV AX,WORD PTR [BX]         ;1       ;BX still is j, so now AX = *j               --117
        LEA SI,[BX-2]                ;1       ;SI now points to (j-1)                      --118
        MOV WORD PTR [BP-92],SI      ;1       ;This is the only usage of [BP-92]           --119
        CMP WORD PTR [SI],AX         ;!3      ;Comparing *(j-1) with AX, which is *j       --120
        JLE $FB211                   ;1/3     ;(we can break out of the loop if <=)        --121
        MOV DX,WORD PTR [SI]         ;1       ;C code: tmp=*(j-1);*(j-1)=*j;*j=tmp;        --122
        MOV AX,WORD PTR [BX]         ;1       ;In this exchange, as oft seen before,       --123
        MOV WORD PTR [SI],AX         ;1       ;we're loading [SI] value just after         --124
        MOV WORD PTR [BX],DX         ;1       ;we use [SI] in a compare instruction.       --125
        MOV BX,SI                    ;1       ;C code: j--;(SI is still "(j-1)")           --126
        CMP BX,WORD PTR [BP+4]       ;2       ;[BP+4] is the passed "base" parameter       --127
        JA $FC210                    ;1/3     ;(loop if j>base) BX register is j           --128
$FB211: ADD CX,2                     ;1       ;C code: i++;} CX register is i              --129
        CMP CX,WORD PTR [BP-8]       ;2       ;[BP-8] contains "limit"                     --130
        JB $FC207                    ;1/3     ;(loop if i < limit) CX register is i        --131
$FB208: MOV CX,WORD PTR [BP-10]      ;1       ;[BP-10] is "sp", the stack pointer          --132
        LEA AX,WORD PTR [BP-90]      ;1       ;C code: if (sp > stack) {                   --133
        CMP CX,AX                    ;1       ;AX now points to the start of stack         --134
        JBE $EX175                   ;1/3     ;(if sp <= stack address end function)       --135
        SUB CX,4                     ;1       ;C code: sp -= 2;                            --136
        MOV BX,CX                    ;1       ;C code: base = *sp;                         --137
        MOV DX,WORD PTR [BX]         ;!3      ;Now we're using BX register for sp          --138
        MOV AX,WORD PTR [BX+2]       ;1       ;C code: limit = *(sp+1);}                   --139
        MOV WORD PTR [BP-8],AX       ;1       ;[BP-8] holds a copy of "limit"              --140
        JMP short $L239              ;3       ;Restore "sp", re-start outer loop           --141
$EX175: POP SI                       ;1       ;Counteracts PUSH SI at function start       --142
        POP DI                       ;1       ;Counteracts PUSH DI at function start       --143
        MOV SP,BP                    ;1                                                    --144
        POP BP                       ;!3      ;Counteracts PUSH BP at function start       --145
        RET                          ;5       ;Near return (it's a small model)            --146
_quicksort ENDP
```

Lab Notes

To a point, Microsoft's translation of `quicksort` illustrates how well a good C compiler handles a relatively complex input. This is not to say that Microsoft had to use a plethora of tricks though: over half of the instructions generated are simple `MOV`s, and most of the remainder are well-known instructions like `ADD`, `SUB`, and conditional jumps.

Use of the registers `AX`, `BX`, `CX`, `DX`, `SI`, `DI`, and `BP` is common in the translation; Microsoft has pressed into service every register that it can possibly use. Even so, it's necessary to juggle the registers quite a bit because Intel machines simply don't supply enough registers for a function with so many variables in it. Actually, the `quicksort` algorithm gave the compiler a leg up by using direct pointers. Had the code used `array[n]` instead of `*array`, the Microsoft compiler would have been forced to keep track of two separate variables, causing even more overloading of the precious register resources.

Lab Note A

The only register that isn't in direct use is SP. That's as expected: although there's a stack in the function, a C stack never gets translated into a real assembler stack. This is the point at which we can make the first improvement in Microsoft's translation. Since the code at label $FB208 (line 132ff) is really referring to the stack, this code:

```
MOV CX,WORD PTR [BP-10]     ;1      ;[BP-10] is "sp", the stack pointer
LEA AX,WORD PTR [BP-90]     ;1      ;C code: if (sp > stack) {
CMP CX,AX                   ;1      ;AX now points to the start of stack
JBE $EX175                  ;1/3    ;(if sp <= stack address end function)
SUB CX,4                    ;1      ;C code: sp -= 2;
MOV BX,CX                   ;1      ;C code: base = *sp;
MOV DX,WORD PTR [BX]        ;!3     ;Now we're using BX register for sp
MOV AX,WORD PTR [BX+2]      ;1      ;C code: limit = *(sp+1); }
```

can be replaced with the faster and more elegant:

```
CMP SP,<original stack position>    ;2
JZ $EX175                           ;1/3
POP AX                              ;1
POP DX                              ;1
```

Similar replacements can be put in wherever the stack is used. Although this means that SP's original value has to be saved when the function starts, it also means the stack pointer itself won't need to be kept in [BP-10] as Microsoft is doing.

Lab Note B

On a few occasions, Microsoft runs out of registers when doing an exchange and the translation gets convoluted. For example, notice how it handles tmp=*j; *j=*i; *i=tmp; in the loop beginning at label $L223 (line 68ff):

```
                         Size        Cycles
MOV AX,WORD PTR [SI]     ; 2         2 (includes a penalty)
MOV WORD PTR [BP-2],AX   ; 3 tmp     1
MOV AX,WORD PTR [BX]     ; 2         1
MOV WORD PTR [SI],AX     ; 2         1
MOV AX,WORD PTR [BP-2]   ; 3 tmp     1
MOV WORD PTR [BX],AX     ; 2         1
;Total                   ;14 bytes, 7 cycles
```

This is the second opportunity to improve Microsoft's code. When there are no more registers available to do an exchange, we can use the stack again and save some space with this code:

```
                        Size        Cycles
MOV AX,WORD PTR [SI]    ;2          2
PUSH AX                 ;1          1
MOV AX,WORD PTR [BX]    ;2          1
MOV WORD PTR [SI],AX    ;2          1
POP AX                  ;1          1
MOV WORD PTR [BX],AX    ;2          1
;Total                  ;10 bytes, 7 cycles
```

Incidentally, one reason we chose to repeat the exchange code several times instead of calling a procedure is that we calculated the overhead involved. It takes 10 cycles to PUSH two parameters, make a CALL, and do a RET from the called procedure. Since calling a procedure saves at most 4 bytes over using the exchange code, we felt it wasn't worth doing.

There's a more important consideration, though. When Microsoft sees a CALL, it has to assume that the called procedure might change some of the registers. This means the compiler either has to save the registers it's using at the time, or it would have to use fewer registers. Either way, the compiler wouldn't be able to generate its best possible translation. This is another way that the compiler was given a leg up by the original C code.

This brings us to a general observation about the code that we started with. At this stage in the optimization process, we only want to do the optimizations that cannot be done in C. The optimizations that were possible in C — using pointers rather than offsets, repeating the swap operation rather than making it into a function — have already been done. (Exception: it might have helped to explicitly declare i or j as a register variable. But that's hindsight. If we hadn't been examining the assembler output we wouldn't have noticed that Microsoft is juggling i and j in and out of registers.)

Lab Note C
Microsoft usually uses DI for i, BX for j, and SI for base. Our improvements tidy the code so those register assignments are always true. Doing this frees up both the DX and BX registers since both were being used to store base too. As soon as the code reliably uses SI, we don't need DX or BX any more. Microsoft's code also uses [BP+4] for base, and it too becomes redundant once use of SI becomes consistent. Our tidying broke a bit of a logjam, and we found

that once this was done it wasn't necessary to save and restore i and j at all — saving several cycles overall.

We're now ready to make some observations about individual instructions in the Microsoft translation.

Lab Note D

Line 1 is hit by the Call-Plus-Stack-Use Rule; lines 4 and 145 are hit by the Change-SP-Then-Use-Stack Rule. If these instructions were in loops we'd try to do something about the penalties, but they're not so we let them lie.

Lab Note E

In Chapter 4 we covered various tricks that one can play with shifts. Microsoft is using one of these tricks in line 10: to multiply by 2, Microsoft now uses the instruction ADD AX , AX, a 1-cycle instruction. Microsoft just figured this out last year — their version 7.0 C compiler generated SHL AX , 1, a 3-cycle instruction.

Lab Note F

In a similar vein, compare what Microsoft outputs now against what Microsoft used to produce with Microsoft C v7.0, in three places in the code we've listed:

```
Position in code  Latest Microsoft C version  Prior Microsoft C version
line 50           MOV SI,DX                   MOV SI,DX
line 51           ADD DI,2                    MOV AX,[SI]
line 52           MOV AX,[SI]                 ADD DI,2

line 56           SUB BX,2                    MOV AX,[SI]
line 57           MOV AX,[SI]                 SUB BX,2
line 58           CMP [BX],AX                 CMP [BX],AX

line 93           MOV SI,CX                   MOV AX,[BP-6]
line 94           MOV AX,[BP-6]               MOV SI,CX
line 95           MOV [SI],AX                 MOV [SI],AX
```

If you look closely you'll see that the difference in all three cases is a transposition: Microsoft has put some space between the instructions that change SI (or BX), and the instructions that use SI (or BX) as a pointer. This is clear proof that sometime in 1994 Microsoft discovered the Register-Address Rule. In all three cases the code that Microsoft produces now is 1 cycle faster than the code they produced earlier, even though a reduced 1-cycle penalty still applies.

Lab Note G

Notice how instructions like `LEA SI,[BX-2]` (at line 118) are used instead of the equivalent:

```
MOV SI,BX
SUB SI,2
```

Microsoft is saving 1 cycle with this trick.

Lab Note H

`MOV WORD PTR [BP-92],SI` at line 119 and `MOV SP,BP` at line 144 are both utterly pointless instructions. Perhaps they're left over from an earlier stage before optimization. Since nothing uses `[BP-92]` we'll get rid of the instruction at line 119, and since `BP` must already equal `SP` at line 144, we'll get rid of this instruction as well.

Lab Note I

Microsoft is trying the trick of ANDing with an 8-bit register in order to save a byte with the `AND BL,254`, `AND AL,254` and `AND CL,254` instructions at lines 16, 79, and 82 respectively. In Chapter 2 we discussed this trick and warned that it can lead to violations of the Hi/Lo Rule or the Bytes-and-Pointers Rule. Sure enough: look at the instruction that will be executed 1 cycle after the `AND BL,254` instruction at line 16 — an indirect reference using a register, which violates the Bytes-and-Pointers Rule. Notice too the violation of the Hi/Lo Rule after the `AND CL,254` instruction at line 82. We've marked the cycle counts with a ! to show the penalties.

Actually, if it weren't for this `AND` trick, there would be no byte-related stalls in this function. That's only because it's an integer array though. When we compiled a `quicksort` in which we'd changed `int` to `char`, we found that Microsoft frequently generated stalling code — as did Borland and Symantec.

Lab Note J

The occasional `NOP`s are there to cause word alignment of the code. It seems the compiler is forcing such alignment whenever it can freely do so; that is, when the previous instruction was a `JMP`. Although word alignment is useful, the important thing is to prevent violation of the Cache-Straddling Rule.

Lab Note K

The `MOV AX,WORD PTR [BX][SI]` (line 18) and
`MOV WORD PTR [BX][SI],AX` (line 21) instructions aren't deep
in the inner loop, so it's not terribly important that Microsoft's translation loses cycles for violating the Register-Pointer-Doubled Rule. The
occurrence at line 18 is interesting, though: not only is it a double register pointer reference, it's got two penalties. The previous instruction
was a load of the `BX` register and the one before that was a load of an
8-bit register. Our optimized code shifts the instructions in this area
around a bit and saves several cycles.

Lab Note L

There's an opportunity to save another cycle at lines 103 and 104
where Microsoft generates:

```
SAR CX,1
CMP CX,7
```

This operation can be handled as easily with `CMP CX,14`. The `CX`
register is used later so the `SAR` does have to be done, but only along one
branch. One other improvement uses the faster `SAR CX,1` version that
we showed you in Chapter 4.

Lab Note M

The loop that starts at label `$FC210` (line 117) uses two registers. One
register (`BX`) stands for `j`, the other register (`SI`) stands for (`j-1`). This
was once a great optimization: it was cheaper to refer to `[BX]` than to
`[BX-2]`. On a 486 though, it's just a waste of a register. Optimizing
this code is simple: we'll use `CMP [BX-2],AX` rather than:

```
LEA SI,[BX-2]
...
CMP [SI],AX
```

This saves 1 cycle and makes it unnecessary to reload `SI` later.

Lab Note N

Microsoft has generated a strange loop beginning at line 50:

```
$D197: MOV SI,DX              ;1 cycle
       ADD DI,2               ;1 cycle
       MOV AX,WORD PTR [SI]   ;!2 cycles (Register-Address Rule)
       CMP WORD PTR [DI],AX   ;2 cycles
       JL $D197               ;1 or 3 cycles
```

Not only is this code constantly recreating SI and AX unnecessarily, it's violating the Register-Address Rule. Much better would be:

```
$D197: MOV SI,DX          ;1 cycle — outside the loop
       MOV AX,[SI]        ;!3 cycles — outside the loop
$D198: CMP [DI+2],AX      ;2 cycles
       LEA DI,[DI+2]      ;1 cycle
       JL $D198           ;1 or 3 cycles
```

A similar enhancement is possible in the loop that follows at line 56. That's not quite what we ended up with, though, because we found that the CMP could be improved too.

Lab Note O
CMP <memory>,<register> appears frequently (incidentally, the operands are always in that order because on older processors CMP <register>,<memory> was a slower instruction). This is a 2-cycle instruction. We've discussed this situation several times throughout this book: if the memory location will be loaded into a register anyway, the load is free if a MOV is done prior to the CMP. That happens several times deep in the loop, so our savings can be considerable. For example, consider the code at lines 27ff:

```
MOV AX,WORD PTR [DI]      ;2 bytes, 1 cycle
CMP WORD PTR [BX],AX      ;2 bytes, 2 cycles
...
MOV AX,WORD PTR [BX]      ;2 bytes, 1 cycle
```

Since the final MOV shown above loads [BX] anyway, 1 cycle can be saved with this code:

```
MOV AX,[DI]      ;2 bytes, 1 cycle
MOV CX,[BX]      ;2 bytes, 1 cycle
CMP AX,CX        ;2 bytes, 1 cycle
...
```

Lab Note P
The routine:

```
MOV CX,AX
MOV AX,[BX]
MOV [DI],AX
MOV [BX],CX
```

at lines 30ff could be better expressed as:

```
MOV CX,[BX]
MOV [BX],AX
MOV [DI],CX
```

It's not easy to see what the general rule is here. It just appears that on occasion Microsoft uses two moves when one will do.

Lab Note Q
Finally, there are a few places in Microsoft's code where a register is being reloaded even though the register already contains the correct value. Our optimized code makes changes to jump around these re-loadings.

That's the end of our Lab Notes. After we'd made them, we started modifying the assembler code generated by Microsoft in its translation of the `quicksort` algorithm. It isn't productive to simply add a few inline assembly instructions in a routine like this because inline assembly discourages the compiler from doing its own optimizations. It also doesn't provide the opportunity to correct some of the complex problems we described above.

When making our changes, we made no attempt to change the structure of the code. The jumps are in the same places and they go to the same places. Possibly we should have adjusted some structural details — why, for instance, does the code switch to an insertion sort when there's seven elements left, rather than eight elements? — but, as we've said before, the optimization stage is the wrong place to change such details. We'd modify and test the C code before we got to this stage if we thought such changes would make a significant difference to our target program.

As we worked, we changed only one thing at a time. Then we stopped and checked that our tweaking hadn't wrecked something. (Well, truth-fully we didn't always do that, but every time we didn't we ended up wishing we had.) We aren't going to show the routine's evolution through each intermediate stage, though. What we will show here is our final result, as a C function with inline assembly:

```
void QUICKSORT (int*,int);
void QUICKSORT (int *a,int b)
{        /* Comments refer to cycle times only. For further comments see the
            original assembler listing earlier in this chapter. The
            instructions at the beginning and end are actually generated by
            the C compiler. Cache-Straddling Rule penalties are not shown. */
         /* PUSH     BP */                     // ;!2 Call-Plus-Stack-Use Rule
         /* MOV      BP,SP */                  // ;1
         /* PUSH     SI */                     // ;1
         /* PUSH     DI */                     // ;1
         __asm SUB   SP,92;                    // ;1 Reserve more than needed.
         __asm MOV   SI,a;                     // ;1 MOV SI,[BP+4]
         __asm MOV   [BP-10],SP;               // ;!2 Change-SP-Then-Use-Stack Rule
         __asm MOV   AX,b;                     // ;1 MOV AX,[BP+6]
         __asm ADD   AX,AX;                    // ;1 Not SHL AX,1: Lab Note E
         __asm ADD   AX,SI;                    // ;1
         __asm MOV   [BP-8],AX;                // ;1
         __asm JMP   L238;                     // ;3
FC185:   __asm AND   BX,0FFFEh;                // ;1 Not AND BL,254: Lab Note I
         __asm ADD   BX,SI;                    // ;1
         __asm LEA   DI,[SI+2];                // ;1 Lab Note K
         __asm MOV   AX,[SI];                  // ;1
         __asm MOV   DX,[BX];                  // ;1 Evades Register-Address Rule
         __asm MOV   [BX],AX;                  // ;1
         __asm MOV   BX,WORD PTR [BP-8];       // ;1
         __asm SUB   BX,2;                     // ;1
         __asm MOV   [SI],DX;                  // ;1
         __asm MOV   AX,WORD PTR [DI];         // ;1 Lab Note O
         __asm MOV   CX,[BX];                  // ;1 Evades Register-Address Rule
         __asm CMP   CX,AX;                    // ;1
         __asm JGE   short I191A;              // ;3/1
         __asm MOV   [DI],CX;                  // ;1 Lab Note O
         __asm MOV   [BX],AX;                  // ;1
I191:    __asm MOV   DX,WORD PTR [SI];         // ;1
         __asm MOV   CX,[BX];                  // ;1
I191A:   __asm CMP   CX,DX;                    // ;1
         __asm JGE   short I192A;              // ;3/1
         __asm MOV   [BX],DX;                  // ;1
         __asm MOV   [SI],CX;                  // ;1
I192:    __asm MOV   DX,WORD PTR [SI];         // ;1
I192A:   __asm MOV   CX,[DI];                  // ;1 CMP [DI],DX would be slow
         __asm CMP   CX,DX;                    // ;1
         __asm JLE   short D197A;              // ;3/1
         __asm MOV   [SI],CX;                  // ;1
         __asm MOV   [DI],DX;                  // ;1
L220:
D197:    __asm MOV   DX,WORD PTR [SI];         // ;1 Lab Note N
D197A:
D198:    __asm CMP   WORD PTR [DI+2],DX;       // ;2
         __asm LEA   DI,[DI+2];                // ;1 LEA doesn't change flags set by CMP
         __asm JL    short D198;               // ;3/1
D200:    __asm MOV   DX,WORD PTR [SI];         // ;1
```

```
D201:     __asm MOV    CX,[BX-2];                  // ;1
          __asm CMP    CX,DX;                      // ;1
          __asm LEA    BX,[BX-2];                  // ;1 LEA doesn't change flags set by CMP
          __asm JG     short D201;                 // ;3/1
          __asm CMP    BX,DI;                      // ;1
          __asm JB     short L223;                 // ;3/1
          __asm MOV    AX,WORD PTR [DI];           // ;1
          __asm MOV    WORD PTR [DI],CX;           // ;1
          __asm MOV    WORD PTR [BX],AX;           // ;1
          __asm JMP    short L220;                 // ;3
L223:     __asm MOV    DX,[SI];                    // ;1 Exchange.
          __asm MOV    CX,[BX];                    // ;1
          __asm MOV    [SI],CX;                    // ;1
          __asm MOV    [BX],DX;                    // ;1
          __asm MOV    AX,[BP-8];                  // ;1
          __asm SUB    AX,DI;                      // ;1
          __asm AND    AX,0FFFEh;                  // ;1 Not AND AL,254: Lab Note I
          __asm MOV    CX,BX;                      // ;1
          __asm SUB    CX,SI;                      // ;1
          __asm AND    CX,0FFFEh;                  // ;1 Not AND CL,254: Lab Note I
          __asm CMP    AX,CX;                      // ;1
          __asm JGE    short I204;                 // ;3/1
          __asm PUSH   SI;                         // ;1
          __asm PUSH   BX;                         // ;1
          __asm MOV    SI,DI;                      // ;1
          __asm JMP    short L240;                 // ;3
                                                   //    No NOP here: Lab Note J
I204:     __asm PUSH   DI;                         // ;1
          __asm MOV    AX,[BP-8];                  // ;1
          __asm PUSH   AX;                         // ;1
          __asm MOV    [BP-8],BX;                  // ;1
L240:
L239:
L238:     __asm MOV    BX,WORD PTR [BP-8];         // ;1
          __asm SUB    BX,SI;                      // ;1
          __asm CMP    BX,14;                      // ;1 Lab Note L
          __asm JLE    short JCC236;               // ;3/1 JG FC185 would work too.
          __asm _EMIT  0C1h;                       // ;2 These 3 lines constitute
          __asm _EMIT  0FBh;                       //    the fast way to say
          __asm _EMIT  001h;                       //    SAR BX,1.
          __asm JMP    FC185;                      // ;3
JCC236:   __asm LEA    DI,[SI+2];                  // ;1
          __asm CMP    DI,WORD PTR [BP-8];         // ;2
          __asm JAE    short FB208;                // ;3/1
FC207:    __asm MOV    BX,DI;                      // ;1
          __asm CMP    BX,SI;                      // ;1
          __asm JBE    short FB211;                // ;3/1
FC210:    __asm MOV    CX,WORD PTR [BX];           // ;1
          __asm MOV    DX,[BX-2];                  // ;1 Lab Note M
          __asm SUB    BX,2;                       // ;1
          __asm CMP    DX,CX;                      // ;1
          __asm JLE    short FB211;                // ;3/1
          __asm MOV    [BX+2],DX;                  // ;1
          __asm MOV    [BX],CX;                    // ;1
          __asm CMP    BX,SI;                      // ;1
          __asm JA     short FC210;                // ;3/1
FB211:    __asm ADD    DI,2;                       // ;1
          __asm CMP    DI,WORD PTR [BP-8];         // ;!4 Register-Address Rule
          __asm JB     short FC207;                // ;3/1
```

```
FB208:    __asm CMP      SP,[BP-10];                // ;2 Lab Note A
          __asm JZ       short EX175;               // ;3/1
          __asm POP      AX;                        // ;1
          __asm POP      SI;                        // ;1
          __asm MOV      WORD PTR [BP-8],AX;        // ;1
          __asm JMP      short L239;                // ;3
EX175:    __asm ADD      SP,92                      // ;1
          /*    POP      DI */                      // ;!1 Change-SP-Then-Use-Stack Rule
          /*    POP      SI */                      // ;1
          /*    POP      BP */                      // ;1
          /*    RET */                              // ;5
}
```

We ran our optimized `quicksort` through the timing tests described on page 253. Read on for the results.

Where You Are

We expected our optimized version of the `quicksort` algorithm to be faster than the original code that Microsoft produced. By extension, our code should also be faster than the code produced by Borland and Symantec, since they happened to be a little slower than Microsoft in this example. As a test of whether the work involved was worthwhile then, we did one further comparison: we timed our optimized routine and the `qsort` routine which comes with the standard C library of the test compilers. The results, in seconds elapsed for the test, follow.

Test #1: at the start, all array elements are in order.
Array contains: { 1,2,3,4,5,6,7,8,9,10,11,12,13,14,15,16,17,18,19,20 }

	Borland	**Microsoft**	**Symantec**
original `quicksort`	29	25	36
"optimized" `quicksort`	20	20	20
`qsort` function in C library	131	34	71

Test #2: at the start, all array elements are in reverse order.
Array contains: { 20,19,18,17,16,15,14,13,12,11,10,9,8,7,6,5,4,3,2,1 }

	Borland	**Microsoft**	**Symantec**
original `quicksort`	38	31	44
"optimized" `quicksort`	23	23	23
`qsort` function in C library	144	299	101

Test #3: at the start, all array elements are in order except the last. Array contains: { 1,1,1,1,1,1,1,1,1,1,1,1,1,1,1,1,1,1,0 }

	Borland	**Microsoft**	**Symantec**
original `quicksort`	34	28	39
"optimized" `quicksort`	22	22	22
`qsort` function in C library	58	56	88

It took us about 4 hours to make the changes and test as we went along. Naturally, someone who's new to this game will have to put more effort in than we did. In exchange for the effort, the routine goes considerably faster.

It's as simple as that.

Chapter 11

C String Functions

This chapter presents alternative code for functions that manipulate strings — that is, those functions that begin with *str* in the standard C library, plus the string/numeric conversion functions `atoi`, `atol`, `itoa`, and `ltoa`.

The code is simple. In keeping with the fact that these are general purpose library routines, we avoided anything that wouldn't work on 8086s and 80286s, and we avoided any ideas that would require checking for protected mode segment limits — so we don't use all the tricks that we've described in earlier chapters. The tricks we do use are so basic they're not tricks at all: use 1-cycle instructions instead of instructions that take longer, avoid the penalties, unroll the loops, and you'll see code that's faster than what comes with your C compiler.

Figure 11.1 shows how fast our functions go in our tests, compared with equivalents from Borland, Microsoft and Symantec. As usual we must disclaim: your mileage may vary, because compilers change and because not all strings are alike. That doesn't change what we're proving, which is — if we can beat those guys (at this moment, in this situation), then you can beat anybody (at some moment, in some situation) provided you see what we're doing.

Definitions

A string in C is an array of bytes or characters whose end is signaled by a byte with a value of zero (this book designates the null terminator with \0 to distinguish it from the numeral 0). Strings often contain textual information, and when that is the case we will use the term character rather than byte in describing them.

While it is possible to read each section of this chapter in isolation, it is probably best to read them in order, to see how we build up the repertoire of tricks and techniques for shaving cycles out of loops over the course of the discussions. The following style notes and definitions apply throughout:

❖ Procedure names are in uppercase, for example _ATOI. This prevents conflict with the standard C _atoi routine during testing stages. After testing, you can change the procedure name to lowercase and remove the old _atoi routine from your standard C library.

❖ Most of the assembler instructions in our routines are followed by a comment. In these comments, the symbol BX --> string means "BX is a pointer to string." Comments enclosed in parentheses ( ) occur only after conditional jump instructions and refer to the action or situation which applies if the condition is TRUE. For a quick primer on the assembler instructions used in this book, refer to Appendix A.

❖ Instructions that are not followed by comments are "framing" code. All functions begin with

```
PUSH BP
MOV BP,SP
<PUSH other registers>
...
```

and all functions end with

```
<POP other registers>
POP BP
RET
```

❖ The BP register is always saved, and the SI and DI registers are saved when they are used — a conventional practice which is not always necessary with Borland applications. PUSH BP causes a Call-Plus-Stack-Use Rule penalty because it's the first instruction in the function, but we won't pay special attention to penalties that occur in the initialization of the function. It's *inside* the loops that penalties matter, and we'll only comment on penalties inside the loops.

FUNCTION	OUR ROUTINE	BORLAND v3.1	MICROSOFT v2.0	SYMANTEC v7.0	% GAIN
atoi	9	15	19	14	53%
atol *	8	11	14	13	43%
itoa	11	19	17	14	42%
ltoa	12	19	18	31	61%
strcat *	15	20	21	20	29%
strchr *	15	20	30	28	50%
strcmp *	12	24	23	21	50%
strcpy *	24	39	43	34	44%
strcspn *	29	53	41	48	45%
stricmp	70	126	110	100	44%
strlen *	32	46	47	42	32%
strlwr	79	134	127	210	62%
strncat *	61	125	81	99	51%
strncmp	4	7	8	14	71%
strncpy *	29	38	53	43	45%
strnset *	29	52	45	46	44%
strpbrk *	14	46	18	44	70%
strrchr *	28	79	46	71	65%
strrev *	63	118	92	144	56%
strset *	44	75	74	66	41%
strspn	9	13	20	12	55%
strstr *	69	106	102	989	93%
strupr	64	99	95	143	55%

Figure 11.1 Timing Tests Run on a 486. The numbers in the columns entitled "OUR ROUTINE," "BORLAND," "MICROSOFT," and "SYMANTEC" show the length of time, in seconds, required to execute 8 million iterations of the function on a 486 by the routines in this book and by the standard C small model library supplied by the indicated vendor. The final column, "% GAIN," shows the gain in percentage terms that occurs when our code is substituted for the standard code supplied by the slowest of the three vendors. Gains vary greatly depending on string size, string contents, and processor — see the text under the discussion of the function for more details on the actual code used in the test. An asterisk (*) following the function name in the first column denotes a routine which is not recommended for use with older CPUs (i.e., 8086s, 80286s or 80386s) because the routine contains code optimizations which enhance speed on newer Intel processors only.

❖ When referencing values on the stack, the routines shown in this chapter use the BP register and an offset that is correct for the small model only (for example, [BP+4]). The routines also assume that DS=SS and that parameter addresses are offsets only, as in the small model. These routines thus work only with small model C programs, but adapting to other C models should require very little modification.

❖ We frequently use the assembler directive ALIGN 16 to avoid Cache-Strad-dling Rule penalties. You'll have to get rid of ALIGN 16 if you put these routines into a C program — using inline assembly, you'll just have to tolerate the 5 percent performance penalty that straddling cache lines causes. Other than that there's no problem using these routines in C programs: just enclose them in braces after the directive __asm, that is, use:

```
__asm {
   ... routine ...
   }
```

❖ This chapter uses the word *gain* to refer to an amount of acceleration which can normally be expected by replacing slower code with faster code (see, for example, Figure 11.1).

Let's review what's special about string routines.
In C, the string ABCD is stored as:

	A	B	C	D	\0
position	0	1	2	3	4

Since the null terminator is stored at the end of the string, it is generally impossible to find out an essential characteristic — the string length — without testing every byte to see if it is equal to \0. Knowing the string length is, of course, important because an application must avoid writing to, or even reading from, memory beyond the end of the string. Using the assembler instruction

```
MOV AX,string+4
```

to find the length of the string ABCD is not sound practice because the byte at string+5 is not merely irrelevant, it may be past the end of the segment. If string+5 is past the end of the segment, the instruction could cause a General Protection Fault. Primarily because of this funda-mental characteristic, routines for strings are not similar to routines for byte arrays with a known length.

atoi

Prototype: `int atoi(char *string)`

Function: Convert an ASCII string containing optional whitespace, an optional sign, and a series of decimal digits to a signed 16-bit integer.

Method: Beginning with an accumulator value of zero, for each decimal digit: multiply the accumulator by 10 and add the digit. Stop when a non-digit, for example \ 0, is encountered. When the string is invalid, for example 65536, results are undefined and will not equal the undefined results returned by all C compilers' libraries.

Return: AX = 16-bit integer, undefined value if string isn't valid

Gain: (Borland C) on 486: 40% — on 386SX: 10%
(Microsoft C) on 486: 53% — on 386SX: 19%
(Symantec C) on 486: 36% — on 386SX: 7%
Amount of gain varies depending on string contents. With smaller numbers the gain is smaller. The test run was `i=atoi("1234");`.

The following _ATOI routine shows a gain because it avoids Intel's multiply instruction. Instead of IMUL, which takes 13 cycles, this routine uses five ADDs which take 1 cycle each; that is, _ATOI uses

```
AX = (AX*2) + ((AX*2)*2)*2)
```

instead of simply

```
AX = AX*10
```

_ATOI also uses

```
ADD AX,AX
```

to express AX*2 — remember that this instruction is faster than

```
SHL AX,1
```

on a 486 but not on earlier CPUs. According to Intel, ADD should run fastest (or at least equally as fast) on all CPUs since the 8086 assuming all other factors are equal. However, our tests have shown that there is no appreciable difference between ADD AX,AX and SHL AX,1 on a 386, so this trick will not work well on 386s or earlier. (In 32-bit mode, LEA EAX,[EAX*2] could also be used.)

```
        public _ATOI                   ;Ascii TO Integer
ALIGN 16
_ATOI proc
        PUSH BP                        ;Call-Plus-Stack-Use penalty unavoidable here
        MOV BP,SP
        MOV BX,[BP+4]                  ;BX --> string. Register-Address penalty.
        XOR AX,AX                      ;AX = accumulator, starts = 0
        MOV DL,0                       ;DL is our sign flag; 0 means unsigned
@@init:                               ;skip whitespace till we come to a sign,
                                       ;a digit, or the string's end.
        MOV CL,[BX]                    ;get CL = an initial byte in string
        SUB CL,30h                     ;30h is ASCII code for "0", so SUB CL,"0"
        JGE @@digit                    ;(CL = [BX] >= "0", possibly a digit)
        INC BX                         ;point BX to next byte in string
        CMP CL,2Dh - 30h               ;2Dh is ASCII code for "0", so CMP CL,"-"-"0"
        JZ @@sign                      ;(CL="-", set flag. digits should follow)
        INC BX
        CMP CL,20h - 30h               ;20h is ASCII code for " ", so CMP CL," "-"0"
        JZ @@init                      ;(original was space, skip till nonwhitespace)
        CMP CL,09h - 30h               ;09h is ASCII code for tab, i.e. was this tab?
        JZ @@init                      ;(original was tab, skip till nonwhitespace)
        JMP short @@ret                ;[BX] = 0, string contains no digits.
ALIGN 16
@@sign: INC DL                         ;CL = "-". set the sign flag to 1.
@@next: MOV CL,[BX]                    ;get CL = byte in string
        SUB CL,"0"
        JL @@eos                       ;(CL = [BX] < "0" so it's string end)
@@digit: CMP CL,9                      ;is (string byte - "0") > 9?
        JA @@eos                       ;(CL > "9" so it's string end)
        INC BX                         ;point BX to next byte in string
        MOV CH,0                       ;XOR CH,CH would be better on 386s
        ADD AX,AX                      ;multiply accumulator by 10
        ADD CX,AX
        ADD AX,AX
        ADD AX,AX
        ADD AX,CX                      ;ADD current digit that came from [BX]
        JMP @@next                     ;go and repeat for next digit
@@eos:                                ;We've reached the end of the string.
                                       ;AX has the absolute number.
        TEST DL,DL                     ;is the "sign" flag 1?
        JZ @@ret                       ;(no, string didn't start with "-")
        NEG AX                         ;yes, so the number should be negative
@@ret:  POP BP
        RET                            ;return AX = result
_ATOI endp
```

atol

Prototype: `long atol(char *string)`

Function: Convert an ASCII string containing optional whitespace, an optional sign, and a series of decimal digits to a signed 32-bit integer.

Method: Beginning with an accumulator value of zero, for each decimal digit: multiply the accumulator by 10 and add the digit. Stop when a non-digit, for example \0, is encountered.

Return: DX : AX = 32-bit integer, undefined value if string isn't valid

Gain: (Borland C) on 486: 27% — on 386SX: –7%
         (Microsoft C) on 486: 43% — on 386SX: 11%
         (Symantec C) on 486: 38% — on 386SX: 14%

This routine is recommended for 486s only, although a gain can also be achieved on older machines if your compiler is Microsoft or Symantec. Amount of gain varies slightly depending on string contents. The test run was `i=atol("1234");`.

    The _ATOL routine could use a 32-bit accumulator, but then _ATOL would look just like _ATOI. Instead, the following routine illustrates how the principles used in _ATOI can be extended with large numbers. _ATOL uses two registers — DX : AX — for accumulation and for the negation which occurs if the string is signed. It's no longer possible to use DL for the sign flag as the _ATOI routine does because DX is the high word of the accumulator now. It is, however, possible to use the BP register. This possibility, of using BP as a scratch register after the parameter value has been loaded, is easily overlooked.

```
ALIGN 16
    public _ATOL            ;Ascii TO Long
_ATOL proc
        PUSH BP
        MOV BP,SP
        PUSH DI
        MOV BX,[BP+4]       ;BX --> string. Register-Address penalty.
        XOR AX,AX           ;AX = accumulator, starts = 0
        XOR DX,DX
        XOR BP,BP           ;BP is our sign flag; 0 means unsigned
```

```
@@init:                         ;skip whitespace till we come to a sign,
                                ;a digit, or the string's end.
          MOV CL,[BX]           ;get CL = an initial byte in string
          SUB CL,30h            ;30h is ASCII "0". We could say SUB CL,"0".
          JGE @@digit           ;(CL = [BX] >= "0", possibly a digit)
          CMP CL,2Dh - 30h      ;2Dh is ASCII "-". Was the original byte "-"?
          JZ @@sign             ;(CL = "-", set flag. digits should follow)
          INC BX
          CMP CL,20h - 30h      ;20h is ASCII " ". Was the original byte " "?
          JZ @@init             ;(yes, skip till it's not whitespace)
          CMP CL,09h - 30h      ;09h is ASCII tab. Was the original byte tab?
          JZ @@init             ;(yes, skip till it's not whitespace)
          JMP short @@ret       ;[BX] = 0, string contains no digits.
ALIGN 16
@@sign:   INC BP                ;CL = "-", set the sign flag to 1.
@@next:   MOV CL,[BX]           ;get CL = byte in string
          SUB CL,30h            ;30h is ASCII "0". We could say SUB CL,"0".
          JL @@eos              ;(CL = [BX] < "0" so it's string end)
@@digit:  CMP CL,9              ;is (string byte - "0") > 9?
          JA @@eos              ;(CL > "9" so it's string end)
          INC BX                ;point BX to next byte in string
          MOV CH,0              ;XOR CH,CH would be better on 386s
          XOR DI,DI
          ADD AX,AX             ;multiply accumulator by 10
          ADC DX,0
          ADD CX,AX
          ADC DI,0
          ADD AX,AX
          ADC DX,0
          ADD AX,AX
          ADC DX,0
          ADD AX,CX             ;ADD current digit that came from [BX]
          ADC DX,DI
          JMP @@next            ;go and repeat for next digit
@@eos:                          ;We've reached the end of the string.
                                ;AX has the absolute number.
          TEST BP,BP            ;is the "sign" flag 1?
          JZ @@ret              ;(no, string didn't start with "-")
          NEG DX                ;yes, so the number should be negative
          NEG AX
          SBB DX,0
@@ret:    POP DI
          POP BP
          RET                   ;return DX:AX = result
_ATOL endp
```

itoa

Prototype: `char *itoa(int value,char *string,int radix)`

Function: Convert a signed 16-bit integer to an ASCII string.

Method: Divide the integer by the radix and concatenate the remainder (which is inevitably 1 byte long) to the string. Repeat division and concatenation until the integer is zero, then reverse the bytes in the string (division produces them with the least significant byte first), adding zero to convert them to ASCII. For negative numbers, put out a minus sign (–), but not for any other radix than 10.

Return: AX = char *string

Gain: (Borland C) on 486: 42% — on 386SX: 31%
(Microsoft C) on 486: 35% — on 386SX: 18%
(Symantec C) on 486: 21% — on 386SX: 15%
Amount of gain varies slightly depending on string contents. The test run was itoa(10,tmp,10);.

The radix of a number is often 10, and then _ITOA is the reverse of _ATOI. Remember that, to save cycles, _ATOI replaced Intel's multiply instruction with a series of multiply-by-2 instructions — ADD AX,AX — which take only 1 cycle each. Unfortunately, there is no such trick for the reverse of a multiply — _ITOA must employ DIV, the most expensive of all Intel instructions.

_ITOA's opportunity to save cycles lies in the limited range of the radix. By definition, the radix can only be a number between 2 and 36 — not because division by 37 presents special problems, but because the string representation must consist of the 10 digits and 26 letters of the alphabet. That means the radix will always fit in an 8-bit register, so the routine can switch to the cheaper DIV CL instruction as soon as AX becomes small enough that dividing by the radix won't cause an overflow. If the radix is known, it is possible to be more exact about the maximum number that can be divided without getting an overflow.

From now on we're going to show constants that represent ASCII values within quote marks. CMP AH,"9" means the same thing as CMP AH,39h (the ASCII code for 9 is 39h).

```
ALIGN 16
NOP
      public _ITOA              ;Integer TO Ascii
_ITOA proc
            ;The next instruction is subject to the Call-Plus-Stack-Use Rule
          PUSH BP
          MOV BP,SP
          PUSH DI
            ;The next instruction is subject to the Register-Address Rule
          MOV CX,[BP+8]        ;CX = radix, we use DIV CX later
          MOV DI,[BP+6]        ;DI --> destination string
          CMP CX,36            ;Check if radix > 36.
          JA @@radix           ;(radix > 36, which is out of range.)
          CMP CL,2             ;Check if radix < 2. We know CH = 0.
          JB @@radix           ;(radix < 2, which is out of range.)
          MOV AX,[BP+4]        ;AX = integer value
          MOV BX,DI            ;BX = DI --> destination string
```

```
@@test:  TEST AH,AH              ;If high byte of AX is not equal to 0:
         JL @@sign               ;(AH<0 so AX<0, the value is signed)
                  ;The next instruction is not subject to the Double-Jump Rule. Waived.
         JZ @@zero               ;(AH=0 so AX<256, let's check AL too)
                                 ;(AH>0 so AX>=256, start with long DIV)
@@long:  XOR DX,DX               ;DX = high part of value = 0
         DIV CX                  ;24 cycles
              ;The next instruction is subject to the Delayed-Bytes-and-Pointers Rule
         MOV [DI],DL             ;DL = remainder, DH will be 0
         INC DI
         TEST AH,AH              ;is the value less than 256 now?
         JA @@long               ;(no, we must repeat the long DIV)
                                 ;AX is now < 256, we can use the short DIV
@@short:MOV AH,0                 ;AH = high part of value = 0
         DIV CL                  ;16 cycles
              ;The next instruction is subject to the Delayed-Bytes-and-Pointers Rule
         MOV [DI],AH             ;AH = remainder
         INC DI
         TEST AL,AL              ;is the value 0 now?
         JNZ @@short             ;(no, we must repeat the short DIV)
         MOV [DI],AL             ;dump the terminating \0 byte
@@rev:   DEC DI                  ;DIVs are done. Now reverse bytes.
         CMP DI,BX               ;Has downgoing DI met upgoing BX?
         JB @@ret                ;(They passed, reversing is finished)
                                 ;Notice the order of the next two instructions.
                  ;If we put MOV AL,[DI] before MOV AH,[BX] then ADD AX would
                  ;get a Hi/Lo penalty.
         MOV AH,[BX]
         MOV AL,[DI]
         ADD AX,3030h            ;Add "0" to AH, ADD "0" to AL
         CMP CL,10               ;CL still has the "radix" byte
         JA @@rad11              ;(radix>10 so test for alpha digits)
@@rad10:MOV [DI],AH              ;Put bytes back, exchanging so that
         MOV [BX],AL             ;what was in [DI] is now in [BX],
         INC BX                  ;and vice versa
         JMP @@rev               ;go and reverse the next byte pair
ALIGN 16
@@rad11:CMP AH,"9"               ;since radix was > 10, remainders
         JBE @@rad12             ;could have been more than 9, and
         ADD AH,"a"-("9"+1)      ;we check both of the bytes that
@@rad12:CMP AL,"9"               ;we're reversing for that chance.
         JBE @@rad10             ;In either case, we change "9"+1 to
         ADD AL,"a"-("9"+1)      ;"A", "9"+2 to "B", and so on, then
         JMP @@rad10             ;join the radix-10 mainstream again.
ALIGN 16
@@zero:                          ;AH=0 so AX<256. Check if the rest of the
                                 ;value, i.e. AL is 0 too.
                                 ;If so that's a special case: put a leading
                                 ;'0' before we stop.
         TEST AL,AL              ;AH=0 so AX<256. Check if the rest of
         JNZ @@short             ;of the value is 0, a special case.
         MOV WORD PTR [DI],"0"   ;value = 0 so: [DI] = '0', [DI+1]='\0'
@@ret:   MOV AX,[BP+6]           ;Return AX = char *string.
         POP DI
         POP BP
         RET
```

```
        ALIGN 16
        @@radix:  MOV BYTE PTR [DI],0      ;Radix < 2 OR radix > 36. That's out
                  JMP @@ret                ;of range, so we just return nothing.
        @@sign:   CMP CL,10                ;We don't use signed numbers unless
                  JNZ @@long               ;radix is 10.
                  NEG AX                   ;AH<0 so AX (integer value) < 0, so
                  MOV BYTE PTR [DI],"-"    ;negate it and put a minus sign at the
                  INC BX                   ;start of the destination string. Then
                  INC DI                   ;(with AX as a positive number now) we
                  JMP @@test               ;go to check again if AL=0, etc.
        _ITOA endp
```

ltoa

Prototype: `char *ltoa(long value,char *string,int radix)`

Function: Convert a signed 32-bit integer to an ASCII string.

Method: Divide the integer by the radix and concatenate the remainder (which is inevitably 1 byte long) to the string. Repeat division and concatenation until the integer is zero, then reverse the bytes in the string (division produces them with the least significant byte first), adding zero to convert them to ASCII.

Return: AX = `char *string`

Gain: (Borland C) on 486: 37% — on 386SX: 21%
         (Microsoft C) on 486: 33% — on 386SX: 12%
         (Symantec C) on 486: 61% — on 386SX: 74%
Amount of gain varies slightly depending on string contents. The test run was `ltoa(1000000,tmp,10);`.

The _LTOA function is pretty much the same as _ITOA. The only complications caused by the doubling of the integer size are that:

(a) there are fewer registers available so BP is pressed into service;

(b) the method of number negation is a little tricky, involving a carry from the negation of the low half to the negation of the high half of the integer; and

(c) the high half of the passed integer must be used until the DIVs cause it to become zero.

Fortunately, _LTOA only has to divide a 32-bit number by a 16-bit number — dividing a 32-bit number by a 32-bit number is far more difficult.

```
        ALIGN 16
            public _LTOA                     ;Long TO Ascii
        _LTOA proc
                    PUSH BP
                    MOV BP,SP
                    PUSH [BP+8]              ;At the end we'll POP AX = string1
                    PUSH DI
                    MOV CX,[BP+10]           ;CX = radix, we don't check validity
                    MOV DI,[BP+8]            ;DI --> destination string
                    CMP CX,36                ;Check if radix > 36.
                    JA @@radix               ;(radix > 36, which is out of range.)
                    CMP CL,2                 ;Check if radix < 2. We know CH = 0.
                    JB @@radix               ;(radix < 2, which is out of range.)
                    MOV BX,DI                ;BX = DI --> destination string
                    MOV AX,[BP+4]            ;AX = long value, low word
                    MOV BP,[BP+6]            ;BP = long value, high word
        @@test:     TEST BP,BP               ;If high word of BP:AX is not equal to 0:
                    JL @@sign                ;(BP<0 so BP:AX<0, the value's signed)
                    JZ @@zero                ;(BP=0 so BP:AX<65536, let's check AX too)
                                             ;BP>0 so BP:AX>=65536, start with dword DIV
        @@dword:    TEST BP,BP               ;Switch to @@long's DIV when you can.
                    JZ @@long                ;(We can switch now, high word = 0.)
                    XCHG AX,BP               ;Exchange: bottom word, top word.
                    XOR DX,DX                ;DX:AX = 0000:<top word>
                    DIV CX                   ;24 cycles, Divide DX:AX by radix.
                    XCHG AX,BP               ;DX:AX = <DIV remainder>:<bottom word>
                    DIV CX                   ;24 cycles, Divide DX:AX by radix.
                    MOV [DI],DL              ;DL = remainder. Penalty here.
                    INC DI
                    JMP @@dword
        ALIGN 16
        @@long:     XOR DX,DX                ;DX = high part of value = 0
                    DIV CX                   ;24 cycles
                    MOV [DI],DL              ;DL = remainder, DH will be 0. Penalty here.
                    INC DI
                        ;Jumping if (AH>0) is the same thing as jumping if (AX>255).
                    TEST AH,AH               ;is the value less than 256 now?
                    JA @@long                ;(no, we must repeat the long DIV)
                                             ;AX is now < 256, we can use the short DIV
        @@short:    MOV AH,0                 ;AH = high part of value = 0
                    DIV CL                   ;16 cycles
                        ;Next instruction is subject to the Delayed-Bytes-and-Pointers Rule
                    MOV [DI],AH              ;AH = remainder. Penalty here.
                    INC DI
                    TEST AL,AL               ;is the value 0 now?
                    JNZ @@short              ;(no, we must repeat the short DIV)
                    MOV [DI],AL              ;dump the terminating \0 byte
        @@rev:      DEC DI                   ;DIVs are done. Now reverse bytes.
                    CMP DI,BX                ;Has downgoing DI met upgoing BX?
                    JB @@ret                 ;(They passed, we finished reversing)
                    MOV AH,[BX]              ;As with _ITOA, the order matters here.
                    MOV AL,[DI]
                    ADD AX,3030h             ;ADD "0" to AH, ADD "0" to AL
                    CMP CL,10                ;CL still has the "radix" byte
                    JA @@rad11               ;(radix>10 so test for alpha digits)
        @@rad10:    MOV [DI],AH              ;Put bytes back, exchanging so that
                    MOV [BX],AL              ;what was in [DI] is now in [BX],
                    INC BX                   ;and vice versa
                    JMP @@rev                ;go and reverse the next byte pair
```

```
          ALIGN 16
@@rad11:  CMP  AH,"9"                ;Since radix was > 10, remainders
          JBE  @@rad12               ;could have been more than 9, and
          ADD  AH,"a"-("9"+1)        ;we check both of the bytes that
@@rad12:  CMP  AL,"9"                ;we're reversing for that chance.
          JBE  @@rad10               ;In either case, we change "9"+1 to
          ADD  AL,"a"-("9"+1)        ;"A", "9"+2 to "B", and so on, then
          JMP  @@rad10               ;join the radix-10 mainstream again.
          ALIGN 16
@@zero:                             ;BP=0 so BP:AX<65536. Check if the rest of the
                                    ;value i.e. AX is 0 too.
                                    ;If so that's a special case: put a leading
                                    ;'0' before we stop.
          TEST AH,AH
          JNZ  @@long
          TEST AL,AL
          JNZ  @@short
          MOV  WORD PTR [DI],"0"     ;value = 0 so: [DI] = '0', [DI+1]='\0'
@@ret:    POP  DI
          POP  AX                    ;Return AX = string (we PUSHed
          POP  BP                    ;[BP+8] at the start of the routine).
          RET
          ALIGN 16
@@radix:  MOV  BYTE PTR [DI],0       ;Radix < 2 OR radix > 36. That's out
          JMP  @@ret                 ;of range, so we just return nothing.
@@sign:   CMP  CL,10                 ;We don't do signed numbers unless
          JNZ  @@dword               ;the radix is 10.
                                    ;BP<0 so BP:AX i.e. the integer value is < 0,
               ;so negate it and put a minus sign at the start of the destination
               ;string. This shows how to negate double-word integers.
          NEG  BP
          NEG  AX
          SBB  BP,0
          MOV  BYTE PTR [DI],"-"
          INC  BX
          INC  DI
          JMP  @@test                ;Check again if BP=0, etc.
_LTOA endp
```

A simpler _LTOA routine can be written using 32-bit registers if the machine it will run on is not an 8086 or 80286. The gain with such an alternative, shown below as _LTOA2, is about 10 percent — this is one of the cases where using 32-bit registers in 16-bit mode does not pay huge dividends. Though it works fine with MS-DOS, we've deliberately restricted ourselves to 16-bit registers for the other code in this chapter.

```
_LTOA2 proc                         ;A variant of _LTOA, above
          PUSH BP
          MOV  BP,SP
          PUSH SI
          PUSH DI
.386
          MOVZX ECX,WORD PTR [BP+10] ;CX = radix
          CMP  CX,36                 ;Check if radix > 36.
          JA   @@radix               ;(radix > 36, which is out of range.)
          CMP  CL,2                  ;Check if radix < 2. We know CH = 0.
          JB   @@radix               ;(radix < 2, which is out of range.)
          MOV  EAX,[BP+4]            ;AX = value
          XOR  EDX,EDX               ;high part of value
```

```
.8086
        MOV DI,[BP+8]               ;DI --> destination
        MOV SI,DI
@@long:
.386
        XOR EDX,EDX                 ;high part of value
        DIV ECX
.8086
        MOV [DI],DL                 ;DL = remainder
        INC DI
.386
        TEST EAX,EAX
.8086
        JNZ @@long
        MOV [DI],AL
@@rev:  DEC DI                      ;Reverse the bytes
        CMP DI,SI
        JBE @@ret
        MOV AL,[DI]
        ADD AL,"0"
        XCHG AL,[SI]
        ADD AL,"0"
        MOV [DI],AL
        INC SI
        JMP @@rev
@@ret:  MOV AX,[BP+8]              ;Return AX = *string
        POP DI
        POP SI
        POP BP
        RET
@@radix: MOV BYTE PTR [DI],0       ;Radix < 2 or radix > 36. That's out
         JMP @@ret                 ;of range, so we just return nothing.
_LTOA2 endp
```

strcat

Prototype: char *strcat(char *destination,char *source)

Function: Add the source string to the end of the destination string.

Method: Increment the destination pointer till it points to the terminating \0 byte. Then copy each byte in the source string to the destination string.

Return: AX = char *destination

Gain: (Borland C) on 486: 25% — on 386SX: –56%
         (Microsoft C) on 486: 29% — on 386SX: –68%
         (Symantec C) on 486: 25% — on 386SX: –43%

This routine is recommended for 486s only. Amount of gain varies slightly depending on string contents. The test run was strcat(string1,string2); where string1 and string2 are both equal to "1234567890abcdefghij".

The end of the destination string can be found using the _STRLEN function. Copying each byte is done with the _STRCPY function. So if the _STRLEN and _STRCPY routines are fast, you can expect that the _STRCAT routine will be fast too. That, in fact, proves to be the case with the following routine, although with small strings the overhead of making the calls is significant. The overhead involved in pushing parameters and making two calls is around 30 cycles — that's about the amount of time it takes to find the end and move 5 bytes. _STRCAT can be made faster for short strings by copying in the code for _STRLEN and _STRCPY, rather than calling _STRLEN and _STRCPY.

After _STRCAT calls _STRCPY, the stack has to be restored. This is done by adding 4 to the SP register the straightforward way: ADD SP, 4. Borland still generates dummy POP commands, i.e.:

```
POP CX
POP CX
```

While these two stack cleanup methods work the same (since nobody cares what happens to the CX register), Borland's method is an optimization for 8086s. On 486s, our routine is faster. (Incidentally, it's perfectly safe to take out the ADD SP, 2 instruction and just say ADD SP, 4+2 at the end.)

```
ALIGN 16
    public _STRCAT        ;STRing conCATenate
_STRCAT proc
    PUSH BP
    MOV BP,SP
    PUSH [BP+4]           ;PUSH the destination address
    CALL _STRLEN          ;This will return AX = length
    ADD SP,2
    PUSH [BP+6]           ;PUSH: address of string2
    ADD AX,[BP+4]         ;PUSH: address of (string1+length)
    PUSH AX
    CALL _STRCPY
    ADD SP,4
    MOV AX,[BP+4]
    POP BP
    RET
_STRCAT endp
```

strchr

Prototype: `char *strchr(char *string,int character)`

Function: Find a specified character in a string.

Method: Compare the character to a byte of the string. If the character and byte are equal, stop. If it's the end of the string, stop. Otherwise repeat for the next byte of the string.

Return: AX = `char *string` + offset of character

Gain: (Borland C) on 486: 25% — on 386SX: –24%
      (Microsoft C) on 486: 50% — on 386SX: 7%
      (Symantec C) on 486: 46% — on 386SX: 10%

This routine is recommended for 486s only, although a gain can also be achieved on older machines if your compiler is Microsoft or Symantec. The test run was `strchr("ABCDEFGHIJKLMNOPQRSTUVWXYZ",'q');`. If q is halfway in the string, the gain is halved. If q is at the start of the string, the gain is 0 percent.

The Intel instruction `REPNZ SCASB` appears to be tailor-made for precisely this purpose. For instance, the comparison could be done with:

```
PUSH BP
MOV BP,SP
PUSH DS
POP ES
CLD
MOV AL,[BP+6]
MOV DI,[BP+4]
MOV CX,-1
REPNZ SCASB
LEA AX,[DI-1]
POP BP
RET
```

This code is much faster than that used in the following _STRCHR routine, but has one crippling problem — the length of the string is unknown. So if the character being looked for isn't found in the string, the above procedure will keep looking past the end of string. Eventually it will crash. Normally, then, it is necessary to search first for the string's terminating \0 in order to determine the string length, and then search for the character itself. That's two passes through the string. Our _STRCHR routine only has to do one pass.

Since it's a single pass, _STRCHR does two comparisons for every byte. The first comparison is with \0. That is, the code checks to see if the string is ending. The second comparison is with the character — the byte value must be loaded into a register. Compare the code we actually use (on the left) with the obvious and slow code (on the right):

```
MOV AL,[BX+1]    ;1 cycle     CMP BYTE PTR [BX+1],0  ;4 cycles
CMP AL,0         ;1 cycle     JZ ...                 ;1 cycle
JZ ...           ;1 cycle     CMP BYTE PTR [BX],DL   ;2 cycles
CMP AL,DL        ;1 cycle     JZ ...                 ;1 cycle
JZ ...           ;1 cycle
```

_STRCHR does comparisons in sets of four bytes. That is, rather than incrementing the pointer and looping back after every byte, _STRCHR does this after every four bytes. This method saves the cost of INC and JMP instructions and costs nothing but space, since MOV AL,[BX] takes the same number of cycles as MOV AL,[BX+1] on a 486. (On earlier processors, MOV AL,[BX+1] takes more cycles than MOV AL,[BX].)

In Chapter 9 we discussed various ways to search a string for a character. The method _STRCHR uses is often not the fastest, but it's simple and consistent.

```
ALIGN 16
    public _STRCHR                  ;STRing compare CHaRacter
_STRCHR proc
        PUSH BP
        MOV BP,SP
        MOV DL,[BP+6]               ;DL = character
        TEST DL,DL                  ;Check for DL = character = '\0'
        JZ @@dleq0                  ;(It's \0, this is a special case)
        MOV BX,WORD PTR [BP+4]      ;BX --> string
@@loop: MOV AL,[BX]                 ;Move byte to AL
        TEST AL,AL                  ;Is the byte '\0'?
        JZ @@eos                    ;(AL = [BX] = 0, the string is ended)
        CMP AL,DL                   ;does AL = the character we want?
        JZ @@ret                    ;(yes, so we can stop now)
        MOV AL,[BX+1]               ;Move byte to AL
        TEST AL,AL                  ;Is the byte '\0'?
        JZ @@eos                    ;(AL = [BX] = 0, the string is ended)
        CMP AL,DL                   ;does AL = the character we want?
        JZ @@byte1                  ;(yes, so we can stop now)
        MOV AL,[BX+2]               ;Move byte to AL
        TEST AL,AL                  ;Is the byte '\0'?
        JZ @@eos                    ;(AL = [BX] = 0, the string is ended)
        CMP AL,DL                   ;does AL = the character we want?
        JZ @@byte2                  ;(yes, so we can stop now)
        MOV AL,[BX+3]               ;Move byte to AL
        TEST AL,AL                  ;Is the byte '\0'?
        JZ @@eos                    ;(AL = [BX] = 0, the string is ended)
        ADD BX,4                    ;One increment for all 4 bytes
        CMP AL,DL
        JNZ @@loop                  ;One jump for all 4 bytes
        DEC BX                      ;Matching character seen at [BX+3]
        JMP short @@ret
```

```
            ALIGN 16
@@byte2:    INC BX                          ;Matching character seen at [BX+2]
@@byte1:    INC BX                          ;Matching character seen at [BX+1]
@@ret:      MOV AX,BX
            POP BP
            RET                             ;Return AX = pointer within string
@@eos:      XOR AX,AX                       ;End of string seen, i.e. [BX] = 0
            POP BP
            RET                             ;Return AX = 0
@@dleq0:                                    ;If (DL = character = 0, it's sort of
                   ;a special case: '\0' is both the end of the string and the item
                   ;we're seeking. We handle it with a _STRLEN call, which is OK
                   ;if the length is longer than 2 or 3 bytes. We aren't really
                   ;expecting the special case to occur very often anyway.
            PUSH [BP+4]
            CALL _STRLEN
            ADD SP,2
            ADD AX,[BP+4]
            POP BP
            RET
_STRCHR endp
```

strcmp

Prototype: int strcmp(char *string1,char *string2)

Function: Compare string1 to string2.

Method: Get the first character in string1 into a register. Compare the register to the character in string2. If it's equal, repeat for the next pair of characters. If it's not equal, stop. An alternate method (used by all C compiler vendors) is: search for the terminating \0 in string1 using REPNZ SCASB. Subtract the original pointer to string1, yielding the string size. Compare string1 to string2 for <string size> bytes, using REPNZ CMPSB.

Return: AX = 0 if strings are equal
              AX < 0 if string1 < string2
              AX > 0 if string1 > string2

In fact, AX is the difference in the last character, e.g., strcmp("1","9"); returns AX = –8, but the C vendors' documentation is not specific about this point.

Gain: Four separate tests were run. This routine is recommended for 486s only.

Test#1: both strings are 4096 bytes long, both are equal, word alignment
(Borland C) on 486: 17% — on 386SX: –89%
(Microsoft C) on 486: 17% — on 386SX: –89%
(Symantec C) on 486: 17% — on 386SX: –86%

Test#2: both strings are 3 bytes long, both are equal, no word alignment
(Borland C) on 486: 33% — on 386SX: –14%
(Microsoft C) on 486: 10% — on 386SX: –10%
(Symantec C) on 486: 17% — on 386SX: –41%

Test#3: both strings are 15 bytes long, they become unequal on the 6th byte, word alignment. This is the test whose results are shown in Figure 11.1.
(Borland C) on 486: 50% — on 386SX: 0%
(Microsoft C) on 486: 49% — on 386SX: 12%
(Symantec C) on 486: 43% — on 386SX: –3%

Test#4: both strings are 4096 bytes long, unequal on the first byte, word alignment
(Borland C) on 486: 97% — on 386SX: 44%
(Microsoft C) on 486: 76% — on 386SX: 51%
(Symantec C) on 486: 76% — on 386SX: 49%

When it comes to the `_strcmp` routine, the C compiler vendors are using a method which works best with yesterday's computers. With a 486, regardless of string size, the following `_STRCMP` routine is simpler and is faster even when all bytes are equal. This is because in each iteration of the loop, it is only necessary to compare the byte in `string1` to zero, and if they match, to exit the loop. If the byte in `string2` is zero and the byte in `string1` is not zero, then the two bytes are unequal and the loop is exited anyway. If, however, the byte in `string2` is zero and the byte in `string1` is also zero, then the two bytes are equal. A single final `CMP` instruction is needed to provide this information only if the loop hasn't been exited.

An additional advantage becomes obvious when you consider what happens with (for example) 1,000-byte strings in which the first byte is unequal — `_STRCMP` breaks off after the first byte, but the traditional method searches all 1,000 bytes for the terminating \0 regardless — taking 1,000 times longer.

We should warn here against making a slight "improvement" to this routine. For example, if the loop in the routine looked like this:

```
@loop: MOV AL,[BX]
       OR AL,AL
       JZ @@ret0
       INC BX
       INC DI          ;NB: DI is being incremented here
       SUB AL,[DI-1]
       JZ @@loop
```

then the routine would be 15 percent slower! To make the simplest possible example, because of the Register-Address Rule, the set of instructions shown below on the left are faster than their exact inverse, shown on the right:

```
MOV AL,[BX]          INC BX
INC BX               MOV AL,[BX]
```

As usual, the rule to follow is change BX *after* accessing memory using [BX] if at all possible. That way the address decoder doesn't get stalled. Other changes, such as putting the INC BX instruction immediately after the MOV AL,[BX] instruction or incrementing DI before the MOV AL,[BX] instruction, also make the routine slower.

One change that could speed _STRCMP up is to use word-at-a-time techniques. These are shown later on for the _STRNCMP routine.

```
ALIGN 16
       public _STRCMP        ;STRing CoMPare
_STRCMP proc
       PUSH BP
       MOV BP,SP
       PUSH DI
       MOV BX,[BP+4]    ;BX is our pointer to string1
       MOV DI,[BP+6]    ;DI is our pointer to string2
@@loop: MOV AL,[BX]     ;Get AL = a byte from string1
       TEST AL,AL       ;Check if it's '\0'
       JZ @@ret0        ;(AL = *string1 = '\0', string1 is ended)
       INC BX           ;Add 1 to string1 pointer, the classical way.
       SUB AL,[DI]      ;Subtract *string2 from AL i.e. from *string1
       LEA DI,[DI+1]    ;Before looping, add 1 to string2 pointer.
       JZ @@loop        ;(Bytes are equal, so repeat for next bytes)
@@ret:  CBW             ;AL has the difference.  Convert AL to AX.
       POP DI
       POP BP
       RET              ;return AX = difference
@@ret0: SUB AL,[DI]     ;String1 ended, so we'll stop. Our return
       JMP @@ret        ;will be the comparison with the last *string2
_STRCMP endp
```

strcpy

Prototype: `char *strcpy(char *string1,char *string2)`

Function: Move `string2` to `string1`.

Method: Get the byte `*string2` into the low half of a 16-bit register. Stop if it's `\0`. Get the byte `*(string2+1)` into the high half of a 16-bit register. Stop if it's `\0`. Dump the 16-bit register `*string1`. Add 2 to both `string2` and `string1`, so the pointers are to the next words in each of the strings. Repeat.

Return: `AX = *string1`

Gain: (Borland C) on 486: 38% — on 386SX: –8%
       (Microsoft C) on 486: 44% — on 386SX: –4%
       (Symantec C) on 486: 29% — on 386SX: –18%
This routine is recommended for 486s only. Amount of gain varies slightly depending on string lengths. The test run was `strcpy(tmp,"1234567890");`.

The gain produced by _STRCPY has two causes. First, it works with multiple bytes before looping (see the comments on _STRCHR, where these tricks were introduced). Second, two bytes at a time are being stored to `string1`, taking advantage of the fact that a `MOV` of a word takes no longer than a `MOV` of a byte.

Remember that when working with words, it's best if addresses are on word boundaries or penalties for misalignment are applied. In other words, the initial address values should be divisible by 2. It's easy to check for such alignment and move a single byte if it's not aligned — this is illustrated in the instructions following the label `@@align:` in the following routine. If these lines are left out, the procedure becomes 5 percent slower if called with a misaligned destination-string address.

_STRCPY uses `TEST AL,AL` to compare `AL` with 0. We could use `CMP AL,0` and wouldn't lose a thing by doing so — that's a matter of taste. What's not a matter of taste is using `OR AL,AL` to compare `AL` with 0. If the routine used `OR AL,AL`, Bytes-and-Pointers Rule penalties would be triggered. `TEST AL,AL` and `CMP AL,0` never trigger the Bytes-and-Pointers Rule.

There is a TEST AH,AH instruction that looks out of place, following the label @@place:. In version one of this function we had this instruction following the MOV [BX-2],AX instruction, but the MOV was then penalized by the Register-Address Rule, so we moved TEST AH,AH in front. Since MOV never changes the flags register, it's easy to shift TEST or CMP instructions in front of MOV and do the conditional jumping later.

```
ALIGN 16
    public _STRCPY          ;STRing CoPY
_STRCPY proc
        PUSH BP
        MOV BP,SP
        PUSH SI
        MOV SI,[BP+6]       ;SI --> source string
        MOV BX,[BP+4]       ;BX --> destination string
@@align: TEST BX,1          ;Is BX = string1 aligned nicely?
        JZ @@loop           ;(yes it's already on a word boundary)
        MOV AL,[SI]         ;The calling routine has sent us a
        TEST AL,AL
        JZ @@eos
        MOV [BX],AL         ;misaligned destination string, we'll
        INC SI              ;fix the alignment by moving a single
        INC BX              ;byte before entering the main loop.
@@loop: MOV AL,[SI]         ;AL = the next byte *string2
        TEST AL,AL          ;Check if this byte = '\0'
        JZ @@eos            ;(stop if *(string2) was '\0')
        MOV AH,[SI+1]       ;AH = the next byte *string2
        TEST AH,AH          ;Check if this byte = '\0'
        JZ @@ret1           ;(stop if *(string2+1) was '\0')
        MOV [BX],AX
        MOV AL,[SI+2]       ;Repeat the 7 instructions that we
        TEST AL,AL          ;used beginning with "@@loop:...",
        JZ @@eos1           ;varying only the addresses, which are
        MOV AH,[SI+3]       ;now 1 word (2 bytes) forward.
        TEST AH,AH
        JZ @@ret2
        MOV [BX+2],AX
        MOV AL,[SI+4]       ;Repeat the 7 instructions that we
        TEST AL,AL          ;used beginning with "@@loop:...",
        JZ @@eos2           ;varying only the addresses, which are
        MOV AH,[SI+5]       ;now 2 words (4 bytes) forward.  Along
        ADD BX,6            ;the way add 6 to SI  (the string2
        ADD SI,6            ;pointer) and to BX (the string1
@@place: TEST AH,AH         ;pointer), so e.g. [BX-2] is [prev BX+4]
        MOV [BX-2],AX
        JNZ @@loop          ;(go to repeat for the next 6 bytes)
        JMP short @@ret     ;There's a Double-Jump penalty here.
@@eos2: ADD BX,2            ;we ended on the third word
@@eos1: ADD BX,2            ;we ended on the second word
@@eos:  MOV [BX],AL         ;we ended on the second byte of a word
@@ret:  MOV AX,[BP+4]       ;return pointer to destination string
        POP SI
        POP BP
        RET
@@ret2: ADD BX,2
@@ret1: MOV [BX],AX
        JMP @@ret
_STRCPY endp
```

strcspn

Prototype: `int strcspn(char *string1,char *string2)`

Function: Find the first byte within `string1` that's in `string2`.

Method: This is an exhaustive search using a loop within a loop. Compare a byte in `string1` to a byte in `string2`. If they match, increment the `string1` pointer and repeat. If they don't match, increment the `string2` pointer and repeat. When `string2` ends, return.

Return: `AX` = `*string1` + offset of byte

Gain: (Borland C) on 486: 45% — on 386SX: 31%
    (Microsoft C) on 486: 29% — on 386SX: –21%
    (Symantec C) on 486: 40% — on 386SX: 36%
This routine is recommended for 486s only, although a gain can also be achieved for earlier machines if your compiler is Borland or Symantec. Amount of gain varies slightly depending on the string lengths. The test run was `strcspn("ABCDEFGHIJKLMNOPQRSTUVWXYZ!","QV?");`.

_STRCSPN doesn't introduce any new ideas. The large gain it produces is due to the loop-unrolling concepts discussed previously — repeating instructions to avoid the overhead of incrementing and jumping. One innovative way to speed this function up is to sort the characters in one of the strings. This will be illustrated in the _STRPBRK routine, which is functionally very similar to _STRCSPN.

One notable detail in _STRCSPN is the set of instructions following the label `@@note:`, where `BX` (the `string2` pointer) is incremented before the final byte comparison. A conventional (admittedly more easy to follow) way would use this code:

```
@@note: CMP AL,DL
        JZ @@ret0
        ADD BX,4
        JMP @@loop2
```

_STRCSPN doesn't use this conventional way because conditional jumps like `JNZ` and `JZ` take 1 cycle if the jump is not done but take 3 cycles if the jump is done. The latter figure — 3 cycles — is the same number of cycles that a straight `JMP` takes. Therefore, each time the loop above is repeated, it takes 1 cycle for the `JZ` and 3 cycles for the `JMP`, or 4 in all. The loop in _STRCSPN on the other hand, only takes 3 cycles for the JNZ each time it is repeated — saving 1 cycle. You can often save a cycle in a loop this way.

```
ALIGN 16
    public _STRCSPN          ;STRing Character SPaN
_STRCSPN proc
        PUSH BP
        MOV BP,SP
        PUSH SI
        MOV SI,[BP+4]        ;SI --> string1, what we're searching
@@loop1: MOV AL,[SI]          ;AL = [SI] = next character in string1
        TEST AL,AL           ;Test if AL is '\0'
        JZ @@ret             ;(AL = [SI] = '\0' so return offset)
        MOV BX,[BP+6]        ;BX --> string2, the list of bytes
        INC SI               ;increment string1 pointer for next time
                             ;The MOV BX,... + INC SI + MOV ....,[BX] combo gets a 1 cycle penalty.
@@loop2: MOV DL,[BX]          ;DL = [BX] = next byte in string2
        TEST DL,DL           ;first check for '\0', then check for match
        JZ @@loop1           ;(it's '\0' so no string2 byte matches AL)
        CMP AL,DL            ;Does this string2 byte match AL i.e. [SI]?
        JZ @@ret0            ;(yes, we've found a match so we can return)
        MOV DL,[BX+1]        ;From here to @@note, we are being repetitive:
        TEST DL,DL           ;getting bytes from [BX] and comparing them to
        JZ @@loop1           ;AL, just as we did at the start of @@loop2.
        CMP AL,DL            ;The process goes on for two words (4 bytes).
        JZ @@ret0
        MOV DL,[BX+2]
        TEST DL,DL
        JZ @@loop1
        CMP AL,DL
        JZ @@ret0
        MOV DL,[BX+3]
        TEST DL,DL
        JZ @@loop1
@@note:  ADD BX,4             ;Increment the pointer to string2
        CMP AL,DL            ;See if the last byte from string2 matched
        JNZ @@loop2          ;(It didn't, so we repeat the compare loop)
@@ret0:  DEC SI               ;We incremented SI after we moved [SI] to AL
@@ret:   MOV AX,SI            ;Jump to here if we reach end of string1
        SUB AX,[BP+4]        ;Return is an offset, not a pointer
        POP SI
        POP BP
        RET                  ;Return AX = offset of first non-matching byte
_STRCSPN endp
```

stricmp

Prototype: `int stricmp(char *string1,char *string2)`

Function: Like `_strcmp`, but this time the comparison is case insensitive.

Method: Get a byte from `string1`. If it's less than or equal to Z, add 20h to it — this will convert it to lowercase if it's an uppercase letter. (There is no need to check if it is greater than or equal to A — adding 20h to a non-letter will not invalidate the comparison.) Get a byte from `string2` and do the same process. Get another pair of bytes from `string1` and `string2`, again doing the same process.

Compare 16-bit words. If they're equal, add 2 to the `string1` and `string2` pointers and repeat from the start. If they're not equal, stop. Although this method produces "A" < "[", which is technically a wrong answer, we use it because it's the same answer that all the compiler vendors return.

Return: $AX < 0$ if `string1` < `string2`
$AX = 0$ if `string1` = `string2`
$AX > 0$ if `string1` > `string2`

In fact, AX is the difference in the last character, e.g.: `stricmp("1","9");` returns $AX = -8$, but the C vendors' documentation is not specific about this point.

Gain: (Borland C) on 486: 44% — on 386SX: 10%
(Microsoft C) on 486: 36% — on 386SX: 11%
(Symantec C) on 486: 30% — on 386SX: 0%

There is no significant gain unless most bytes are letters, with a mix of both uppercase and lowercase letters. The test run was `stricmp("abcdefghijklmnopqrstuvwxyz!"` `,"abcdefghijklmnopqrstuvwxyz!");`.

After initialization, _STRICMP has the instruction `JMP short @@nxtwd`. Right after the `JMP` is a handy place to put an `ALIGN 16` statement in.

Sometimes when a change is made to avoid a penalty, it's such a little change that nobody appreciates it. An example is this three-line combination:

```
        ADD DX,' '        ;1 cycle    ;ADD instruction, changes DX
@@getb2: MOV AH,[SI+1]    ;1 cycle    ;MOV instruction, in the middle
        MOV DH,[BX+1]     ;1 cycle    ;MOV instruction, loads DH
```

Why are we using the entire `DX` register in the first instruction when we really only want to add a constant to the `DL` register? Well, the truth is that at first we did use only `DL`. Originally these three instructions were:

```
        ADD DL,' '
@@getb2: MOV AH,[SI+1]
        MOV DH,[BX+1]
```

which looks more natural. But when we were doing our final touching up of the code, our TACHO.EXE utility program alerted us that there's a Bytes-and-Pointers Rule penalty on the `MOV DH,[BX+1]` instruction. By changing `DL` to `DX` we avoid the penalty, we save 2 cycles, and we don't change the meaning — `ADD DX,20h` can affect `DH` (the upper half of `DX`) too, but we're going to wipe out `DH` anyway.

```
ALIGN 16
    public _STRICMP                     ;STRing case-Insensitive CoMPare
_STRICMP proc
        PUSH BP
        MOV BP,SP
        PUSH SI
        MOV SI,[BP+4]                   ;SI --> string1 start
        MOV BX,[BP+6]                   ;BX --> string2 start
        JMP short @@nxtwd               ;First time, skip increments.
ALIGN 16
@@aled1: TEST AL,AL                     ;Jump here if 1st bytes equal.
        JZ @@eq                         ;(AL = 0, string1 is ended)
        MOV AH,[SI+1]                   ;Get 2nd byte from string1
        MOV DH,[BX+1]                   ;Get 2nd byte from string2
        ADD SI,2                        ;SI --> next word in string1
        ADD BX,2                        ;BX --> next word in string2
        CMP AX,DX                       ;Compare by word. Notice that
        JNZ @@chkah                     ;the 1st bytes are high bytes.
@@axedx: TEST AH,AH                     ;Ready for next word, maybe.
        JZ @@eq                         ;(AH = 0, string1 is ended)
@@nxtwd: MOV AL,[SI]                    ;Get 1st byte from string1
        MOV DL,[BX]                     ;Get 1st byte from string2
        CMP AL,DL       ;Redundant.     ;Don't bother with conversion
        JZ @@aled1      ;Redundant.     ;unless this test says "!=".
        CMP AL,"Z"
        JA @@chkd1                      ;(AH > 'Z', so no conversion)
        TEST AL,AL                      ;AL = string1 byte < 'Z'
        JZ @@lt                         ;(AL=0, DL<>0, so return "<")
        ADD AL," "                      ;Convert AL to lower case.
@@chkd1: CMP DL,"Z"
        JA @@getb2                      ;(DL > 'Z', so no conversion)
        ADD DX," "                      ;Convert DL to lower case.
@@getb2: MOV AH,[SI+1]                  ;Get 2nd byte from string1.
        MOV DH,[BX+1]                   ;Get 2nd byte from string2.
        ADD SI,2                        ;SI --> next word in string1
        ADD BX,2                        ;BX --> next word in string2
        CMP AX,DX       ;Redundant.     ;Compare by word. Notice that
        JZ @@axedx      ;Redundant.     ;the 1st bytes are high bytes.
@@chkah: CMP AH,"Z"
        JA @@chkdh                      ;(AH > 'Z', so no conversion)
        ADD AH," "                      ;Convert AH to lower case.
@@chkdh: CMP DH,"Z"
        JA @@cmpax                      ;(DH > 'Z', so no conversion)
        ADD DH," "                      ;Convert DH to lower case.
@@cmpax: ADD SI,2                       ;SI --> next word in string1
        ADD BX,2                        ;BX --> next word in string2
        SUB AX,DX                       ;Compare by word. Notice that
        JZ @@nxtwd                      ;the 1st bytes are high bytes.
        TEST AL,AL
        JNZ @@ret
        MOV AL,AH
@@ret:   CBW
        POP SI
        POP BP
        RET
@@eq:    XOR AX,AX
        JMP @@ret
@@lt:    SUB AL,DL
        JMP @@ret
_STRICMP endp
```

strlen

Prototype: `int strlen(char *string)`

Function: Return the length of the string.

Method: Get a byte from the string, compare with \0, end if equal. Repeat eight times before incrementing the string pointer and looping.

Return: AX = number of bytes not including the \0

Gain: (Borland C) on 486: 30% — on 386SX: –33%
       (Microsoft C) on 486: 32% — on 386SX: –11%
       (Symantec C) on 486: 24% — on 386SX: –62%

This routine is recommended for 486s only. The amount of gain varies depending on the size of the string. There is no gain on a zero-length or tiny string. The test run was `strlen("ABCDEGHIJKLMNOPQRSTUVWXYZ");`.

In Chapter 9 we found that there are lots of ways to skin the _strlen cat. We won't repeat the listing of what is probably the fastest way, since you can refer back to Chapter 9 for details. The way that we do it here involves no tricks: we just unroll the loop eight times. If you like the idea that "trick-free code is bug-free code," you might even prefer the approach we're using for this version of _STRLEN. You might also find that this approach is somewhat clearer than the classic approach that every C compiler's library uses, namely, a REPNZ SCASB with a high value of CX:

```
PUSH DS                                                 ;3 cycles
POP ES                                                  ;3 cycles
CLD             ;Scanning in a forward direction,       ;2 cycles
XOR AL,AL       ;with AL = \0,                          ;1 cycle
MOV CX,0FFFFh   ;repeating the SCASB "indefinitely",    ;1 cycle
REPNZ SCASB     ;scan bytes until AL = [DI] = \0.        ;7+5*CX cycles
NOT CX                                                  ;1 cycle
DEC CX                                                  ;1 cycle
```

In any case, every iteration of REPNZ SCASB takes 5 cycles to scan a byte. Every iteration of the loop in our _STRLEN routine takes 27 cycles and scans 8 bytes, for an average of 3.4 cycles per byte — perhaps not as fast as the tricky stuff we described in Chapter 9, but still faster than 5 cycles per byte. In other words the classic way is uncompetitive according to cycle counting, and as usual this translates to "uncompetitive in practice." Only on 386s is the classic method faster.

_STRLEN uses MOV AL,0 to set the 8-bit AL register to zero. This is unlike the method — XOR AX,AX — used to set the 16-bit AX register to zero in _STRCHR. The difference lies in the sizes of the registers — for an 8-bit register, the MOV instruction and the XOR instruction are the same size (2 bytes) and take the same amount of time, so we use MOV because it's clearer.

AL is also being used as a register constant. If _STRLEN used CMP BYTE PTR [BX+n],0 rather than CMP AL,[BX+n], the function would be 10 percent slower.

```
ALIGN 16
    public _STRLEN    ;STRing LENgth
_STRLEN proc
          PUSH BP
          MOV BP,SP
          MOV BX,[BP+4]   ;BX --> string
          MOV CX,BX       ;CX = BX --> string, we use CX at end
          MOV AL,0        ;AX = 0
@@loop:   CMP AL,[BX+0]   ;If *(string+0) == '\0' we're done
          JZ @@byte0
          CMP AL,[BX+1]   ;If *(string+1) == '\0' we're done
          JZ @@byte1
          CMP AL,[BX+2]   ;If *(string+2) == '\0' we're done
          JZ @@byte2
          CMP AL,[BX+3]   ;If *(string+3) == '\0' we're done
          JZ @@byte3
          CMP AL,[BX+4]   ;If *(string+4) == '\0' we're done
          JZ @@byte4
          CMP AL,[BX+5]   ;If *(string+5) == '\0' we're done
          JZ @@byte5
          CMP AL,[BX+6]   ;If *(string+6) == '\0' we're done
          JZ @@byte6
          CMP AL,[BX+7]   ;If *(string+7) == '\0' we're done
          LEA BX,[BX+8]   ;ADD 8 to BX without changing flags.
          JNZ @@loop      ;(Repeat for next 8 non-zero bytes)
          DEC BX          ;We're done @ string+7.
@@byte0:  MOV AX,BX       ;We're done @ string+0.
          SUB AX,CX
          POP BP
          RET
@@byte1:  LEA AX,[BX+1]   ;We're done @ string+1.
          SUB AX,CX
          POP BP
          RET
@@byte2:  LEA AX,[BX+2]   ;We're done @ string+2.
          SUB AX,CX
          POP BP
          RET
@@byte3:  LEA AX,[BX+3]   ;We're done @ string+3.
          SUB AX,CX
          POP BP
          RET
@@byte4:  LEA AX,[BX+4]   ;We're done @ string+4.
          SUB AX,CX
          POP BP
          RET
```

```
@@byte5: LEA AX,[BX+5]    ;We're done @ string+5.
         SUB AX,CX
         POP BP
         RET
ALIGN 16
@@byte6: LEA AX,[BX+6]    ;We're done @ string+6.
         SUB AX,CX
         POP BP
         RET              ;Return AX = length prior to '\0'
_STRLEN endp
```

strlwr

Prototype: `char *strlwr(char *string)`

Function: Convert all uppercase letters in the string to lowercase.

Method: Get a byte from the string. See if it's in the range between A and Z. If it is, add 20h to it (20h is the distance between a and A). Follow different execution paths for the next byte in the string, depending on whether the first byte was converted or not.

Return: `AX = *string`

Gain: (Borland C) on 486: 41% — on 386SX: 13%
            (Microsoft C) on 486: 38% — on 386SX: 15%
            (Symantec C) on 486: 62% — on 386SX: 49%

The test run was

`strlwr("abcdefghijklmnopqrztuvwxyz1234567890");.`

The key to the success of _STRLWR is that, depending on whether a byte from the string was converted or not, different execution paths are followed for the next byte in the string. The advantage is that, if both bytes are uppercase, they can both be converted to lowercase with a single word operand. (Note that, since a word instruction is used, performance will be adversely affected if the string isn't on a word boundary.) The ability to use a word operand has no value if most bytes in the string are already in lowercase or are not letters at all, but _STRLWR will still achieve an overall gain due to the multiple execution paths method.

There are other fast ways to do case conversions. If you're using Windows, the Windows "ANSI" character set allows conversion even of the majority of the non-English characters by adding/subtracting 20h. The fastest way of all would be with a table lookup rather than a calculation.

Why don't we use a table lookup since the fastest conversion is with a fixed table? In our imagination, we see a table named *table1* which contains all the ASCII characters from 0 to 255. But at the 65th position (65 is the ASCII code for the letter A), we have a value of 97 (97 is the ASCII code for the letter a). The table lookup code seems simple enough:

```
MOV BH,0              ;Ensure that the upper part of BX is always 0
...
MOV BL,[SI]           ;Get a character from the input string
MOV AL,table1[BX]     ;Convert that to lower case using table1
MOV [SI],AL           ;Put converted character back in the string
```

Although this code is faster than what we're going to use, it has the concomitant problem of what segment *table1* is in. If the _STRLWR routine isn't small model MS-DOS, a large amount of work will have to be done to ensure the DS register has the right value in it. So we rejected table lookup as not being generalizable.

_STRLWR's code is ugly. It contains 11 jump and conditional jump instructions. It repeats some instructions several times in different places. It's 39 lines long and results nearly as good can be achieved with a routine only 24 lines long (see "elegant alternative _STRLWR" at the end of this section for one example, and the code for _STRUPR for a short solution to a very similar problem). And yet, nothing generalizable is faster than the following _STRLWR routine, so we'll excuse ourselves by saying, "Here is an instructive example of assembler brutality that works very well, but generally we prefer to use cleaner-looking alternatives."

```
ALIGN 16
    public _STRLWR                  ;STRing LoWeR
_STRLWR proc
         PUSH BP
         MOV BP,SP
         MOV BX,[BP+4]              ;BX --> string
         ;Set up CX as Register Constant, to avoid Constant-to-Memory Rule
         MOV CX,2020h               ;Both CH and CL = 20h i.e. "a"-"A"
@@next:  MOV DL,[BX]                ;DL = [BX] = *string
         ADD BX,2
         CMP DL,"A"                 ;Is DL in range A-Z?
         JB @@dllea                 ;(DL = [BX] < "A")
         CMP DL,"Z"
         MOV DH,[BX-1]              ;DH = [BX+1] = *(string+1)
         JA @@dlgez                 ;(DL = [BX] > "Z")
                                    ;DL is in the range between 'A' and 'Z'
         CMP DH,"A"                 ;Is DH in range A-Z?
         JB @@dhlea                 ;(DH = [BX+1] < 'A')
         CMP DH,"Z"
         JA @@dhgez                 ;(DH = [BX+1] > 'Z')
                                    ;Both DH and DL are in the range between 'A' and 'Z'.
         ;The next instruction is bad news if BX happens to be misaligned. We
         ;figured the chances of misalignment are only 1 in 4, and risked it.
         ADD WORD PTR [BX-2],CX     ;Convert both bytes in one instruction
         JMP @@next                 ;Go to get the next bytes.
```

```
        ALIGN 16
@@dhgez: ADD BYTE PTR [BX-2],CL    ;DH = [BX+1] > 'Z'. CL = 20h. Convert.
        JMP @@next                 ;Go to get the next bytes.
        ALIGN 16
@@dllea: TEST DL,DL                ;DL = [BX] < 'A'. Is it = '\0'?
        JZ @@eos                   ;(Yes, this is the end of the string.)
        MOV DH,[BX-1]
@@dlgez:                           ;DL is not in the range. It's < 'A' or it's > 'Z'
        CMP DH,"A"                 ;Is DH in range A-Z?
        JB @@isdh0                 ;(DH = [BX+1] < 'A', out of range.)
        CMP DH,"Z"'
        JA @@next                  ;(DH = [BX+1] > 'Z', out of range.)
        ADD BYTE PTR [BX-1],CL     ;We've already added 2 to BX. Convert.
        JMP @@next                 ;Go to get the next bytes.
        ALIGN 16
@@dhlea: ADD BYTE PTR [BX-2],CL    ;DH = [BX+1] < 'A'. CL = 20h. Convert.
@@isdh0: TEST DH,DH
        JNZ @@next                 ;Go to get the next bytes, if DH!='\0'
@@eos:  MOV AX,[BP+4]              ;return pointer to passed string
        POP BP
        RET
_STRLWR endp
```

An alternate way to do _STRLWR follows. Its loop contains only one main line. It contains no repetitions. It's only 24 lines long. This code is the "elegant alternative _STRLWR" mentioned earlier. Although it's not as speedy as our recommended _STRLWR routine, _STRLWR2 is still somewhat faster (about a 10 percent gain) than the usual solutions.

_STRLWR2 also illustrates what can be done with the carry flag if you're determined to avoid jumping back and forth depending on whether the letter is less than A, is equal to 0, or is greater than Z. Briefly: the CMP instruction sets the carry flag, and both the ADC and SBB instructions use the carry flag's status to decide whether the operation needs to carry (or borrow) to determine the result. What _STRLWR2 is doing is storing zero in a register, incrementing the register if *string is greater than Z, decrementing the register if *string is less than A, then testing whether the register is zero — which is only possible if *string is less than or equal to A.

```
        public _STRLWR2            ;variant of _STRLWR, above
_STRLWR2 proc
        PUSH BP
        MOV BP,SP
        MOV BX,[BP+4]              ;BX --> start of string
        MOV AX,5B40h               ;i.e. AH='Z'+1, AL='A'-1
        MOV DX,0020h               ;i.e. DH=0, DL='a'-'A'
@@ge_z: MOV CL,0                   ;start with CL = 0. Use XOR CH,CH on 386s.
@@next: MOV CH,[BX]
        INC BX                     ;Increment pointer to string.
        CMP CH,AH                  ;Is the letter > 'Z'?
        ADC CL,CL                  ;If letter > 'Z', CL becomes 1.
        CMP AL,CH                  ;Is 'A' greater than the letter? (Hi/Lo penalty)
        SBB CL,DH                  ;If letter < 'A', CL gets decremented.
        JL @@ge_z                  ;(CL < 0, meaning letter > 'Z')
        JG @@le_a                  ;(CL > 0, meaning letter < 'A') (Double-Jump penalty)
        ADD [BX-1],DL              ;CL = 0 meaning letter between 'A' and 'Z'
        JMP @@next                 ;Repeat for next letter.
@@le_a: TEST CH,CH                 ;The letter is < 'A'. Specifically: is it \0?
        JNZ @@ge_z                 ;(no it's not 0, so repeat for next letter)
        MOV AX,[BP+4]              ;return AX = pointer to passed string
        POP BP
        RET
_STRLWR2 endp
```

strncat

Prototype: `char *strncat(char *string1,`
`char *string2,int maximum)`

Function: Like `_strcat`, but no more than `maximum` bytes are copied.

Method: Find the end of `string1`. Move `maximum` or `strlen(string2)` bytes, whichever is shorter, from `string2` to `string1`. End with `\0`.

Return: `AX = *string1`

Gain: (Borland C) on 486: 51% — on 386SX: 32%
(Microsoft C) on 486: 25% — on 386SX: –26%
(Symantec C) on 486: 38% — on 386SX: –28%

This routine is recommended for 486s only, although a gain can also be achieved on older machines if your compiler is Borland. Amount of gain varies slightly depending on string contents. The test run was `strncat(tmp,"abcdefghijklmnop7890123456!",10);` where `tmp` is equal to "ABCDEFGHIJKLMNOPQRSTUVWXYZ!".

The only difference between _STRCAT and _STRNCAT is that _STRNCAT only copies up to a specified number of bytes. While the _STRCAT routine is merely a combination of the _STRLEN and _STRCPY routines, it isn't possible to follow the same procedure for _STRNCAT because of one subtle detail — the function `strncpy(string1,"string2",7);` only copies `string2` to `string1`, while the function `strncat(string1,"string2",7);` not only appends `string2` to `string1`, it adds a terminating `\0` too. The following _STRNCAT routine thus illustrates some of the points of the classic method for doing this.

There's a loop in _STRNCAT which does two bytes at a time. This loop has to stop if CX changes from a value of greater than or equal to zero to a value of less than zero. The potential trap here is that this bad code looks good:

```
@@loop: ...
        SUB CX,2        ;Subtract 2 from CX
        JGE @@loop      ;Repeat as long as CX is >= 0
```

This doesn't answer the question! If CX's initial value is 0x8004 and 2 is subtracted from it, the result is 0x8002. The sign bit is on so the result is less than zero, which causes the looping to immediately stop. Since the loop should happen 0x8004/2 times, something's wrong. Clearly it's the JGE instruction because JGE only answers the question "Is the result less than zero?" The question "Is the result less than zero and was it greater than or equal to zero previously?" is answered by a different conditional jump instruction: JNB.

There's a CALL instruction in _STRNCAT because we figured it was easier to CALL _STRLEN than to repeat all the _STRLEN instructions inside _STRNCAT. The CALL takes time, so this _STRNCAT is inefficient for really short strings (less than 5 bytes long).

```
ALIGN 16
    public _STRNCAT
_STRNCAT proc                   ;STRing Number-of-bytes conCATenate
        PUSH BP
        MOV BP,SP
        PUSH DI
        PUSH [BP+4]             ;Pass string2 to _STRLEN function
        CALL _STRLEN            ;Returns AX = size of string2
        ADD SP,2                ;Cleans up the stack after the call
        MOV DI,[BP+4]           ;DI --> string2
        ADD DI,AX               ;DI --> string2 end
        MOV BX,[BP+6]           ;BX --> string1
        MOV CX,[BP+8]           ;CX = maximum string2 bytes to copy
        JMP short @@loop1       ;Join the loop in midstream
        ;The following loop usually takes 6.5 cycles per byte.
        ;We could speed it up a bit by unrolling more.
ALIGN 16
@@loop: MOV AL,[BX]             ;AL = next byte *string1
        TEST AL,AL
        JZ @@loope
        MOV AH,[BX+1]           ;AL = next byte *(string1+1)
        TEST AH,AH
        JZ @@ahend
        MOV [DI],AX             ;Risks misalignment
        ADD BX,2
        ADD DI,2
@@loop1: SUB CX,2
        JNB @@loop              ;(there's at least 2 bytes left)
        CMP CX,-2
        JZ @@loope              ;(there's no bytes left, we're done)
        MOV AL,[BX]             ;there's one byte left, move it+stop
@@ahend: MOV [DI],AL
        INC DI
@@loope: MOV BYTE PTR [DI],0    ;The final byte output must be '\0'
@@end:  MOV AX,[BP+4]          ;Return a pointer to string1
        POP DI
        POP BP
        RET
_STRNCAT endp
```

strncmp

Prototype: `int strncmp(char *string1,`
`char *string2,int maximum)`

Function: Like `_strcmp`, but no more than `maximum` bytes are compared.

Method: For `maximum` or `strlen(string2)` bytes, whichever is shorter, compare bytes in `string1` to bytes in `string2`. Stop if an inequality is encountered.

Return: AX< 0 if `string1` < `string2`
AX = 0 if `string1` = `string2`
AX > 0 if `string1` > `string2`

Gain: (Borland C) on 486: 43% — on 386SX: 17%
(Microsoft C) on 486: 50% — on 386SX: 17%
(Symantec C) on 486: 71% — on 386SX: 46%
The gain depends on the number of initial unequal bytes in the string. The test run was `strncmp("ABCDEFGHIJKLMNOPQRSTUVWXYZ!"` `,"abcdefghijklmnop7890123456!",5);`.

When commenting on _STRCMP, we made the observation that one of the reasons the compiler vendors' implementations are slow was the fact that they had to go all the way to the end of the string to find the size before doing any actual comparing. The same problem exists with _strncmp; it doesn't go away unless _memcmp is used. Our _STRNCMP routine, on the other hand, faces a large overhead on the final byte (that is, on the last byte of the string or the first byte that's not equal). So if the strings being compared are both short, or if the first bytes are unequal, the code shown in this book will experience a "negative gain."

_STRNCMP uses SUB rather than CMP to neatly solve a problem that comes up in word comparisons. Intel machines are smallendian, which means that the small end of a number comes first. Consider, then, the strings az and bc. If these strings are compared by word, then az is less than bc because the top halves of the words are compared first — i.e., z is compared with c. But the question is, what was the result if the lower halves of the words are compared first? This question can't be answered by using CMP — the flags don't tell us. If SUB is used instead, though, then the result is in a register and examining the bottom half of the register will show the result of a – b.

As for the LEA BP, [BP] instruction, which accomplishes precisely nothing: it's for alignment. We talked about the idea in Chapter 3 in our discussion of the NOP instruction.

```
ALIGN 16
    public _STRNCMP          ;STRing Number-of-bytes CoMPare
_STRNCMP proc
          PUSH BP
          MOV BP,SP
          PUSH SI
          MOV SI,[BP+4]       ;SI --> string1
          MOV BX,[BP+6]       ;BX --> string2
          MOV CX,[BP+8]       ;CX = maximum number of bytes
          LEA BP,[BP]         ;ALIGN 16 would work but this is faster.
@@loop:   SUB CX,2
          JC @@max            ;(reached or passed maximum)
          MOV AL,[SI]
          TEST AL,AL
          JZ @@eos1           ;(no more bytes in string1)
          MOV DL,[BX]         ;DL = *string2
          TEST DL,DL
          JZ @@ret            ;(no more bytes in string2, string1 > string2)
          MOV DH,[BX+1]       ;DH = *(string2+1)
          MOV AH,[SI+1]
          TEST AH,AH
          JZ @@eos2           ;(no more bytes in string1)
          ADD SI,2
          ADD BX,2
          SUB AX,DX           ;This compares 2 bytes at once
          JZ @@loop           ;(Strings are equal in the last 2 bytes)
@@0:                          ;There's a word inequality i.e. [SI]>[BX].
          ;The AL register has the comparison of *string1/*string2. It could be
          ;0, in which case we use the AH register which has the comparison of
          ;*(string1+1)/*(string2+1)
          TEST AL,AL
          JNZ @@ret
          MOV AL,AH
@@ret:    CBW                 ;We must return AX, so AH = sign of AL
          POP SI
          POP BP
          RET
ALIGN 16
@@eos1:   SUB AL,[BX]         ;We're at end of string1. CMP last byte only.
          JMP @@ret
@@eos2:   SUB AX,DX
          JMP @@0
@@max:    MOV AL,0
          CMP CL,-1           ;Really checking if CX = -1, we know CH = -1.
          JL @@ret            ;(CX was 0, now it's -2, the strings are =)
          MOV AL,[SI]
          SUB AL,[BX]
          JMP @@ret
_STRNCMP endp
```

strncpy

Prototype: char *strncpy(char *string1,
                                   char *string2,int maximum)

Function: Like _strcpy, but no more than maximum bytes are copied.

Method: Move maximum or strlen(string2) bytes, whichever is shorter, from string2 to string1. End with \0.

Return: AX = *string1

Gain: (Borland C) on 486: 24% — on 386SX: –30%
       (Microsoft C) on 486: 45% — on 386SX: –3%
       (Symantec C) on 486: 33% — on 386SX: –27%
This routine is recommended for 486s only. If length of string2 is less than maximum, gain is less. If maximum is less than 10, gain is less. The test run was strncpy(string2,"ABCDEFGHIJK",10);.

Although the length of a string is often not known, there are a few situations where the number of bytes is known — in CX — and that number of bytes either needs to be moved with REP MOVSx — or needs to be stored with REP STOSx. It's common practice to do this in words rather than bytes, and simply dividing CX by 2 provides the number of words for the bytes. However, this calculation doesn't provide information on whether the division has a remainder. If there is a remainder, then after manipulating the correct number of words, one more byte also needs to be manipulated, so knowing the remainder is vital. The remainder of a division by 2 is in the carry flag if the division is done with a SHR instruction, so the following two alternatives exist:

```
        SHR CX,1              SHR CX,1
        REP MOVSW             REP MOVSW
        JNC @@done            ADC CX,0
        MOVSB                 REP MOVSB
@@done: ...
```

On 486s, the set of instructions on the left is faster; on older machines, however, the set on the right is preferable.

When using REP STOSx, the additional duty of ensuring the AH register equals the AL register before using words exists. In this routine that's no problem because, by definition, _STRNCPY pads string1 to zero. Both registers are set to zero by setting the AX register to zero (using XOR AX,AX as usual).

In _STRNCPY, it does no good to replace the constant 2 with a register constant which equals 2.

```
ALIGN 16
    public _STRNCPY            ;STRing Number-of-bytes CoPY
_STRNCPY proc
        PUSH BP
        MOV BP,SP
        PUSH DI
        MOV CX,[BP+8]          ;CX = maximum
        MOV BX,[BP+6]          ;BX --> string2 (the source)
        MOV DI,[BP+4]          ;DI --> string1 (the destination)
        JMP short @@loop1      ;Join the loop in mid stream
ALIGN 16
@@loop:  MOV AL,[BX]
        TEST AL,AL
        JZ @@eos               ;(end of string2, dump out AL = last byte = 0)
        MOV AH,[BX+1]
        TEST AH,AH
        JZ @@eos1              ;(end of string2)
        MOV [DI],AX            ;Dump 2 bytes at a time into string1
        ADD BX,2
        ADD DI,2
@@loop1: SUB CX,2             ;This is our loop control. We subtract 2 at
        JNC @@loop             ;a time from maximum since we've done 2 bytes
        ;We've just subtracted 2 from CX and now it's less than 0.
        CMP CX,-1             ;CX = -1 or -2. Find out which it is.
        JL @@ret             ;(It's -2, dead stop.)
        MOV AL,[BX]          ;CX = -1, there's one more byte to dump
        MOV [DI],AL
@@ret:   MOV AX,[BP+4]        ;return AX = string1 start
        POP DI
        POP BP
        RET
ALIGN 16
@@eos1:  MOV [DI],AX          ;AH = *(string2+1) = '\0'. AL has a value.
        JMP short @@eos2     ;Dump AL+AH in string2, then pad.
@@eos:   MOV WORD PTR [DI],0  ;Just pad the rest of string1 to nulls.
@@eos2:  ADD DI,2
        SUB CX,2
        JNC @@eos
        CMP CX,-1
        JL @@ret
        MOV BYTE PTR [DI],0
        JMP @@ret
_STRNCPY endp
```

strnset

Prototype: `char *strnset(char *string,`
`int character,int maximum)`

Function: Set characters in the string to a value.

Method: For up to `strlen(string1)` or `maximum` bytes, which-ever is less: move `character` into `string1`. There is also a variant of `_strnset` without a maximum; see our discussion of `_STRSET`.

Return: `AX` = `char *string1`

Gain: (Borland C) on 486: 44% — on 386SX: 31%
       (Microsoft C) on 486: 36% — on 386SX: –29%
       (Symantec C) on 486: 37% — on 386SX: 24%
This routine is recommended for 486s only, although a gain can also be achieved on older machines if your compiler is Borland or Syman-tec. The test run was `strnset(tmp,'a',10);`.

Once again we're being optimistic about alignment: our `_STRNSET` routine is not checking whether `BX` is an even number before it begins the loop. Our reasoning is that misalignment isn't a huge risk because there's only one instruction that moves a word value to memory here.

Other than that, we're making the usual sensible choices. `_STRNSET` uses a register constant for zero to avoid Constant-to-Memory Rule penalties — that saves 1 cycle. The code duplicates the `character` value so that the value can be dumped one word at a time instead of one byte at a time — that saves 1 cycle. We've checked that the alignment is okay — so that 1 cycle isn't lost whenever the code jumps back to `@@loop`. Having done this much, we've stopped. There's no loop unrolling.

Since `_STRNSET` is not doing anything particularly clever, it might seem surprising that it's 44 percent faster than Borland's `_strnset`. The reason is that Borland's `_strnset` is particularly unclever — it calls `_strlen` to get the actual size of the string, compares the actual size with `maximum`, and uses whichever is smaller. That's not efficient design.

```
ALIGN 16
    public _STRNSET ;STRing Number-of-bytes SET
_STRNSET proc
        PUSH BP
        MOV BP,SP
        MOV BX,[BP+4]          ;BX --> string start.
        MOV AL,[BP+6]          ;AL = the character we want to set bytes to
        MOV CX,[BP+8]          ;CX = maximum
        MOV AH,AL             ;AH is a duplicate of AL
        MOV DL,0             ;DH is a Register Constant equal to 0, always
        JMP short @@loop1      ;Join the loop in mid stream
@@loop: CMP DL,[BX]           ;DL=0. Check if this is the end of the string
        JZ @@eos             ;(*string = '\0', we can stop now)
        CMP DL,[BX+1]         ;DL=0. Check if this is the end of the string
        JZ @@eos1            ;(*(string+1) = '\0', we can stop now)
        MOV WORD PTR [BX],AX   ;*string = *(string+1) = the character
        ADD BX,2
@@loop1: SUB CX,2
        JNB @@loop
        CMP CX,-1             ;CX = -1 or else CX = -2
        JNZ @@eos            ;(CX = -2, we've cleared exactly CX bytes)
@@eos1: MOV BYTE PTR [BX],AL   ;*string isn't '\0', but *(string+1) is.
@@eos:  MOV AX,[BP+4]         ;Return AX = pointer to the string, as passed.
        POP BP
        RET
_STRNSET endp
```

strpbrk

Prototype: `char *strpbrk(char *string1,char *string2)`

Function: Find a character in `string1` that matches any of the characters in `string2`.

Method: Get a 7-byte subset of `string2` into 7 registers. Sort the registers. For each byte of `string1`: do a binary search of the 7 registers. If that fails, then get another 7 bytes.

The following table shows a sorted register list (in the last three columns, a 1 means the register is checked first, a 2 means the register is checked second, and a 3 means the register is checked third):

REGISTER NAME	CHECKED FIRST	CHECKED SECOND	CHECKED THIRD
AH			3
AL		2	
BH			3
BL	1		
CH			3
CL		2	
DH			3

Return: `AX` = `string1`
An alternate routine is `_strcspn`, which returns an offset.

Gain: (Borland C) on 486: 70% — on 386SX: 77%

(Microsoft C) on 486: 22% — on 386SX: –7%

(Symantec C) on 486: 68% — on 386SX: 77%

This routine is recommended for 486s only, although a gain can also be achieved on older machines if your compiler is Borland or Symantec. There is no gain if both strings are small or a match exists in the first few bytes of string1, but the gain is huge in other circumstances. Performance goes down markedly if strlen(string2); is greater than 7; in fact, _STRPBRK is slower than Microsoft's _strpbrk in that circumstance. The test run was strpbrk("ABCDEFGHIJKLMNOPQRSTUVWXYZ!","1234Q67");.

There's an overhead doing the initial sort of the bytes, so if the SI register is tiny, or the first byte of SI matches the first byte of the DI register, _STRPBRK is slower than the standard routines. But the bigger SI is, the greater the gain achieved with _STRPBRK. If the characters in string2 are presorted highest to lowest, _STRPBRK shows an even bigger gain.

One notable detail about _STRPBRK is that it doesn't use any data memory. Using data memory would be helpful, but problems arise with each of the three available methods. Firstly, _malloc can't be called from _STRPBRK because there is no way to inform the C program that _STRPBRK failed if the _malloc itself fails. Secondly, using static memory gets too complicated for our purposes. Finally, although using the stack is the best choice for a temporary sort set when a significant number of characters is being sorted (the maximum is 255, providing there are no duplicates), we've assumed from our own practice that the size of string2 is unlikely to be greater than 7.

```
ALIGN 16
    public _STRPBRK        ;STRing Per Binary checK
_STRPBRK proc
        PUSH BP
        MOV BP,SP
        PUSH SI
        PUSH DI
        MOV SI,[BP+6]      ;SI --> string2
@@start:XOR AX,AX          ;Begin with all registers = 0.
        XOR BX,BX
        XOR CX,CX
        XOR DX,DX
```

```
@@setup:MOV DH,[SI]          ;DH = *(string2+0), stop if it's '\0'
        TEST DH,DH
        JZ @@sort
        MOV CL,[SI+1]        ;CL = *(string2+1), stop if it's '\0'
        TEST CL,CL
        JZ @@sort
        MOV CH,[SI+2]        ;CH = *(string2+2), stop if it's '\0'
        TEST CH,CH
        JZ @@sort
        MOV BL,[SI+3]        ;BL = *(string2+3), stop if it's '\0'
        TEST BL,BL
        JZ @@sort
        MOV BH,[SI+4]        ;BH = *(string2+4), stop if it's '\0'
        TEST BH,BH
        JZ @@sort
        MOV AL,[SI+5]        ;AL = *(string2+5), stop if it's '\0'
        TEST AL,AL
        JZ @@sort
        MOV AH,[SI+6]        ;AH = *(string2+6)
@@sort:                      ;Sort the register list using a primitive bubble.
@@sort1: CMP AH,AL           ;Interchange AH,AL if AH>AL.
        JBE @@sort2
        XCHG AL,AH
@@sort2: CMP AL,BH           ;Interchange AL,BH if AL>BH.
        JBE @@sort3
        XCHG AL,BH
        JMP @@sort1
@@sort3: CMP BH,BL           ;Interchange BH,BL if BH>BL.
        JBE @@sort4
        XCHG BH,BL
        JMP @@sort2
@@sort4: CMP BL,CH           ;Interchange BL,CH if BL>CL.
        JBE @@sort5
        XCHG BL,CH
        JMP @@sort3
@@sort5: CMP CH,CL           ;Interchange CH,CL if CH>CL.
        JBE @@sort6
        XCHG CH,CL
        JMP @@sort4
@@sort6: CMP CL,DH           ;Interchange CL,DH if CL>DH.
        JBE @@sort7
        XCHG CL,DH
        JMP @@sort5
ALIGN 16
@@sort7:                     ;The sort is over. Registers are in order: AH,AL,BH,BL,CH,CL,DH.
        MOV DI,[BP+4]        ;DI --> string1 start
        DEC DI
@@2:    INC DI               ;increment string1 pointer
        MOV DL,[DI]          ;DL = *string1
        CMP DL,BL            ;Comparison #1.
        JA @@3
        JB @@4
        JMP short @@match
@@3:    CMP DL,CL            ;DL>BL. Comparison #2.
        JA @@3a
        JB @@3b
        JMP short @@match
@@3a:   CMP DL,DH            ;DL>BL, DL>CL.Comparison #3.
        JNZ @@2
        JMP short @@match
@@3b:   CMP DL,CH            ;DL>BL, DL<CL. Comparison #3.
        JNZ @@2
        JMP short @@match
```

```
@@4:        CMP DL,AL           ;DL<BL. Comparison #2.
            JA @@4a
            JB @@4b
            JMP short @@match
@@4a:       CMP DL,BH           ;DL<BL, DL>AL. Comparison #3.
            JNZ @@2
            JMP short @@match
@@4b:       CMP DL,AH           ;DL<BL, DL<AL. Comparison #3.
            JA @@2
            JZ @@match
                                ;DL < all the registers. Is that because DL = 0?
            TEST DL,DL
            JNZ @@2
                                ;DL = 0 so we're out of [DI] but
                                ;DL<>AH, so we're not out of [SI]
            ADD SI,7            ;Very unfortunate, there's more to
            JMP @@start         ;string2 than we're designed for.
ALIGN 16
@@match:                        ;DL=one of the registers. Because they're both 0 or a real match?
            MOV AX,DI
            TEST DL,DL
            JNZ @@ret           ;(they're not both 0, string1 pointer)
            XOR AX,AX           ;Both registers are 0, we return 0
@@ret:      POP DI
            POP SI
            POP BP
            RET
_STRPBRK endp
```

Since `_strpbrk` isn't a commonly called function, the above implementation might appear as overkill. The following variant, called
_STRPBRK2, is a less complex but still reasonably fast way to do it.
(This routine is nearly a duplicate of _STRCSPN; the differences are
noted.) Because _STRPBRK2 starts by finding the size of string2, it
loses on performance if the first byte of string1 is in string2. But
if the searching is longer, the gain is 20 percent.

```
    public _STRPBRK2        ;variant of _STRPBRK, above
_STRPBRK2 proc
            PUSH BP
            MOV BP,SP
            PUSH SI
            MOV SI,[BP+4]       ;SI --> string1, what we're searching
@@loop1:    MOV AL,[SI]         ;AL = [SI] = next character in string1
            TEST AL,AL          ;Test if AL is '\0'
            JZ @@ret            ;(AL = [SI] = '\0' so return offset)
            INC SI              ;increment string1 pointer for next time
            MOV BX,[BP+6]       ;BX --> string2, the list of bytes
@@loop2:    XOR DX,DX           ;DH = 0, DL = 0 -- so the OR trick will work
            OR DL,[BX]          ;DL = [BX] = next byte in string2
            JZ @@loop1          ;(it's '\0' so no string2 byte matches AL)
            CMP AL,DL           ;Does this string2 byte match AL i.e. [SI]?
            JZ @@ret0           ;(Yes, we've found a match so we can return)
            OR DH,[BX+1]        ;From here to @@note, we are being repetitive:
            JZ @@loop1          ;getting bytes from [BX] and comparing them to
            CMP AL,DH           ;AL, just as we did at the start of @@loop2.
            JZ @@ret0           ;The process goes on for two words.
            XOR DX,DX
            OR DL,[BX+2]
            JZ @@loop1
            CMP AL,DL
            JZ @@ret0
            OR DH,[BX+3]
            JZ @@loop1
@@note:     ADD BX,4            ;Increment the pointer to string2
            CMP AL,DH           ;See if the last byte from string2 matched
            JNZ @@loop2         ;(It didn't, so we repeat the compare loop)
@@ret0:     DEC SI              ;We incremented SI after we moved [SI] to AL
```

```
@@ret:    MOV AX,SI        ;Jump to here if we reach end of string1
;         SUB AX,[BP+4]    ;Take out the ";" here and you'd have _strcspn
          POP SI
          POP BP
          RET              ;Return AX = offset of first non-matching byte
_STRPBRK2 endp
```

strrchr

Prototype: `char *strrchr(char *string,int character)`

Function: Find the last byte in the string that matches the character.

Method: Get a byte from `string`. If it matches `character`, save the current string pointer value. If it's the end of `string`, return the saved string pointer value (which is zero if it was never set).

Return: AX = pointer to last character
AX = 0 if character does not appear in string.

Gain: (Borland C) on 486: 65% — on 386SX: 52%
(Microsoft C) on 486: 39% — on 386SX: –23%
(Symantec C) on 486: 61% — on 386SX: 46%

This routine is recommended for 486s only, although a gain can also be achieved on older machines if your compiler is Borland or Symantec. The gain is a function of position of `character` in `string`. The gain is 0 percent for
`strrchr("ABCDEFGHIJKLMNOPQRSTUVWXYZ",'Z');`.
The test run was
`strrchr("ABCDEFGHIJKLMNOPQRSTUVWXYZ",'A');`.

The classic way to approach this problem is to search for the end of the string (with `REPNZ SCASB`), then search backwards for the `character`. So if `character` does not appear in the string at all, the classic approach will go through the entire string twice. In the best case, `character` is at the end of the string, in which case the classic approach will go through the entire string once.

Our approach involves a single pass. _STRRCHR compares to the string terminator byte (\0) and to `character` for every byte, going forward. This double comparison takes longer than `SCASB`, so our approach is inferior to the classic best case, that is, when `character` is at the end of the string. However, our approach is definitely superior for the average case, and has the extra advantage of being consistent. For

_STRRCHR, the time consumed is not affected by the absence or by the relative position of `character` in the string.

One notable detail about _STRRCHR is the instruction `MOV AX,0`. We've often made the point that the `AX` register can be cleared using `XOR AX,AX`, which takes only 2 bytes. `MOV AX,0`, on the other hand, is a 3-byte instruction. It looks like we're being wasteful, but we're just doing a subtle alignment. If we used `XOR AX,AX`, the following instruction, at `@@loop`, would be exactly 1 byte before a 0-mod-16 address and Cache-Straddling Rule penalties would be applied.

```
ALIGN 16
        public _STRRCHR        ;STRing Reverse CHaRacter
_STRRCHR proc
        PUSH BP
        MOV BP,SP
        MOV CL,[BP+6]          ;CL will always = the 'character' we want
        TEST CL,CL
        JZ @@cleq0
        MOV BX,[BP+4]          ;BX --> string
        MOV AX,0               ;AX will = 0 or it will = last match position
@@loop: MOV DL,[BX]
        TEST DL,DL
        JZ @@eos               ;(DL = [BX] = '\0', end of string encountered)
        MOV DH,[BX+1]
        TEST DH,DH
        JZ @@eos1              ;(DH = [BX+1] = '\0', end but check [BX] too)
        ADD BX,2
        CMP DH,CL              ;First compare DH (the later byte)
        JZ @@dheq              ;(DH = AL = [BX+1], save position and go on)
        CMP DL,CL
        JNZ @@loop             ;(neither DH nor DL = AL, get next two bytes)
@@dleq: LEA AX,[BX-2]          ;AX = BX = address of match for 'character'
        JMP @@loop
@@dheq: LEA AX,[BX-1]          ;AX = BX+1 = address of match for 'character'
        JMP @@loop
@@eos1: CMP DL,CL             ;[BX+1] = '\0' but we haven't checked [BX] yet
        JNZ @@eos             ;(DL = [BX] != 'character', we're finished)
        MOV AX,BX             ;AX = BX = address of match for 'character'
@@eos:  POP BP
        RET
@@cleq0:                      ;If (CL = character = 0, it's sort of a special
        ;case: '\0' is both the end of the string and the item we're seeking.
        ;We handle it with a _STRLEN call, which is OK if the length is longer
        ;than 2 or 3 bytes. We aren't really expecting the special case to
        ;occur very often anyway. We do precisely the same thing in _STRCHR.
        PUSH [BP+4]
        CALL _STRLEN
        ADD SP,2
        ADD AX,[BP+4]
        POP BP
        RET
_STRRCHR endp
```

strrev

Prototype: `char *strrev(char *string)`

Function: Reverse the order of bytes in the string.

Method: Find the end of the string. Interchange the first and last words of the string. Interchange the second and second-last words of the string. Interchange the third and third-last words of the string. Continue the interchanging process until all words have been interchanged once.

Return: `AX` = `char *string`

Gain: (Borland C) on 486: 47% — on 386SX: –7%
      (Microsoft C) on 486: 32% — on 386SX: 4%
      (Symantec C) on 486: 56% — on 386SX: 45%

This routine is recommended for 486s only, although a gain can also be achieved on older machines if your compiler is Microsoft or Symantec. The test run was `strrev("ABCDEFGHIJKLMNOPQRSTUVWXYZ");`.

"There is nothing new under the sun" is a common saying and it's certainly true here — there is nothing new about our method for doing `_strrev`. The innovation lies in the insight that words can be reversed almost as easily as bytes. The C vendors' implementations of `_strrev` all use bytes so they cannot hope to match `_STRREV`'s performance provided the length of the string is greater than 5. (If you expect strings to be long, calculate the string size with the method we used in `_STRLEN`.)

Note that simply reversing the words in the string ABCD results in CDBA. The correct result is DCBA, so `_STRREV` has to exchange the bytes within the words before exchanging the words themselves. A straightforward way to do this is with the `XCHG` instruction, as follows:

```
XCHG AL,AH
XCHG DL,DH
MOV [DI],AX
MOV [SI],DX
```

`XCHG` is too slow though, so `_STRREV` uses a slightly less straightforward way: the code `MOV`s a word in memory into a word register, then `MOV`s the top half of the register back to the bottom half of the word in memory, then `MOV`s the bottom half of the register back to the top half of the word in memory.

Notice the function's eighth instruction: MOV BX,DI. At an earlier point, _STRREV loaded the DI register with a pointer to the string, and we expect that it still has that value. Our expectation is safe, because CALL _STRLEN won't change the values in DI, SI, or BP. That, not incidentally, is why the function's third and third-to-the-last lines are PUSH DI and POP DI. Other routines may make the same assumption: that normal functions don't change DI's value.

```
ALIGN 16
    public _STRREV             ;STRing REVerse
_STRREV proc
        PUSH BP
        MOV BP,SP
        PUSH DI
        MOV DI,[BP+4]          ;DI --> string
        PUSH DI                ;Pass address of string to _STRLEN
        CALL _STRLEN           ;Returns AX = number of bytes in string
        ADD SP,2               ;Cleans up stack, we don't need what we PUSHed
        ;The next lines could be a bit shorter: LEA DI,[BX-2]; ADD DI,AX.
        MOV BX,DI              ;BX --> string
        ADD DI,AX              ;DI --> end of string, pointing to '\0' byte
        SUB DI,2               ;now DI --> last word in the string
        JMP short @@loop1      ;Begin the loop with a check: are we done?
@@loop: MOV AX,[BX]            ;AX = a word from the front of the string
        MOV DX,[DI]            ;DX = a word from the back of the string
        MOV [DI],AH            ;Put bytes-reversed AX value at back of string
        MOV [DI+1],AL
        MOV [BX],DH            ;Put bytes-reversed DX value at back of string
        MOV [BX+1],DL
        SUB DI,2               ;The back-of-the-string pointer goes down.
        ADD BX,2               ;The front-of-the-string pointer goes up.
@@loop1: CMP BX,DI            ;Has upgoing pointer met downgoing?
        JA @@eos               ;(it passed it)
        JNZ @@loop             ;(repeat for next word) (Double-Jump penalty)
@@2byte: MOV AX,[BX]          ;When a string has precisely 2 bytes, we don't
        MOV [BX],AH           ;have two words to interchange so we do this.
        MOV [BX+1],AL
@@eos:  MOV AX,[BP+4]         ;return a pointer to the reversed string
        POP DI
        POP BP
        RET
_STRREV endp
```

strset

Prototype: char *strset(char *string,int character)

Function: Set all bytes in string to the value of character.

Method: Get byte from string. If it's \0, stop. Replace *string with character. Repeat.

Return: AX = char *string

Gain: (Borland C) on 486: 41% — on 386SX: 11%

(Microsoft C) on 486: 41% — on 386SX: –9%

(Symantec C) on 486: 33% — on 386SX: 23%

This routine is recommended for 486s only, although a gain can also be achieved on older machines if your compiler is Borland or Symantec. The test run was strset("ABCDEFGHIJKLMNOPQRSTUVWXYZ",'a');.

Despite its small size, _STRSET is a review of most of the tips we've shown you before: use of a register constant, manipulating 2 bytes at a time with a word-sized instruction, minimizing the number of conditional jumps in a loop, and using XOR to set a register to zero.

One notable detail about _STRSET is that every time the code goes through the loop, it's necessary to add 2 to the BX register (which is being used as the pointer to the string). The obvious instruction for the purpose is ADD BX,2. What is not so obvious is where this instruction should be placed.

Putting ADD BX,2 before MOV [BX],AX or CMP DL,[BX] or CMP DL,[BX+1] isn't optimal — if BX is changed before using [BX], the address decoder stalls — so the answer appears to be to put ADD BX,2 before JZ @@eos or JNZ @@loop. Further consideration indicates this isn't correct either because ADD BX,2 will change the zero flag. The solution is to add 2 to the BX register *without* changing the flags. If this sounds like a puzzle problem, that's because it was — for us. You have it easy: the answer is below in the code following the label @@loop:. In case you think that this last consideration is trivial, we present here both _STRSET (the recommended routine) and _STRSET2. The two routines are exactly the same except for the placement and syntax of the instruction that adds 2 to the BX register. _STRSET uses this code:

```
@@loop: MOV [BX-2],AX    ;The two bytes *string become = 'character'
```

_STRSET2, on the other hand, uses this code:

```
@@loop: MOV [BX],AX    ;The two bytes *string become = 'character'
        ADD BX,2       ;Add size of 16-bit word to string pointer
```

_STRSET is 10 percent faster than _STRSET2 on a 486. So, use this routine:

```
ALIGN 16
    public _STRSET          ;STRing SET to character
_STRSET proc                ;Do it the correct way ...
        PUSH BP
        MOV BP,SP
        XOR DX,DX            ;DL will always = 0; DH's value doesn't matter
        MOV BX,[BP+4]        ;BX --> start of string
        MOV AL,[BP+6]        ;Both halves of the AX register, AL and AH,
        MOV AH,AL            ;will contain 'character', making MOV easy.
        TEST BX,1            ;Standard check for misalignment
        JZ @@start          ;(BX is even, alignment won't be a problem)
        CMP DL,[BX]          ;BX is uneven, align before entering the loop
        JZ @@eos            ;(no need to enter the loop, string is blank)
        MOV [BX],AL          ;We'll set the first byte to the desired value
        INC BX              ;And we'll add 1 to BX, so now BX is even.
        JMP short @@start    ;Jump to within the loop.
ALIGN 16
@@loop: MOV [BX-2],AX        ;The two bytes *string become = 'character'.
@@start: CMP DL,[BX]         ;Is [BX] = '\0' i.e. is this end of string?
        JZ @@eos            ;(Yes, so stop.)
        CMP DL,[BX+1]        ;Is [BX+1] = '\0' i.e. next byte is the end?
        LEA BX,[BX+2]        ;Add size of 16-bit word to string pointer.
        JNZ @@loop          ;([BX+1] !='\0', so we can dump a word out.)
        MOV [BX-2],AL        ;Next byte is the end, only one byte to set.
@@eos:  MOV AX,[BP+4]        ;strset returns pointer to passed string
        POP BP
        RET
_STRSET endp
```

Don't use this routine:

```
    public _STRSET2
_STRSET2 proc               ;Or do it the wrong way.
        PUSH BP
        MOV BP,SP
        MOV AL,[BP+6]        ;Both halves of the AX register, AL and AH,
        MOV AH,AL            ;will contain 'character', making STOSW easy.
        MOV BX,[BP+4]        ;BX --> start of string (Bytes-and-Pointers penalty)
        MOV DL,0            ;DL will always = 0
        JMP short @@start    ;Jump to within the loop.
@@loop: MOV [BX],AX          ;The two bytes *string become = 'character'.
        ADD BX,2            ;Add size of 16-bit word to string pointer.
@@start: CMP DL,[BX]         ;Is [BX] = '\0' i.e. is this end of string?
        JZ @@eos            ;(Yes, so stop.)
        CMP DL,[BX+1]        ;Is [BX+1] = '\0' i.e. next byte is the end?
        JNZ @@loop          ;(No, so we can dump a word out.)
        MOV [BX],AL          ;Next byte is the end, only one byte to set.
@@eos:  MOV AX,[BP+4]        ;strset returns pointer to passed string
        POP BP
        RET
_STRSET2 endp
```

strspn

Prototype: `int strspn (char *string1, char *string2)`

Function: Find the first character in `string1` that doesn't appear in `string2`. This is equivalent to saying: Count initial characters in `string1` that are in `string2`.

Method: For each byte in `string1`, search for the byte in `string2`. Repeat search if byte is found. Stop search if byte is not found.

Return: `AX` = offset of the non-matching character within `string1`

Gain: (Borland C) on 486: 31% — on 386SX: 39%
(Microsoft C) on 486: 55% — on 386SX: 21%
(Symantec C) on 486: 25% — on 386SX: 27%
The gain decreases if `string1` is shorter and depends on the strings' contents. The test run was
`strspn("ABCDEFGHIJKLMNOPQRSTUVWXYZ","ABC");`.

Because _STRSPN doesn't begin by finding the size of `string2`, the routine gains if the characters in `string1` are found at the start of `string2`. _STRSPN loses, however, if `string2` is a long string and the matches between it and `string1` occur towards the end of `string2`. A greater gain occurs if the bytes in `string2` are guaranteed to be in sorted order. (This is the method we used in _STRPBRK to solve a similar problem. In effect, _STRPBRK and _STRSPN make different assumptions about the probability of a match being found quickly in `string2`.)

Notice that _STRSPN uses

```
MOV AL,[SI]
INC SI
```

shortly after the label `@@loop:`. We tested a variant of this routine where these two instructions were replaced by the `LODSB` instruction, which does exactly the same thing. The `LODSB` variant of the routine turned out to be a bit slower than this _STRSPN routine shown here.

```
        ALIGN 16
            public _STRSPN          ;STRing to string SPaN
        _STRSPN proc
                PUSH BP
                MOV BP,SP
                PUSH SI
                MOV SI,[BP+4]     ;SI --> string1 start
                MOV DX,[BP+6]     ;DX --> string2 start, always
@@loop:         MOV BX,DX         ;BX --> string2 start
                MOV AL,[SI]       ;AL = [SI] = next byte from string1
                INC SI            ;Increment pointer to string1.
                TEST AL,AL        ;Check if string1 has ended.
                JZ @@eos          ;(AL = [SI] = '\0', string1's over)
@@loop2:        MOV AH,[BX]       ;AH = [BX] = next byte from string2
                TEST AH,AH        ;Check if string2 has ended.
                JZ @@eos          ;(AH = [BX] = '\0', string2's over)
                INC BX            ;Increment pointer to string2.
                CMP AL,AH         ;Compare string1 byte to string2 byte.
                JNZ @@loop2       ;(They're not equal, get another string2 byte)
                ;The next instruction is subject to a Double-Jump Rule penalty
                JMP @@loop        ;AL has a match somewhere in string2
@@eos:                            ;Either string1 ended (equality all the way to
                ;the end of the string so return the offset of the '\0'), or string2
                ;ended (inequality seen when comparing AL to AH so return the offset
                ;of the unequal byte).
                MOV AX,SI         ;SI is currently pointing somewhere in string1
                DEC AX            ;SI was one greater than the offset we wanted
                SUB AX,[BP+4]
                POP SI
                POP BP
                RET               ;Return AX = offset of '\0' or of non-match.
        _STRSPN endp
```

strstr

Prototype: char *strstr (char *string1,char *string2)

Function: Find the first occurrence in string1 of the complete contents of string2.

Method: Get the first word in string2. Search for this word in string1. If the word is in string1, compare the rest of string2 with the rest of string1. If the comparison fails, backtrack — i.e., go back to the place where the words matched and start the search again.

Return: AX = pointer to matching string, or 0

Gain: (Borland C) on 486: 35% — on 386SX: –24%
(Microsoft C) on 486: 32% — on 386SX: –13%
(Symantec C) on 486: 93% — on 386SX: 93%

This routine is recommended for 486s only, although a gain can also be achieved on older machines if your compiler is Symantec. There is a gain if the characters in string1 that precede the characters that match string2 are random — that is, if the first characters in

`string1` do not match `string2`. So _STRSTR loses on
`strstr("aaaaaaaaaaardvark","ard");` but gains on
`strstr("there is ard","ard");`. The test run was
`strstr("The rain in Spain","in Spain");`.

When writing a _STRSTR routine, we'd like to compare the two
strings a word at a time. Although doing so would give an incorrect result
if the function was checking whether the word in `string1` is greater
than the word in `string2` (because the comparison's result is on the
high byte of the word first), a word comparison works for _STRSTR
because the result is based only on whether or not the words are equal.
Although `CMPSW` is normally used in word comparisons, this is a case
where, if the words being compared are unequal, then the register index
should only be incremented by 1 — which makes `CMPSW` inappropriate
(it changes the register index by 2).

The possible flaw in the method we chose for _STRSTR is its
optimism. The routine searches very quickly for the first 2 matching
bytes, but after that the search goes slowly. So if _STRSTR finds several
times that the first 2 bytes compared are equal, but then that the sub-
sequent bytes are not equal, it has to pay for that optimism by backtracking.

Note that if `string2` is only 1 byte long, then _STRSTR is really
being asked to find a single character within `string1`. That's the
function of _STRCHR, so _STRSTR will just call _STRCHR for that
special case. If you think that such an eventuality will happen often, put
the _STRCHR function inline here instead of calling it.

```
ALIGN 16
    public _STRSTR              ;STRing in STRing
_STRSTR proc
        PUSH BP
        MOV BP,SP
        PUSH SI
        MOV BX,[BP+4]           ;BX --> start of string1
        MOV SI,[BP+6]           ;SI --> start of string2
        MOV AL,[SI]             ;Check for a special case, namely, whether
        TEST AL,AL              ;string2 is blank or contains just 1 byte.
        JZ @@true               ;(string2 size = 0, so we can't ever fail)
        CMP BYTE PTR [SI+1],0
        JNZ @@start             ;(string2 size > 1, proceed as expected)
                                ;Since string2 size is 1, this is effectively
                                ;the same as _strchr.

        PUSH AX
        PUSH [BP+4]
        CALL _STRCHR
        ADD SP,4
        POP SI
        POP BP
        RET
```

```
        ALIGN 16
@@start: MOV AL,[BX]          ;AL = low byte of next word in string1
        TEST AL,AL            ;If AL = '\0' now, then we've failed.
        JZ @@eos
@@loop:  MOV AH,[BX+1]        ;AH = high byte of next word in string1
        TEST AH,AH            ;If AH = '\0' now, then we've failed (because
        JZ @@eos             ;remaining string1 size = 1 < string2 size).
        CMP AX,[SI]          ;Compare a word from string1 with the first
        JZ @@match           ;word in string2. If match, check the rest.
@@next:  INC BX               ;There's no match on the word. Point to the
        MOV AL,AH            ;next byte (not the next word!) in string1,
        JMP @@loop           ;and go further on in string1.
@@match: MOV DX,BX            ;Save string1 position in case we backtrack.
        ADD SI,2
        ADD BX,2
@@cmp:   MOV CL,[SI]
        TEST CL,CL
        JZ @@z               ;(end of SI. Success. DX still = address)
        CMP CL,[BX]
        JNZ @@nz             ;(non-matching byte, continue with string1)
        INC SI
        INC BX
        JMP @@cmp
@@nz:    MOV BX,DX            ;We're going to have to backtrack.
        MOV SI,[BP+6]
        JMP @@next
@@eos:   XOR DX,DX            ;Failure. Return AX = 0
@@z:     MOV AX,DX
        POP SI
        POP BP
        RET                  ;Return AX = 0 or address within string1.
@@true:  MOV AX,BX            ;When string2 size = 0, by convention, we say
        POP SI               ;that we've matched on the first character of
        POP BP               ;string1 -- even if string1 is also blank. It
        RET                  ;is like saying "all/none of the bytes are =".
_STRSTR endp
```

strupr

Prototype: char *strupr(char *string)

Function: Convert all lowercase characters in string to uppercase.

Method: Get byte from string. If byte is \0, stop. If byte is between a and z, subtract 20h from it. Repeat.

Return: AX = pointer to string

Gain: (Borland C) on 486: 35% — on 386SX: 24%
  (Microsoft C) on 486: 33% — on 386SX: 33%
  (Symantec C) on 486: 55% — on 386SX: 51%

The test run was strupr(a);, where a contains
"ABCDEFGHIJKLMNOPQRSTUVWXYZ".

We used a variety of interesting tricks when we wrote _STRLWR and we could use the same tricks again for _STRUPR, since _STRUPR is the reverse of _STRLWR. But we decided to show that even without the _STRLWR-style speedups, it was possible to write a faster routine with simple principles.

Note that _STRUPR uses BX for the string pointer. It's possible to use any register as a pointer on a 486, but the traditional choices are BX, SI, DI, and BP because those are the only registers which can be used as pointers on 8086s. We chose BX because:

(a) BP works best as a pointer to the stack segment; using it to point to the string would require a segment override instruction or an assumption that the stack segment register equals the data segment register, i.e., that SS = DS.

(b) The Microsoft and Symantec C compiler manuals say that the values of SI and DI may not be permanently changed, and the Borland C manual says the SI and DI values may not be changed when using register variables. If SI and DI are used in a function, then they have to be saved and restored with PUSH and POP instructions.

That leaves BX as the only register that can be used for addressing that doesn't require the use of a segment override and that doesn't have to be saved.

```
ALIGN 16
    public _STRUPR              ;STRing convert to UPpeR case
_STRUPR proc
        PUSH BP
        MOV BP,SP
        MOV BX,[BP+4]           ;BX --> string
        MOV CL,20h              ;CL = 20h i.e. 'a' - 'A'
@@loop: MOV AL,[BX]            ;AL = [BX] = byte in string
        TEST AL,AL              ;Check if AL = [BX] = '\0'
        JZ @@eos                ;(Yes, we've reached end of string.)
        INC BX                  ;Increment pointer before you loop.
        CMP AL,"a"              ;Is AL in range 'a'-'z'
        JB @@loop               ;(AL = [BX] < 'A', it's out of range)
        CMP AL,"z"
        JA @@loop               ;(AL = [BX] > 'Z', it's out of range)
        SUB BYTE PTR [BX-1],CL  ;CL always = 20h i.e. 'a' - 'A'
        JMP @@loop              ;Go to repeat for the next byte.
@@eos:  MOV AX,[BP+4]           ;return a pointer to the passed string
        POP BP
        RET
_STRUPR endp
```

The mem Functions

All C libraries contain these functions: `_memcmp`, `_memcpy`, `_memset`, `_memchr`.

There's one big difference between mem functions and string functions: there is no more need to worry about the terminating `\0` byte because the size of the memory block is known in advance. That makes it easy to switch from byte-size memory accesses to word-size memory accesses, so `_memcmp`, `_memcpy`, and `_memset` are faster than their string counterparts `_strcmp`, `_strcpy`, and `_strset`, for the same number of bytes regardless of whose C library you use.

In this section, we'll present substitute mem functions which work faster than the ones in the standard C libraries. Our timing tests (see Figure 11.2) show gains between 25 percent and 74 percent.

Our mem functions are specialized. Two of them will only work with post-80286 CPUs. All four of them are geared for large data movements/comparisons; they work badly with small buffers. So there's a tradeoff: in return for the large speed gains, you get reduced applicability.

FUNCTION	OUR ROUTINE	BORLAND v3.1	MICROSOFT v2.0	SYMANTEC v7.0	% GAIN
memcmp	36	141	140	139	74%
memcpy	16	33	32	60	73%
memset *	16	40	40	39	60%
memchr *	76	100	101	100	25%

Figure 11.2 Timing Test Run on a 486. The numbers in the columns entitled "OUR ROUTINE," "BORLAND," "MICROSOFT" and "SYMANTEC" show the length of time, in seconds, required to execute eight million iterations of the function on a 486 by the routines in this book and by the standard C small model library supplied by the indicated vendor. The final column, "% GAIN," shows the gain in percentage terms that occurs when our code is substituted for the standard code supplied by the slowest of the three vendors. These timing tests apply only for 8,192-byte buffers on 80486s. An asterisk (*) following the function name in the first column denotes a routine which is not recommended for use with older CPUs (i.e., 8086s, 80286s, or 80386s) because the routine contains code optimizations which enhance speed on newer Intel processors only.

In other words, beginning now, we will throw off the constraint that bound us with our string functions — our string functions will work on all CPUs and offer gains even if string sizes are small. Our mem functions won't but do show some of the extra speed gains we can get with some new tricks, such as using 32-bit registers and Intel string instructions.

memcmp

Prototype: `int memcmp (const void *string1,`
                         `const void *string2,int n)`

Function: Compare two blocks of data.

Method: Take a double-word from `string1` and compare it to a double-word from `string2`. If they're not equal or if the maximum has been compared: stop. Otherwise increment the `string1` and `string2` pointers and repeat.

Return: AX = 16-bit integer.
            AX < 0 if `string1` < `string2`
            AX = 0 if `string1` = `string2`
            AX > 0 if `string1` > `string2`
In fact, the value of AX is the difference in the first non-equal bytes, but this detail is undocumented.

Gain: (Borland C) on 486: 74% — on 386SX: 64%
          (Microsoft C) on 486: 74% — on 386SX: 52%
          (Symantec C) on 486: 74% — on 386SX: 64%
This test was taken for two equal memory blocks. If blocks differ within the first few bytes, there is no gain. The test run was `memcmp(a,a,8192);`.

_MEMCMP uses the repeated Intel string instructions REP CMPSD and REP CMPSB. Any function that uses repeated Intel string instructions must begin by setting up the ES segment register. We do this by moving the contents of DS to ES, thus:

```
PUSH DS     ;This instruction takes at least 3 cycles.
POP ES      ;This instruction takes at least 3 cycles.
REP CMPSD   ;This instruction has two prefixes.
```

We could have put PUSH DS and POP ES at the very start of the function but chose to put them immediately before REP CMPSD to trigger the Prefix-Waiver Rule. This saves the 2 cycles normally taken by REP CMPSD's prefixes.

If the inequality happens on the very first byte, _MEMCMP takes 30 cycles to find this out. However if the inequality happens on the 10,000th byte of two huge and nearly-equal buffers, _MEMCMP rattles along comparing 4 bytes every 7 cycles. The fact that REP CMPSD takes only 7 cycles per iteration, and compares 4 bytes at a time, makes this a good implementation for large buffers.

Now consider the REP CMPSD instruction itself. The idea is that 4 bytes can be compared at once, in the same time that it takes to compare 1 byte (after initialization, each iteration of REP CMPSD takes 7 cycles, the same amount of time that REP CMPSB would take). The problem with this method is that when inequality is hit, we don't know *which* byte was unequal. So if REP CMPSD turns the zero flag OFF, it's necessary to back up 4 bytes and re-compare them 1 byte at a time.

It's easy to miss the subtle beauties of the four lines that finish off the comparison:

```
AND CX,3
REP CMPSB
SBB AX,AX
SBB AX,-1
```

First subtlety: REP CMPSB often has a trap — it's easy to forget that if CX equals 0, REP CMPSB won't set the zero flag. _MEMCMP avoids the trap — the preceding AND instruction sets the zero flag ON if CX was 0.

Second subtlety: after the REP CMPSB there is a result in the flags — either "greater," "equal," or "less." At this time the AX register happens to contain 0 (because a XOR AX,AX instruction was part of the initialization). Given this situation, the two SBB instructions accomplish this effect:

❖ AX will become + 1 if the flags are "greater."

❖ AX will become – 1 if the flags are "less than."

We call this the Double-SBB Trick. It always works for converting flag results of unsigned comparisons into a register, which is what we always want when we're returning from C memory comparison or string comparison functions. The Double-SBB Trick takes 2 cycles, not counting any time needed to initialize the AX register.

Avoid using _MEMCMP with buffers that might be misaligned. There should be no misalignment problem with buffers that you created with `GlobalAlloc` or similar functions.

```
ALIGN 16
    public _MEMCMP
_MEMCMP proc
.486       ;We'll use SHR CX,2 and CMPSD, instructions that 8086s can't handle.
        PUSH BP                     ;No attempt is made to avoid Call-Plus-Stack-Use Rule
        MOV BP,SP
:       CLD                         ;We don't need CLD, this is just a reminder
        XOR AX,AX                   ;The Double-SBB Trick: Setup
        PUSH SI
        PUSH DI
        MOV CX,[BP+8]               ;CX = count of bytes to compare
        MOV SI,[BP+4]               ;SI --> string1
        MOV DI,[BP+6]               ;DI --> string2
        SHR CX,2                    ;Divide CX by 4
        PUSH DS                     ;The next two lines are part of the usual
        POP ES                      ;initialization needed for string instructions
        ;The next instruction is subject to the Prefix-Waiver Rule, twice.
        REP CMPSD                   ;Compare 4 bytes at a time
        JNZ short @@check           ;(Inequality on last double-word)
        MOV CX,[BP+8]               ;Get original value of CX again
        AND CX,3                    ;The maximum count of bytes remaining is 3
@@cmpsb: REP CMPSB                  ;Compare the last 0, 1, 2, or 3 bytes
        JZ short @@ret
        SBB AX,AX                   ;The Double-SBB Trick: Part I
        SBB AX,-1                   ;The Double-SBB Trick: Part II
@@ret:  POP DI
        POP SI
        POP BP
        RET                         ;Return with an appropriate value in AX.
@@check: MOV CX,4                   ;REP CMPSD said the last double-words weren't
        SUB SI,CX    ;(SUB SI,4) ;equal. So back up the SI and DI pointers to
        SUB DI,CX    ;(SUB DI,4) ;point to the unequal double-word, and then
        JMP @@cmpsb                 ;go to compare them, a byte at a time.
_MEMCMP endp
```

memcpy

Prototype: `void *_memcpy (void *block1,`
                              `void *block2,int n)`

Function: Move a block of data.

Method: Take a double-word from `string2`. Put it in `string1`. Repeat until $n/4$ double-words have been moved. If n is not perfectly divisible by 4, move the last few bytes.

Return: $AX = $ `*block1`

Gain: (Borland C) on 486: 52% — on 386SX: 25%

(Microsoft C) on 486: 50% — on 386SX: 25%

(Symantec C) on 486: 73% — on 386SX: 62%

Our version of `_memcpy` does not reverse direction if there's overlap. `_MEMCPY` is thus not a complete replacement for the `_memcpy` function in the standard C library. The test run was `memcpy(a,a,8192);`.

Everybody has figured out that the way to make `_memcpy` move is to use words. The essential routine, which works on all 80x86 chips, involves `REP MOVSW`:

```
                 ;get SI = string2, DI = string1, CX = number of bytes
     SHR CX,1    ;Divide CX by 2. Carry flag ON if remainder.
     REP MOVSW   ;Move CX words from SI to DI
     JNC @@1     ;(if carry flag OFF that means CX was even)
     MOVSB       ;Move the last byte if original CX was odd
@@1:             ;clean up and return
```

Since it's good to move words instead of bytes, is it even better to move double-words instead of words? Yes — the Prefix Rule penalty is negligible (see Chapter 9), so if there's more than a few bytes to move, our version of `_MEMCPY` is faster.

Avoid using `_MEMCPY` with buffers that might be misaligned. There should be no misalignment problem with buffers that you created with `GlobalAlloc` or similar functions.

```
ALIGN 16
   public _MEMCPY
_MEMCPY proc
.486    ;We'll use SHR CX,2 and MOVSD, instructions that 8086s can't handle.
        PUSH    BP
        MOV     BP,SP
;       CLD               ;We don't need CLD, this is just a reminder.
        PUSH SI
        PUSH DI
        MOV CX,[BP+8]     ;CX = number of bytes to move
        MOV SI,[BP+6]     ;SI --> source buffer
        MOV DI,[BP+4]     ;DI --> destination buffer
        SHR CX,2          ;Divide CX by 4
        PUSH DS           ;The next two lines are part of the usual
        POP ES            ;initialization needed for string instructions
        ;The next instruction is subject to the Prefix-Waiver Rule, twice.
        REP MOVSD         ;Move CX double-words from SI to DI
        MOV CX,[BP+8]     ;Restore original CX value
        AND CX,3          ;Only the last 2 bits matter (the "remainder")
        REP MOVSB         ;Move CX bytes from SI to DI (from 0 to 3)
        MOV AX,[BP+6]     ;Return AX --> source buffer
        POP DI
        POP SI
        POP BP
        RET
_MEMCPY endp
```

memset

Prototype: `void *_memset (void *block,int n)`

Function: Set all bytes in a block of data to a passed value.

Method: Set a 32-bit register to contain 4 copies of the 8-bit byte. Move the register to `*block`. Repeat, incrementing `*block`, until `n/4` double-words have been moved. If `n` is not perfectly divisible by 4, move the last few bytes.

Return: `AX = *block`

Gain: (Borland C) on 486: 60% — on 386SX: –42%
        (Microsoft C) on 486: 60% — on 386SX: –41%
        (Symantec C) on 486: 59% — on 386SX: –42%
This routine is recommended for 486s only. The test run was `memset(a,'a',8192);`.

As with _MEMCPY, _MEMSET gains by transferring double-words instead of words. Unlike _MEMCPY, _MEMSET has only one block pointer to worry about so it's easy to align to a 4-byte boundary right at the start of the routine. Although we chose to emphasize the 60 percent gain that one gets with a large block, we aren't hiding that there's a lot of potential overhead. This function is strictly for large memory blocks.

In the comments, we've marked the seven instructions that are in the main loop by adding a comment: the instruction's cycle time. These comments make it easy to see that every iteration of the loop takes 13 cycles. The calculation is easy too — each iteration of the loop sets 16 bytes, so _MEMSET's speed is (13/16) cycles per byte. That's not quite as fast as the `MOVSD` trick we talked about in Chapter 9, but it would be faster if the loop was unrolled a few times. As for `REP STOSD`: forget it, it takes 1 cycle per byte. In any case we like this method because it's much more adaptable than code based on `REP STOSx` (e.g., an array-add can be done just by changing some `MOV` instructions to `ADD`s).

The fact that _MEMSET puts together several `MOV`-to-memory instructions might lead you to worry that we're going to cause a pipeline stall. This won't be a problem though. Because there's a Prefix Rule penalty on every `MOV` in the loop, the CPU has time to catch its breath.

_MEMSET is usable even if the buffer is misaligned. We can take care of misalignment problems easily when there's only one buffer.

```
        ALIGN 16
          public _MEMSET
        _MEMSET proc
        .486     ;We'll use the EAX register, which 8086s can't handle.
                 PUSH BP
                 MOV BP,SP
                 MOV CX,[BP+8]           ;CX = number of bytes to set
                 MOV AX,[BP+6]           ;AL = the byte value we're setting to
                 MOV BX,[BP+4]           ;BX = block --> where we do the set
                 CMP CX,16               ;We're going to do 16 bytes at a time,
                 JB short @@final        ;so if CX < 16 skip the main body.
        @@align: TEST BL,3              ;We want to ensure that the pointer is
                 JZ short @@setal        ;on a double-word boundary, that is,
                 MOV [BX],AL             ;that the pointer is divisible by 4.
                 INC BX
                 DEC CX                  ;and to ensure this we move a byte at
                 JMP @@align             ;a time, possibly repeating 3 times.
        @@setal: MOV AH,AL              ;We're going to use the 32-bit EAX
                 MOV DX,AX               ;register, in which all 4 bytes (AL,
                                         ;AH, EAX & 0FF000h, EAX & 0FF0000h)
                 SHL EAX,16              ;have the same value: these lines show
                 MOV AX,DX               ;how we do an appropriate duplication.
                 JMP short @@start       ;Start at a late spot in "@@loop" loop
        @@loop:  ;The next four instructions are subject to the Prefix Rule.
                 MOV [BX],EAX    ;2 cycles  ;Next 4 bytes = {byte,byte,byte,byte}.
                 MOV [BX+4],EAX  ;2 cycles  ;Next 4 bytes = {byte,byte,byte,byte}.
                 MOV [BX+8],EAX  ;2 cycles  ;Next 4 bytes = {byte,byte,byte,byte}.
                 MOV [BX+12],EAX ;2 cycles  ;Next 4 bytes = {byte,byte,byte,byte}.
        .8086    ;We don't need 486-specifics any more.
                 ADD BX,16       ;1 cycle   ;4*4=16 so next round we're 16 later.
        @@start:SUB CX,16        ;1 cycle   ;There's 16 fewer bytes to process now
                 JNC @@loop      ;3 cycles  ;(We still have >0 bytes, do again.)
                 ADD CX,16                  ;SUB's flags are good, results aren't.
        @@final: TEST CX,CX                ;There's <16 bytes left. Are there 0?
                 JZ short @@ret             ;(yes, we're done)
                 MOV [BX],AL               ;These last few bytes are being done
                 INC BX                     ;a byte a time, and we could repeat 15
                 DEC CX                     ;times -- which is inefficient, but we
                 JMP @@final               ;concentrated on the main loop's gain.
        @@ret:   MOV AX,[BP+4]            ;Return AX = pointer to block
                 POP BP
                 RET
        _MEMSET endp
```

memchr

Prototype: void *_memchr (void *block,int char,int n)

Function: Find the first byte in a block of data which equals the passed char value.

Method: Load char into AL. Load pointer to block into BX. Compare AL with [BX]; if they're equal, stop. Otherwise compare AL with [BX+1], [BX+2], [BX+3], and so on. Stop once n comparisons are done.

Return: AX = pointer to byte within block (or, if failure, AX = 0)

Gain: (Borland C) on 486: 24% — on 386SX: –43%

(Microsoft C) on 486: 25% — on 386SX: –43%

(Symantec C) on 486: 24% — on 386SX: –42%

This routine is recommended for 486s only. The test run was `memchr(a,'a',8192);`.

_MEMCHR does not use 32-bit registers — it's hard to use the top 16 bits of a 32-bit register for byte-size comparisons. It's still fast though. Just counting the cycles between the beginning of the loop (from `@@loop:`) and the end of the loop (`JNC @@loop`), we find that each iteration takes 15 cycles. Since each iteration handles 4 bytes, that's (15/4) = 3.75 cycles per compared byte. Contrast this with `REP SCASB`, which takes 5 cycles per compared byte.

_MEMCHR does a single loop unroll. The first five instructions in the loop are, nearly exactly, repeated in the next five instructions. If the loop was unrolled one more time, an additional 0.5 cycles per compared byte would be saved. If a third loop unroll was done after that, an additional 0.08 cycles would be saved. The more the loop is unrolled, the greater the gain, but a law of diminishing returns does set in. We chose to stop while the code still looks simple.

_MEMCHR is usable even if the buffer is misaligned. We can take care of misalignment problems easily when there's only one buffer. _MEMCHR is not efficient unless the buffer is large and the character is not likely to be at the very beginning of the buffer.

```
ALIGN 16
    public _MEMCHR
_MEMCHR proc
        PUSH BP
        MOV BP,SP
        MOV CX,[BP+8]
        TEST CX,CX              ;Make sure there's stuff to compare
        JZ @@end                ;(there isn't, so return AX = 0)
        MOV AX,[BP+6]           ;MOV AL,[BP+6] would be enough
        MOV BX,[BP+4]
        TEST BX,1               ;Is BX aligned on a word boundary?
        JZ @@loop1              ;(yes, proceed directly to loop)
        CMP AL,[BX]             ;CMP first byte, on uneven boundary
        JZ @@ok0                ;(the first byte was a match)
        INC BX                  ;Increment BX, now it's aligned even
        DEC CX                  ;Decrement CX, there's one less byte
        JZ @@end                ;(whoops, that was the only byte)
        JMP short @@loop1       ;Proceed to loop, start at end check
```

```
@@loop:     MOV DX,[BX]      ;1 cycle
            CMP AL,DL        ;1 cycle
            JZ @@ok0         ;1 cycle      ;(there's a match at [BX])
            CMP AL,DH        ;1 cycle
            JZ @@ok1         ;1 cycle      ;(there's a match at [BX+1])
            MOV DX,[BX+2]    ;1 cycle
            CMP AL,DL        ;1 cycle
            JZ @@ok2         ;1 cycle      ;(there's a match at [BX+2])
            CMP AL,DH        ;1 cycle
            JZ @@ok3         ;1 cycle      ;(there's a match at [BX+3])
            ADD BX,4         ;1 cycle
@@loop1:    SUB CX,4         ;1 cycle
            JNC @@loop       ;3 cycles
@@loop2:    CMP CX,-4                      ;if CX == -4 now, it was 0 before
            JZ @@end                       ;(we've done all the checks we can)
            CMP AL,[BX]                     ;There's 1 or 2 or 3 bytes left now
            JZ @@ok0                        ;(a match on one of the final bytes)
            INC BX                          ;Not a match on this final byte, but
            DEC CX                          ;there still might be one or two
            JMP @@loop2                     ;left.
@@end:      XOR AX,AX                       ;Still nothing is =, so return AX = 0
            JMP short @@ret
@@ok3:      INC BX
@@ok2:      INC BX
@@ok1:      INC BX
@@ok0:      MOV AX,BX
@@ret:      POP BP
            RET
_MEMCHR endp
```

Chapter 12

Counting Cycles with TACHO.EXE

Penalties incurred by breaking a secret rule of assembler use can overlap. For instance, consider this pair of instructions:

```
MOV BX,OFFSET mema    ;1 cycle
ADD [BX+4],10         ;2 cycles — plus penalties
```

The second instruction is subject to the Constant-to-Memory Rule (lose 1 cycle) because a constant is being added to a Register Pointer plus Constant memory location. ADD [BX+4],10 is also subject to the Register-Address Rule (lose 2 cycles) because a register is being used as an address immediately after the register was loaded. If the penalties are combined, the ADD instruction would take an extra 3 cycles, for a total of 5 cycles. In reality though, the two penalties *don't* combine — they overlap. The total penalization on the second instruction is not 3, but 2 cycles. The complicating factor is that not all penalties overlap. Misalignment penalties, for instance, are in full force no matter what else is going on.

We've shown you that, in assembler, there are many rules that cause penalties. Some of them are complicated. Others are forgettable. Sometimes penalties are waived. At other times they overlap. Even without penalties, instruction times vary. Given all this, don't you wish you could just ask the computer to tell you what penalties are in effect? Well, you can — using the cycle-counting utility provided on this book's diskette, TACHO.EXE.

Illiterate people shouldn't use spelling checkers. Innumerate people shouldn't use calculators. And people who don't understand cycle times shouldn't use TACHO.EXE. That's why we waited until the last chapter of this book to describe the program. We didn't want you to try using it before gaining an understanding of what it will show you. On the other hand, just because you should know what the rules and subtleties are, that doesn't mean you ought to have to memorize them. A computer program can do that for you.

TACHO stands for TACHOMETER. Like the tachometer on a car, TACHO tells you how fast the engine is turning over. So, while it's not an exact indicator of your speed, it will give you a pretty fair idea of how fast you're going. TACHO can tell you:

❖ the number of cycles an instruction in a program takes on a 486. Note the words "in a program" — instruction timings vary depending on context, and TACHO allows for that.

❖ the penalties that apply on an instruction. TACHO explains what SECRET RULE applies and how many extra cycles are in force. Conversely, TACHO will note when an instruction takes less than the usual time (due to the Prefix-Waiver Rule, for instance).

Copyright

Requirements and Limitations

Installation is simple: copy TACHO.EXE from this book's diskette to your hard disk. Alternatively, you can run TACHO.EXE directly from the diskette.

TACHO.EXE is supplied with *Optimizing C with Assembly Code* so that readers of *Optimizing C with Assembly Code* have a convenient way to estimate cycle times in critical loops. It is not designed as a general replacement for DEBUG.COM and it is not warranted for any non-educational purposes. The display of cycle times may be incorrect in certain circumstances, for reasons described in this book.

TACHO is an MS-DOS program. It won't handle Windows or OS/2 executables, and it won't handle programs which were written for use with a 32-bit DOS Extender. It won't handle most instructions which run only in protected mode. True application programs won't use specialized protected-mode instructions anyway.

TACHO won't handle floating-point instructions, except for a few instructions that C compilers might generate to initialize the floating-point processor. TACHO won't handle programs that do exotic forms of I/O (for instance, reading directly from the serial port). However, TACHO will handle programs that do I/O in the normal fashion, via an MS-DOS command.

Finally, TACHO is designed to handle tiny programs. Although it is capable of loading and running programs that are 200Kb or larger, it is too slow to be useful on millions or billions of instruction iterations.

TACHO is a timing program. It bears a superficial resemblance to the common MS-DOS utility DEBUG.COM in that both TACHO and DEBUG display registers and instructions, and both TACHO and DEBUG respond to the T and Q commands in a similar fashion. The similarities end there though. TACHO can display the entire register set (DEBUG only displays the lower 16 bits and misses some segment registers); TACHO can display the names of almost all 80486 instructions (DEBUG only understands instructions which existed on 8086s); and most importantly, TACHO displays cycle times and penalties. DEBUG doesn't.

There is also a difference in the way the programs are made. DEBUG is using certain features of the 80x86 architecture which make it possible to "single step" (i.e., execute one instruction and then call a DEBUG routine) and to "go until" (i.e., execute instructions until a breakpoint is reached and then call a DEBUG routine). TACHO, on the other hand, is an *interpreter*. It loads an instruction and performs a simulation of the instruction using a TACHO routine — it never yields control of the program it's operating on.

How to Run TACHO.EXE

To run TACHO, type the following from the command line:

```
TACHO <program name> <cr>
```

    `<program name>` must be the name of an executable program. `<cr>` stands for "hit the carriage return key." The program must be the product of a LINK utility (or an equivalent such as TLINK) in .EXE format. Usually, the extension of such a program is .EXE. TACHO cannot read .COM files.

    The program will display a dash (-) as a prompt. At this stage, you may type any one of these commands, followed by a carriage return:

Q	"Quit."	Return to MS-DOS command line.
T	"Trace."	Execute a single instruction and display the results.
G `<instruction name>`	"Go."	Proceed with program execution until the next occurrence of an instruction of type `<instruction name>`.

What TACHO.EXE Displays

Typically, after a T or G command, TACHO will print the following data on the screen:

❖ A list of registers and their contents. All 32-bit registers are shown in full (EAX, EBX, ECX, EDX, ESI, EDI, EBP, ESP). All segment registers are shown, including the new segment registers which were introduced with the 80386 processor and which we have not discussed in this book (CS, DS, SS, ES, FS, GS). Contents display is hexadecimal.

❖ The current instruction, that is, the instruction which the program is about to execute.

❖ The size of the instruction in bytes.

❖ The number of cycles required for this instruction, on a 486, in normal circumstances.

❖ Any penalties applicable to this instruction. Generally this is shown as the name of the relevant SECRET RULE.

Important: the display of cycle times does not take into account any stalling that may occur due to cache misses or pre-fetching failures. Therefore in many cases the actual elapsed time will be greater than what TACHO indicates.

A Sample TACHO.EXE Session

The program XX.EXE on this book's diskette can be used to try out TACHO.EXE in this sample session. This is a listing of XX.EXE:

```
MOV DL,5
SUB AX,5
MOV DH,5
SUB BX,5
ADD BH,5
XCHG BH,BL
MOV EAX,150
```

(1) Start the program. Type:

```
TACHO XX.EXE <cr>
```

You will see the following display on your screen:

```
[**] TACHO — a tachometer for programs on Intel486 computers

[**] Copyright (c) 1988, 1994 by Ocelot Computer Services Inc.
[**] All rights reserved.

[**] This program can only be distributed along with the book:
[**]   OPTIMIZING C WITH ASSEMBLY CODE
[**]   by Peter Gulutzan and Trudy Pelzer

EAX=00000000 EBX=00000000 ECX=00000000 EDX=00000000
ESP=00000000 EBP=00000000 ESI=00000000 EDI=00000000
DS=0040 ES=0040 SS=0050 CS=0050 FS=0000 GS=0000 O- D- S- Z- A- P- C-
0050:0000 b205 MOV DL,5 2 bytes 1 cycle
-
```

The display shows that all the registers except the segment registers contain 0 (e.g., EAX=00000000 but DS=0040). The flags — Overflow, Direction, Sign, Zero, Auxiliary, Parity and Carry — are all OFF as indicated by the minus sign (–) after the first letter of each flag's name in the third line of the instruction display (e.g., O– means Overflow OFF). The final line is a dash (-), a prompt indicating that you can type a command in.

(2) Trace an instruction. Type:

```
T <cr>
```

You will see the following display on your screen:

```
EAX=00000000 EBX=00000000 ECX=00000000 EDX=00000005
ESP=00000000 EBP=00000000 ESI=00000000 EDI=00000000
DS=0040 ES=0040 SS=0050 CS=0050 FS=0000 GS=0000 O- D- S- Z- A- P- C-
0050:0002 2d0500 SUB AX,5 3 bytes 1 cycle
-
```

Notice that the display now shows the current contents of the EDX register (5) set by the previous MOV DL, 5 instruction. As yet no other registers or flags have changed.

(3) Go to the ADD instruction (executing but not displaying intervening instructions). Type:

```
G ADD <cr>
```

You will see the following display on your screen:

```
EAX=0000fffb EBX=0000fffb ECX=00000000 EDX=00000005
ESP=00000000 EBP=00000000 ESI=00000000 EDI=00000000
DS=0040 ES=0040 SS=0050 CS=0050 FS=0000 GS=0000 O- D- S- Z- A+ P- C+
0050:000a 80c705 ADD BH,5 3 bytes 1+ cycle
 +Hi/Lo Penalty
-
```

Notice that the EAX register, the EBX register, and some of the flags have changed during instructions that TACHO has executed without displaying. The cycle time display for ADD BH,5 is 1+ cycle: the plus sign is an indication that there is a penalty on this instruction. The nature of the penalty is explained on the following line: +Hi/Lo Penalty. This penalty is applied because the previous instruction was SUB BX,5.

(4) Go to the MOV instruction. Type:

```
G MOV <cr>
```

You will see the following display on your screen:

```
EAX=0000004b EBX=0000fb04 ECX=00000000 EDX=00000505
ESP=00000000 EBP=00000000 ESI=00000000 EDI=00000000
DS=0050 ES=0040 SS=0050 CS=0050 FS=0000 GS=0000 O- D- S- Z- A+ P- C+
0050:001c 66b896000000 MOV EAX,00000096 (prefix cost waived) 6 bytes 1 cycle
-
```

The EAX, EBX, EDX, and DS registers have changed but the status of the flags register is the same. The cycle time display for MOV EAX, 150 is 1 cycle: the cycle normally applied for the 32-bit operand has been waived by the Prefix-Waiver Rule because the previous instruction (XCHG BH, BL) was a lengthy instruction.

(5) End the program. Type:

```
Q <cr>
```

You are now back at the MS-DOS command line.

You can use TACHO in a similar way with any program. With C programs, it is probably handy to insert an obscure instruction at the start of the code that you want to examine so you can "Go" to it immediately. Otherwise, you will have to "Trace" through quite a few lines of C initialization code before you reach your goal.

Benefits

TACHO.EXE is especially handy in these situations:

❖ You want to know the size and speed of a particular instruction. For this, you just have to create a one-line program containing that instruction, load with TACHO, and "Trace." Depending on your typing speed, this may be faster than looking up the instruction in Appendix A. It's also simpler, since it's easy to get confused by the plethora of instruction variants.

❖ You might have a procedure or a function that you want to optimize. TACHO will tell you how well that routine is doing now: how fast each of its instructions is going, and what penalties (if any) are slowing it down.

Afterword

At this point you know everything worth knowing about optimizing C and/or assembler application programs on 486s, according to the definition of optimizing we gave you in the Preface. If your interests are broader, we endorse the items in the following list without guaranteeing that they are necessarily the best values in any given category.

For proven ideas that work at the C-function level, try Robert Sedgewick's *Algorithms in C* (Addison Wesley 1994, ISBN 0-201-51059-6).

A primary source is the *Intel486 (tm) Microprocessor Family Programmer's Reference Manual* (ISBN 1-55512-159-4), available in the United States from: Intel Literature Sales, P.O. Box 7641, Mount Prospect IL 60056 (phone 800-548-4725). For machine opcode descriptions, operating-system-level instructions, and floating-point examples, this 817-page, chart-filled document is good.

A general source for all processors in the Intel family is Michael Abrash's *Zen of Code Optimization* (Coriolis Group Books 1994, ISBN 1-883577-03-9). This book has tips on 8086, 8088, 80286, and 80386 processors that do not appear anywhere else. On the back cover is a diskette with The Zen Timer, which uses the 8523 (or equivalent) timer chip that comes with all true IBM-PC compatibles and is accurate within a microsecond or so (for MS-DOS programs only).

If you want to see some assembler routines for real numbers or the elementary functions, you want Don Morgan's *Numerical Methods: Real-Time and Embedded Systems Programming* (M&T Books 1992, ISBN 1-55851-232-2). Though marred by typos, the extensive code listings are interesting.

You'll find further information in the following appendices.

Quick Guide to Assembler Instructions and Cycle Times

This appendix lists all the assembler instructions we've used in this book, showing our calculated cycle count for every possible format of each instruction on an Intel 486 in 16-bit mode. It also makes special note of every case where our cycle count differs from the number predicted in Intel documents (see Notes, at the end). Our tests were done in real mode, with MS-DOS, on typical Intel 486 machines, so we believe that our cycle counts are more accurate than Intel's (the secret rules of assembler use probably have something to do with this).

One point to note about the penalties applicable to the instructions shown here. Sometimes penalties add up (e.g., two Prefix Rule penalties on one instruction), and sometimes penalties are served concurrently (e.g., moving a constant to a double register pointer memory location violates both the Constant-to-Memory Rule and the Register-Pointer-Doubled Rule but only 1 extra cycle is applied for this). Misalignment is never concurrent. A penalty is equivalent to a no-operation preceding the current instruction.

This appendix is just a synopsis of this book's instructions. It should not be taken as a definitive assembler reference guide — there are assembler instructions which are not listed herein. In some cases, there are also additional allowable formats for the instructions we do list that we have chosen to ignore because they are beyond the scope of this book.

Note: in the form charts that follow, "register operand" is abbreviated as *reg* and "memory operand" is abbreviated as *mem*. The "Notes" referenced in the righthand columns of the form charts begin on page 381.

AAM

ASCII Adjust AX register after Multiply.

AAM divides the AL register by 10, putting the quotient in the AH register and the remainder in the AL register. The format discussed in this book is:

Instruction Mnemonic	Destination	Source	Byte Size	Cycle Count
AAM			2	15

ADC

ADd with Carry.

ADC adds <source operand> to <destination operand>, checking the status of the carry flag to decide whether a carry is needed when adding. The formats discussed in this book are:

Instruction Mnemonic	Destination	Source	Byte Size	Cycle Count
ADC	<8-bit reg>	,<8-bit constant>	2	1
ADC	<8-bit reg>	,<8-bit reg>	2	1
ADC	<8-bit reg>	,<byte-size mem>	4	2
ADC	<byte-size mem>	,<8-bit constant>	5	3 Note 1
ADC	<byte-size mem>	,<8-bit reg>	4	3
ADC	<16-bit reg>	,<8-bit constant>	3	1
ADC	<16-bit reg>	,<16-bit constant>	3	1
ADC	<16-bit reg>	,<16-bit reg>	2	1
ADC	<16-bit reg>	,<word-size mem>	4	2 Note 2
ADC	<word-size mem>	,<8-bit constant>	5	3 Note 1, Note 2
ADC	<word-size mem>	,<16-bit constant>	6	3 Note 1, Note 2
ADC	<word-size mem>	,<16-bit reg>	4	3 Note 2
ADC	<32-bit reg>	,<8-bit constant>	4	2 Note 3
ADC	<32-bit reg>	,<32-bit constant>	6	2 Note 3
ADC	<32-bit reg>	,<32-bit reg>	3	2 Note 3
ADC	<32-bit reg>	,<long-size mem>	5	3 Note 2, Note 3
ADC	<long-size mem>	,<8-bit constant>	6	4 Note 1, Note 2, Note 3
ADC	<long-size mem>	,<32-bit constant>	9	4 Note 1, Note 2, Note 3
ADC	<long-size mem>	,<32-bit reg>	5	4 Note 2, Note 3

ADD

ADD without carry.

ADD adds <source operand> to <destination operand> without checking the status of the carry flag. The formats discussed in this book are:

Instruction Mnemonic	Destination	Source	Byte Size	Cycle Count
ADD	<8-bit reg>	,<8-bit constant>	2	1
ADD	<8-bit reg>	,<8-bit reg>	2	1
ADD	<8-bit reg>	,<byte-size mem>	4	2
ADD	<byte-size mem>	,<8-bit constant>	5	3 Note 1
ADD	<byte-size mem>	,<8-bit reg>	4	3
ADD	<16-bit reg>	,<8-bit constant>	3	1
ADD	<16-bit reg>	,<16-bit constant>	3	1
ADD	<16-bit reg>	,<16-bit reg>	2	1
ADD	<16-bit reg>	,<word-size mem>	4	2 Note 2
ADD	<word-size mem>	,<8-bit constant>	5	3 Note 1, Note 2
ADD	<word-size mem>	,<16-bit constant>	6	3 Note 1, Note 2
ADD	<word-size mem>	,<16-bit reg>	4	3 Note 2
ADD	<32-bit reg>	,<8-bit constant>	4	2 Note 3
ADD	<32-bit reg>	,<32-bit constant>	6	2 Note 3
ADD	<32-bit reg>	,<32-bit reg>	3	2 Note 3
ADD	<32-bit reg>	,<long-size mem>	5	3 Note 2, Note 3
ADD	<long-size mem>	,<8-bit constant>	6	4 Note 1, Note 2, Note 3
ADD	<long-size mem>	,<32-bit constant>	9	4 Note 1, Note 2, Note 3
ADD	<long-size mem>	,<32-bit reg>	5	4 Note 2, Note 3

AND

AND <destination operand> with <source operand> and place the results in <destination operand>.

AND is a bitwise logical operator — each bit of the result is 1 if both corresponding bits of the two operands are 1; otherwise, each bit is 0. The formats discussed in this book are:

Instruction Mnemonic	Destination	Source	Byte Size	Cycle Count
AND	<8-bit reg>	,<8-bit constant>	2	1
AND	<8-bit reg>	,<8-bit reg>	2	1
AND	<8-bit reg>	,<byte-size mem>	4	2
AND	<byte-size mem>	,<8-bit constant>	5	3 Note 1
AND	<byte-size mem>	,<8-bit reg>	4	3
AND	<16-bit reg>	,<8-bit constant>	3	1
AND	<16-bit reg>	,<16-bit constant>	3	1
AND	<16-bit reg>	,<16-bit reg>	2	1
AND	<16-bit reg>	,<word-size mem>	4	2 Note 2
AND	<word-size mem>	,<8-bit constant>	5	3 Note 1, Note 2
AND	<word-size mem>	,<16-bit constant>	6	3 Note 1, Note 2
AND	<word-size mem>	,<16-bit reg>	4	3 Note 2
AND	<32-bit reg>	,<8-bit constant>	4	2 Note 3
AND	<32-bit reg>	,<32-bit constant>	6	2 Note 3
AND	<32-bit reg>	,<32-bit reg>	3	2 Note 3
AND	<32-bit reg>	,<long-size mem>	5	3 Note 2, Note 3
AND	<long-size mem>	,<8-bit constant>	6	4 Note 1, Note 2, Note 3
AND	<long-size mem>	,<32-bit constant>	9	4 Note 1, Note 2, Note 3
AND	<long-size mem>	,<32-bit reg>	5	4 Note 2, Note 3

BSR

Bit Scan <source operand> in Reverse.

BSR scans the bits in <source operand> from the most significant (highest) bit to the least significant (lowest) bit and writes the bit index of the first set bit found into <destination operand>. The formats discussed in this book are:

Instruction Mnemonic	Destination	Source	Byte Size	Cycle Count
BSR	<16-bit reg>	,<16-bit reg>	3	7 to 55 Note 4
BSR	<16-bit reg>	,<word-size mem>	5	8 to 56 Note 2, Note 5
BSR	<32-bit reg>	,<32-bit reg>	4	8 to 104 Note 3, Note 6
BSR	<32-bit reg>	,<long-size mem>	6	9 to 105 Note 2, Note 3, Note 6

Note: BSR takes 6 cycles to set up plus another 3 cycles for each bit that is scanned. Its opcode includes a 0Fh prefix, so an extra cycle is added unless the Prefix-Waiver Rule is in effect.

CALL

CALL the procedure located at <destination operand>.

CALL pushes the current code address on the stack and jumps to <destination operand> to execute the procedure found there. The formats discussed in this book are:

Instruction Mnemonic	Destination	Source	Byte Size	Cycle Count
CALL	<distant_label>		3	3 Note 7
CALL	<16-bit reg>		2	5
CALL	<word-size mem>		4	5
CALL	<32-bit reg>		3	6 Note 3
CALL	<long-size mem>		4	6 Note 3

CBW

Convert Byte in AL to Word in AX.

CBW converts the signed byte in the AL register to a signed word in the AX register by extending the sign bit of AL into all the bits of AH. The format discussed in this book is:

Instruction Mnemonic	Destination	Source	Byte Size	Cycle Count
CBW			1	3

CLC

CLear Carry flag.

CLC clears the carry flag; that is, it turns the carry flag OFF. The format discussed in this book is:

Instruction Mnemonic	Destination	Source	Byte Size	Cycle Count
CLC			1	2

CLD

CLear Direction flag.

CLD clears the direction flag; that is, it turns the direction flag OFF. The format discussed in this book is:

Instruction Mnemonic	Destination	Source	Byte Size	Cycle Count
CLD			1	2 Note 8

CLI

CLear Interrupt flag.

CLI clears the interrupt flag; that is, it turns the interrupt flag OFF. The format discussed in this book is:

Instruction Mnemonic	Destination	Source	Byte Size	Cycle Count
CLI			1	5

CMC

CoMplement Carry flag.

CMC sets the carry flag to the complement of its current status; that is, if the carry flag is ON, CMC turns it OFF, and if the carry flag is OFF, CMC turns it ON. The format discussed in this book is:

Instruction Mnemonic	Destination	Source	Byte Size	Cycle Count
CMC			1	2

CMP

CoMPare <source operand> to <destination operand>.

CMP acts exactly like the SUB instruction, except that it doesn't affect the <destination operand> by actually writing to it — that is, CMP simulates a subtraction of <source operand> from <destination operand> without checking the status of the carry flag only in order to set the flags of the flags register appropriately. The formats discussed in this book are:

Instruction Mnemonic	Destination	Source	Byte Size	Cycle Count
CMP	<8-bit reg>	,<8-bit constant>	2	1
CMP	<8-bit reg>	,<8-bit reg>	2	1
CMP	<8-bit reg>	,<byte-size mem>	4	2
CMP	<byte-size mem>	,<8-bit constant>	5	2 Note 1
CMP	<byte-size mem>	,<8-bit reg>	4	2
CMP	<16-bit reg>	,<8-bit constant>	3	1
CMP	<16-bit reg>	,<16-bit constant>	3	1
CMP	<16-bit reg>	,<16-bit reg>	2	1
CMP	<16-bit reg>	,<word-size mem>	4	2 Note 2
CMP	<word-size mem>	,<8-bit constant>	5	2 Note 1, Note 2
CMP	<word-size mem>	,<16-bit constant>	6	2 Note 1, Note 2
CMP	<word-size mem>	,<16-bit reg>	4	2 Note 2
CMP	<32-bit reg>	,<8-bit constant>	4	2 Note 3
CMP	<32-bit reg>	,<32-bit constant>	6	2 Note 3
CMP	<32-bit reg>	,<32-bit reg>	3	2 Note 3
CMP	<32-bit reg>	,<long-size mem>	5	3 Note 2, Note 3
CMP	<long-size mem>	,<8-bit constant>	6	3 Note 1, Note 2, Note 3
CMP	<long-size mem>	,<32-bit constant>	9	3 Note 1, Note 2, Note 3
CMP	<long-size mem>	,<32-bit reg>	5	3 Note 2, Note 3

CMPSx

CMPSB: CoMPare String one Byte at a time, increment (decrement) SI/DI by 1.

CMPSW: CoMPare String one Word at a time, increment (decrement) SI/DI by 2.

CMPSD: CoMPare String one Double-word at a time, increment (decrement) SI/DI by 4.

CMPSx compares a byte, word, or double-word pointed to by DS:SI with one pointed to by ES:DI, incrementing both SI and DI in the process (or decrementing if the direction flag is ON). The formats discussed in this book are:

Instruction Mnemonic	Destination	Source	Byte Size	Cycle Count
CMPSB			1	8
CMPSD			2	9 Note 3, Note 9
CMPSW			1	8

CWD

Convert Word in AX to Double-word in DX:AX.

CWD converts the signed word in the AX register to a signed double-word in the pair of registers DX:AX by extending the sign bit of AX into all the bits of DX. The format discussed in this book is:

Instruction Mnemonic	Destination	Source	Byte Size	Cycle Count
CWD			1	3

DEC

DECrement <destination operand> by 1.

DEC subtracts 1 from <destination operand>. The formats discussed in this book are:

Instruction Mnemonic	Destination	Source	Byte Size	Cycle Count
DEC	<8-bit reg>		2	1
DEC	<byte-size mem>		4	3
DEC	<16-bit reg>		1	1
DEC	<word-size mem>		4	3
DEC	<32-bit reg>		2	2 Note 3
DEC	<long-size mem>		5	4 Note 3

DIV

Unsigned DIVide AX, DX:AX or EDX:EAX by <source operand> and place the result in AL (remainder to AH), AX (remainder to DX), or EAX (remainder to EDX).

DIV performs unsigned division with the <source operand> as the divisor. The dividend, quotient, and remainder are implicitly assigned to fixed registers based on the size of the divisor. The formats discussed in this book are:

Instruction Mnemonic	Destination	Source	Byte Size	Cycle Count
DIV		<8-bit reg>	2	16 Note 10
DIV		<byte-size mem>	4	16
DIV		<16-bit reg>	2	24
DIV		<word-size mem>	4	24
DIV		<32-bit reg>	3	41 Note 3
DIV		<long-size mem>	5	41 Note 3

IDIV

Integer (signed) DIVide AX, DX : AX or EDX : EAX by <source operand> and place the result in AL (remainder to AH), AX (remainder to DX) or EAX (remainder to EDX).

IDIV performs signed division with the <source operand> as the divisor. The dividend, quotient, and remainder are implicitly assigned to fixed registers based on the size of the divisor. The formats discussed in this book are:

Instruction Mnemonic	Destination	Source	Byte Size	Cycle Count
IDIV		<8-bit reg>	2	19 Note 11
IDIV		<byte-size mem>	4	20
IDIV		<16-bit reg>	2	27
IDIV		<word-size mem>	4	28
IDIV		<32-bit reg>	3	44 Note 3
IDIV		<long-size mem>	5	45 Note 3

IMUL

Form 1:
Integer (signed) MULtiply AL, AX, or EAX with <source operand> and place the result in AX, DX : AX or EDX : EAX.

The first form of IMUL performs signed multiplication with <source operand> as the multiplier. The multiplicand and result are implicitly assigned to fixed registers based on the size of <source operand>. The formats discussed in this book are:

Instruction Mnemonic	Destination	Source (Multiplier)	Byte Size	Cycle Count
IMUL		<8-bit reg>	2	13 to 18
IMUL		<byte-size mem>	4	13 to 18
IMUL		<16-bit reg>	2	13 to 26
IMUL		<word-size mem>	4	13 to 26
IMUL		<32-bit reg>	3	14 to 43 Note 3, Note 13
IMUL		<long-size mem>	5	14 to 43 Note 3

Form 2:

Integer (signed) MULtiply <destination operand> with <source operand> and place the result in <destination operand>.

The second form of IMUL performs signed multiplication with <source operand> as the multiplier and <destination operand> as the multiplicand. The result is assigned to <destination operand>. The formats discussed in this book are:

Instruction Mnemonic	Destination (Result & Multiplicand)	Source (Multiplier)	Byte Size	Cycle Count
IMUL	<16-bit reg>	,<8-bit constant>	3	13 to 26
IMUL	<16-bit reg>	,<16-bit constant>	4	13 to 26
IMUL	<16-bit reg>	,<16-bit reg>	3	14 to 27 Note 6
IMUL	<16-bit reg>	,<word-size mem>	5	14 to 27 Note 6
IMUL	<32-bit reg>	,<8-bit constant>	4	14 to 43 Note 3
IMUL	<32-bit reg>	,<32-bit constant>	7	14 to 43 Note 3
IMUL	<32-bit reg>	,<32-bit reg>	4	15 to 44 Note 3, Note 6
IMUL	<32-bit reg>	,<long-size mem>	6	15 to 44 Note 3, Note 6

Form 3:

Integer (signed) MULtiply <source operand_1> with <source operand_2> and place the result in <destination operand>.

The third form of IMUL performs signed multiplication with <source operand_2> as the multiplier and <source operand_1> as the multiplicand. The result is assigned to <destination operand>. The formats discussed in this book are:

Instruction Mnemonic	Destination (Result)	Source_1 (Multiplicand)	Source_2 (Multiplier)	Byte Size	Cycle Count
IMUL	<16-bit reg>	,<16-bit reg>	,<8-bit constant>	3	13 to 26
IMUL	<16-bit reg>	,<word-size mem>	,<8-bit constant>	5	13 to 26
IMUL	<32-bit reg>	,<32-bit reg>	,<8-bit constant>	4	14 to 43 Note 3
IMUL	<32-bit reg>	,<long-size mem>	,<8-bit constant>	6	14 to 43 Note 3

Note: the cycle count is dependent on the position of the most significant bit in the multiplier. To calculate actual cycles use:

```
cycles = 13 or (11 + (magnitude of multiplier)), whichever is higher.
```

Note: Intel's description of IMUL says an extra 3 cycles are added to the cycle count if the multiplier is a memory operand. This appears to be false.

Note: Intel's description of IMUL says the instruction takes only 9 cycles if the multiplier is zero. This is false. The minimum number of cycles is 13.

INC

INCrement <destination operand> by 1.

INC adds 1 to <destination operand>. The formats discussed in this book are:

Instruction Mnemonic	Destination	Source	Byte Size	Cycle Count
INC	<8-bit reg>		2	1
INC	<byte-size mem>		4	3
INC	<16-bit reg>		1	1
INC	<word-size mem>		4	3
INC	<32-bit reg>		2	2 Note 3
INC	<long-size mem>		5	4 Note 3

JA

Jump to <destination operand> if Above.

JA jumps short if the zero flag and the carry flag are both OFF (i.e., if ZF=0 and CF=0), else it goes on to the next instruction. This instruction is used for unsigned comparisons. The format discussed in this book is:

Instruction Mnemonic	Destination	Source	Byte Size	Cycle Count
JA	<near_label>		2	3 if TRUE, 1 if FALSE

JAE

Jump to <destination operand> if Above or Equal.

JAE jumps short if the carry flag is OFF (i.e., CF=0) and goes on to execute the next instruction if the carry flag is ON. An alternate mnemonic is JNC (Jump if Not Carry flag ON). The format discussed in this book is:

Instruction Mnemonic	Destination	Source	Byte Size	Cycle Count
JAE	<near_label>		2	3 if TRUE, 1 if FALSE

JB

Jump to <destination operand> if Below.

JB jumps short if the carry flag is ON (i.e., CF=1) and goes on to execute the next instruction if the carry flag is OFF. An alternate mnemonic is JC (Jump if Carry flag ON). The format discussed in this book is:

Instruction Mnemonic	Destination	Source	Byte Size	Cycle Count
JB	<near_label>		2	3 if TRUE, 1 if FALSE

JBE

Jump to <destination operand> if Below or Equal.

JBE jumps short if either the zero flag or the carry flag is ON (i.e., ZF=1 or CF=1), else it goes on to the next instruction. This instruction is used for unsigned comparisons. The format discussed in this book is:

Instruction Mnemonic	Destination	Source	Byte Size	Cycle Count
JBE	<near_label>		2	3 if TRUE, 1 if FALSE

JC

Jump to <destination operand> if Carry flag ON.

JC jumps short if the carry flag is ON (i.e., CF=1) and goes on to execute the next instruction if the carry flag is OFF. An alternate mnemonic is JB (Jump if Below). The format discussed in this book is:

Instruction Mnemonic	Destination	Source	Byte Size	Cycle Count
JC	<near_label>		2	3 if TRUE, 1 if FALSE

JCXZ

Jump to <destination operand> if CX register equals 0.

JCXZ jumps short if CX=0. JCXZ does not affect the contents of CX. The format discussed in this book is:

Instruction Mnemonic	Destination	Source	Byte Size	Cycle Count
JCXZ	<near_label>		2	8 if TRUE, 5 if FALSE

JE

Jump to <destination operand> if Equal.

JE jumps short if the zero flag is ON (i.e., ZF=1) and goes on to execute the next instruction if the zero flag is OFF. An alternate mnemonic is JZ (Jump if Zero flag ON). The format discussed in this book is:

Instruction Mnemonic	Destination	Source	Byte Size	Cycle Count
JE	<near_label>		2	3 if TRUE, 1 if FALSE

JG

Jump to <destination operand> if Greater.

JG jumps short if the zero flag is OFF (i.e., ZF=0) and the status of the sign flag equals the status of the overflow flag, else it goes on to the next instruction. This instruction is used for signed comparisons. The format discussed in this book is:

Instruction Mnemonic	Destination	Source	Byte Size	Cycle Count
JG	<near_label>		2	3 if TRUE, 1 if FALSE

JGE

Jump to <destination operand> if Greater or Equal.

JGE jumps short if the status of the sign flag equals the status of the overflow flag, else it goes on to the next instruction. This instruction is used for signed comparisons. The format discussed in this book is:

Instruction Mnemonic	Destination	Source	Byte Size	Cycle Count
JGE	<near_label>		2	3 if TRUE, 1 if FALSE

JL

Jump to <destination operand> if Less.

JL jumps short if the status of the sign flag is not equal to the status of the overflow flag, else it goes on to the next instruction. This instruction is used for signed comparisons. The format discussed in this book is:

Instruction Mnemonic	Destination	Source	Byte Size	Cycle Count
JL	<near_label>		2	3 if TRUE, 1 if FALSE

JLE

Jump to <destination operand> if Less or Equal.

JLE jumps short if the zero flag is ON (i.e., ZF=1) or if the status of the sign flag is not equal to the status of the overflow flag, else it goes on to the next instruction. This instruction is used for signed comparisons. The format discussed in this book is:

Instruction Mnemonic	Destination	Source	Byte Size	Cycle Count
JLE	<near_label>		2	3 if TRUE, 1 if FALSE

JMP

JuMP to <destination operand>.

JMP jumps near. The format discussed in this book is:

Instruction Mnemonic	Destination	Source	Byte Size	Cycle Count
JMP	<distant_label>		2	3

JNC

Jump to <destination operand> if Not Carry flag ON.

JNC jumps short if the carry flag is OFF (i.e., CF=0) and goes on to execute the next instruction if the carry flag is ON. An alternate mnemonic is JAE (Jump if Above or Equal). The format discussed in this book is:

Instruction Mnemonic	Destination	Source	Byte Size	Cycle Count
JNC	<near_label>		2	3 if TRUE, 1 if FALSE

JNE

Jump to <destination operand> if Not Equal.

JNE jumps short if the zero flag is OFF (i.e., ZF=0) and goes on to execute the next instruction if the zero flag is ON. An alternate mnemonic is JNZ (Jump if Zero flag Not ON). The format discussed in this book is:

Instruction Mnemonic	Destination	Source	Byte Size	Cycle Count
JNE	<near_label>		2	3 if TRUE, 1 if FALSE

JNO

Jump to <destination operand> if Not Overflow flag ON.

JNO jumps short if the overflow flag is OFF (i.e., OF=0) and goes on to execute the next instruction if the overflow flag is ON. The format discussed in this book is:

Instruction Mnemonic	Destination	Source	Byte Size	Cycle Count
JNO	<near_label>		2	3 if TRUE, 1 if FALSE

JNP

Jump to <destination operand> if Not Parity flag ON.

JNP jumps short if the parity flag is OFF (i.e., PF=0) and goes on to execute the next instruction if the parity flag is ON. An alternate mnemonic is JPO (Jump if Parity Odd). The format discussed in this book is:

Instruction Mnemonic	Destination	Source	Byte Size	Cycle Count
JNP	<near_label>		2	3 if TRUE, 1 if FALSE

JNS

Jump to <destination operand> if Not Sign flag ON.

JNS jumps short if the sign flag is OFF (i.e., SF=0) and goes on to execute the next instruction if the sign flag is ON. The format discussed in this book is:

Instruction Mnemonic	Destination	Source	Byte Size	Cycle Count
JNS	<near_label>		2	3 if TRUE, 1 if FALSE

JNZ

Jump to <destination operand> if Not Zero flag ON.

JNZ jumps short if the zero flag is OFF (i.e., ZF=0) and goes on to execute the next instruction if the zero flag is ON. An alternate mnemonic is JNE (Jump if Not Equal). The format discussed in this book is:

Instruction Mnemonic	Destination	Source	Byte Size	Cycle Count
JNZ	<near_label>		2	3 if TRUE, 1 if FALSE

JO

Jump to <destination operand> if Overflow flag ON.

JO jumps short if the overflow flag is ON (i.e., OF=1) and goes on to execute the next instruction if the overflow flag is OFF. The format discussed in this book is:

Instruction Mnemonic	Destination	Source	Byte Size	Cycle Count
JO	<near_label>		2	3 if TRUE, 1 if FALSE

JP

Jump to <destination operand> if Parity flag ON.

JP jumps short if the parity flag is ON (i.e., PF=1) and goes on to execute the next instruction if the parity flag is OFF. An alternate mnemonic is JPE (Jump if Parity Even). The format discussed in this book is:

Instruction Mnemonic	Destination	Source	Byte Size	Cycle Count
JP	<near_label>		2	3 if TRUE, 1 if FALSE

JPE

Jump to <destination operand> if Parity Even.

JPE jumps short if the parity flag is ON (i.e., PF=1) and goes on to execute the next instruction if the parity flag is OFF. An alternate mnemonic is JP (Jump if Parity flag ON). The format discussed in this book is:

Instruction Mnemonic	Destination	Source	Byte Size	Cycle Count
JPE	<near_label>		2	3 if TRUE, 1 if FALSE

JPO

Jump to <destination operand> if Parity Odd.

JPO jumps short if the parity flag is OFF (i.e., PF=0) and goes on to execute the next instruction if the parity flag is ON. An alternate mnemonic is JNP (Jump if Not Parity flag ON). The format discussed in this book is:

Instruction Mnemonic	Destination	Source	Byte Size	Cycle Count
JPO	<near_label>		2	3 if TRUE, 1 if FALSE

JS

Jump to <destination operand> if Sign flag ON.

JS jumps short if the sign flag is ON (i.e., SF=1) and goes on to execute the next instruction if the sign flag is OFF. The format discussed in this book is:

Instruction Mnemonic	Destination	Source	Byte Size	Cycle Count
JS	<near_label>		2	3 if TRUE, 1 if FALSE

JZ

Jump to <destination operand> if Zero flag ON.

JZ jumps short if the zero flag is ON (i.e., ZF=1) and goes on to execute the next instruction if the zero flag is OFF. An alternate mnemonic is JE (Jump if Equal). The format discussed in this book is:

Instruction Mnemonic	Destination	Source	Byte Size	Cycle Count
JZ	<near_label>		2	3 if TRUE, 1 if FALSE

LDS

Load DS : <register> with pointer from memory.

LDS reads a full pointer from <source operand> and stores it in <destination operand>. The format discussed in this book is:

Instruction Mnemonic	Destination	Source	Byte Size	Cycle Count
LDS	<DS:16-bit reg>	,<mem address>	4	6 Note 2

LEA

Load Effective Address from <source operand> to <destination operand>.

LEA calculates the offset of <source operand> and puts it in <destination operand>. The formats discussed in this book are:

Instruction Mnemonic	Destination	Source	Byte Size	Cycle Count
LEA	<16-bit reg>	,<mem address>	2	1 Note 2
LEA	<32-bit reg>	,<mem address>	3	2 Note 2, Note 3

LES

Load ES : <register> with pointer from memory.

LES reads a full pointer from <source operand> and stores it in <destination operand>. The format discussed in this book is:

Instruction Mnemonic	Destination	Source	Byte Size	Cycle Count
LES	<ES:16-bit reg>	,<mem address>	4	6 Note 2

LODSx

LODSB: LOaD String one Byte at a time, increment (decrement) SI by 1.

LODSW: LOaD String one Word at a time, increment (decrement) SI by 2.

LODSD: LOaD String one Double-word at a time, increment (decrement) SI by 4.

LODSx loads a byte, word, or double-word pointed to by DS:SI into the AL, AX or EAX registers respectively, incrementing SI in the process (or decrementing if the direction flag is ON). The formats discussed in this book are:

Instruction Mnemonic	Destination	Source	Byte Size	Cycle Count
LODSB			1	5
LODSD			2	6 Note 3
LODSW			1	5

LOOP

Decrement the CX register by 1. If CX is not equal to 0, jump to LOOP's <destination operand>.

LOOP decrements CX by 1, then checks CX's value. If CX<>0, LOOP jumps short, else it goes on to the next instruction. The format discussed in this book is:

Instruction Mnemonic	Destination	Source	Byte Size	Cycle Count
LOOP	<near_label>		2	7 if TRUE, 6 if FALSE Note 18

LSL

Load Segment Limit from <source operand> into <destination operand>.

LSL loads a register with a segment limit. LSL is strictly a protected mode instruction; it won't work inside an MS-DOS program. The formats discussed in this book are:

Instruction Mnemonic	Destination	Source	Byte Size	Cycle Count
LSL	<16-bit reg>	,<16-bit reg>	1	1 Note 6
LSL	<16-bit reg>	,<word-size mem>	1	1 Note 2, Note 6
LSL	<32-bit reg>	,<32-bit reg>	1	2 Note 3, Note 6
LSL	<32-bit reg>	,<long-size mem>	1	2 Note 2, Note 3, Note 6

MOV

MOVe <source operand> to <destination operand>.

MOV assigns the value of <source operand> to <destination operand>. The formats discussed in this book are:

Instruction Mnemonic	Destination	Source	Byte Size	Cycle Count
MOV	<8-bit reg>	,<8-bit constant>	2	1
MOV	<8-bit reg>	,<8-bit reg>	2	1
MOV	<8-bit reg>	,<byte-size mem>	4	1
MOV	<byte-size mem>	,<8-bit constant>	5	1 Note 1
MOV	<byte-size mem>	,<8-bit reg>	4	1
MOV	<16-bit reg>	,<16-bit constant>	3	1
MOV	<16-bit reg>	,<16-bit reg>	2	1
MOV	<16-bit reg>	,<word-size mem>	4	1 Note 2
MOV	<word-size mem>	,<16-bit constant>	6	1 Note 1, Note 2
MOV	<word-size mem>	,<16-bit reg>	4	1 Note 2
MOV	<32-bit reg>	,<32-bit constant>	6	2 Note 3
MOV	<32-bit reg>	,<32-bit reg>	3	2 Note 3
MOV	<32-bit reg>	,<long-size mem>	5	2 Note 2, Note 3
MOV	<long-size mem>	,<32-bit constant>	9	2 Note 1, Note 2, Note 3
MOV	<long-size mem>	,<32-bit reg>	5	2 Note 2, Note 3
MOV	<16-bit reg>	,<segment-reg>	2	3
MOV	<word-size mem>	,	4	3 Note 2
MOV	<segment-reg>	,<16-bit reg>	2	3
MOV	<segment-reg>	,<word-size mem>	4	3 Note 2, Note 14

MOVSx

MOVSB: MOVe String one Byte at a time, increment (decrement) SI/DI by 1.

MOVSW: MOVe String one Word at a time, increment (decrement) SI/DI by 2.

MOVSD: MOVe String one Double-word at a time, increment (decrement) SI/DI by 4.

MOVSx copies a byte, word, or double-word pointed to by DS:SI to the location pointed to by ES:DI, incrementing both SI and DI in the process (or decrementing if the direction flag is ON). The formats discussed in this book are:

Instruction Mnemonic	Destination	Source	Byte Size	Cycle Count
MOVSB			1	7
MOVSD			2	8 Note 3
MOVSW			1	7

MOVSX

MOVe with Sign-eXtension <source operand> to <destination operand>.

MOVSX reads <source operand>, sign-extends the value to the size of <destination operand>, and writes the result to <destination operand>. The formats discussed in this book are:

Instruction Mnemonic	Destination	Source	Byte Size	Cycle Count
MOVSX	<16-bit reg>	,<8-bit reg>	3	4 Note 6
MOVSX	<16-bit reg>	,<byte-size mem>	5	4 Note 6
MOVSX	<32-bit reg>	,<8-bit reg>	4	5 Note 3, Note 6
MOVSX	<32-bit reg>	,<byte-size mem>	6	5 Note 3, Note 6
MOVSX	<32-bit reg>	,<16-bit reg>	4	5 Note 3, Note 6
MOVSX	<32-bit reg>	,<word-size mem>	6	5 Note 2, Note 3, Note 6

MOVZX

MOVe with Zero-eXtension <source operand> to <destination operand>.

MOVZX reads <source operand>, zero-extends the value to the size of <destination operand>, and writes the result to <destination operand>. The formats discussed in this book are:

Instruction Mnemonic	Destination	Source	Byte Size	Cycle Count
MOVZX	<16-bit reg>	,<8-bit reg>	3	4 Note 6
MOVZX	<16-bit reg>	,<byte-size mem>	5	4 Note 6
MOVZX	<32-bit reg>	,<8-bit reg>	4	5 Note 3, Note 6
MOVZX	<32-bit reg>	,<byte-size mem>	6	5 Note 3, Note 6
MOVZX	<32-bit reg>	,<16-bit reg>	4	5 Note 3, Note 6
MOVZX	<32-bit reg>	,<word-size mem>	6	5 Note 2, Note 3, Note 6

MUL

Unsigned MULtiply AL, AX, or EAX with <source operand> and place the result in AX, DX:AX or EDX:EAX.

MUL performs unsigned multiplication with the <source operand> as the multiplier. The multiplicand and result are implicitly assigned to fixed registers based on the size of the multiplier. The formats discussed in this book are:

Instruction Mnemonic	Destination	Source	Byte Size	Cycle Count
MUL		<8-bit reg>	2	13 to 18 Note 12
MUL		<byte-size mem>	4	13 to 18
MUL		<16-bit reg>	2	13 to 26
MUL		<word-size mem>	4	13 to 26
MUL		<32-bit reg>	3	14 to 43 Note 3
MUL		<long-size mem>	5	14 to 43 Note 3

Note: the cycle count is dependent on the position of the most significant bit in the multiplier. To calculate actual cycles, use:

```
cycles = 13 or (11 + (magnitude of multiplier)), whichever is higher.
```

NEG

NEGate <destination operand> with its two's complement.

NEG replaces <destination operand> with its two's complement. The formats discussed in this book are:

Instruction Mnemonic	Destination	Source	Byte Size	Cycle Count
NEG	<8-bit reg>		2	1
NEG	<byte-size mem>		4	3
NEG	<16-bit reg>		2	1
NEG	<word-size mem>		4	3
NEG	<32-bit reg>		3	2 Note 3
NEG	<long-size mem>		5	4 Note 3

NOP

No OPeration.

NOP takes up space but does nothing. The format discussed in this book is:

Instruction Mnemonic	Destination	Source	Byte Size	Cycle Count
NOP			1	1

Note: Intel's description of NOP states NOP is an alias mnemonic for XCHG AX,AX. This is false.

NOT

Negate <destination operand> with its One's complemenT.

NOT replaces <destination operand> with its one's complement. The formats discussed in this book are:

Instruction Mnemonic	Destination	Source	Byte Size	Cycle Count
NOT	<8-bit reg>		2	1
NOT	<byte-size mem>		4	3
NOT	<16-bit reg>		2	1
NOT	<word-size mem>		4	3
NOT	<32-bit reg>		3	2 Note 3
NOT	<long-size mem>		5	4 Note 3

OR

Calculate the inclusive OR of <destination operand> and <source operand> and place the results in <destination operand>.

OR is a bitwise logical operator — each bit of the result is 0 if both corresponding bits of the two operands are 0; otherwise, each bit is 1. The formats discussed in this book are:

Instruction Mnemonic	Destination	Source	Byte Size	Cycle Count
OR	<8-bit reg>	,<8-bit constant>	2	1
OR	<8-bit reg>	,<8-bit reg>	2	1
OR	<8-bit reg>	,<byte-size mem>	4	2
OR	<byte-size mem>	,<8-bit constant>	5	3 Note 1
OR	<byte-size mem>	,<8-bit reg>	4	3
OR	<16-bit reg>	,<8-bit constant>	3	1
OR	<16-bit reg>	,<16-bit constant>	3	1
OR	<16-bit reg>	,<16-bit reg>	2	1
OR	<16-bit reg>	,<word-size mem>	4	2 Note 2
OR	<word-size mem>	,<8-bit constant>	5	3 Note 1, Note 2
OR	<word-size mem>	,<16-bit constant>	6	3 Note 1, Note 2
OR	<word-size mem>	,<16-bit reg>	4	3 Note 2
OR	<32-bit reg>	,<8-bit constant>	4	2 Note 3
OR	<32-bit reg>	,<32-bit constant>	6	2 Note 3
OR	<32-bit reg>	,<32-bit reg>	3	2 Note 3
OR	<32-bit reg>	,<long-size mem>	5	3 Note 2, Note 3
OR	<long-size mem>	,<8-bit constant>	6	4 Note 1, Note 2, Note 3
OR	<long-size mem>	,<32-bit constant	9	4 Note 1, Note 2, Note 3
OR	<long-size mem>	,<32-bit reg>	5	4 Note 2, Note 3

POP

POP top of stack to <destination operand>, increment SP.

POP copies the contents from the stack location to <destination operand>, then increments SP by 2 if the size of <destination operand> is 16 bits or by 4 if the size of <destination operand> is 32 bits. The formats discussed in this book are:

Instruction Mnemonic	Destination	Source	Byte Size	Cycle Count
POP	<16-bit reg>		1	1 Note 15
POP	<segment-reg>		1	3
POP	<word-size mem>		4	5 Note 16
POP	<32-bit reg>		2	2 Note 3, Note 15
POP	<long-size mem>		5	6 Note 3, Note 16

Note: POP CS is not allowed on 486s.

PUSH

Decrement SP, PUSH <source operand> onto top of stack.

PUSH decrements SP by 2 if the size of <source operand> is 16 bits and by 4 if the size of <source operand> is 32 bits, then copies <source operand> to the new top of stack location. The formats discussed in this book are:

Instruction Mnemonic	Destination	Source	Byte Size	Cycle Count
PUSH		<16-bit constant>	3	1
PUSH		<16-bit reg>	1	1
PUSH		<segment-reg>	1	3
PUSH		<word-size mem>	4	4
PUSH		<32-bit constant>	6	2 Note 3
PUSH		<32-bit reg>	2	2 Note 3
PUSH		<long-size mem>	5	5 Note 3

REP CMPSx

REPeat <CMPSx> instruction until CX register is 0 or while zero flag ON.

REP CMPSx: if CX is 0 then go on to next instruction; do a CMPSx; decrement CX by 1; if zero flag is OFF then go on to next instruction; repeat loop. The formats discussed in this book are:

Instruction Mnemonic	Destination	Source	Byte Size	Cycles To Initialize	Cycles Per Iteration
REP CMPSB			1		6 if CX=0 Note 19
REP CMPSB			2	8 Note 19	7 if CX>0
REP CMPSD			2		7 if CX=0 Note 3, Note 19
REP CMPSD			3	9 Note 3, Note 19	7 if CX>0
REP CMPSW			1		6 if CX=0 Note 19
REP CMPSW			2	8 Note 19	7 if CX>0

REP MOVSx

REPeat <MOVSx> instruction until CX register is 0.

REP MOVSx: if CX is 0 then go on to next instruction; do a MOVSx; decrement CX by 1; repeat loop. The formats discussed in this book are:

Instruction Mnemonic	Destination	Source	Byte Size	Cycles To Initialize	Cycles Per Iteration
REP MOVSB			1		6 if CX=0 Note 19
REP MOVSB			2		14 if CX=1 Note 19
REP MOVSB			2	11 Note 19, Note 20	3 if CX>1
REP MOVSD			2		7 if CX=0 Note 3, Note 19
REP MOVSD			3		15 if CX=1 Note 3, Note 19
REP MOVSD			3	12 Note 3, Note 19 Note 20	3 if CX>1
REP MOVSW			1		6 if CX=0 Note 19
REP MOVSW			2		14 if CX=1 Note 19
REP MOVSW			2	11 Note 19, Note 20	3 if CX>1

REPNZ CMPSx

REPeat <CMPSx> instruction until CX register is 0 or while Not Zero flag ON.

REPNZ CMPSx: if CX is 0 then go on to next instruction; do a CMPSx; decrement CX by 1; if zero flag is ON then go on to next instruction; repeat loop. The formats discussed in this book are:

Instruction Mnemonic	Destination	Source	Byte Size	Cycles To Initialize	Cycles Per Iteration
REPNZ CMPSB			1		6 if CX=0 Note 19
REPNZ CMPSB			2	8 Note 19	7 if CX>0
REPNZ CMPSD			2		7 if CX=0 Note 3, Note 19
REPNZ CMPSD			3	9 Note 3, Note 19	7 if CX>0
REPNZ CMPSW			1		6 if CX=0 Note 19
REPNZ CMPSW			2	8 Note 19	7 if CX>0

REPNZ SCASx

REPeat <SCASx> instruction until CX register is 0 or while Not Zero flag ON.

REPNZ SCASx: if CX is 0 then go on to next instruction; do a SCASx; decrement CX by 1; if zero flag is ON then go on to next instruction; repeat loop. The formats discussed in this book are:

Instruction Mnemonic	Destination	Source	Byte Size	Cycles To Initialize	Cycles Per Iteration
REPNZ SCASB			1		6 if CX=0 Note 19
REPNZ SCASB			2	8 Note 19	5 if CX>0
REPNZ SCASD			2		7 if CX=0 Note 3, Note 19
REPNZ SCASD			3	9 Note 3, Note 19	5 if CX>0
REPNZ SCASW			1		6 if CX=0 Note 19
REPNZ SCASW			2	8 Note 19	5 if CX>0

REP SCASx

REPeat <SCASx> instruction until CX register is 0 or while zero flag ON.

REP SCASx: if CX is 0 then go on to next instruction; do a SCASx; decrement CX by 1; if zero flag is OFF then go on to next instruction; repeat loop. The formats discussed in this book are:

Instruction Mnemonic	Destination	Source	Byte Size	Cycles To Initialize	Cycles Per Iteration
REP SCASB			1		6 if CX=0 Note 19
REP SCASB			2	8 Note 19	5 if CX>0
REP SCASD			2		7 if CX=0 Note 3, Note 19
REP SCASD			3	9 Note 3, Note 19	5 if CX>0
REP SCASW			1		6 if CX=0 Note 19
REP SCASW			2	8 Note 19	5 if CX>0

REP STOSx

REPeat <STOSx> instruction until CX register is zero.

REP STOSx: if CX is 0 then go on to next instruction; do a STOSx; decrement CX by 1; repeat loop. The formats discussed in this book are:

Instruction Mnemonic	Destination	Source	Byte Size	Cycles To Initialize	Cycles Per Iteration
REP STOSB			1		6 if CX=0 Note 19
REP STOSB			2	8 Note 19	4 if CX>0
REP STOSD			2		7 if CX=0 Note 3, Note 19
REP STOSD			3	9 Note 3, Note 19	4 if CX>0
REP STOSW			1		6 if CX=0 Note 19
REP STOSW			2	8 Note 19	4 if CX>0

RET

RETurn from procedure.

RET pops an address off the stack and jumps to it. The format discussed in this book is:

Instruction Mnemonic	Destination	Source	Byte Size	Cycle Count
RET			1	5

ROL

ROtate <destination operand> to the Left by <source operand> bits.

ROL is like a SHL (SHift Left), but the bits that get shifted out on the left get shifted in on the right. The formats discussed in this book are:

Instruction Mnemonic	Destination	Source	Byte Size	Cycle Count
ROL	<8-bit reg>	,CL	2	3
ROL	<byte-size mem>	,CL	4	4
ROL	<8-bit reg>	,1	2	3
ROL	<byte-size mem>	,1	4	4
ROL	<8-bit reg>	,<8-bit constant>	3	2
ROL	<byte-size mem>	,<8-bit constant>	5	4 Note 1
ROL	<16-bit reg>	,CL	2	3
ROL	<word-size mem>	,CL	4	4 Note 2
ROL	<16-bit reg>	,1	2	3
ROL	<word-size mem>	,1	4	4 Note 2
ROL	<16-bit reg>	,<8-bit constant>	3	2
ROL	<word-size mem>	,<8-bit constant>	5	4 Note 1, Note 2
ROL	<32-bit reg>	,CL	3	4 Note 3
ROL	<long-size mem>	,CL	5	5 Note 2, Note 3
ROL	<32-bit reg>	,1	3	4 Note 3
ROL	<long-size mem>	,1	5	5 Note 2, Note 3
ROL	<32-bit reg>	,<8-bit constant>	4	3 Note 3
ROL	<long-size mem>	,<8-bit constant>	6	5 Note 1, Note 2, Note 3

SAR

Shift <destination operand> to the Arithmetic Right by <source operand> bits.

SAR shifts <destination operand> to the right by the number of bits in <source operand>, moving the low-order bit into the carry flag. SAR leaves the sign bit in the same state it was in before the shift and is therefore used to shift right a signed value. The formats discussed in this book are:

Instruction Mnemonic	Destination	Source	Byte Size	Cycle Count
SAR	<8-bit reg>	,CL	2	3
SAR	<byte-size mem>	,CL	4	4
SAR	<8-bit reg>	,1	2	3
SAR	<byte-size mem>	,1	4	4
SAR	<8-bit reg>	,<8-bit constant>	3	2
SAR	<byte-size mem>	,<8-bit constant>	5	4 Note 1
SAR	<16-bit reg>	,CL	2	3
SAR	<word-size mem>	,CL	4	4 Note 2
SAR	<16-bit reg>	,1	2	3
SAR	<word-size mem>	,1	4	4 Note 2
SAR	<16-bit reg>	,<8-bit constant>	3	2
SAR	<word-size mem>	,<8-bit constant>	5	4 Note 1, Note 2
SAR	<32-bit reg>	,CL	3	4 Note 3
SAR	<long-size mem>	,CL	5	5 Note 2, Note 3
SAR	<32-bit reg>	,1	3	4 Note 3
SAR	<long-size mem>	,1	5	5 Note 2, Note 3
SAR	<32-bit reg>	,<8-bit constant>	4	3 Note 3
SAR	<long-size mem>	,<8-bit constant>	6	5 Note 1, Note 2, Note 3

SBB

SuBtract with Borrow.

SBB subtracts <source operand> from <destination operand>, checking the status of the carry flag to decide whether a borrow is needed when subtracting. The formats discussed in this book are:

Instruction Mnemonic	Destination	Source	Byte Size	Cycle Count
SBB	<8-bit reg>	,<8-bit constant>	2	1
SBB	<8-bit reg>	,<8-bit reg>	2	1
SBB	<8-bit reg>	,<byte-size mem>	4	2
SBB	<byte-size mem>	,<8-bit constant>	5	3 Note 1
SBB	<byte-size mem>	,<8-bit reg>	4	3
SBB	<16-bit reg>	,<8-bit constant>	3	1
SBB	<16-bit reg>	,<16-bit constant>	3	1
SBB	<16-bit reg>	,<16-bit reg>	2	1
SBB	<16-bit reg>	,<word-size mem>	4	2 Note 2
SBB	<word-size mem>	,<8-bit constant>	5	3 Note 1, Note 2
SBB	<word-size mem>	,<16-bit constant>	6	3 Note 1, Note 2
SBB	<word-size mem>	,<16-bit reg>	4	3 Note 2
SBB	<32-bit reg>	,<8-bit constant>	4	2 Note 3
SBB	<32-bit reg>	,<32-bit constant>	6	2 Note 3
SBB	<32-bit reg>	,<32-bit reg>	3	2 Note 3
SBB	<32-bit reg>	,<long-size mem>	5	3 Note 2, Note 3
SBB	<long-size mem>	,<8-bit constant>	6	4 Note 1, Note 2, Note 3
SBB	<long-size mem>	,<32-bit constant>	9	4 Note 1, Note 2, Note 3
SBB	<long-size mem>	,<32-bit reg>	5	4 Note 2, Note 3

SCASx

SCASB: SCAn String one Byte at a time, increment (decrement) DI by 1.

SCASW: SCAn String one Word at a time, increment (decrement) DI by 2.

SCASD: SCAn String one Double-word at a time, increment (decrement) DI by 4.

SCASx compares the AL, AX, or EAX registers to a byte, word or double-word pointed to by ES:DI, incrementing DI in the process (or decrementing if the direction flag is ON). The formats discussed in this book are:

Instruction Mnemonic	Destination	Source	Byte Size	Cycle Count
SCASB			1	6
SCASD			2	7 Note 3
SCASW			1	6

SHL

SHift <destination operand> to the Left by <source operand> bits.

SHL shifts <destination operand> to the left by the number of bits in <source operand>, moving the high-order bit into the carry flag and clearing the low-order bit. The formats discussed in this book are:

Instruction Mnemonic	Destination	Source	Byte Size	Cycle Count
SHL	<8-bit reg>	,CL	2	3
SHL	<byte-size mem>	,CL	4	4
SHL	<8-bit reg>	,1	2	3
SHL	<byte-size mem>	,1	4	4
SHL	<8-bit reg>	,<8-bit constant>	3	2
SHL	<byte-size mem>	,<8-bit constant>	5	4 Note 1
SHL	<16-bit reg>	,CL	2	3
SHL	<word-size mem>	,CL	4	4 Note 2
SHL	<16-bit reg>	,1	2	3
SHL	<word-size mem>	,1	4	4 Note 2
SHL	<16-bit reg>	,<8-bit constant>	3	2
SHL	<word-size mem>	,<8-bit constant>	5	4 Note 1, Note 2
SHL	<32-bit reg>	,CL	3	4 Note 3
SHL	<long-size mem>	,CL	5	5 Note 2, Note 3
SHL	<32-bit reg>	,1	3	4 Note 3
SHL	<long-size mem>	,1	5	5 Note 2, Note 3
SHL	<32-bit reg>	,<8-bit constant>	4	3 Note 3
SHL	<long-size mem>	,<8-bit constant>	6	5 Note 1, Note 2, Note 3

SHLD

SHift <destination operand> to the Left Double-word by <bit-count operand> bits.

SHLD shifts <destination operand> to the left by <bit-count operand> bits and takes the bits to shift in from the right (starting with bit 0) from <source operand> without changing <source operand>. The formats discussed in this book are:

Instruction Mnemonic	Destination	Source	Bit-Count	Byte Size	Cycle Count
SHLD	<16-bit reg>	,<16-bit reg>	,<8-bit constant>	4	3 Note 6
SHLD	<word-size mem>	,<16-bit reg>	,<8-bit constant>	6	4 Note 1, Note 6
SHLD	<32-bit reg>	,<32-bit reg>	,<8-bit constant>	5	4 Note 3, Note 6
SHLD	<long-size mem>	,<32-bit reg>	,<8-bit constant>	7	5 Note 1, Note 3, Note 6

SHR

SHift <destination operand> to the Right by <source operand> bits.

SHR shifts <destination operand> to the right by the number of bits in <source operand>, moving the low-order bit into the carry flag. SHR sets the sign bit to 0 and is therefore used to shift right an unsigned value. The formats discussed in this book are:

Instruction Mnemonic	Destination	Source	Byte Size	Cycle Count
SHR	<8-bit reg>	,CL	2	3
SHR	<byte-size mem>	,CL	4	4
SHR	<8-bit reg>	,1	2	3
SHR	<byte-size mem>	,1	4	4
SHR	<8-bit reg>	,<8-bit constant>	3	2
SHR	<byte-size mem>	,<8-bit constant>	5	4 Note 1
SHR	<16-bit reg>	,CL	2	3
SHR	<word-size mem>	,CL	4	4 Note 2
SHR	<16-bit reg>	,1	2	3
SHR	<word-size mem>	,1	4	4 Note 2
SHR	<16-bit reg>	,<8-bit constant>	3	2
SHR	<word-size mem>	,<8-bit constant>	5	4 Note 1, Note 2
SHR	<32-bit reg>	,CL	3	4 Note 3
SHR	<long-size mem>	,CL	5	5 Note 2, Note 3
SHR	<32-bit reg>	,1	3	4 Note 3
SHR	<long-size mem>	,1	5	5 Note 2, Note 3
SHR	<32-bit reg>	,<8-bit constant>	4	3 Note 3
SHR	<long-size mem>	,<8-bit constant>	6	5 Note 1, Note 2, Note 3

SHRD

SHift <destination operand> to the Right Double-word by <bit-count operand> bits.

SHRD shifts <destination operand> to the right by <bit-count operand> bits and takes the bits to shift in from the left (beginning with bit 31) from <source operand> without changing <source operand>. The formats discussed in this book are:

Instruction Mnemonic	Destination	Source	Bit-Count	Byte Size	Cycle Count
SHRD	<16-bit reg>	,<16-bit reg>	,<8-bit constant>	4	3 Note 6
SHRD	<word-size mem>	,<16-bit reg>	,<8-bit constant>	6	4 Note 6
SHRD	<32-bit reg>	,<32-bit reg>	,<8-bit constant>	5	4 Note 1, Note 3, Note 6
SHRD	<long-size mem>	,<32-bit reg>	,<8-bit constant>	7	5 Note 1, Note 3, Note 6

STC

SeT Carry flag.

STC sets the carry flag; that is, it turns the carry flag ON. The format discussed in this book is:

Instruction Mnemonic	Destination	Source	Byte Size	Cycle Count
STC			1	2

STD

SeT Direction flag.

STD sets the direction flag; that is, it turns the direction flag ON. The format discussed in this book is:

Instruction Mnemonic	Destination	Source	Byte Size	Cycle Count
STD			1	2

STI

SeT Interrupt flag.

STI sets the interrupt flag; that is, it turns the interrupt flag ON. The format discussed in this book is:

Instruction Mnemonic	Destination	Source	Byte Size	Cycle Count
STI			1	5

STOSx

STOSB: STOre String one Byte at a time, increment (decrement) DI by 1.

STOSW: STOre String one Word at a time, increment (decrement) DI by 2.

STOSD: STOre String one Double-word at a time, increment (decrement) DI by 4.

STOSx copies the AL, AX, or EAX registers to a byte, word or double-word pointed to by ES:DI, incrementing DI in the process (or decrementing if the direction flag is ON). The formats discussed in this book are:

Instruction Mnemonic	Destination	Source	Byte Size	Cycle Count
STOSB			1	5
STOSD			2	6 Note 3
STOSW			1	5

SUB

SUBtract without borrow.

SUB subtracts <source operand> from <destination operand> without checking the status of the carry flag. The formats discussed in this book are:

Instruction Mnemonic	Destination	Source	Byte Size	Cycle Count
SUB	<8-bit reg>	,<8-bit constant>	2	1
SUB	<8-bit reg>	,<8-bit reg>	2	1
SUB	<8-bit reg>	,<byte-size mem>	4	2
SUB	<byte-size mem>	,<8-bit constant>	5	3 Note 1
SUB	<byte-size mem>	,<8-bit reg>	4	3
SUB	<16-bit reg>	,<8-bit constant>	3	1
SUB	<16-bit reg>	,<16-bit constant>	3	1
SUB	<16-bit reg>	,<16-bit reg>	2	1
SUB	<16-bit reg>	,<word-size mem>	4	2 Note 2
SUB	<word-size mem>	,<8-bit constant>	5	3 Note 1, Note 2
SUB	<word-size mem>	,<16-bit constant>	6	3 Note 1, Note 2
SUB	<word-size mem>	,<16-bit reg>	4	3 Note 2
SUB	<32-bit reg>	,<8-bit constant>	4	2 Note 3
SUB	<32-bit reg>	,<32-bit constant>	6	2 Note 3
SUB	<32-bit reg>	,<32-bit reg>	3	2 Note 3
SUB	<32-bit reg>	,<long-size mem>	5	3 Note 2, Note 3
SUB	<long-size mem>	,<8-bit constant>	6	4 Note 1, Note 2, Note 3
SUB	<long-size mem>	,<32-bit constant>	9	4 Note 1, Note 2, Note 3
SUB	<long-size mem>	,<32-bit reg>	5	4 Note 2, Note 3

TEST

TEST for the logical AND of <destination operand> and <source operand>.

TEST acts exactly like the AND instruction, except that it doesn't affect the <destination operand> by actually writing to it — that is, TEST calculates the bitwise logical AND of <destination operand> and <source operand> only in order to set the flags of the flags register appropriately. The formats discussed in this book are:

Instruction Mnemonic	Destination	Source	Byte Size	Cycle Count
TEST	<8-bit reg>	,<8-bit constant>	2	1
TEST	<8-bit reg>	,<8-bit reg>	2	1
TEST	<8-bit reg>	,<byte-size mem>	4	2
TEST	<byte-size mem>	,<8-bit constant>	5	2 Note 1
TEST	<byte-size mem>	,<8-bit reg>	4	2
TEST	<16-bit reg>	,<16-bit constant>	3	1
TEST	<16-bit reg>	,<16-bit reg>	2	1
TEST	<16-bit reg>	,<word-size mem>	4	2 Note 2
TEST	<word-size mem>	,<16-bit constant>	6	2 Note 1, Note 2
TEST	<word-size mem>	,<16-bit reg>	4	2 Note 2
TEST	<32-bit reg>	,<32-bit constant>	6	2 Note 3
TEST	<32-bit reg>	,<32-bit reg>	3	2 Note 3
TEST	<32-bit reg>	,<long-size mem>	5	3 Note 2, Note 3
TEST	<long-size mem>	,<32-bit constant>	9	3 Note 1, Note 2, Note 3
TEST	<long-size mem>	,<32-bit reg>	5	3 Note 2, Note 3

XCHG

eXCHanGe <first operand> with <second operand>.

XCHG exchanges the values of two operands. The formats discussed in this book are:

Instruction Mnemonic	First	Second	Byte Size	Cycle Count
XCHG	<8-bit reg>	,<8-bit reg>	2	3
XCHG	<8-bit reg>	,<byte-size mem>	4	10 Note 17
XCHG	<byte-size mem>	,<8-bit reg>	4	10 Note 17
XCHG	<16-bit reg>	,<16-bit reg>	1	3
XCHG	<16-bit reg>	,<word-size mem>	4	10 Note 2, Note 17
XCHG	<word-size mem	,<16-bit reg>	4	10 Note 2, Note 17
XCHG	<32-bit reg>	,<32-bit reg>	2	4 Note 3
XCHG	<32-bit reg>	,<long-size mem>	5	11 Note 2, Note 3, Note 17
XCHG	<long-size mem>	,<32-bit reg>	5	11 Note 2, Note 3, Note 17

XOR

Calculate the eXclusive OR of <destination operand> and <source operand> and place the results in <destination operand>.

XOR is a bitwise logical operator — each bit of the result is 1 if the corresponding bits of the two operands are different; each bit is 0 if the corresponding bits of the two operands are the same. The formats discussed in this book are:

Instruction Mnemonic	Destination	Source	Byte Size	Cycle Count
XOR	<8-bit reg>	,<8-bit constant>	2	1
XOR	<8-bit reg>	,<8-bit reg>	2	1
XOR	<8-bit reg>	,<byte-size mem>	4	2
XOR	<byte-size mem>	,<8-bit constant>	5	3 Note 1
XOR	<byte-size mem>	,<8-bit reg>	4	3
XOR	<16-bit reg>	,<8-bit constant>	3	1
XOR	<16-bit reg>	,<16-bit constant>	3	1
XOR	<16-bit reg>	,<16-bit reg>	2	1
XOR	<16-bit reg>	,<word-size mem>	4	2 Note 2
XOR	<word-size mem>	,<8-bit constant>	5	3 Note 1, Note 2
XOR	<word-size mem>	,<16-bit constant>	6	3 Note 1, Note 2
XOR	<word-size mem>	,<16-bit reg>	4	3 Note 2
XOR	<32-bit reg>	,<8-bit constant>	4	2 Note 3
XOR	<32-bit reg>	,<32-bit constant>	6	2 Note 3
XOR	<32-bit reg>	,<32-bit reg>	3	2 Note 3
XOR	<32-bit reg>	,<long-size mem>	5	3 Note 2, Note 3
XOR	<long-size mem>	,<8-bit constant>	6	4 Note 1, Note 2, Note 3
XOR	<long-size mem>	,<32-bit constant>	9	4 Note 1, Note 2, Note 3
XOR	<long-size mem>	,<32-bit reg>	5	4 Note 2, Note 3

Note 1: If <mem> is not [SI] or [DI] or [BX], add a 1-cycle penalty because of the Constant-to-Memory Rule.

Note 2: If <mem> contains a double register (e.g., [BX][SI]) or a register plus constant (e.g., [BX+n]), add a 1-cycle penalty because of the Register-Pointer-Doubled Rule.

Note 3: One extra cycle is due to the 32-bit operand size override prefix. The cycle may be waived by the Prefix-Waiver Rule.

Note 4: One extra cycle is due to the 0Fh prefix. The cycle may be waived by the Prefix-Waiver Rule. Intel's documentation says this form of BSR takes 6 to 103 cycles.

Note 5: One extra cycle is due to the 0Fh prefix. The cycle may be waived by the Prefix-Waiver Rule. Intel's documentation says this form of BSR takes 7 to 104 cycles.

Note 6: One extra cycle is due to the 0Fh prefix. The cycle may be waived by the Prefix-Waiver Rule.

Note 7: All CALLs are near.

Note 8: Intel's description of CLD mentions only that SI and DI will be incremented during Intel string instructions. These registers are changed during 16-bit mode. In 32-bit mode, the registers involved are ESI and EDI.

Note 9: Intel's description of CMPSx states that the comparison is of DS:SI with ES:DI or ES:EDI. DS:SI is compared with ES:DI in 16-bit mode. DS:ESI is compared with ES:EDI in 32-bit mode.

Note 10: Intel's description of DIV shows that the instruction accepts two operands — an explicit AL, AX, or EAX dividend followed by the explicit <source operand> divisor. These formats will not work. The dividend (AL, AX, or EAX) is always implied.

Note 11: Intel's description of IDIV shows that, for 16-bit and 32-bit divisions, the instruction accepts two operands — an explicit AX or EAX dividend followed by the explicit <source operand> divisor. These formats will not work. The dividend (AL, AX, or EAX) is always implied.

Note 12: Intel's description of MUL shows that the instruction accepts two operands — an explicit AL, AX, or EAX multiplicand followed by the explicit <source operand> multiplier. These formats will not work. The multiplicand (AL, AX, or EAX) is always implied.

Note 13: Intel's description of IMUL shows that IMUL <32-bit reg> takes from 12 to 42 cycles before the Prefix Rule cycle is applied. Since all other forms of IMUL take at least 13 cycles, we assume this is a typographical error.

Note 14: Intel's description of MOV shows that this is a 9-cycle instruction in protected mode.

Note 15: Intel's description of POP says this is a 4-cycle instruction.

Note 16: Intel's description of POP says this is a 6-cycle instruction.

Note 17: Intel's description of XCHG says this is a 5-cycle instruction. On some machines, it's 2 cycles faster than our count.

Note 18: Intel's description of LOOP says this is a 2-cycle instruction if the jump is made.

Note 19: One extra cycle is due to the REP or REPNZ prefix. The cycle may be waived by the Prefix-Waiver Rule.

Note 20: Intel's description of REP MOVSx says this loop takes 12+(3*CX) cycles before the Prefix Rule cycle is applied.

Quick Guide to Secret Rules of Assembler

This appendix lists all the secret rules of assembler use described in this book, in the order that we introduced them. The page number next to each rule's heading indicates the page the rule is discussed on.

Secret Rules in Chapter 1

◆ **SECRET "CONSTANT-TO-MEMORY" RULE: page 8**
If you move a constant to a Register Pointer plus Constant Mode memory location, you lose 1 cycle.

◆ **SECRET "REGISTER-POINTER-DOUBLED" RULE: page 9**
If you use an address that contains two registers, you lose 1 cycle.

◆ **SECRET "REGISTER-ADDRESS" RULE: page 23**
If you set a register value just before using the register for an address, you lose 2 cycles. Further, if you set a register value, then execute any 1-cycle instruction, and then use the register for an address, you lose 1 cycle.

◆ **SECRET "BYTES-AND-POINTERS" RULE: page 24**
If you move a value to a byte register, then use any instruction that runs in precisely 1 cycle, then use a register pointer such as [BX] or [SI+n], you lose 1 cycle. Further, if you move a value to a byte register, then move a value to another byte register, then use an address register, you lose 2 cycles. (The only known exception to this is the use of: MOV <Register Pointer plus Constant memory addressing mode>,<constant>).

◆ **SECRET "CACHE-SMASH" RULE: page 29**
If you access several memory addresses which are exactly or nearly 800h bytes (2048 decimal) apart, you risk a huge penalty. The penalty is usually between 70 and 90 cycles but may be masked if the computer has an external cache.

◆ **SECRET "PREFIX" RULE: page 33**
Whenever you use a segment override (CS: or DS: or ES: or SS:), the assembler will begin with a 1 byte, 1-cycle instruction (the segment override instruction). Although generally used and referred to as a prefix, the segment override is really a separate instruction, and it can exist independently. Other prefixes that this rule applies to are the 32-bit operand override (DB 66h) prefix, the 0Fh prefix, the REP prefix, and the REPNZ prefix.

◆ **SECRET "PREFIX-WAIVER" RULE: page 34**
There is no charge for using a prefix if the previous instruction takes more than 1 cycle unless the previous instruction is JMP or CALL. This rule is cumulative so that if, for example, an instruction has 2 prefixes and the previous instruction takes 3 or more cycles, both prefixes are free.

Secret Rules in Chapter 2

◆ **SECRET "HI/LO" RULE: page 59**
Part 1:
((If you execute two consecutive instructions which contain references to the same 16-bit register or to the high and low halves of a 16-bit register)
and (the first instruction changes one half of the register)
and (the second instruction is MOV
and either
    ((the source operand is the other half of the register)
    or (the source operand is the entire register)))
then you lose 1 cycle.)

Part 2:
((If you execute two consecutive instructions which contain references to the same 16-bit register or to the high and low halves of a 16-bit register)
and (the first instruction changes one half of the register)
and (the second instruction does ARITHMETIC
and either
    ((the source or the destination is the other half of the register)
    or (the source or the destination is the entire register))
and (neither source nor destination is a <memory> operand))
then you lose 1 cycle.)

Part 3:
((If you execute two consecutive instructions which contain references to the same 16-bit register or to the high and low halves of a 16-bit register)
and (the first instruction changes the entire register)
and (the second instruction is MOV
    and (the source operand is the high half of the register))
then you lose 1 cycle.)

Part 4:
((If you execute two consecutive instructions which contain references to the same 16-bit register or to the high and low halves of a 16-bit register)
and (the first instruction changes the entire register)
and (the second instruction does ARITHMETIC
   and (either source or destination is the high half of the register)
    and (neither source nor destination is a <memory> operand))
then you lose 1 cycle.)

(NOTE: In the Hi/Lo Rule, ARITHMETIC means any one of ADD, SUB, OR, AND, XOR, INC, DEC, ADC, SBB, CMP, SHR, SAR, SHL, ROL, TEST, NEG, and NOT.)

◆ SECRET "MISALIGNMENT" RULE: page 76
If your <source operand> is misaligned, you lose at least 3 cycles. If your <destination operand> is misaligned, you lose at least 6 cycles.

Secret Rules in Chapter 3

◆ SECRET "DOUBLE-JUMP" RULE: page 92
If a conditional jump instruction whose condition is false (i.e., the jump is not done) is immediately followed by a second jump instruction, you lose 1 cycle on the second jump instruction unless the next instruction that is executed after that begins on a 0-mod-8 address.

◆ SECRET "LONG-JUMP" RULE: page 95
If you use the long form of conditional jump, you lose 1 cycle whether or not the jump happens, unless the previous instruction (which can't be JMP or CALL) takes more than 1 cycle. That is, the long form takes 4 cycles if the condition is true and 2 cycles if the condition is false, subject to the Prefix-Waiver Rule.

◆ **SECRET "CACHE-STRADDLING" RULE: page 97**
If you jump to an instruction which straddles a 16-byte boundary (that is, an instruction which begins in one cache line and ends in the next cache line), you lose 2 cycles. Further, if you jump to a 1-cycle instruction which doesn't straddle, but is followed by an instruction which either straddles or begins in a new 16-byte boundary (i.e., the two instructions together straddle), you lose 1 cycle.

◆ **SECRET "JCXZ-COSTS-MORE" RULE: page 103**
JCXZ costs 5 cycles more if true, and 4 cycles more if false, than the other conditional jump instructions.

Secret Rules in Chapter 4

◆ **SECRET "DELAYED-BYTES-AND-POINTERS" RULE: page 131 and 184**
If you move a value to a byte register then use a register pointer such as [BX] or [SI+n], you lose 2 cycles if the first instruction is XCHG. If you move a value to a byte register then use a register pointer such as [BX] or [SI+n], you lose 1 cycle if the first instruction is IMUL, MUL, IDIV, or DIV.

Secret Rules in Chapter 5

◆ **SECRET "LOAD-POINTER-WITH-MOV" RULE: page 143**
If you use LDS or LES instead of two MOVs to load a pointer, you lose 2 cycles.

Secret Rules in Chapter 6

◆ **SECRET "CALL-PLUS-STACK-USE" RULE: page 169**
In 16-bit mode, if the first instruction after a CALL is PUSH or POP or RET, you lose 1 cycle.

◆ **SECRET "CHANGE-SP-THEN-USE-STACK" RULE: page 172**
If the first instruction after an explicit change to SP is PUSH or
POP or RET, you lose 2 cycles. If the first instruction after an
explicit change to ESP is PUSH or POP or RET, you lose 1 cycle.

◆ **SECRET "HI/LO-PUSH" RULE: page 173**
If an instruction that changes one half of a register is immediately
followed by a PUSH of an entire register, you lose 1 cycle.

Secret Rules in Chapter 7

◆ **SECRET "MULTIPLY-BIG-TO-SMALL" RULE: page 183**
Multiplication works faster if the value of <source operand_1> —
the multiplicand — is greater than the value of <source operand_2>
— the multiplier. This is true whether the multiplicand is specified
or merely implied (i.e., AL, AX, EAX, or the <destination operand>).

Appendix C

A Routine To Determine What CPU Your Program Is Running On

During the course of this book, we've often stressed that our optimization suggestions are specifically geared for Intel 486 machines. Because of this, if you're in a situation where you'll be using several different machines, or if you intend to distribute your program to others, you need a routine in your install program that can determine what kind of CPU your program will be running on. A common `cputype` routine can be found in Symantec's library as:

```
int cputype(void)
```

Notes on the `cputype` source code state that the code was "Placed into public domain by Compaq Computers."

In the following CPUTYPE routine, we've made a few style changes and added comments to the cputype code as included in Symantec's library. CPUTYPE uses extended registers, so the warnings about using extended registers with old versions of OS/2 apply. CPUTYPE returns a value from 0 to 5 as follows:

VALUE RETURNED	PROCESSOR TYPE
0	8088/8086/V20
1	80186
2	80286
3	80386
4	80486
5	Pentium

Although the differences among processor types are not tiny, a routine like this can't simply try to use an 80386 instruction on an 80286 machine and see if it blows up or not to determine the processor. Instead, it must check for very subtle differences, mostly in the way that obscure bits of the flags register are handled. We ignored these bits in this book, and you'll be able to ignore them as well until you become a protected mode programmer. The subtleties in CPUTYPE are not useful in a general way.

Note: CPUTYPE uses two variants of the PUSH and POP instructions (PUSHF, PUSHFD and POPF, POPFD) which we haven't covered in this book. These instructions PUSH and POP flags on and off the stack. It isn't necessary for you to understand the code, though. You'll find the routine, ready to use, on the diskette that comes with this book.

```
public _CPUTYPE

    ;This routine's first division is between the CPUs which are >= 80286
    ;and those which are < 80286. There is a way of telling whether CPU =
    ;80286: MOV AX,1 | MOV DS,AX | MOV AX,DS | CMP AX,1 (the 80286 in
    ;protected mode would move in a 0). However, this routine uses a more
    ;useful fact: with the 8086 and 80186 it was possible to set all the
    ;bits in the flag register to 0 but with the 80286 and later, some bits
    ;can't be changed. (The 80286 came with protected mode, and disallowed
    ;switching to protected mode by simply changing bits.)

        PUSHF
        XOR AX,AX
        PUSH AX
        POPF
        PUSHF
        POP AX
        AND AH,0F0h
        CMP AH,0F0h
        JNZ @@new          ;(it's a 286 or 386 or 486)
```

```
            ;Jump failed. CPU is an 8086 or 80186. With the 80186 a change was
            ;introduced to the SHL AX,CL instruction — if CL is 32 then a 32-bit
            ;shift occurs on an 8086, leaving AX = 0, but an 80186 does nothing
            ;because only the lowest 5 bits of CL matter in the shift. This routine
            ;could have used that fact, but instead utilizes another difference in
            ;the PUSH SP instruction. The PUSH instruction itself subtracts 2 from
            ;the SP register, so the question is: does the subtract happen first or
            ;does the push happen first? The 8086 pushes the new pointer while the
            ;80186 pushes the current one.

                XOR AX,AX
                PUSH SP
                POP BX
                CMP BX,SP
                JZ @@80186          ;(it's a 186)
@@8086:         MOV AX,0            ;It's an 8086 (or 8088 or V20, we can't
                JMP short @@ret     ;distinguish).
@@80186:        MOV AX,1            ;It's a 186.
                JMP short @@ret

@@new:          ;CPU is later than an 8086 or 80186. 80286s allow the use of a few
                ;more instructions: PUSH <constant>; IMUL reg,memory,constant;
                ;SHL <operand>,<constant>. Compilers rarely make use of these
                ;advantages. Again, resolve the difference between processors by
                ;pushing flags.

                MOV AX,0F000h
                PUSH AX             ;try to force high bits on in flags
                POPF
                PUSHF
                POP AX              ;AX = what was actually stored
                AND AH,0F0h
                JNZ @@newer
@@80286:        MOV AX,2            ;It's a 286.
                JMP short @@ret

@@newer:        ;CPU is an 80386 or 80486. These processors allow the use of a few more
                ;instructions, but the big change is that 32-bit registers and operands
                ;can now be used. At this point, the routine needs to distinguish
                ;between 386 and 486. Yet again, the matter hinges on the way that
                ;flags are pushed — this time, using the rare double-word push
                ;instruction PUSHFD.

.386
                MOV BX,SP
                AND SP,0FFFCh       ;round down to a dword boundary
                PUSHFD
                PUSHFD
                POP EDX
                MOV ECX,EDX
                XOR EDX,40000h      ;toggle AC bit
                AND ECX,40000h
                PUSH EDX
                POPFD
                PUSHFD
                POP EDX
                POPFD               ;restore original flags
                MOV SP,BX           ;restore original stack pointer
                AND EDX,40000h
                CMP EDX,ECX
                JNZ @@newst
@@80386:        MOV AX,3            ;It's an 80386.
                JMP short @@ret
```

```
@@newst:    ;CPU is at least an 80486. There aren't many more instructions
            ;available to use, but this is an important break because knowing the
            ;CPU is a 486 affects timing. (For example, some of the suggestions in
            ;this book will speed up your code if the CPU is a 486 but may slow it
            ;down if the CPU is a 386.)

            ;Determine if chip supports CPUID. Not all 486s can (which is why
            ;the CPUID instruction isn't documented), but the ones that can will
            ;have a bit on in the flags register.

            PUSHFD
            POP EAX
            MOV ECX,EAX
            XOR EAX,200000h      ;toggle ID bit
            PUSH EAX
            POPFD
            PUSHFD
            POP EAX
            XOR EAX,ECX
            JNZ @@later
@@80486:    MOV AX,4             ;It's a 486 but it doesn't support CPUID.
            JMP short @@ret

@@later:    ;With some 486s, and all Pentiums, the CPUID instruction can be used
            ;to determine the processor type. Since TASM and MASM don't have a
            ;mnemonic for CPUID, it's necessary to put the machine code in directly.

            MOV EAX,1
            DB 0Fh,0A2h          ;CPUID opcode
            MOV AL,AH
            AND AX,0Fh
@@ret:      POPF                 ;original flags
            RET
_CPUTYPE ends
```

List of this Book's Diskette Contents

The diskette that comes with this book contains the following files:

ATOI.ASM —   routine to replace C library _atoi

ATOL.ASM —   routine to replace C library _atol

CPUTYPE.ASM —   routine to determine what CPU type
                  a program is running on

ITOA.ASM —   routine to replace C library _itoa

LTOA.ASM —   routine to replace C library _ltoa

MEMCMP.ASM —   routine to replace C library _memcmp

MEMCPY.ASM —   routine to replace C library _memcpy

MEMSET.ASM —   routine to replace C library _memset

MEMCHR.ASM —   routine to replace C library _memchr

STRCAT.ASM —   routine to replace C library _strcat

STRCHR.ASM —   routine to replace C library _strchr

`STRCMP.ASM` —	routine to replace C library `_strcmp`
`STRCPY.ASM` —	routine to replace C library `_strcpy`
`STRCSPN.ASM` —	routine to replace C library `_strcspn`
`STRICMP.ASM` —	routine to replace C library `_stricmp`
`STRLEN.ASM` —	routine to replace C library `_strlen`
`STRLWR.ASM` —	routine to replace C library `_strlwr`
`STRNCAT.ASM` —	routine to replace C library `_strncat`
`STRNCMP.ASM` —	routine to replace C library `_strncmp`
`STRNCPY.ASM` —	routine to replace C library `_strncpy`
`STRNSET.ASM` —	routine to replace C library `_strnset`
`STRPBRK.ASM` —	routine to replace C library `_strpbrk`
`STRRCHR.ASM` —	routine to replace C library `_strrchr`
`STRREV.ASM` —	routine to replace C library `_strrev`
`STRSET.ASM` —	routine to replace C library `_strset`
`STRSPN.ASM` —	routine to replace C library `_strspn`
`STRSTR.ASM` —	routine to replace C library `_strstr`
`STRUPR.ASM` —	routine to replace C library `_strupr`
`TACHO.EXE` —	cycle-counting utility program
`TIMEDOS.EXE` —	16-bit DOS timing program
`TIMEWIN.EXE` —	Windows timing program
`TIME32.EXE` —	32-bit DOS timing program
`XX.EXE` —	sample program for testing out TACHO.EXE
`ZOOMIMUL.ASM` —	macro for fast multiplication

Index

.486   *15, 73, 114, 151*

0-mod-16 address   *26, 98*

0-mod-four address   *13*

OFh prefix   *42*

16-bit constant   *2 - 4, 6, 8, 105, 150, 152, 161*

16-bit mode   *18, 65, 105, 147, 154 - 155, 164, 169, 194, 220, 339, 381*

16-bit register   *2, 4, 25, 59 - 60, 64 - 65, 70, 93, 131 - 132, 141 - 142, 146, 149, 152 - 153, 158, 161, 165, 181, 192, 205, 245, 281, 289*

32-bit constant   *2 - 3, 72, 135, 161*

32-bit mode   *32, 65, 154 - 155, 162 - 164, 169, 218 - 220, 231, 273, 381*

32-bit register   *2 - 3, 15 - 17, 19, 23, 54, 63, 65, 73, 104 - 105, 128, 132, 141, 146 - 147, 153 - 155, 161, 165, 171, 179 - 180, 189, 192, 205, 245, 281, 327, 329, 334*

8-bit constant   *2 - 3, 6, 44, 70, 72, 74, 79, 111, 126, 132, 137, 139, 152, 161 - 162, 180, 192, 213*

8-bit register   *2, 4, 52 - 54, 70, 141, 149, 152 - 153, 181, 193, 203, 261 - 262, 277, 296*

80286   *73 - 74, 95, 119, 269, 281, 322, 390*

80386   *334, 390*

80486   *151, 333, 390*

8086   *113, 179, 269, 281, 283, 321, 390*

__asm   *10, 16, 272*

_emit   *16*

A

AAM   *201, 211 - 212, 340*

ADC   *69 - 72, 76, 105 - 106, 128, 134, 299, 340, 386*

ADD   *24 - 25, 43 - 78, 104 - 105, 114 - 115, 117 - 118, 128, 134, 138, 147, 168 - 169 184 - 186, 191, 193 - 194, 260, 273, 283, 315, 331, 336, 341* address   *4 - 9, 13 - 14, 17, 22 - 24, 26, 29, 31 - 32, 35 - 37, 49, 51, 58, 74, 76, 92, 95, 117 - 118, 138, 142, 146 - 148, 152, 157 - 160, 165 - 173, 218 - 228, 238, 288 - 289, 331, 358*

AH   *3, 60, 64, 150, 189, 202, 212, 304, 307, 340, 343, 347 - 348*

AL   *3, 60, 64, 72, 124, 148, 150, 179 - 181, 183, 189 - 190, 202, 212, 220, 222, 225 - 226, 261, 304, 307, 328, 340, 343, 347 - 348, 359, 362, 372, 376, 381 - 382*

ALIGN 16   *98 - 100, 272, 293*

ALIGN 2   *100*

alignment   *97 - 98, 159, 261, 287, 289, 303, 312*

AND   *43 - 46, 50, 56, 62, 66 - 68, 72 - 76, 136 - 137, 139, 155, 261, 342, 378*

arithmetic operation   *46, 70, 76*

assignment operator   *2*

atoi   *269 - 271, 273, 275*

atol   *269, 271, 275*

automatic variable   *51, 159-160, 163, 168, 170, 246*

auxiliary carry flag   *66*

AX   *3, 15, 19, 28, 60 - 64, 66, 85, 128, 145, 148 - 150, 158, 171, 179 - 182, 185, 189 - 191, 194, 201 - 202, 204, 207 - 208, 211 - 212, 220, 222, 225 - 226, 257, 273, 275, 277, 279, 282, 284, 286, 289, 291, 293, 295 - 297, 300 - 302, 304, 306 - 307, 311 - 315, 317 - 318, 320, 323 - 325, 327 - 328, 340, 343, 346 - 348, 359, 362, 372, 376, 381 - 382*

B

Base Pointer   *168*

BH   *3, 60, 62, 307*

bitwise logical operator   *44 - 45, 342, 364, 380*

BL   *60, 62, 150, 190, 307*

Boolean value   *144 - 145*

Borland C++   *ix, 18*

BP   *17, 31, 36, 51, 157 - 158, 160, 164, 168 - 173, 257 - 258, 261, 270, 275, 279, 314, 321*

BSR   *205 - 206, 342, 381*

BX   *3, 5, 17, 19, 37, 60, 62, 149, 155, 157, 185, 246, 257, 259 - 260, 262, 288, 291, 306, 315, 321, 328*

byte operand   *73 - 74, 189*

BYTE PTR   *33, 73*

C

C function   *98, 177, 265*

C procedure   *159*

cache line   *26, 29 - 30, 37, 97 - 99, 272*

caching   *22, 25 - 30, 239*

CALL   *34, 95, 165 - 167, 169, 259, 314, 343, 381*

carry flag   *55, 66 - 72, 74, 80 - 81, 83, 85 - 86, 88 - 89, 105 - 106, 112 - 114, 126, 128, 133, 136, 140, 144 - 145, 151 - 152, 154 - 155, 163, 181, 189, 202, 205, 236, 299, 304, 340 - 341, 343 - 345, 350 - 351, 354, 370 - 371, 373 - 375, 377*

casting   *148 - 149, 151 - 152, 154*

CBW   *148 - 152, 154, 156, 171, 343*

CH *60, 62*

CL *3, 60, 62, 111 - 112, 120 - 122, 126 - 127, 150*

CLC *144 - 145, 343*

CLD *218 - 219, 344, 381*

CLI *158, 239, 344*

CMC *144 - 145, 344*

CMP *79 - 81, 91 - 92, 106, 138, 145, 157 - 158, 225, 262 - 263, 287 - 290, 302, 345*

CMPSB *220 - 222, 240 - 241, 346*

CMPSD *220 - 222, 233 - 234, 346*

CMPSW *220 - 222, 319, 346*

CMPSx *220 - 222, 229 - 231, 346, 366 - 367, 381*

Code Segment *31*

compare Intel string instruction *220*

comparison *81, 85, 89, 92, 158, 176, 186, 221, 225, 240 - 242, 252 - 253, 267, 284 - 285, 291 - 292, 302, 311, 318 - 319, 322, 324, 328 - 329, 350 - 353, 381*

conditional jump instruction *65, 82, 84, 88, 90 - 92, 94 - 95, 101 - 103, 109 - 110, 138, 270, 298, 301, 386 - 387*

CPUTYPE *389 - 390*

CS *31, 33, 36, 161, 334, 365*

CWD *148 - 152, 154, 346*

CX *3, 19, 52, 60, 62, 72, 101 - 103, 105, 128, 138 - 139, 148 - 149, 154, 168, 204, 214 - 215, 220, 229 - 243, 257, 262, 283, 295, 301, 304, 324, 352, 359, 366 - 368, 382*

cycle times *28, 36, 39, 69, 115, 255, 332 - 333, 335*

cycle-counting utility program *394*

D

Data Segment *31, 157, 219*

DB 66h *16 - 17, 34 - 35, 65, 233, 384*

DEC *54 - 56, 62, 64, 66 - 68, 76, 96 - 97, 101 - 102, 104 - 106, 108 - 109, 133, 154, 159, 176, 196, 204, 216, 238, 240 - 241, 243 - 244, 310, 347, 386*

DELAYED-BYTES-AND-POINT-ERS RULE *131, 184*

Destination Index *219*

DH *3, 60, 130, 242 - 244, 293*

DI *3, 17, 19 - 20, 48, 58, 117, 128, 154 - 155, 157, 169, 177, 218 - 222, 224 - 228, 234, 237 - 239, 257, 259, 270, 288, 308, 314, 321, 346, 361, 372, 376, 381*

direction flag *218 - 227, 236, 239, 247, 344, 346, 359, 361, 372, 375 - 376*

DIV *184, 201 - 204, 206 - 207, 211 - 215, 277, 279, 347, 381, 387*

divide-by-2 instruction *113*

DL *3, 20, 37, 60 - 63, 128, 150, 242 - 244, 293, 315, 336*

Double-SBB Trick *324*

DS *31, 33 - 34, 36, 100, 142, 147, 155 - 157, 164, 176, 219 - 222, 226 - 227, 244, 272, 298, 321, 323, 334, 358*

DS:ESI *219, 381*

DS:SI *219 - 223, 346, 359, 361, 381*

DWORD PTR *33, 35*

DX *3, 19, 33, 60, 62, 86, 128, 130, 145, 149-150, 154, 166, 189, 201 - 202, 242, 257, 259, 275, 293, 346 - 348*

DX:AX *148 - 149, 171, 179 - 180, 182, 189, 202, 275, 346 - 348, 362*

E

EAX   *15, 35, 105, 154, 163, 179 -
    181, 183, 189, 202, 220, 222,
    225, 242, 273, 334 - 337, 347 -
    348, 359, 362, 372, 376, 381 - 382*

EBP   *15, 164, 171, 334, 337*

EBX   *15, 17, 65, 164, 334 - 337*

ECX   *15, 220, 231, 334*

EDI   *15, 164, 218 - 219, 334, 381*

EDX   *15, 65, 73, 189, 202, 242, 334,
    337, 347 - 348*

EDX:EAX   *179 - 181, 189, 202, 213,
    347 - 348, 362*

effective address   *146*

embed assembler instructions in C
    programs   *10*

ES   *31 - 36, 142, 164, 219 - 222, 224 -
    227, 236, 323, 334, 381*

ES:DI   *219 - 221, 224 - 226, 346, 361,
    372, 376, 381*

ES:EDI   *219, 381*

ESI   *15, 164, 218 - 219, 334, 381*

ESP   *162 - 163, 170 - 171, 334*

EVEN   *100*

extended register   *15, 36, 390*

Extended Stack Pointer *163*

Extra Segment   *31, 219*

F

far pointer   *32, 34, 143, 155, 168, 174 -
    175, 177*

FASTIMUL   *187, 191 - 193, 195*

flag OFF   *66 - 69, 71, 81, 83, 85, 136,
    144 - 145, 205, 218, 236, 245,
    324, 343 - 344*

flag ON   *66, 68 - 69, 71, 74, 81, 83,
    85, 105, 128, 144 - 145, 163, 202,
    205, 218, 231, 245, 324, 350 -
    352, 354 - 357, 366 - 368, 375 -
    376*

flags register   *65, 69, 77, 80 - 82, 88,
    90 - 91, 99, 101 - 102, 104, 112,
    126, 128, 136, 142, 144 - 148,
    153, 161, 163, 165, 192, 202,
    210, 218, 221 - 227, 231, 236,
    240, 290, 337, 345, 378, 390*

FS   *334*

function calls   *19*

G

General Protection Fault   *244, 246 -
    247, 272*

global variable   *14, 169 - 170*

GS   *334*

H

huge pointer   *174*

I

IDIV   *184, 201 - 204, 206 - 208, 211,
    348, 381, 387*

IMUL   *179 - 194, 204, 273, 348 - 349,
    382*

INC   *54 - 58, 62, 66 - 68, 76, 105,
    107, 223, 227, 288, 350*

index register   *218, 234*

inline assembly   *19, 47 - 48, 88, 90,
    98, 168, 188, 194, 264 - 265, 272*

Intel   *x, 2, 26 - 27, 29 - 30, 39, 48, 65,
    99, 129, 139 - 140, 142 - 143, 161
    - 162, 194, 202, 205, 257, 273,
    277, 284, 302, 335, 338 - 339,
    349, 363, 382, 389*

Intel string   *34, 217 - 248, 381*

Intel string instruction   *34, 217 - 220, 228 - 232, 234, 246 - 248, 323, 381*

interrupt flag   *344, 376*

itoa   *269, 276 - 277, 279*

J

JA   *88 - 89, 350*

JAE   *85, 350, 354*

JB   *85, 92 - 93, 351*

JBE   *88 - 89, 351*

JC   *82 - 85, 88, 351*

JCXZ   *102 - 104, 352*

JE   *84, 352, 357*

JG   *88 - 90, 92, 352*

JGE   *88 - 90, 301, 353*

JL   *88 - 90, 92 - 93, 353*

JLE   *88 - 90, 353*

JMP   *34, 90 - 91, 94 - 95, 166, 169 - 170, 261, 285, 291, 293, 354*

JNC   *82 - 85, 329, 350, 354*

JNE   *85, 354 - 355*

JNO   *82 - 84, 354*

JNP   *82 - 85, 355, 357*

JNS   *82 - 84, 355*

JNZ   *82 - 85, 94, 291 - 292, 315, 354 - 355*

JO   *82 - 84, 87 - 88, 356*

JP   *82 - 85, 356*

JPE   *85, 356*

JPO   *85, 355, 357*

JS   *82 - 84, 357*

L

LDS   *142 - 144, 358*

LEA   *146 - 148, 163, 194, 223, 226 - 227, 261, 273, 303, 358*

LES   *7, 13, 33, 41, 48, 77, 110, 142 - 144, 155 - 156, 178, 195, 358, 387*

LODSB   *222 - 223, 228, 317, 359*

LODSD   *222 - 223, 359*

LODSW   *222 - 223, 359*

LODSx   *220, 222 - 223, 228 - 229, 247, 359*

logic operation   *76 - 77*

lookup table   *216 - 217*

LOOP   *101 - 104, 109, 206, 359, 382*

loop control   *12, 102, 105, 107, 110, 154, 206*

loop unroll   *37, 107, 126, 241, 243, 306, 329*

LSL   *244 - 246, 248, 360*

ltoa   *269, 271, 279, 281, 393*

M

macros   *117, 193 - 194*

mem function   *322 - 323*

memchr   *322, 328 - 329, 393*

memcmp   *302, 322 - 325, 393*

memcpy   *175, 236, 322, 325 - 327, 393*

memset   *239, 322, 327, 393*

misaligned address   *38, 74, 109, 138, 148*

misalignment   *14, 17, 39, 41, 63, 97, 109, 124, 152, 162, 234, 238, 240, 289, 298, 301, 306, 325 - 327, 329*

MOV *1 - 17, 21 - 27, 31 - 37, 46, 48, 50, 52 - 53, 58 - 60, 63 - 65, 72, 75 - 76, 87, 91, 104, 117 - 118, 124 - 126, 129 - 130, 143, 148 - 149, 151, 160, 164, 167, 169 - 173, 184, 191, 210, 222, 240, 244, 257, 261 - 263, 285, 288 - 290, 293, 296, 312 - 315, 327, 336 - 337, 360, 382*

MOVSB *223 - 224, 234, 237, 361*

MOVSD *223 - 224, 233 - 234, 327, 361*

MOVSW *223 - 224, 229, 232, 237, 361*

MOVSX *148, 153 - 154, 220, 224 - 225, 229 - 231, 239, 361, 366*

MOVZX *148, 153 - 156, 362*

MUL *179, 184, 189 - 191, 194, 204, 362, 382*

multiply-by-2 instruction *113, 277*

N

near pointer *33, 174 - 175, 177*

NEG *140 - 141, 144 - 145, 155, 187, 191, 193, 195, 200, 363, 386*

NOP *99 - 100, 109, 130, 148, 261, 284, 291, 295, 300, 302 - 303, 308, 311, 313, 315, 317, 320, 363*

NOT *141 - 142, 145, 155, 243, 364, 386*

O

OFFSET *4, 17, 23, 37, 109, 125, 176 - 177*

one's complement *142, 364*

opcode *115, 128, 130, 133 - 134, 154, 161, 213, 245, 338, 342*

operand size override prefix *35, 65, 381*

OR *43 - 46, 50, 56, 62 - 63, 66 - 68, 72 - 74, 76, 102, 104, 139, 154, 289, 364, 380*

overflow flag *66, 68 - 69, 82 - 83, 86 - 89, 113, 126, 133, 135 - 136, 352 - 354, 356*

P

parity flag *66, 69, 80 - 81, 83, 85, 133, 136, 181, 189, 212, 355 - 357*

passing parameters *169*

penalty *7 - 8, 14, 17, 23 - 30, 34, 36, 38, 41, 46, 48, 53, 58, 60 - 62, 64 - 65, 71 - 72, 74, 76, 81, 93 - 94, 97, 99, 104, 106, 108 - 109, 118 - 120, 123 - 124, 127, 130 - 131, 137, 139, 148, 152, 154, 162, 169, 171 - 173, 183, 189, 202 - 203, 205, 219, 228, 233 - 234, 240, 255, 260, 270, 272, 293, 299, 326 - 327, 336, 339, 381, 384*

pipeline stall *22 - 25, 39, 97, 108, 148, 239, 327*

pointer *4 - 6, 8 - 9, 14, 18, 24, 29, 32 - 34, 40 - 41, 48, 51, 57 - 58, 97, 107, 125, 130 - 131, 134, 138, 142 - 143, 147, 155 - 157, 159 - 160, 163 - 164, 166 - 168, 170, 172, 174 - 175, 177, 184, 195, 219, 235 - 236, 242, 245, 257 - 260, 262, 270, 282, 285 - 286, 289, 291, 293, 295, 299, 301, 307, 310 - 311, 314 - 315, 318, 320 - 321, 323, 327 - 328, 339, 358, 384, 387*

pointer register *5 - 6, 160, 177*

POP *151 - 152, 160 - 173, 176 - 178, 200, 204, 206, 235 - 236, 239 - 240, 270, 283, 299, 301, 307, 310 - 311, 314, 321, 323, 365, 382, 387 - 388, 390*

POPF   *390*

POPFD *390*

prefix byte   *16, 34*

PUSH   *28, 151 - 152, 160 - 173, 176 -
178, 200, 204, 206, 235 - 236,
239 - 240, 259, 270, 298 - 299,
301, 307, 310, 314, 321, 323,
365, 387 - 388, 390*

PUSHF   *390*

PUSHFD   *390*

R

register list   *307*

Register Pointer Doubled address
mode   *6 - 7, 9, 40, 81, 104*

Register Pointer plus Constant address mode   *6 - 9, 24, 35, 38, 40 -
41, 46, 49, 81, 104 - 105, 173,
183, 331, 383 - 384*

register variable   *18 - 20, 41, 52, 91,
93, 109, 259, 321*

REP   *28, 34, 42, 229 - 234, 236 - 244,
248, 284, 286, 295, 304, 311, 323
- 324, 326 - 327, 329, 366 - 368,
382, 384*

REP CMPSB   *230, 232 - 233, 240 -
241, 323 - 324, 366*

REP CMPSD   *230, 232 - 233, 323 -
324, 366*

REP CMPSW   *230, 232 - 233, 366*

REP CMPSx   *231, 240 - 241, 248, 366*

REP MOVSB   *230, 232 - 234, 236 -
237, 239, 366*

REP MOVSD   *230, 232 - 233, 237 -
239, 366*

REP MOVSW   *230, 232 - 233, 236 -
237, 239, 326, 366*

REP MOVSx   *231, 234, 238 - 239,
248, 304, 366, 382*

REP SCASB   *230, 232 - 233, 241 -
243, 329, 368*

REP SCASD   *230, 232 - 233, 368*

REP SCASW   *230, 232 - 233, 242,
368*

REP SCASx   *231, 241 - 242, 244,
248, 368*

REP STOSB   *230, 232 - 233, 237,
239, 368*

REP STOSD   *230, 232 - 233, 238 -
240, 327, 368*

REP STOSx   *231, 237 - 239, 248, 304,
327, 368*

REPE *231 - 232*

repeat prefix   *231 - 232*

repeated Intel string instruction   *220,
230, 232, 234, 248, 323*

REPNE *231 - 232*

REPNZ *34, 42, 229 - 234, 240 - 241,
243, 248, 284, 286, 295, 311,
367, 382, 384*

REPNZ CMPSB   *230, 232 - 233, 240,
286, 367*

REPNZ CMPSD *230, 232 - 233, 367*

REPNZ CMPSW *230, 232 - 233, 367*

REPNZ SCASB   *230, 232 - 233, 241,
243, 284, 286, 295, 311, 367*

REPNZ SCASD   *230, 232 - 233, 367*

REPNZ SCASW *230, 232 - 233, 367*

REPZ   *231*

RET   *13, 23 - 24, 29, 33 - 34, 41 - 42,
48 - 49, 59 - 60, 76 - 78, 92, 95,
97, 103, 110, 131, 134, 143, 145,
156, 165 - 167, 169 - 173, 178,
183 - 184, 195, 206, 259, 270,
299, 301, 307, 310 - 311, 332,
335, 368, 383 - 388, 390*

ROL   *111, 126 - 129, 131 - 132, 134,
369, 386*

rotl *126*

S

SAR   *111 - 113, 115 - 118, 120 - 122, 128, 134, 206 - 208, 210, 217, 262, 370, 386*

saving bytes   *72*

SBB   *69 - 72, 76, 106, 144, 151 - 152, 299, 324, 371, 386*

SCASB   *225 - 226, 228, 230, 232 - 233, 241 - 243, 284, 286, 295, 311, 329, 367 - 368, 372*

SCASD   *225 - 226, 230, 232 - 233, 367 - 368, 372*

SCASW   *225 - 226, 230, 232 - 233, 242, 367 - 368, 372*

SCASx   *220, 225 - 226, 229 - 231, 241 - 242, 244, 247 - 248, 367 - 368, 372*

Secret Rule   *383, 385 - 388*

segment   *31 - 36, 38, 40, 42, 63 - 64, 90, 142 - 143, 155, 157, 161 - 162, 164, 175 - 176, 219, 222, 224, 226 - 227, 244 - 246, 248, 269, 272, 298, 321, 323, 333 - 334, 336, 360, 365, 384*

segment identifier   *31 - 32*

segment limit   *244, 246, 248, 269, 360*

segment override   *33 - 35, 42, 63, 321, 384*

segment register   *31 - 32, 36, 40, 64, 142, 155, 157, 162, 164, 222, 224, 226 - 227, 244 - 245, 321, 323, 333 - 334, 336*

self-test   *138*

Shift and Subtract method   *206*

SHL   *111 - 115, 117 - 126, 128, 132 - 134, 184 - 187, 191, 193 - 194, 196 - 197, 199 - 200, 204, 206, 260, 273, 369, 373, 386*

SHLD   *111, 132 - 134, 373*

SHR   *111 - 113, 115 - 122, 124, 128, 132 - 134, 137, 140, 151 - 152, 204, 206 - 208, 215, 217, 236 - 238, 240, 304, 374 - 375, 386*

SHRD   *111, 132 - 134, 375*

SI   *3 - 7, 9 - 10, 17, 19 - 20, 23 - 24, 27 - 28, 37 - 38, 40 - 41, 45, 56 - 58, 81, 91, 93, 96 - 97, 105, 115, 117 - 118, 128, 130 - 131, 134, 148, 154 - 155, 157, 164, 169, 174 - 177, 184, 195, 198 - 200, 218 - 224, 228 - 229, 234 - 240, 248, 257, 259 - 263, 270, 297, 308, 310 - 311, 314, 321, 334 - 337, 346, 359, 361, 381, 384, 387*

sign bit   *66, 112, 138 - 139, 148 - 151, 208, 210, 301, 343, 346, 370, 374*

sign flag   *66 - 67, 69, 80 - 81, 83, 85, 89, 112, 136, 138 - 139, 209, 275, 352 - 353, 355, 357*

signed division   *201, 217, 347 - 348*

signed multiplication   *179, 189, 192, 195, 348 - 349, 362*

signed value   *66, 112, 370, 374*

Source Index   *219*

SP   *1, 22, 44 - 45, 54, 69 - 70, 72 - 73, 80, 83, 89 - 90, 99, 101 - 102, 111, 117, 126, 128, 132, 135, 140 - 142, 144 - 146, 148, 153, 157 - 165, 167 - 173, 177 - 178, 180 - 182, 189 - 190, 192, 202, 205 - 206, 212, 218, 221 - 225, 227, 230 - 231, 236 - 237, 239, 245 - 246, 250 - 251, 253, 258 - 264, 267 - 268, 270, 272 - 273, 275 - 277, 279, 282 - 284, 286 - 287, 289, 291 - 293, 295, 297 - 302, 304, 306 - 308, 310 - 311, 313 - 315, 317 - 318, 320, 323, 325 - 329, 332, 334 - 337, 346, 349, 359, 361, 363, 365, 372, 376, 381 - 382, 388, 390, 393 - 394*

SS   *23, 31, 33, 36, 40 - 42, 157, 161, 177, 246, 272, 321, 334 - 337, 383 - 384, 390*

stack   *152, 157 - 159, 161 - 162, 165 - 169, 171 - 172, 177 - 178, 246, 258 - 259, 272, 283, 301, 308, 321, 343, 365, 368, 390*

stack cleanup   *168, 283*

Stack Pointer   *157, 159, 163, 177*

Stack Segment   *31, 157, 177, 246*

STC   *144 - 145, 156, 375*

STD   *218 - 219, 247, 375*

STI   *98, 158, 187, 191 - 193, 195 - 196, 198 - 200, 239, 376*

STOSB   *226 - 228, 230, 232 - 233, 237, 239, 368, 376*

STOSD   *226 - 227, 230, 232 - 233, 238 - 240, 327, 368, 376*

STOSW   *28, 226 - 228, 230, 232 - 234, 237 - 240, 368, 376*

STOSx   *220, 227 - 231, 237 - 239, 247 - 248, 304, 327, 368, 376*

strcat   *271, 282 - 283, 300, 393*

strchr   *271, 284 - 285, 289, 296, 319, 393*

strcmp   *271, 286 - 288, 292, 302, 322, 394*

strcpy   *96, 271, 283, 289, 300, 304, 322, 394*

strcspn   *271, 291, 307, 310 - 311, 394*

stricmp   *271, 292 - 293, 394*

string function   *322 - 323*

strlen   *96, 243, 246, 271, 283, 295 - 296, 300 - 302, 304, 306, 308, 313 - 314, 394*

strlwr   *271, 297 - 299, 321, 394*

strncat   *271, 300 - 301, 394*

strncmp   *271, 288, 302, 394*

strncpy   *271, 300, 304 - 305, 394*

strnset   *271, 306 - 307, 394*

strpbrk   *271, 291, 307 - 308, 310 - 311, 317, 394*

strrchr   *271, 311 - 312, 394*

strrev   *271, 313 - 314, 394*

strset   *271, 306, 314 - 316, 322, 394*

strspn   *271, 317, 394*

strstr   *271, 318 - 319, 394*

strupr   *271, 298, 320 - 321, 394*

swap two halves of a register   *128*

Symantec C++   *ix*

T

TACHO.EXE   *39, 64, 293, 331 - 335, 337, 394*

TEST   *98, 135 - 140, 145, 148, 155, 204, 208, 238, 240 - 241, 243 - 244, 247, 289 - 290, 299, 301, 310, 378, 386*

Trick Shift method   *150 - 152*

two's complement   *140, 155, 363*

U

Unified Cache Penalty   *26*

unsigned division   *201, 217, 347*

unsigned multiplication   *189, 195, 362*

unsigned value   *66, 112, 374*

V

Visual C++   *ix, 250*

W

word operand   *73 - 74, 189, 297*

WORD PTR   *32 - 35, 73, 158, 261 - 262*

Write-through Cache Penalty   *27*

X

XCHG   *28, 111, 128 - 132, 134, 184,*
       195, 313, 337, 363, 379, 382, 387

XOR   *43 - 46, 50, 52, 56, 62 - 64, 66 -*
        68, 72 - 74, 76, 93, 108, 125 -
        126, 130, 139, 142, 149, 158,
        296, 304, 312, 315, 324, 380

XX.EXE   *335, 394*

Z

zero flag   *66, 69 - 70, 77, 79 - 81, 83 -*
            84, 86, 88 - 89, 109, 126, 135 -
            136, 138, 140, 145, 155, 167,
            202, 205, 221, 225, 230 - 231,
            240 - 241, 244 - 245, 315, 324,
            350 - 355, 357, 366 - 368

ZOOMIMUL.ASM   *194, 196 - 200*

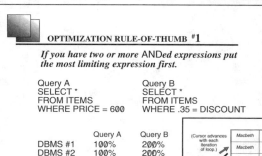
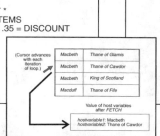